THE ENCYCLOPEDIA OF
PROPAGANDA

THE ENCYCLOPEDIA OF PROPAGANDA

Volume 3

Russia: 1918-1953 – Zionism
Index

Editor
Robert Cole

Foreword by
Philip M. Taylor

SHARPE REFERENCE

An imprint of M.E. Sharpe, INC.

e Edition published by Sharpe Reference

ace is an imprint of M.E. Sharpe, INC.

M.E. Sharpe, INC.
80 Business Park Drive
Armonk, NY 10504

Library of Congress Cataloging-in-Publication Data

The Encyclopedia of propaganda / editor, Robert Cole ; foreword by Philip M. Taylor
p.   cm.
Includes bibliographical references and index.
ISBN 0-7656-8009-2 (set : alk. paper)
1. Propaganda—Encyclopedias. 2. Persuasion (Psychology)—Encyclopedias.
3. Public opinion—Encyclopedias. 4. History, Modern—19th century—Encyclopedias.
5. History, Modern—20th century—Encyclopedias. I. Cole, Robert, 1939-
HM263.E53   1998
303.3′75′03—DC21
97-18036
CIP

Printed and bound in the United States of America

The paper used in this publication meets the minimum requirements of the American National Standard for Information Sciences—Permanence of Paper for Printed Library Materials, ANSI Z39.48-1984

10   9   8   7   6   5   4   3   2   1

Frontispiece: This 1971 anti-Vietnam War poster plays on the Uncle Sam
"I Want You" theme introduced during World War I.
(*Library of Congress*)

Project Editors: Juliane Brand and R. Kent Rasmussen   *Development Editor:* R. Kent Rasmussen
Production Editor: Cynthia Breslin Beres   *Research Supervisor:* Jeffry Jensen
Acquisitions Editor: Mark Rehn   *Photo Editor:* Karrie Hyatt
Proofreading Supervisor: Yasmine A. Cordoba   *Layout:* William Zimmerman

Cover and page design: Lee Goldstein

CONTENTS

THE ENCYCLOPEDIA OF
PROPAGANDA

■ Russia: 1918-1953

Era spanning the Russian Revolution and the dictatorship of Joseph Stalin

As a means of increasing the class consciousness needed for a proletarian revolution, propaganda was central to Marxist-Leninist ideology long before the Bolshevik Revolution of 1917. A little-known leader of a small but highly disciplined party, V. I. Lenin's ability to reduce Bolshevik objectives to the simple slogan "Peace, Bread, and Land," was a major factor in gaining him popular support. Seizing power over a barely functioning, half-starved remnant of a once powerful empire faced with a catastrophic world war, a tearing civil war, and occupation and invasion by foreign expeditionary forces, Lenin turned to propaganda as one of his most powerful weapons.

WAR COMMUNISM AND THE NEW ECONOMIC POLICY (1918-1924) During the precarious early years of the Soviet regime, large numbers of party loyalists were sent throughout the countryside in propaganda trains loaded with brochures and posters. These "agit-trains" (and "agit-ships" for port cities) were decorated with large frescoes that depicted for the illiterate population the battle of good versus evil. The Bolsheviks were portrayed as champions of the people, struggling against the coalition of exploiters (landlords, priests, aristocrats, and capitalists). In the cities similar themes appeared on streetcars, posters, and buildings (*see* MURAL ART). AGITPROP street theater and open-air theater, sometimes with casts of many thousands as in the 1920 productions of *The Winter Palace* and *The Blockade of Russia*, were used as Soviet heroic epics.

Short propaganda films were produced from 1918 to 1920 to appeal to mass audiences and to their fascination with the new form of entertainment.

From the start of Bolshevik control, education became a state monopoly and was used for mass propaganda. By 1918 all schools, both public and private, had become the state's responsibility. In 1922 the organization Pioneers was founded to propagandize children who might one day be party members. Literacy remained high on the educational agenda, as did the substitution of atheism for Orthodoxy as a belief for the young. Many churches were closed and their valuables collected and turned into needed revenues. Orthodox priests were included in agit-court show trials in 1922 that were intended to document the activities of the people's enemies. Newsworthy events, such as the trials, and their meaning, were reported to the people in *Pravda* (truth), the party newspaper designed to control the dissemination of news and motivate the masses.

Lenin used news, education, literature, and the visual and performing arts to begin the process of creating a "New Soviet Man." His cultural commissar, Anatolii Lunacharskii, was put in charge of the effort to construct a proletarian culture. Artists and writers not speaking the language of proletarian culture were silenced. All the politically correct themes for the 1920's were guided by the Russian Association of Proletarian Writers (RAPP), an organization that itself was guided by the slogan "The Book Is an Instrument of Production."

INTERNATIONAL POLICIES UNDER LENIN Initially Lenin and the Bolshevik leadership viewed developments in Russia as the

Члены Политбюро ЦК ВКП(б) за обсуждением плана второй пятилетки   С картины художника П.Малы

This idealized painting of Soviet dictator Joseph Stalin (center) chairing a Central Committee meeting contrasted with the reality of his regime's bloody purges during the 1930's. (*Library of Congress*)

catalyst that would set off a chain reaction of similar revolutions in war-weary Europe. To coordinate worldwide revolutionary activity from one center, the Third International, or COMINTERN was organized in March, 1919. With its base in Moscow, and the presidency in the hands of Grigorii Zinoviev, one of Lenin's intimate circle, the Comintern was clearly Soviet directed. By the end of 1920 revolutionary hopes for Europe faded, yet the fear that the White Russian armies might win the civil war had also vanished. Hence Comintern propaganda shifted from advocating immediate world revolution to building Soviet Russia as a center of world revolution. A secondary theme was the support of national liberation efforts in the colonial world so as to undermine imperialism, which Lenin believed was the economic foundation of capitalism. The Comintern's role was to urge peaceful coexistence and

recognition of the Soviet Union as a legitimate nation. To guarantee uniformity in propaganda themes, centralized party newspapers were to be operated in each nation along the lines of *Pravda* while remaining sensitive to local conditions (in the United States the *Daily Worker* fulfilled this task). In foreign policy peace and DISARMAMENT were favorite themes.

Also of considerable significance was Lenin's propaganda effort to win influential supporters who could portray the Soviet Union as a democratic society with social, racial, gender, and economic equality. To achieve this end, the Soviet Union made liberal and socialist intellectuals welcome, among them the American news reporter John REED, who did much to popularize the Bolshevik Revolution. Reed's tremendously popular *Ten Days That Shook the World*, published in 1919 with an introduction by Lenin, romanticized the revolution as a heroic epic. Others who helped legitimize the revolution include the American writers Lincoln Steffens and Harold Laski, the British scholars Sidney and Beatrice Webb, and such writers as H. G. Wells. Lenin grasped the significance of a friendly foreign press; hence entry and exit visas were granted only after considerable scrutiny. Lenin cooperated only with journalists who were themselves cooperative. News dissemination was centralized early, in September, 1918, with the creation of the Russian Telegraphic Agency (renamed TASS in 1925) to handle news releases, which were often a mixture of selective information and propaganda.

Another successful effort initiated by Lenin, based on the idea of a German communist, Willie Munzenberg, was to set up front groups in nations otherwise hostile to communism. Such groups attempted to gain support for Soviet policies as well as economic aid. Thus numerous workers' aid organizations were established in the Western industrialized nations, along with workers' book clubs and organizations to feed starving children.

THE RISE OF STALIN The years following Lenin's death in 1924 witnessed a creative period in Soviet propaganda, particularly in cinema. Sergei Eisenstein's brilliant films *Strike* (1925), THE BATTLESHIP PO-TEMKIN (1926), and *October* (1927) were widely seen in Europe and the United States, where they did much to expose czarist horrors and to justify and heroize the revolution. Dziga Vertov's *Forward Soviet* (1926) and *A Sixth Part of the World* (1926) produced similar effects. For internal use only were antireligious films such as *Judas* and *Opium*, meant to move the masses further in the direction of atheism.

In 1928 Lenin's 1921 New Economic Policy (NEP) was replaced by a Five-Year Plan designed to transform heavy industry and collectivize agriculture. The Stalinist revolution for the transformation of Russia had begun, and with it propaganda soared to heights that Lenin could not have imagined nor deemed acceptable. Within ten years the entire old party membership, a sizeable portion of military officers, and millions of common people had been imprisoned or executed as class enemies.

As a sign of things to come, show trials were held from 1928 to 1930, in which engineers, technicians, and economists were accused of wrecking the economy, and historians, social scientists, and philosophers were dismissed and charged with being Trotskyists, Mensheviks, or national deviationists. However, for Joseph STALIN, the most threatening class enemy were the wealthy private farmers (*Kulaks*) who resisted collectivization by slaughtering their animals and burning their crops. In 1930 Stalin called for liquidation of the Kulaks as a class by mass executions and forced deportations.

Not only within the central and local party levels but on the international level as well, left-and right-wing deviationists were denounced. In the Comintern new leaders came to the fore (among them Palmiro Togliatti in Italy, Maurice Thorez in France, Ernst Thälmann in Germany, and Earl Browder in the United States) whose absolute obedience could be trusted. All varieties of other socialists were labeled as "the moderate wing of fascism." Indeed, during the early years of the Great Depression, socialists, not fascists, were portrayed as the main enemy of the Left and the last refuge of the bourgeoisie. Yet by 1934 Soviet foreign-policy propaganda made an about-face.

POPULAR FRONT AND PARTY PURGES By 1934 the dual military threat of Japan and Nazi Germany could no longer be ignored. In response, Comintern was ordered to form a popular front with all antifascist parties and work toward collective action with the Western democracies. Sanctions and rearmament themes of the LEAGUE OF NATIONS replaced former anti-imperialism, anticapitalism, and peace themes. Undoubtedly the most active propaganda role was taken during the SPANISH CIVIL WAR (1936-1939). The Soviets not only advocated collective international action through the League to stop fascist aggression but ordered their front organizations to urge volunteers from all nations to fight in Spain. In the United States many rallies were held and the Lincoln Brigade was formed to join the other international brigades fighting to preserve Republican Spain.

The failure of collective security in the wake of continued U.S. isolationism and Anglo-French appeasement caused Stalin to make another about-face by signing the Non-Aggression Pact with Germany in 1939. Propaganda too was put into reverse gear. Because Nazi Germany was now to be portrayed as a peace-loving nation, the Comintern was ordered to launch a peace offensive in that direction and target the imperialist tendencies of England and France as the main obstacle to peace. A considerable number of foreign party members and sympathizers, caught in a credibility gap, left the party to continue their opposition to Adolf HITLER. Their disillusionment was all the greater after the equally incredible purge

trials that had taken place in the Soviet Union since 1934.

Following the assassination of Sergei Kirov in December, 1934, mass arrests and deportations began of party members accused of being tied to a Trotskyite conspiracy to wreck communism. About one hundred people were directly linked to Kirov's assassination and shot. Many were forced to confess to having conspired with Leon Trotsky and Soviet enemies to bring about a counterrevolution. Trials were also held on the local level and spread to army officers (leading to an officer shortage when World War II began) and even to the secret police. The Comintern press dutifully played along with the conspiracy theme, documenting it with the many coerced confessions. At the same time, to accentuate the positive, the press focused on the new constitution of 1936, which was described as the most democratic yet produced in the world and a model of freedoms, including freedom from unemployment.

A plot so widespread at the top inevitably involved the masses below. A minor critical remark, a slight error at work, failure to meet one's production quota, or even a casual conversation could link an individual to the conspiracy. Thus propaganda created an imaginary civil-war atmosphere, as well as providing a ready excuse as to why the infallible party was having problems meeting quotas set in the Second Five Year Plan.

Soviet literature and art during the Second and Third Plans (1933-1941), was directed to produce heroes out of common people, who were to lose their vices and gain heroic stature through hard work and determination. Many novels were written about collectivization and successes in exceeding quotas, often against overwhelming odds. Socialist realist art (*see* SOCIALIST REALISM) portrayed the heroic factory and agricultural worker, and the press, joining in to depict the heroic worker, immortalized Alexis Stakhanov, a coal miner who produced fourteen times his quota in one shift. The party stepped in to create the Stakhanovite movement, giving medals and privileges to those who significantly exceeded their quota. Those writers who did not contribute to Socialist Realist themes were linked to the enemies of the people.

WORLD WAR II During the first years of World War II Soviet propaganda denounced Winston CHURCHILL as a warmonger and imperialist, while the Nazi invasion of France was rationalized as part of the just wars against French imperialism. In the United States communists joined "American Firsters" in denouncing aid to Great Britain; they demonstrated with signs proclaiming "The Yanks Are Not Coming" and "Work Not War." The German invasion of Russia in June, 1941, caused an immediate shift to a popular front, with all antifascist groups joining in resistance groups. After the Third Five-Year Plan was aborted in the Soviet Union, propaganda themes rarely mentioned socialism. Instead, traditional Russian national themes were stressed and heroes from czarist times resurrected. After its entry into the war, the United States portrayed Russia as a fellow democratic nation. The Comintern was abolished in mid-1943 to ease misapprehensions.

POSTWAR PROPAGANDA Themes honed throughout the early Soviet period provided the basis for Soviet propaganda in the post-World War II era. For the occupied states of Eastern Europe, the theme of being joined in a popular front against fascism was repeated innumerable times. Communists joined coalition governments, often taking minor cabinet positions. Former fascist collaborators were tried and convicted, after which the disinformation machinery was put in motion to discredit noncommunist members of the popular front. By 1948 there was no longer any need for collective government in the East European states, which had become satellites controlled by their own communist leaders who were, in turn, controlled by Stalin.

To reprogram a suspect population that had lived under Nazi occupation, or had close contact with the former Western allies, reindoctrination camps were established following World War II. Release, if granted, came only to those who could prove their trustworthiness. Many others, including many military personnel, were executed or sent to Siberian gulags. To take the place of the Comintern, the Cominform was created in 1946. The postwar world rapidly came to resemble the prewar one.

In a speech made in February, 1946, Stalin made it clear to the party that "war is inevitable as long as capitalism exists." By 1947 U.S. imperialism replaced former postwar themes of Anglo-American imperialism. Peace campaigns reached a height in 1948-1949 with the formation of the Soviet-controlled World Peace Council.

A full-fledged anti-Western propaganda campaign was launched in the summer of 1946, headed by Andrei Zhdanov, chief of Soviet ideology. Intellectuals were castigated for their "servile adulation of contemporary bourgeois culture" and for turning away from more meaningful Russian themes. Jazz was banned as decadent (*see* MUSIC). Historians were forced to emphasize themes of class struggle and the progressive nature of Russian developments throughout history. It was claimed that important inventions such as the steam engine, electric lightbulb, radio, and airplane were Russian.

Undoubtedly the largest gaff in party propaganda was that of the official support given in 1948 to Trofim Lysenko's theory that acquired characteristics could be transferred genetically, in other words that good Communists could breed good Communist children, eventually producing the new Soviet utopia. Artists, writers, and scholars who accented the politically correct themes were rewarded with medals and privileges; those who did not were relegated as outcasts. The film producer Sergei Eisenstein had to denounce himself for having produced *Ivan Gronzy, Part Two*, which Stalin detested.

Stalin was clearly upset after the UNITED NATIONS voted to create the state of ISRAEL, and he worried about the resulting divided loyalties of Soviet Jews. By 1949 he had oriented the party toward an anti-Semitic campaign against those Jews guilty of "homeless bourgeois cosmopolitanism" who were subverting Soviet values.

In October, 1952, the Nineteenth Party Congress was held after an interim of thirteen years. Shortly after the event, *Pravda* announced that a plot in which nine doctors (seven of whom were Jewish) had killed high Soviet officials, among them Zhdanov, was part of a wider conspiracy. As arrests began, party members and the general population trembled in fear that another massive purge was beginning. With

Stalin's unexpected death on March 5, 1953, the Doctor's Plot fabrication was terminated. Stalin retained great importance in the Soviet Union for the next three years, after which the propaganda machinery he had played a large role in creating, thrust him into oblivion.

SUGGESTED READINGS:

Barghoorn, Frederick. *Soviet Foreign Propaganda.* Princeton, N.J.: Princeton University Press, 1964. A landmark study of the historical development of Soviet Communism and its use of propaganda to manipulate world opinion.

Borkenau, Franz. *World Communism: A History of the Communist International.* Ann Arbor: University of Michigan Press, 1962. An excellent and well-researched analysis of the evolution and policies of the Communist International.

Martin, Ebon. *The Soviet Propaganda Machine.* New York: McGraw Hill, 1987. An excellent topical study of Soviet propaganda, how agitprop worked, the tactics used, the media and people agenda and ideology involved.

Medvedev, Rhea. *Let History Judge: The Origins and Consequences of Stalinism.* Rev. ed. Revised and translated by George Rhea. New York: Columbia University Press, 1989. A well-documented indictment of Stalin and his policies.

Pipes, Richard. *Russia Under the Bolshevik Regime.* New York: Alfred A. Knopf, 1993. A scholarly and exhaustive study of the Bolshevik seizure of power until the death of Lenin.

Treadgold, Donald. *Twentieth Century Russia.* 8th ed. Boulder, Colo.: Westview Press, 1995. Provides a clear and solid background for the beginning researcher of topical themes spanning the 1918-1953 period.

Ulam, Adam. *Expansion and Coexistence: Soviet Foreign Policy, 1917-1973.* New York: Praeger, 1974. A comprehensive and analytical history of Soviet foreign policy including detailed discussions of propaganda and ideological related components.

— *Irwin Halfond*

■ Russia: 1953-1991

Final era of the Soviet Union

The decline of the Stalinist system after 1953 was exceedingly slow. Its building blocks, described in the previous section, persisted through four more decades, the most important single element being the unique and exclusive role of the Communist Party. Here are traced some of the major developments in the internal and external propaganda scenario, through the collapse of the Soviet Union.

NIKITA KHRUSHCHEV Within three years of Stalin's death, Nikita Khrushchev had shouldered aside the tyrant's official successors, and he remained at the helm of the Soviet Union's central leadership until being abruptly ousted in 1964. As early as 1954, however, there were signs that controls over public expression were beginning to be relaxed; some novels and journal articles were published that would never have been allowed under Stalin. Because LITERATURE held a much more central position in both Russian and Soviet life than it typically has in twentieth century Western countries, the publication of novels that did more than simply reinforce Soviet propaganda was a momentous change. This moment was described

at the time and has ever since been referred to as the "thaw" (of the cruel winter of Stalinism).

In 1956, now assured of full control, Khrushchev took the radical step of denouncing some of Stalin's crimes to a specially convened secret midnight session of the Twentieth Communist Party Congress. Guest delegates from foreign communist parties were not invited but soon knew what had transpired, and Khrushchev's speech was later read to specially convened party meetings throughout the Soviet Union. A Polish Communist leaked the speech to the West.

This action effectively opened the door to an extended period of questioning of the Soviet propaganda image, both inside and outside the Soviet bloc. Khrushchev intended to purify what he saw as a deformation of the system and so to strengthen it, but once it had been publicly admitted that previous Soviet propaganda about Stalin had been a tissue of lies, a certain precedent was set, allowing for the possibility of debate over, rather than blanket submission to, the party line. On the other hand, the explanation Khrushchev gave for Stalin's policies, namely that a cult of his personality had been allowed to develop, was so nebulous as to render a deeper analysis of the true sources of Stalin's dictatorship difficult.

From then until 1964 Khrushchev alternated between allowing a little more freedom of public expression and withdrawing those new freedoms. His switches of position resulted directly from waves of pressure, not apparent to public view, emanating from party officials who feared that openness severely threatened the system and themselves personally. Yet these years saw the first major cracks in the monolithic Soviet propaganda edifice.

Khrushchev is remembered particularly in connection with two events: the 1962 publication of the novel *One Day in the Life of Ivan Denisovich* and his savage attack on Soviet artists in the very same year. The novel, a short work by a former labor-camp inmate, Aleksandr Solzhenitsyn, was the first public statement inside the U.S.S.R. about Stalin's gigantic chain of labor camps and the harsh conditions there. The book's damage to the credibility of Soviet propaganda was enormous, both inside and outside the Soviet Union. With a further speech that same year to yet another Soviet Communist Party congress, Khrushchev denounced Stalin's brutal regime more roundly still. However, the effect of this speech was offset by his fierce denunciation of a December, 1962, exhibit by newer Soviet artists who did not follow the official tenets of SoCIALIST REALISM; this speech sprang from his own philistinism as much as it was a sop to conservative Stalinists maneuvering against him. In this situation struggles between Khrushchev and his opponents over policy in other areas of Soviet life overflowed into the artistic realm, causing a reversion to insisting on purely propagandistic art.

Although Khrushchev's record in dismantling the rigid propaganda system is flawed, his period in office did achieve some lasting positive effects. Among these was his allowing the formation of a network of young, highly able journalists and arts organizers, who more than twenty years later would be in key positions to support Mikhail GORBACHEV's attempts to open up the system and make its propagandistic dimension less absolute.

THE EXPANSION OF TELEVISION   Just as V. I. LENIN and the Bolsheviks had prized cinema for its technical capacity to transmit an identical approved message to all parts of the Soviet Union, thus bypassing the mistakes and awkward public speaking of individual Communist propagandists, so too did television become an enormously attractive communication technology to the later Soviet leadership. Because television actually entered the home, its propaganda was able to penetrate still further into the everyday lives of Soviet citizens.

One index of the weight placed on this technology was the volume of its manufacture, which massively outpaced telephone production. The telephone was an instrument of lateral communication, albeit between no more than a very few people, whereas television permitted one-way communication from the top. Another index was the space given in the press to complaints about the quality of television sets and of the repair services available; complaints concerning other consumer items were given much less attention.

In 1967, to mark the fiftieth anniversary of the Bolshevik Revolution, the Soviets harnessed their new space satellite technology to television broadcasting, thus enabling simultaneous transmission of the celebrations to all eleven time zones of the Soviet Union. This was the beginning of a continuous program of expansion for satellite-delivered television broadcasting. With the aid of later advances in satellite technology, particularly given the higher cost of earth transmitters, two television channels were available to practically the entire population, even in remote areas, by the mid-1980's. The Soviet press boasted that even the

Soviet premier Nikita Khrushchev denouncing U.S. spy plane flights at the United Nations in October, 1960. (AP/Wide World Photos)

crews on icebreaker ships in the Arctic Sea were able to receive television broadcasts.

There were increasingly powerful propaganda reasons for continuing this development. One related to the economic geography of the Soviet Union, the other to the morale of its military conscripts. The prime source of oil and gas and a variety of minerals was in the giant terrain of Siberia, the least populated and physically the least hospitable part of the country. Yet extracting these raw materials was crucial for the Soviet economy, both for domestic use and for export. Even with wages of up to five times higher than average to encourage relocation from west to east, people were reluctant to go, or once having arrived often left within the year. The sense of being cut off was more significant even than the climate. Television, the regime hoped, would act to staunch the flow of returning workers, and thus it became a priority to make the medium available in the remotest Siberian areas.

The Soviet military, mostly conscripts, which by the close of the 1970's probably numbered close to six million, was also stationed in far-flung locations on the Soviet map. Fully one-third of the army was stationed at the Chinese frontier, reflecting the bitter antagonism between Soviet and Chinese Communist leaderships of that era; much of that frontier was in wild and extremely cold terrain. A very large naval base was in Murmansk on the White Sea, again in a very harsh climate and a long way from the rest of the country. Military morale was often extremely low and rates of serious alcohol abuse high in such places. Here again television was perceived as an important calming and encouraging influence.

Much of the television programming was uninteresting by non-Soviet standards—it included such events as a general in full military dress reading poetry for a half hour without looking at his audience and with the camera completely stationary— but comparisons were unavailable, and programming also included sports television events, which were popular, and science documentaries. The news program *Vremya* (time) was watched by nearly one hundred million people every night, notwithstanding its strict conformity to the regime's expectations.

Thus on certain levels the regime's internal propaganda via television could be said to be successful. Some have argued that it was decreasingly successful because of the poor quality of much of the programming; in 1978 Leonid Brezhnev, Khrushchev's successor, publicly attacked Soviet television quality. Some critics have argued that television was more successful in portraying the West's problems and its nuclear threat to Russia than in encouraging loyalty to the Soviet regime. Still others have argued that the main purpose of internal propaganda, whether via television or other channels, was to set up such a barrage of messages that people would be convinced there was no escape possible from the system in force. According to this last viewpoint, the propagandists

never expected to develop active loyalty through propaganda.

DISINFORMATION AND FOREIGN POLICY
The term DISINFORMATION became used among some American sovietologists during the 1980's, a period characterized by some others at the time as a second cold war. These individuals argued that the West was being lulled into relaxing its vigilance against the Soviet threat because agents of the Soviet State Security Committee (KGB) were brilliant in planting false reports, in using prestigious figures as witting or unwitting supporters of Soviet foreign-policy objectives, and even in organizing protests. In this view the antinuclear movements that were especially strong during the 1980's in West Germany, Great Britain, Italy, and The Netherlands were interpreted as a particular target of the KGB. Indeed, some asserted that these movements would not have existed at all were it not for successful Soviet manipulation behind the scenes. Undoubtedly Soviet foreign policy strategists did welcome these movements—by that time the U.S. and Soviet governments had placed unprecedented quantities of nuclear firepower in their respective regions of influence in Europe, and public pressure against nuclear weapons in Europe, if successful, would certainly have had the effect of lessening the West's firepower—but to attribute such widespread political movements to Soviet disinformation would be to ascribe an unrealistically inflated power to the KGB.

A similar disinformation claim at that period was launched concerning the so-called space bridges—satellite-linked television studio discussions between groups of individuals in the United States and the

U.S.S.R.—that flourished briefly in the mid-1980's. Many people believed that negotiations between the two superpowers were a dialogue of the deaf and they hoped that other forms of citizen-based diplomacy might help to lessen tensions. These televised discussions were not much watched in the United States, but they had huge audiences in the U.S.S.R. The Russian host, Vladimir Posner, spoke perfect, idiomatic American English, far removed from the halting, heavily accented speech of customary Soviet spokespeople. His American counterpart, the talk-show host Phil Donahue, was attacked by some as an unwitting and naïve agent of Soviet disinformation for allowing the highly articulate Posner to explain Soviet foreign-policy positions and to present Soviet citizens as reasonable discussants. Others, however, considered this a questionable analysis.

That situation contrasts interestingly with the undoubted success of Soviet disinformation in persuading highly placed American officials that Soviet military increases were exponential in character. Prime examples of this are John F. Kennedy's acceptance that a "missile gap" had opened up between the U.S.S.R. and the United States, which he used as a key plank in his successful bid for the presidency, and Ronald REAGAN's administration's acceptance of greatly inflated Soviet military figures that actually emanated from Soviet double agents.

GORBACHEV AND GLASNOST Like Khrushchev before him, Gorbachev had no intention of bringing about the collapse of the Soviet Union but simply to purify and thereby strengthen it. His famous call in 1986 for reconstruction, acceleration (of technical advance), and openness (*glasnost*) was not a summons to defeat or despair. The openness he called for was based on his analysis that there was a destructive chasm between the confident words spoken publicly by Soviet officials and the widespread cynicism about Soviet realities spoken in private by them and their listeners alike. He correctly perceived that no society could be successful operating on that split level, with self-deception elevated into a standard of public life.

In that sense he was addressing the comprehensive failure of the propaganda and agitation system. By the time he came to power in 1985 the Cultural Centers (*doma kul'tury*) that were meant to be the mainstay of general internal propaganda had virtually lost all effective operation. The Communist Party itself had become primarily a vehicle for upward career mobility. People bought *Pravda*, the party newspaper, because subscribing to it was a requirement for senior officials. Gorbachev hoped to breathe life back into the system.

Moreover, the openness he had in mind was specifically targeted. He certainly did not have in mind the kind and degree of openness characteristic of some Western democracies. He supported certain newspapers and weeklies that would in turn support him against his opponents. When they overstepped the boundaries he had in mind, he threatened their editors publicly with dismissal. Anyone touring the Soviet Union would have found that even the word *glasnost*, which Gorbachev introduced to the English language, was barely known and less understood in Soviet newsrooms.

The initial impact of *glasnost* was on urban intellectual circles and revolved in particular around the unfinished business of Khrushchev's denunciations of Stalin's terror. Archives began to be opened and aged labor-camp survivors began to tell their stories. Yet other forces that capitalized on the new degree of freedom were typically nationalistic. Largely suppressed from public expression until then, voices became louder and louder for the independence of the fourteen non-Russian republics that had originally been annexed under the czars. Also raised were voices of the extremist Right in Russia itself, which often blend anti-Semitism with calls for a return to an idealized and mythical Great Russia.

As this brew fermented, the rescue or revival of the Soviet system became ever more implausible, except to some persistent Western sovietologists. Soviet propaganda lost all suasive powers. Notions of the "new Soviet human being," of the socialist fraternity of the fifteen republics, of moving to an assured global victory of communism, or of the inherent rottenness of capitalism, all became empty shells. Television no longer automatically presented the West in terms of its most acute problems but equally or more so in terms of its successes. As the pace of change accelerated, the Soviet people were able to watch live debates in the new Congress of People's Deputies on television, yet already within a year most had largely dismissed the whole institution as an ineffective talking shop.

In the end it was tiny Lithuania, with its insistent demand for national independence from the U.S.S.R., that pulled the rug out from under the creaking edifice. The Soviet propaganda state, as one sovietologist has called it, had decisively collapsed. The Soviet Union immediately collapsed as well.

SUGGESTED READINGS:

Downing, John. *Internationalizing Media Theory: Reflections on Media in Russia, Poland, and Hungary, 1980-1995*. Thousand Oaks: Sage, 1996. Offers a comparative overview of changes in media during this period.

Lawton, Anna. *Kinoglasnost: Soviet Cinema in Our Time*. New York: Cambridge University Press, 1992. Describes the development of Soviet cinema from the end of the Brezhnev era through 1989.

Mickiewicz, Ellen Propper. *Media and the Russian Public*. New York: Praeger, 1981. Summarizes the beginnings of audience research in the U.S.S.R. during the 1970's.

_____. *Split Signals: Television and Politics in the Soviet Union*. New York: Oxford University Press, 1988. Discusses changes in Soviet television news during the 1980's through 1987.

Remington, Thomas F. *The Truth of Authority: Ideology and Communication in the Soviet Union*. Pittsburgh, Pa.: University of Pittsburgh Press, 1988. Describes both the media system and the parallel lecture-circuit agitational system as institutionalized in the U.S.S.R.

Shanor, Donald R. *Behind the Lines: The Private War Against Soviet Censorship*. New York: St Martin's Press, 1985. A study of radio counterpropaganda by Voice Of America, Radio Liberty, and other foreign stations.

Shultz, Richard H., and Roy Godson. *Dezinformatsiya: The Strategy of Soviet Disinformation*. Berkley, New York: 1986. Presents the "disinformation" interpretation of Soviet propaganda.

Spechler, Dina. *Permitted Dissent in the U.S.S.R.* New York: Praeger, 1982. An analysis of the limits of Khrushchev's changes in the propaganda and censorship systems.

Vachnadze, Georgii Nikolaevich. *Secrets of Jour-

nalism in Russia: Mass Media Under Gorbachev and Yeltsin. Commack, N.Y.: Nova Science, 1992. Describes the Russian media system in the latter 1980's up to the breakup of the Soviet Union.

Zaslavsky, Victor. *The Neo-Stalinist State: Class, Ethnicity, and Consensus in Soviet Society.* Rev. ed. Armonk, N.Y.: M. E. Sharpe, 1994.

— *John D. H. Downing*

■ Russia: Since 1991

Post-Soviet era when the Russian Republic separated from the other former Soviet republics

The turbulent years immediately following the failed August coup of 1991 in the Soviet Union saw a series of clashes between past propaganda traditions and renewed struggles for more democratic media. Although the Communist Party was no longer in power, the major flashpoints were around continued government control of television in particular and the press in general. The bitter civil war over the independence of the Chechen Republic illustrated these conflicts with special clarity. The arts, including cinema, now faced financial starvation rather than censorship. Yet the parallel system of agitation (*see* AGITPROP) vanished without a trace.

TELEVISION AND THE GOVERNMENT So far as post-Soviet politicians were concerned, television was a key resource to which they could not afford to grant real independence. This was evident most sharply in the violent confrontation of October, 1993, outside Ostankino television headquarters between those seeking to depose Russian president Boris Yeltsin and those supporting him. For both sides television was the key prize. For both it was axiomatic that their power depended on controlling television.

The previous Soviet pattern of attempted government control of all media of communication, down to the typewriter, had been replaced by a more targeted strategy. Russian politicians had adopted the values of their Western counterparts in enthroning television as the make-or-break mass medium. Yet they were still a long way from the subtler methods of control common in the West such as SPIN CONTROL, photo opportunities, and privileged briefings to key journalists. The new Russian politicians still believed in repression whenever they felt challenged by television.

Many examples could be cited. One that attracted particular attention was a weekly political satire program called *Kukly* (puppets). Using claymation models, the show mercilessly satirized President Yeltsin, Premier Viktor Chernomyrdin, and other political leaders. The politicians who found themselves the butt of this ridicule did not, however, restrict themselves to denouncing the show. In 1995 the procurator general initiated a case against the producers of the series under criminal, not merely civil, law, for insulting the honor and dignity of top government figures (the penalties for breaking that law included up to two years of corrective prison labor); subsequently, tax-evasion and currency-dealing charges were filed against the producers.

In the end, all charges were dropped, and the courage and persistence of the producers and of the Independent Television Company (NTV) were validated. A small precedent had been set for media independence. Yet the event made clear that the new power structure's basic instincts remained those of the past.

There was, however, no longer a single propaganda line being disseminated from the top, no Communist Party committee responsible for setting news policy. TASS still existed but without its previous authority to dictate news copy. The Soviet State Security Committee (KGB) still existed, under numerous name changes, but the organization had no right to summon television or other media executives to account. There were even nongovernmental television companies, notably but not solely NTV, and cable television was beginning.

What came to be important at this stage was media control for defensive purposes rather than for actively propagandistic ends. Control was designed to prevent politically embarrassing revelations and to ensure that the government policy dominated in hotly contested situations. Thus both Russian Public Television and Ostankino, the national state television channels, were the object of energetic control by the Yeltsin administration. Yeltsin personally fired a series of Ostankino directors because of his displeasure with their failure to support his policies. Yet though there was intermittent talk in the mid-1990's about the need to create a new national ideology to inspire and unify Russia, no propaganda ministry was set up to frame or diffuse such a credo.

NEWSPAPERS   In the aftermath of the failed 1991 coup, a great number of newspapers were effectively taken over by their staffs and formed into independent companies. For financial reasons, many sub-

sequently collapsed. Those that did not collapse either found a strong market niche, such as *Moskovskii Komsomolets* (the young Moscow communist), which retained its old title but transformed itself into a wildly sensationalist rag, or they survived by government subsidy, such as the government's own *Rossiiskaia Gazeta* (the Russian newspaper). Other newspapers also partly depended upon subsidy.

The press situation in these respects was much more variable in Moscow and St. Petersburg than elsewhere in the country. The press in the provinces, however, was rather prone during these early post-Soviet years to yielding to provincial government control because of the need to rely on subsidies.

Indeed one of the continuing points of strife between the Yeltsin administration and those urging a faster transition toward democratic processes was the repeated suggestion from some of his key officials that an organized system of governmental press subsidies should be put into operation. The rationale offered for such a system was that newspapers needed to be saved from extinction for financial reasons, but many journalists and reformers, suspecting a strategy for the government's attaining control, consistently fought against implementation of a state press system. The shadows of the past hung heavily over these years.

As the financial situation of the print media began to stabilize, however, certain patterns of control emerged. Perhaps the most interesting was the ownership of newspapers by firms with quite diversified interests, such as the insurance, banking, and travel industries. It appears that the ability to control a political voice within the Russian media system was seen as worthwhile in itself, even though a newspaper might itself not be a profitable commercial venture. Politics, and public political communication, thus retained exceptionally high status even in post-Soviet Russia.

Given the further frequent practical reality that the editor in chief, the leading shareholder, and the legally defined "founder" of a newspaper were often the same person, a tremendous concentration of power might exist in one individual's hands. In turn that enabled, at least in principle, tight control by a few over the major newspapers and thereby the extrusion of a genuinely competing pluralism in the political sphere. The culturally ingrained impulse to retain central control over propaganda seems to have retained much of its strength. Thus the potential for a propagandistic consensus on issues of major public concern was ever present.

THE CRISIS IN CHECHNYA From December, 1994, through September, 1996, more than eighty thousand Russian troops and an unknown number of Chechen guerrillas and civilians, together with Russian civilians whose homes were in the capital, Grozny, were killed in savage fighting. The sources of the Chechen crisis in southern Russia, generated by the Chechen demand for a separate state, are complex. Certain of its features, however, are generally accepted, and these are important in understanding the significance of this bloody episode in assessing the role of propaganda in post-Soviet Russia.

Hatred between Russians and Chechens was of some centuries' standing, ever since the region's original colonization. Preserving Russian territory was central to the conflict, especially since the collapse of the Soviet system only three years earlier, at which time fourteen outlying republics, part of the Russian empire from well before 1917, had thrown off Moscow's sovereignty. Economic issues were at stake, among them the control of natural-gas revenues in the region, one of Russia's most profitable exports. The prestige of the Russian military was also at stake, which had been heavily battered in the bitter war in Afghanistan from 1979 through 1989, from which it had withdrawn without victory. During the economic free fall of the years that followed troops were often left unpaid for months at a time. The Russian troops sent to fight in Chechnya were often barely trained young conscripts.

The critical question from the point of view of propaganda operations is how the Russian government endeavored to handle the explosive situation.

Generally the attempt was made to pretend that Russia was always within inches of victory, an important claim in most military propaganda given the difficulty in mobilizing public enthusiasm for long-drawn-out wars. The government also appealed to the people's self-interest, by claiming that the Chechen rebellion threatened to bring about the disintegration of Russia and so reduce its importance in the world. Moreover, the government accused Chechnya of being in thrall to an immensely powerful criminal mafia, an accusation many Russians considered plausible because of the visible Chechen presence in underworld activity. Last, although this point was not stated publicly for fear of alienating Russia's southern Islamic neighbors, from Turkey to Pakistan, the government relied on the anti-Muslim bias of many Russians.

That this propaganda did not succeed in shoring up support among Russians for

Boris Yeltsin waves a Russian flag after helping to suppress an attempted coup against Soviet president Mikhail Gorbachev in August, 1991; several months later the Soviet Union was dissolved, leaving Yeltsin as president of an independent Russian Republic. (*AP/Wide World Photos*)

the military campaign had much to do with two factors. One was the vigorous exposure of the failure of the war by sections of the Russian media, notably NTV and a number of newspapers. Indeed, beyond the evidence of the campaign's failure there was also a growing credibility gap, as happened in the United States during the VIETNAM WAR, between the government's extravagant claims on one hand, and the images of actual combat on the other. Despite incessant government denunciations and threats to cancel NTV's license, the company did not buckle. Tight governmental control over war news, as was characteristic of the FALKLANDS WAR, or the U.S. invasions of GRENADA and PANAMA, was absent.

The second reason was military morale. Whereas the Chechens were fighting for what they considered their native land and that they knew intimately, the Russian troops were fighting with minimal supplies on harsh and unfamiliar terrain for a seemingly unattainable victory. At the same time they suffered horrendous casualties as a result of their incompetent generals' decisions and general lack of concern for them. This situation gave a former general, Aleksandr Lebed, a large base of support among enlisted troops and their families when he led a campaign to end the war. In the 1996 presidential election campaign his support became vital for the survival of the Yeltsin administration into a second term. Thus he was given much more space for maneuvering when he negotiated for peace than might otherwise have been the case.

THE 1996 ELECTION President Yeltsin's personal unpopularity, and that of most of his administration, together with the disastrous impact of the ruined Russian economy for the general public, at first suggested that his administration had virtually no chance of winning a second term in 1996. Apart from his visibly failing health and long absences from public view, almost none of his pronouncements seemed to have any real effect. What saved his candidacy were the character of two of his leading opponents for the presidency—the anti-Semitic ultranationalist Vladimir Zhirinovsky and the Communist Gennadi Zyuganov—and the reaction of many Russian media professionals against the prospect of either of those candidates becoming president. Zhirinovsky's focus on certain key themes, such as Russian national pride, the dignity of the Russian military, and the humiliation of most Russians as a result of the economic collapse and spiraling street crime, for a time caused many rural and provincial voters to see him as someone who echoed their deepest concerns. As Zhirinovsky's star began to wane, however, Zyuganov's began to rise. He had the advantage of a nationally organized party behind him, and was able to capitalize on some of the same core issues that had enabled Zhirinovsky to emerge from obscurity. Yet it was clear that to form a government he would have to seek an alliance with Zhirinovsky, or with Lebed, whose authoritarian style was also well known—or with both. It was to forestall this prospect that many media professionals, who foresaw the possibility of an even worse regime than Yeltsin's, one that might again reduce media independence, therefore began to support Yeltsin's reelection. The most striking signal of this trend was the decision of Igor Malashenko, the director of NTV, who had been rather consistently under attack from the Yeltsin camp for his channel's defiance of the government, to accept the post of campaign director for Yeltsin's reelection. Even *Kukly*, though still on the air, noticeably softened its tone.

The early years of post-Soviet life thus present a mixed scenario as regards the propaganda traditions of the former U.S.S.R. While media did gain independence from a centralized propagandistic impulse, the defeat of those who threatened to revive old traditions came about in large part at the cost of some of that newly gained independence.

SUGGESTED READINGS:

Androunas, Elena. *Soviet Media in Transition: Structural and Economic Alternatives.* New York: Praeger, 1993. Describes the economic pressures on Russian media during the transition.

Bonnell, Victoria E., Ann Cooper, and Gregory Freidin, eds. *Russia at the Barricades.* Armonk, N.Y.: M. E. Sharpe, 1994. Part 5 is devoted to the press and the August, 1991, coup.

Condee, Nancy, and Vladimir Padunov. "The ABC of Russian Consumer Culture: Readings, Ratings and Real Estate." In *Soviet Hieroglyphics: Visual Culture in Late Twentieth Century Russia,* edited by Nancy Condee. Bloomington: Indiana University Press, 1995.

————. "Pair-a-dice Lost: The Socialist Gamble, Market Determinism, and Compulsory Postmodernism." *New Formations* 22 (1994): 72-94. These articles review the flux in media and culture characteristic of the transition.

Daniloff, Nicholas. "Educating Russia for a Free Press." In *Education and Society in the New Russia,* edited by Anthony Jones. Armonk, N.Y.: M. E. Sharpe, 1994.

Downing, John. *Internationalizing Media Theory: Reflections on Media in Russia, Poland, and Hungary, 1980-1995.* London: Sage, 1996. Offers a comparative overview of changes in media during this period.

Foster, Frances. "Izvestiia as a Mirror of Russian Legal Reform: Press, Law, and Crisis in the Post-Soviet Era." *Vanderbilt Journal of Transnational Law* 26, no. 4 (1993): 675-747. A detailed study of the relations in a key daily newspaper between government, law, and media immediately following the Soviet Union's collapse.

McNair, Brian. "Media in Post-Soviet Russia: An Overview." *European Journal of Communication* 9 (1994): 115-135.

— *John D. H. Downing*

■ Russo-Japanese War

February 8, 1904—September 6, 1905: Conflict between the Russian Empire and Japan

The Russo-Japanese War resulted in a stunning victory for JAPAN and confirmed its emergence as a great power. The Russian army was battered in Manchuria, and RUSSIA's Pacific and Baltic fleets were chopped to pieces off Port Arthur and at Tsushima Strait. At the time, Japan was in the midst of modernization and desperately wanted to imitate the imperialistic efforts of European countries. CHINA, weak and politically divided, was a perfect target. U.S. president Theodore ROOSEVELT, at the request of Japan's nearly bankrupt government, negotiated a peace settlement, and a treaty was signed at Portsmouth, New Hampshire, on September 6, 1905. Japan acquired rights in the

Liaotung Peninsula and a lease on Port Arthur, whereas Russia was compelled to evacuate Manchuria. Further, Japan's dominance over Korea was confirmed, although it remained technically an independent country.

Propaganda, designed to galvanize PUBLIC OPINION, was important for both combatants. In Japan the Amur Society, popularly known as the Black Dagger Society, strongly encouraged Japanese imperialism. The society was motivated by the fact that after Japan had defeated China in the Sino-Japanese War (1894-1895), three European powers, including Russia, had forced Japan to give up its claim for the Liaotung Peninsula. From 1895 to 1904 Russia expanded its interests in the Liaotung Peninsula and in Port Arthur. The Amur Society capitalized on the enormous resentment this created in Japan.

The society contended that it was Japan's obligation to expand into Manchuria, Mongolia, and Siberia, arguing that Japan had a "civilizing" mission in these backward territories and that the expansion was required to protect Korea, which had come under Japanese influence in 1895, from Russian incursion. Mass meetings were organized to show public support for the society's position, and to reinforce the notion that the Japanese were invincible. Many Japanese newspapers and politicians backed these efforts, and some prominent Japanese leaders formed another propaganda association, the Kogetsukai Alliance, with the aim of further advancing the call for Japanese expansion.

In Russia, Czar Nicholas II, beset by opposition created by Russia's belated industrialization, viewed a war with Japan as the opportunity for an easy victory that would lift his regime's flagging popularity. Throughout Europe, except for England—which had formed an alliance with Japan in 1902—there was encouragement for Russia to deal decisively with the "yellow peril." In England, after a century of anti-Russian propaganda in newspapers and magazines, there was little support for Russia's Far East ambitions. English journalists, cartoonists, and politicians had created an indelible image of the huge Russian "bear" ready to pounce on all corners of the globe.

Nicholas' prejudice against the Japanese had originated during a visit to Japan as heir apparent in 1891, when he had been cut on the forehead by a saber-wielding fanatic. Nicholas thereafter referred to Japanese as "yellow monkeys," and for many years Russian newspaper cartoons and children's songs caricatured the Japanese as puny monkeys who stood no chance against strong Russians. The Russian public generally accepted the anti-Japanese propaganda, and when the humiliating military defeat became known the people were stunned. It is not surprising that revolutionary activity began in Russia in 1905.

SUGGESTED READINGS:

Kotkin, Stephen, and David Wolff, eds. *Rediscovering Russia in Asia: Siberia and the Russian Far East.* Armonk, New York: M.E. Sharpe, 1995.

— *Ronald K. Huch*

S

■ Sandinista National Liberation Front

Nicaraguan revolutionary party that ruled the country from 1979 to 1990

The Sandinista National Liberation Front (FSLN) was founded in July, 1961, in opposition to the Somoza family, which had ruled NICARAGUA as a dictatorship with the support of the United States since 1937. The early leaders of the Sandinistas looked to the writings of Karl Marx (*see* COMMUNIST MANIFESTO, THE), V. I. LENIN, and MAO ZEDONG for their ideology and to the successful revolution in CUBA for their example in organizing at the grassroots level.

From its beginnings the FSLN used religion and religious leaders as means of promoting its political and social message. Father Fernando Cardenal, a Roman Catholic priest, used the power of his pulpit to reach young Nicaraguans who wanted to help the poor of their country. Conducting evening talk sessions with interested parishioners, he persuaded them that Christian duty called them to join the Sandinistas. He also traveled throughout Nicaragua and to Washington, D.C., in the 1960's and 1970's, giving public addresses and interviews about the need for social reform in Nicaragua. Cardenal's message was broadcast widely, in part because he was from an old and influential family and in part because he was a Jesuit priest. It was not known until after the FSLN came to power in 1979 that he was secretly a Sandinista himself.

One of the new FSLN government's first social reforms, an intensive program to increase literacy, used education as a propaganda tool. Overseen by Cardenal, more than eighty thousand high school and college students were quickly trained as teachers and sent out across the rural areas of Nicaragua to teach reading and writing to the peasants. In five months during the first year of Sandinista rule, 400,000 adults completed a basic literacy program. Along the way, they were also exposed to ideological propaganda: The program's reading textbooks included chapters entitled "Our Democracy Is the Power of the Organized People" and "The Revolutionary Workers' Organizations Promote Production and Guide the Revolutionary Process."

The issue of FSLN propaganda through the media has an interesting history. During the early years of the Sandinista movement, *La Prensa*, Nicaragua's leading daily newspaper, was opposed to the Somoza regime and used propaganda techniques to criticize the regime and call for moderate reforms. After the Sandinistas took control of the country in 1979, *La Prensa* became a propaganda tool of the United States government in its efforts to overthrow the Sandinistas. By the mid 1980's, *La Prensa* was receiving some $100,000 a year from the CENTRAL INTELLIGENCE AGENCY (CIA) to conduct a DISINFORMATION campaign, manufacturing stories

Nicaraguans cheer Sandanista leaders as they make their way to the National Palace in Managua to take power in July, 1979. (AP/Wide World Photos)

about Sandinista atrocities to promote distrust and stories about shortages of basic goods to stimulate panic buying. In an attempt to prevent this CIA destabilizing tactic, the Sandinista government began occasionally censoring *La Prensa*. Other opposition newspapers, and radio and television stations, were generally allowed to operate without prior censorship, even when they criticized the government, unless the fairly liberal bounds of "acceptable reporting" were exceeded.

— *Cynthia A. Bily*

■ Saudi Arabia

Islamic Mideast nation and a military ally of the United States

The kingdom of Saudi Arabia is ruled by the Sa'ud family. King Fahd is also the country's chief religious leader and custodian of Mecca and Medina. These two cities are destinations for approximately two million pilgrims from all over the Islamic world during the *haj*, the annual pilgrimage, which takes place during the second week of the twelfth month of the Muslim lunar calendar. The king is guided not by an elected assembly or constitution but by senior family members, the Council of Ulama, which is made up of senior Islamic scholars, and the sixty-member Consultative Council.

Private ownership of the press is permitted in Saudi Arabia, but all newspapers must be published by press organizations and are subject to certain policies, among them the prohibition of criticism of the royal family, the government, or the clergy. The largest Arabic-language newspaper, *Ash-Sharq al-Awsat*, is owned by members of the royal family and is published in Cairo, London, France, Morocco, and Saudi Arabia. The foreign press is censored not only for stories critical of the kingdom but for advertisements that show liquor or immodesty. Only under exceptional circumstances are foreign journalists allowed into the kingdom. Journalists who were permitted into the country during the Persian GULF WAR found their activities and information carefully monitored by their hosts and by the governments cooperating in the war effort.

Radio and television, which are owned by the government, broadcast information and religious programming extensively throughout the Islamic word and into western Europe. Religious and cultural programming make up about one quarter of Saudi television. Television is used to show a society that is happy and economically successful. Public relations companies help the ministries promote a variety of domestic programs designed to keep the environment clean, collect dirty and torn money, encourage respect for traffic laws, and ask citizens to donate blood. One of Saudi Arabia's major goals is to strengthen Islam in other countries. When the Central Asian republics were established after the collapse of the Soviet Union, the Saudis sent support, restored mosques, and provided funds for pilgrimages to Mecca.

The government promotes Arab unity but did not support Gamal Abdel NASSER. The Saudis are careful not to promote radical versions of Arab politics that might have domestic consequences and unseat the monarchy. Moreover, the king is aware that his defense needs are linked to the United States. He faced consider-

■ **Saudi Arabia: History at a Glance**

Year	Event
1500's-1600's	Turks rule much of Arabia.
1901	Ibn Saud takes control of Riyadh; leads an Arab nationalist movement.
1932	Saudi Arabia is created when two kingdoms are united under Ibn Saud's rule.
1936	Oil is discovered.
1948-1949	Saudi Arabia joins other Arab nations in warring against the newly created state of Israel.
1953	Ibn Saud dies.
1982	King Fahd assumes power; continues Saudi Arabia's foreign policy of moderation.
1990-1991	Saudi forces take part in the Gulf War against Iraq.

able criticism for permitting non-Arabs and non-Muslims to come to his defense during the Persian Gulf War, but as the keeper of the shrines that are holy to the Arab world, he considered it his first priority to protect the national interests of his own nation-state. To buttress that claim the kingdom supported a *fatwa* or religious ruling that declared a *jihad* (holy war) against Iraq. Because American soldiers were part of that *jihad*, their presence in Saudi Arabia was proclaimed acceptable by the government-controlled press.

— *Fran J. Hassencahl*

■ **Save the Children Federation**

Charitable foundation established in 1932 to assist children, families, and communities in the United States and abroad

In the words of its own literature, Save the Children's programs are designed "to contribute to the growth, dignity, independence and self-reliance of the individual." Therefore, while much of its work is geared to families and communities, the federation's appeals are for individuals to aid individuals. Save the Children has made extensive use of high-priced media and advertising to broadcast its appeals, using many propaganda techniques to persuade prospective benefactors. Its appeals appear on both network and cable television as well as in magazines appealing to all areas of the political spectrum and to all segments of the population.

Emotional appeal is used on TELEVISION and in the print media. Usually a photograph of a Third World child is accompanied by a blurb giving some details of the child's life. Often the children are portrayed with symptoms of malnutrition and disease. Their surroundings are shown to be harboring disease as well. The appeal is to an individual to help this child (or another child, whose sex and location is the benefactor's choice). The child usually has a name, a family, and a biography. The emphasis is on the difference a few dollars a month will make in the life of such a child. This type of appeal has attracted many individual sponsors. Ironically, some groups aided by the federation have rejected this format because of its stress on the individual rather than the group, which goes contrary to the group's culture. Save the Children also uses celebrities, particularly in its television ADVERTISING. Both its print and electronic appeals present these media stars as sponsors of Save the Children. While these ads continue the agency's appeal for individual sponsorship, in later years they have also emphasized the use of funds for community service as well. In the summer of 1985, when the Non-Governmental Organization Forum on Women convened in Huairou, China, Save the Children sent as its delegate the actor Sally Field. Her address to the delegates was originally billed as one representing culture and communications. However, the gist of the speech focused on the work of Save the Children and her visit to Save the Children projects in Nepal. It was, in fact, an appeal for the agency's work.

Save the Children's techniques have been especially successful. Because of its success in fund-raising, it has attracted many imitators of its techniques, especially its emotional appeal to individuals to sponsor individual children. It is also considered by *Money* magazine as one of the most effective charities in the use of its funds.

— *Patricia J. Huhn*

■ Scapegoating

"Scapegoating" is the process of settling guilt or blame on some person, group, or thing for the crimes and failures of others, or for some misfortune brought about by another agency. The term originated in an ancient Jewish Day of Atonement ritual, in which the high priest confessed the sins of the people over the head of a goat that was then allowed to escape. Examples of scapegoating range from cases where medieval

peasants blamed bad harvests on witches to GERMANY's blaming Jews and communists for the country's defeat in WORLD WAR I (*see also* BIG-LIE TECHNIQUE). Scapegoating is a natural device for propaganda which employs such techniques as hate mongering, paranoia (*see* PARANOIA PROPAGANDA), or CHARACTER ASSASSINATION.

■ Scientology

Religion incorporated in 1953 by the science-fiction writer L. Ron Hubbard

Scientology teaches followers to free the "reactive mind" of unconscious images of pain and injuries called engrams. Once "clear," people can begin to function at their true potential and can advance to operating Thetan. Scientology is an extension of principles expounded in Hubbard's 1950 book *Dianetics: The Modern Science of Mental Health*. Becoming clear can take numerous auditing sessions, which resemble counseling sessions, and attaining higher levels requires the taking of several courses. Both require costly fixed donations.

The church believes that it has been unfairly targeted by critics, including writers, government agencies, the media, the mental health profession, and former Scientologists. It consistently responds forcefully, disseminating its ideas and protecting its position in a variety of ways, including frequent lawsuits, pro-Scientology ADVERTISING, activities (some would say interference) involving the Internet, and the aggressive promotion of Hubbard's books. Several protracted legal battles have involved books or articles critical of Scientology, including a $416 million libel suit against *Time*, filed in 1992 and dismissed in July, 1996. When *Time* published a critical cover story on May 6, 1991, the church also ran a $2 million media campaign, including full-page color ads in *USA Today* and an eighty-page booklet correcting the story's alleged inaccuracies. The Church of Scientology replied to the *Los Angles Times*' critical six-part series in 1990 by extracting some positive comments from the articles and posting them on billboards in Los Angeles. Hubbard's writings are considered the church's scriptures, and the church has repeatedly acted against those who violate copyrights and trademarks by distributing his writings or employing his ideas in their own self-improvement courses.

The church combatted postings to an Internet newsgroup by filing legal communications or lawsuits against system administrators, Internet service providers, operators of anonymous remailer services, and individual posters. It also issued requests to have the entire newsgroup removed from news sites. In late 1994 postings to the Internet site were mysteriously canceled, often with the message "canceled because of copyright infringement." Then, beginning in May, 1996, thousands of messages containing material copyrighted by the church and reproduced with permission of the Hubbard library were posted in a two-week period. In August, 1996, Netcom Online Services settled a suit which the Church of Scientology brought because the Internet access provider refused to remove church-related materials posted by a former Scientologist. Netcom agreed to establish procedures for handling disputed materials.

Scientology has touted Hubbard as a best-selling author in conjunction with an extensive advertising campaign for *Dianetics*. Beginning in late 1985 Hubbard had fourteen consecutive books on *The New York Times* best-seller list. Newspapers reported, however, that individuals were coming into bookstores and paying cash for multiple copies of Hubbard's books, thereby possibly inflating sales figures, and one B. Dalton bookstore received books from Hubbard's publisher with B. Dalton's price stickers already on them. Scientology has opposed various mental health practices, including lobotomies, electroconvulsive therapy, and drugs such as Ritalin and Prozac, perhaps because Hubbard saw Scientology as an alternative to psychiatry. Beginning in 1990 some journals linked the antidepressant Prozac to suicidal or violent behavior in a small number of patients. The Citizens Commission on Human Rights, a group affiliated with the Church of Scientology, urged Congress to remove Prozac from the market. A Food and Drug Administration committee held hearings on the issue in 1991 but rejected the request.

— *Dagny Taggart*

■ Seeger, Pete

Born May 3, 1919, in New York, New York City: American folksinger

Pete Seeger, a leader in the folk-music revival of the 1960's, long used MUSIC to move people to embrace social causes. After leaving Harvard University in 1938, Seeger traveled the country by freight train, collecting folk music and performing wherever people gathered. His songs

Folksinger Pete Seeger refuses to testify at a hearing of the House Committee on Un-American Activities in 1955. (AP/Wide World Photos)

encouraged workers to unite in labor unions. In 1940 he founded the Almanac Singers, a group that included Woody GUTHRIE, who was also known for his politicized music, and in 1948 he founded the Weavers, one of the earliest commercially successful folk groups.

Seeger's involvement in left-wing politics and in the trade-union movement led to his being blacklisted. The victim of anticommunist propaganda, Seeger was in 1955 called before the House Committee on Un-American Activities chaired by Senator Joseph MCCARTHY. Seeger's refusal to answer the questions posed to

him resulted in a 1961 contempt of Congress conviction, which was overturned in 1962. He nevertheless continued to experience blacklisting.

During the 1960's Seeger actively participated in both the Civil Rights movement and the VIETNAM WAR protest. His songs "Where Have All the Flowers Gone?" and "If I Had a Hammer" (written with Lee Hayes) became standards at rallies. When Seeger attempted to perform an antiwar song on national television, network censors cut his segment from the variety show. After protests from the show's hosts, Seeger's spot was eventually aired, dramatically calling attention to the issue of freedom of speech.

During the 1970's and 1980's Seeger was active in the environmental movement, sailing the sloop *Clearwater* on the Hudson River and holding concerts to dramatize the need for river cleanup. He continued to use music as a means of persuading people to take political and social action. In 1994 Seeger received a National Medal of Arts in a ceremony at the Kennedy Center in Washington D.C.

— *Diane Andrews Henningfeld*

■ Selectivity bias

The process of selecting which INFORMATION to present and which to omit or suppress (*see* OMISSION and OBJECTIVITY) is used to direct attention to material deemed by the selector to be of greater relevance. NEWSPAPERS and news magazines follow this procedure selecting news events and personalities. PROPAGANDISTS follow the procedure to manipulate PUBLIC OPINION to favor their interpretation of the cause, policy, or program that they are promoting.

■ Sensory perception manipulation

The sensations transmitted to the brain through nerves connected to organs for seeing, hearing, and feeling can be controlled or managed by an outside agency so that the sensations will be perceived by the brain in a form premeditated by the manipulator. Sensory perception manipulation is basic to propaganda, in particular to FILM and MUSIC used for propagan-

distic purposes. A dark and forbidding landscape as a backdrop to an array of enemy soldiers in a war film may contribute to the sense of fear or anxiety (*see* FEAR CAMPAIGN) that in the mind of the audience becomes linked to the menacing presence of the enemy. On the other hand, lively, energetic music as the background for an equally bright and lively film depicting smiling, happy participants in a patriotic parade may create in the viewer a positive sensation of identity with the participants and with what the parade represents. Another variation is the creation of false images (*see* DISTORTION and SUBLIMINAL MESSAGES) that leave the recipient with an impression of something that is not true: a doctored photograph or cassette tape, for example.

■ Shining Path

Peruvian revolutionary movement from the 1970's through the 1990's

Shining Path was founded by Abimael Guzmán in 1970 to bring about a violent overthrow of Peru's right-wing military dictatorship. Over time, the full name of the movement became "The Communist Party of Peru by the Shining Path of José Carlos Mariátegui and Marxism, Leninism, and the Thoughts of Chairman Gonzolo" ("Gonzolo" is a pseudonym of Guzmán's). The name "Shining Path" is used most frequently by foreigners and opposition groups; the movement refers to itself officially as the Communist Party of Peru.

The movement is driven by an orthodox ideology based on the writings of Karl Marx (*see* COMMUNIST MANIFESTO, THE),

After capturing Abimael Guzmán, the leader of the Shining Path terrorist group, the Peruvian government dressed him in a black-and-white prison suit in order to humiliate him when he was photographed by journalists. (*AP/Wide World Photos*)

V. I. LENIN, and, especially, MAO ZEDONG; it has rejected alignment with Communist governments—including the former Soviet Union—because of the impurity of their ideology. While Shining Path leaders tend to be educated, many of the rebels are young, poor, rural Indians who have been systematically denied access to the country's educational and economic opportunities.

When preparing speeches, documents, banners, and posters, the leadership of Shining Path is constantly aware that many of the peasants in their audience are illiterate or semiliterate, with little formal education. Thus, although the foundations for the revolutionary movement lie in complex ideological and historical premises, speeches to indigenous people refer most often to traditional Andean myths and to the Christian Bible, showing the ways in which these texts can be interpreted to promise and call for Shining Path.

Guzmán adopted a two-color scheme—red and black—to symbolize the reversal of the old order that is Shining Path's mission. Red represents fire, daytime, the sun, and the armed resistance; black stands for rot, night, the moon, and the state. There are no other colors, as in a revolution there can be no bystanders—everyone must choose a side. This struggle between two forces echoes Mao's teachings but also echoes traditional Incan beliefs. Propaganda leaflets and POSTER ART use the color symbolism heavily, layering the revolutionary messages on symbols and images recognizable even by nonreaders.

Throughout Peru, Shining Path set up secret "people's committees," which, among other responsibilities, provide desperately needed and wanted education. Shining Path members are instructed in mathematics, Spanish (the official language of Peru), natural science, and social science—all from viewpoints that will guide students into "Marxism-Leninism-Maoism-Thoughts of Chairman Gonzolo." This use of EDUCATION AS A PROPAGANDA TOOL has spread slowly to Peru's universities and schools as more teachers at all levels were brought into Shining Path.

The movement also speaks through the pro-Shining Path newspaper *El Diario.* The paper ran an important and extensive interview with Guzmán in 1988, giving him the opportunity to present Shining Path's interpretations of recent events, especially of clashes with the government and acts of violence. Typical contents of *El Diario* include essays and poems glorifying bombings, assassinations, and other acts of violent revolution. After numerous arrests and raids by the government, *El Diario* was forced underground in 1989. It has continued to publish, but only sporadically.

— *Cynthia A. Bily*

■ Shortwave radio

Radio braodcast medium that allows low-power signals to be sent over great distances

The use of shortwave radio as a tool to disseminate propaganda, both by established governments and by insurgent groups, began soon after the first transatlantic wireless transmission by the inventor Guglielmo Marconi in 1901. Political leaders quickly grasped that this new form of mass communication—produced by skipping short electronic waves off the ionosphere over long distances to radio receivers—could greatly enlarge the arenas for their thoughts and deeds.

Transcending barriers of geography, censorship, and illiteracy, which throughout civilization had limited the reach of politicians, shortwave radio set the twentieth century apart from earlier eras by reducing the physical and cultural distances between peoples. The great political events of the century (the Russian Revolution, World War I, World War II, and the COLD WAR) were shaped in considerable measure by shortwave radio broadcasts to listeners around the globe, battles of words that could influence events on actual battlefields. At the dawn of the twenty-first century, more than eighty nations, as well as countless unofficial organizations, broadcast thousands of hours of programming every week in hundreds of languages.

Although much of this programming seems devoid of overt political content—it includes popular music, sporting events, hobbies, theater, and religion—the symbolism of language is used by sponsors of shortwave broadcasts to construct disparate versions of reality, thereby accomplishing such specific economic and political goals as the overthrow of tyrants and occupying armies or the move toward capitalism or socialism. This subtle control of communication to influence audiences' beliefs and actions is a constant theme in the ever-changing mosaic of ideologies among nations.

RUSSIA, in 1916, was the first nation to exploit shortwave radio, when its military leaders during World War I urged German soldiers to desert their lines. The next year V. I. LENIN broadcast from a ship to European audiences, telling them about the Russian Revolution. During the 1920's and 1930's a number of European nations used shortwave broadcasts in attempts to reinforce dominion over their overseas colonies.

After Adolf HITLER became chancellor of Germany in 1933, the Nazi government used aggressive shortwave programming to legitimize the regime in Europe. When World War II began, France, Great Britain, and the United Stated overcame early qualms about their own governments' broadcasting in order to fight back. In the United States the OFFICE OF WAR INFORMATION helped form the long-lived VOICE OF AMERICA (VOA), which continually altered the focus of its programming to Europe to reflect shifting strategic needs during combat and reconstruction. Despite policy disagreements between VOA and the influential British Broadcasting Corporation (BBC) democratic capitalism emerged triumphant after World War II.

In the Cold War, which was largely a propaganda war, VOA and the U.S. government's RADIO LIBERTY served as the heavy artillery in Eastern Europe; elsewhere during this period many emerging Third World nations used shortwave radio to help gain independence from former colonial powers.

With the fall of the Berlin Wall in 1989, the urgency for government propaganda via shortwave radio eased. At the same time clandestine shortwave broadcasting within the United Stated began attacking the government from a fanatically right-wing perspective.

— *Nan K. Chase*

■ Sierra Club

Conservation group organized in California in 1892 to preserve wilderness areas

The Sierra Club was founded on June 4, 1892, by John Muir and more than 150 university-trained individuals. A nonprofit group, the Sierra Club organized wilderness outings for its members and lobbies for stricter federal and state environmental protection laws. This vigilant group has made itself responsible for millions of acres of land, and one of its most effective tools has been its use of the legal system.

One of the group's earliest successes was the preservation of Yosemite as a national park. In subsequent years the Sierra Club used full-page newspaper advertisements as part of a campaign against the construction of two dams on the Colorado River where it passed through the Grand Canyon. In the 1960's the group opposed a California power company that proposed building a nuclear power plant (*see* NUCLEAR POWER PRODUCTION) near the rare ecosystem of the Nipomo Santa Maria dunes near the Pacific coast. Both campaigns were successful. The club spent nine years lobbying for the legal protection of the Alaskan wilderness. Members also worked for passage of the 1994 California Desert Protection Act, which safeguards more wilderness and parks in the lower forty-eight states than any previous law.

The relationship of pesticides to the deterioration of human health and plant and animal life was exposed in Rachel Carson's book, *Silent Spring* (1962), the royalties of which are part of a gift bequeathed to the organization after her death. The Sierra Club focused attention on this menace through litigation, *Sierra Club v. Ruckelshaus*, that led in 1973 to the Supreme Court's ordering the Environmental Protection Agency to establish a major program preventing the deterioration of air quality in unpolluted areas. The Sierra Club has also worked for the National Environmental Policy Act of 1969; the Clean Water Act of 1972; the National Forest Management Act of 1976; the Clean Air Act amendments of 1977; the National Acid Precipitation Act of 1980; and the creation of the Environmental Protection Agency in 1970. In addition the organization continues to be concerned about the sale of banned pesticides abroad, the effects of pesticides on the nervous, immune, and reproductive systems, and carcinogenic properties of pesticides.

The Sierra Club's mission is to enjoy, explore, and protect the wild places of the earth; to practice and promote the responsible use of the earth's ecosystems and resources; to educate and enlist humanity to protect and restore the quality of the natural and human environment; and to use all lawful means to carry out these objectives. In one of its slogans the organization reminds the public that there is "One Earth, One Chance."

With more than half a million members, the Sierra Club continues to promote its environmental agenda on issues including urban environment, visual pollution, off-road vehicles, indoor air pollution, electric utility rate structures, public lands user fees, and rainforests. The group has its headquarters in San Francisco, and it further publicizes its concerns by designating individuals to receive the John Muir Award, its highest honor, and individuals who remember the Sierra Club in their estate plans are recognized through the Rachel Carson Society.

— *Suzanne Riffle Boyce*

■ Sinclair, Upton

September 20, 1878, in Baltimore, Maryland—November 25, 1968, in Bound Brook, New Jersey: American novelist and socialist writer

Best known as the author of the 1906 novel *The Jungle*, a work that led to the

Upton Sinclair in 1942. (AP/Wide World Photos)

passage of the Pure Food and Drug Act, Upton Sinclair devoted his career to analyzing the failures of American life and offering potential remedies. Labeled a muckraker and worse, Sinclair argued that American economic, political, and social practices subverted the ideals upon which the United States was founded—ideals better realized, in his view, through socialism. To persuade his audience, Sinclair embraced the role of propagandist, using fiction as well as critical and autobiographical writings to advance the cause and consideration of American socialism in the first half of the twentieth century.

Sinclair did not accept the negative terms with which propaganda was defined in the twentieth century. In *Mammonart* (self-published in 1925) Sinclair stated that he would "study art works as instruments of propaganda and repression, employed by the ruling classes of the community; or as weapons of attack, employed by new classes rising into power." He defined art, including literature, as a vital component of culture that explores the conduct of life and the potential of the human spirit. He argued that any representation of life in art is influenced by the values and understanding of the artist, who seeks to communicate those values to others through his or her creative works. Thus, according to Sinclair, "All art is propaganda."

SINCLAIR'S EARLY CAREER Sinclair's literary career eventually reflected his concept of the artist as propagandist, but he began writing for more pragmatic reasons. To support himself and his mother, Sinclair wrote magazine fiction and jokes while a student at City College of New York; later, as a graduate student at Columbia University, he wrote "potboilers" to earn needed income. He left Columbia in 1900 to pursue a career as a serious author, and in 1901 he published at his own expense *Springtime and Harvest*, reissued as *King Midas* later that year by Funk and Wagnalls. Neither this novel, nor his next, *The Journal of Arthur Stirling* (1903), reflected the socialist values that were to shape Sinclair's future. It was *Manassas* (1904), a novel of the Civil War, that revealed Sinclair's growing interest in political and economic conflict.

By 1904 Sinclair had become more fully immersed in the study of socialism. He accepted a cash advance from the socialist weekly *Appeal to Reason* to begin research on what would become *The Jungle*. Sinclair moved to Chicago, where he interviewed laborers, social workers, and doctors and toured the packing plants, both as an official visitor and disguised as a worker. He was deeply disturbed by what he saw and learned through his research; he wanted his narrative to evoke a similar response on the part of his readers. As he detailed the experiences of Jurgis Rudkis and his family, who suffer unspeakable hardships in the "wage-slave" trap called Packingtown, Sinclair hoped to persuade his readers that unregulated capitalism, with its emphasis on competition and its acceptance of the social Darwinist principle of "survival of the fittest," was destroying Americans and their dreams of democratic equality. While this novel created consumer outrage and led to public policy changes, it failed to accomplish Sinclair's true goal of convincing Americans to accept socialism.

SINCLAIR THE CRUSADER Undaunted by the challenge of persuading his audience, Sinclair continued to write novels that he readily admitted were propaganda (according to his definitions) as well as works of nonfiction. In 1915 he compiled an anthology of protest literature, *A Cry for Justice*. This was followed by *King Coal* (1917), a novel in which Sinclair responded to the violence and exploitation of the American coal industry. That same year he publicly resigned from the American Socialist Labor Party, finding himself in disagreement with party philosophies and practices, especially its pacifism in the face of World War I. He wrote the novel *Jimmie Higgins* (1919) to offer his views on the party's failings, but he rejoined the Socialist Party in 1920. In *The Brass Check* (1921) he critiqued American publishing practices, and in *The Goose-Step* (1923) and *The Goslings* (1924) his target was American education

and its cozy relationship with American industry. His novel *Oil!* (1927) featured a wealthy protagonist who embraces liberal ideologies but struggles with their practical implementation. In the 1920's Sinclair joined other writers in opposing the outcome of the Sacco and Vanzetti case in Massachusetts, eventually the subject of his novel *Boston* (1928). Sinclair continued to write for the next three decades, producing countless novels, dramas, and works of nonfiction. His Lanny Budd series, begun in 1940 with *World's End*, became the focus of his efforts; it ran to eleven volumes, one of which, *Dragon's Teeth* (1943), won the Pulitzer Prize. Though the series is historical fiction, Sinclair was proud of his historical accuracy in the books.

In addition to his career as a writer, Sinclair pursued political office. He ran for Congress and for governor of California as a socialist during the 1920's. In 1934 Sinclair won the Democratic primary for governor but lost in the general election later that year. Sinclair's life was rich in personal associations and in political activism; his *My Lifetime in Letters* (1960) and *The Autobiography of Upton Sinclair* (1962) offer details about the many causes he espoused and individuals he knew. Sinclair was a true idealist who believed that propaganda in the form of literature could serve a noble purpose.

SUGGESTED READINGS:

Bloodworth, William A., Jr. *Upton Sinclair.* Boston: Twayne, 1977.

Herms, Dieter, ed. *Upton Sinclair: Literature and Social Reform.* New York: P. Lang, 1990.

Mitchell, Greg. *The Campaign of the Century: Upton Sinclair's Race for Governor of California and the Birth of Media Politics.* New York: Random House, 1992.

Mookerjee, R. N. *Art for Social Justice: The Major Novels of Upton Sinclair.* Metuchen, N.J.: Scarecrow Press, 1988.

— *Melissa McFarland Pennell*

■ Six-Day War

1967: Israel's defeat of surrounding Arab Arab states and occupation of the West Bank, Gaza Strip, Golan Heights, and Sinai Peninsula

The Six-Day War was a watershed in the Arab-Israeli conflict. All the territory west of the Jordan river, excepting the Gaza Strip and the West Bank, had become part of the nascent state of Israel in 1948. During the nineteen years that followed, both sides waged a war of propaganda in an international arena often more concerned with COLD WAR issues than with regional hostilities. To raise their regional and international visibility the Palestinians, who had been frequently shunted to the political periphery during this time, formed the PALESTINE LIBERATION ORGANIZATION (PLO).

Stronger support for the Palestinians resulted from a coup in SYRIA in 1966, when Syria began to challenge Egypt's leadership of the Arab world. Preoccupied with a war in Yemen, Egypt's president Gamal Abdel NASSER, sought reconciliation with Syria through a mutual defense agreement. However, provocative Syrian policies toward Israel began pushing him into open confrontation with that country. Palestinian activists, and several Arab countries, chided Nasser for a weak policy toward Israel. In May, 1967, Nasser unilaterally ordered the emergency forces of the UNITED NATIONS to stop patrolling the Israeli-Egyptian cease-fire line in the Sinai, which served as a warning to the Israelis of possible future confrontation.

Nasser subsequently blockaded the Gulf of Aqaba at its exit, in violation of international law, and refused Israeli access to the Suez canal, which deprived Israel of sea access to eastern Africa and the Far East. Israel considered this a declaration of war. With the United States heavily involved in the protracted VIETNAM WAR and not expected to offer much assistance, Israel chose to strike preemptively against Egypt. On June 5, 1967, Israel decimated the entire Egyptian air force. Within the next five days the Israeli military occupied the Gaza Strip, Sinai, and the West Bank, driving Egyptian, Jordanian, and Lebanese forces from these regions. After having penetrated deeply into the Golan Heights by the end of the sixth day, Israel agreed to a partial withdrawal as part of a cease-fire agreement with Syria.

Although the war was a propaganda coup for Israel, media reports of Israelis rejoicing intensified the conflict. The quick victory fostered a perception—among Arabs, Israelis, and many others—that Israel's military was invincible. Although Israel offered to surrender much of the captured territory in exchange for recognition and full peace with its Arab neighbors, this was refused. The Arab countries found it impossible to forget the humiliation of their military defeat, and to the international community the war suggested that the strongest and best-equipped Arab states were incapable of successfully prosecuting a modern technological war.

The rapid military victory took a serious political toll on all sides. Combatant Arab states were politically destabilized.

The Arab-Israeli conflict had become an internal problem for Israel, which now found itself responsible for a sizable population of Palestinian refugees. The protracted occupation also challenged the democratic basis of the state of Israel. The situation provided both sides with substantial material for propaganda, which has been exploited in the world media and in international diplomacy.

— *Richard A. Bennett*

■ Slogans

The function of catchwords or mottos associated with specific organizations or groups, or a catchphrase associated with a product ADVERTISING campaign, is, in Jacques ELLUL's words, to represent "the demands, the expectations, the hopes of the mass, and at the same time [to express] the established values of a group." The form of the slogan must catch the eye, and the content must focus attention on some positive aspect of its subject for promotional purposes. The U.S. Army announces that it wants its recruits to "Be all that you can be," whereas the Marines want "A few good men." Coca-Cola promises that "Things go better with Coke," and the French Revolution in 1789 promised that it would bring "Liberty, Fraternity, Equality" to the French people. Slogans, by their nature, are propaganda.

■ Smear campaign

This technique is the process of misrepresenting the character of an individual, the policies of a government, or the platform of a political party or organization through innuendo, half-truths, and lies. Smear campaigns are frequently conducted in the context of POLITICAL CAMPAIGNING, when individuals in political office are smeared to discredit their performances and to pave the way for their defeat in forthcoming elections, or even to force their resignation or dismissal from office. The nature of the smear can include allegations of criminal activity, sexual misconduct, and racial or gender BIAS against subordinates or colleagues (*see* CHARACTER ASSASSINATION and LABELING).

■ Smith, Gerald L. K.

February 27, 1898, in Pardeeville, Wisconsin—April 15, 1976, in Los Angeles, California: American fascist spokesperson

Born into a fundamentalist Christian family that adhered to POPULISM, Gerald Lymann Kenneth Smith was ordained a minister of the Disciples of Christ long before he graduated at the age of nineteen from Valpariso University. When his wife, Elna, became ill with tuberculosis, he relocated to Shreveport, Louisiana, but his interest in social reform prompted church leaders to ask him to leave the pulpit. He became the chief national organizer of the "Share Our Wealth" movement organized by Huey LONG, who described Smith as the "greatest rabble-rouser in the country."

When Long was assassinated in 1935 Smith, the best-known of Long's associates, attempted to take the political reins, but he was defeated in the ensuing power struggle. Smith subsequently allied himself with Francis E. Townsend, the director of the Old Age Pension Movement, and later with Father Charles E. COUGHLIN and William Lemke to campaign against Franklin D. ROOSEVELT.

He traveled all across the nation making religio-political harangues and threatening to seize control of the federal government. His speeches, always impressive extemporaneous events and filled with stock phrases and focusing on the same villains, were essentially the same at every stop, but he was able to work his audiences into a frenzy. Smith's views opposing alcohol, drugs, tobacco, and pornography, as well as his opposition to communism, in many ways fit into the mainstream political discussion. Where Smith differed was in viewing these issues in racial, anti-Semitic terms.

In his five hundred books, pamphlets, and tracts Smith discussed social ills with an anger that has rarely been duplicated. He founded the periodical *Cross and the Flag* in 1942 and contributed most of its contents; slightly smaller than a tabloid, this publication appeared until 1977 but always at a financial loss. Smith claimed to live in constant fear that enemies were trying to kill him before he could complete his messianic mission to save the world.

— *R. Ferrell Ervin*

■ Socialist Labor Party

First significant socialist party in the United States, founded in 1877 as a successor to the Workingmen's Party

The Socialist Labor Party's propaganda was ideological in the sense that it promoted a philosophy of industrial union-ism and utopian socialism as the solution to the problems of society (*see* LABOR MOVEMENTS). Until his death in 1914 Daniel DeLeon, a Columbia University professor born in Curaçao and educated in Europe, was the party's mentor. His platform called exclusively for the abolition of capitalism. The crucial question for socialists was how they should replace the existing political system. DeLeon argued that the socialists should be voted peacefully into power; however, once they achieved power, they would turn over the administration of the state to the workers themselves. DeLeon concluded that the major obstacle to socialism was not the power of the great capitalists; rather, the major obstacle was the conservatism of American labor leaders. DeLeon opposed the actions of unions such as the American Federation of Labor and argued that the seeking of higher wages and shorter hours was useless. He feared that the working class would be corrupted by bourgeois values. Thus he advocated the creation of revolutionary industrial unions to educate the workers and to increase their class consciousness. These unions were to be led by a dedicated cadre of revolutionary leaders who would guide the masses to power.

The Socialist Labor Party's greatest appeal was to revolutionary socialists who believed in political education through speeches and publications. Its greatest support came from working-class radicals who mistrusted the middle-class leaders of other radical groups. The Socialist Labor Party communicated with its followers through a number of newspapers, including an array of Yiddish publications as well as a daily English-language newspaper, the *People*.

Despite DeLeon's intellectual leadership, the party was beset by factional disputes with other socialists. In 1901 the Socialist Party, led by Eugene Debs, was created. From that time forward little remained of the Socialist Labor Party except its newspaper and the New York Labor News Company, its publishing component, which reprinted DeLeon's speeches and the writings of European socialists.

Following the death of DeLeon in 1914, Arnold Peterson, a Swedish immigrant, became national secretary of the party. For decades the party continued to distribute socialist leaflets, published the *Weekly People*, organized local study classes that examined the writings of Karl Marx, Friedrich Engels, and Daniel DeLeon, and collected signatures in order to gain ballot status in some states. It remained loyal to the principles of DeLeon throughout its history.

The membership of the Socialist Labor Party peaked at approximately eight thousand in the 1890's. In the early part of the twentieth century its membership was no more than four to five thousand people, about evenly divided between English-language and foreign-language groups. By the early 1970's party membership was only a few hundred people. But despite its limited membership, it had a significant impact on the socialist movement in the UNITED STATES at the beginning of the twentieth century because of the intellectual leadership of Daniel DeLeon. Through his writings and speeches he introduced thousands of working people and intellectuals in the United States to the ideas and ideals of socialism as a solution to the problems created by industrial capitalism.

— *William V. Moore*

■ Socialist Realism

1932-1953: Soviet cultural movement

Socialist Realism was introduced in the Soviet Union under Joseph STALIN in 1932 (*see* RUSSIA: 1918-1953). It was applied to ART, MUSIC, LITERATURE, and THEATER AND DRAMA, and it was an integral part of Stalin's Second Five-Year Plan, from 1933 to 1938. SOCIALIST REALISM reflected the Communist Party's desire to focus the attention of the Soviet people on the need to achieve maximum production for the benefit of the state. Thus artists, musicians, and writers were to be employed as propaganda tools of the party and government. The intention was not only to inspire Soviet workers but also to impress the world that the Soviet Union was moving forward as a great power.

The origin of Socialist Realism is to be found in the Communist Party's decision in 1932 to create the Maxim GORKY Institute of Literature. The institute's efforts were directed toward two goals: fostering a unity of spirit and endeavor among Soviet writers from all the Socialist Republics, and encouraging writers to emphasize positive themes that would inspire workers.

Sensing that many writers remained vague on the methods and objectives to be pursued, the First All-Union Congress of Soviet Writers meeting in Moscow in August, 1934, established a clear definition of Socialist Realism as accurate historical representation with the purpose of educating workers about the goals of Communism. The roots of this definition were to be found in the works of such great nineteenth century writers as Anton Chekhov and Leo Tolstoy, but whereas

One of the best-known Soviet writers outside of the Soviet Union, Aleksandr Solzhenitsyn was also one of the most outspoken critics of Socialist Realism. (*The Nobel Foundation*)

With the invasion of Nazi troops into the U.S.S.R. in June, 1941 (*see* GERMANY), Socialist Realism was, for a time, turned on its head. Stalin ordered Soviet writers and artists to resurrect the wartime leaders of the Russian past, especially the emperors Ivan IV and Peter the Great. This propaganda attempt to establish for Stalin a reputation as a great wartime ruler was highly successful.

When the Soviet Union began to rebuild after the war, Socialist Realism returned to its original objectives. There were severe penalties for those artists who did not follow, or who tried to skirt, the propaganda aims of the state. Although some writers and artists, among them Aleksandr Solzhenitsyn, issued periodic condemnations of Socialist Realism, most stayed within the government guidelines. Socialist Realism did not end with Stalin's death in March, 1953. Although there was some relaxation under Nikita Khrushchev, it continued in effect, with varying levels of enforcement, until Mikhail GORBACHEV became leader of the Soviet Union in 1985.

— *Ronald K. Huch*

those writers had produced works critical of their societies, the writers of Socialist Realism were expected to create heroes who embraced the ideals of the "New Soviet Man and Woman."

The practical result of this directive was to limit the creative range of all Soviet artists. Painters were to eschew all subjects that evoked romantic memories of the czarist regime. They were to depict the honor and dignity of hard labor by showing people at work in factories and fields. Likewise musicians and composers were to emphasize musical scores characterized by optimistic, rousing, martial sounds.

■ Society for the Prevention of Cruelty to Animals

Animal-welfare society founded in England in l824

Successful in his attempts to move an animal-welfare bill through Great Britain's Parliament on June 10, 1822, Richard Martin believed that only through organizational efforts could attitudes regarding treatment of animals be changed. He and eleven other anticruelty advocates founded the Society for the Prevention of Cruelty to Animals (SPCA) in June, 1824. The campaign that Martin and other reformers formulated to effect change entailed the distribution of tracts, MEDIA coverage, sermons, discourses, passage of legislation, enforcement and prosecution of persons who committed cruelty crimes, and the placement of literature in educational institutions. The rationale that was the core of the SPCA's work was based on nineteenth century Protestant tenets and concepts of stewardship; animals were created to serve humankind and were not believed to have souls. They were, however, to be treated with kindness and their suffering alleviated.

The work of the English SPCA quickly produced positive outcomes in the forms of changes in public attitudes and legislation. From the 1820's onward, Parliament continued to enlarge the scope and strength of animal-welfare legislation. Yet, well into the modern era, SPCA workers found it difficult to eliminate the sport of animal fights, baiting, and hunting.

The work of the animal-welfare advocates in England did not go unnoticed. Henry Bergh, a wealthy American, learned of the work of the English SPCA. He carefully familiarized himself with welfare activities in England, and in 1866 he founded the first animal-welfare organization in the United States, using the British society as a model. The mission of the American Society for the Prevention of Cruelty to Animals (ASPCA) was the same as the British mission—welfare—but Bergh emphasized that anticruelty work was not simply moral, nor was it political; rather, it was a matter of conscience infused with mercy.

The ASPCA distributed literature, lobbied for legislation, and conducted lectures; it also pointedly campaigned for change through the media and direct-action activities. Highly visible campaigns conducted by the ASPCA were devised to change the methods for the transport and slaughter of cattle, the transport and sale of turtles, the plucking of live chickens, the use of animal power for omnibuses and street railways, and animal sport fighting. The latter type of animal cruelty, Bergh discovered, as had his English counterparts, was difficult to eradicate. He learned quickly that it was easier to change laws then attitudes.

More noticeable in America than England was the support given by print journalists, editors, and publishers, such as Frank Leslie and James Gordon Bennet, to the various campaigns undertaken by animal-welfare activists. The ASPCA's "Swill Milk" campaign, for example, received extensive and favorable media coverage.

From 1866 onward, various interest groups opposed some of the ASPCA's campaigns. Yet the ASPCA fostered concern for animals in the United States and helped pass legislation, starting with the Animal Welfare Act in 1866. Furthermore, the ASPCA's efforts to awaken public sentiment to the animal-welfare cause led to the formation of other groups, such as the American Rescue League (1874), the Antivivisection Society (1883), and the American Humane Society (1877), which also sought for a time the protection of children. The work of the American and English societies received global attention, and soon their organizational form, mission, and activities became models for similar societies in other countries.

The welfare mission of the SPCA has remained unchanged. By the 1970's, however, many anticruelty activists began to consider the nature of animal rights, and new organizations, such as PEOPLE FOR THE ETHICAL TREATMENT OF ANIMALS (PETA), were established by activists who sought to make animal welfare an unquestionable right.

— *Loretta Ellen Zimmerman*

■ Somalia relief campaign

1992: International effort to address the famine resulting from a civil war in Somalia

After the flight of President Siyad Barrah in January, 1991, Somalia experienced civil war as rival, clan-based groups maneuvered for control. The conflict increasingly inhibited food production. UNITED NATIONS (U.N.) efforts to ensure the transportation and security of relief supplies failed and were marred by disputes over how best to negotiate a U.N. presence. In November, 1992, the United States proposed a major relief and security operation known as Operation Restore Hope. This operation, which was eventually turned over to the U.N., contributed to the reduction of the famine but failed to resolve the deeper and underlying conflicts in the country.

From the start of the crisis, propaganda tactics and issues were used by the governments involved, by international and nongovernmental organizations (NGOs), and by various media. As early as 1991 United Nations secretary-general Boutros Boutros-Ghali blamed Western governments for being more concerned with the "rich man's war" in Yugoslavia than with the black people in Somalia's civil war. He was chastised for these comments, but the United Nations took action to address relief needs the following year. U.S. president George BUSH promised to deploy nearly 30,000 troops to restore order and secure relief supply lines to Somalia; to obtain domestic support he promised that U.S. involvement would be brief.

Most of the humanitarian agencies that had long demanded international action appeared to be satisfied, but some of them resented the American action and criticized it with increasing vigor. The French agency Médecins sans Frontières (Doctors Without Borders), for example, claimed that its work was compromised by the military presence. Other NGOs, however, claimed that the humanitarian intervention had not adequately addressed either the need for political resolution of clan conflicts or the need to disarm the country. In actuality, it was international efforts to disarm the Somali clan armies that eventually provoked resistance and led to the ultimate failure of U.N. efforts to resolve the political crisis in Somalia.

Another problematic issue in the Somali relief operation was whether U.S. forces should be under U.N. command. Republican members of the U.S. Congress, appealing to public doubts and fears, effectively maneuvered the new administration of President Bill Clinton into announcing a complete withdrawal from Somalia after U.S. forces sustained casualties fighting a local war lord's military supporters.

What had initially been portrayed as a humanitarian exercise motivated by the best of intentions gradually evolved into a nightmare of errors and the eventual acknowledgment of defeat and international withdrawal. Relief agencies and governments accused each other of being to blame, and propaganda was used by all the participants in the relief program to disseminate their individual versions of events. Diplomats involved in the situation wrote books to justify their positions, and governments and NGO's produced reports and news releases. The event demonstrated that any relief operation acting in a complex emergency in a country where central government had ceased to exist must face great difficulties. When the difficulties in Somalia became overwhelming, the humanitarian instincts of all parties deteriorated into SCAPEGOATING.

— *Robert F. Gorman*

■ South Africa

African country long dominated by white colonizers

Although Great Britain won the SOUTH AFRICAN WAR in 1902, it gave the defeated Afrikaners virtual control of the region when it granted the Union of South Africa dominion status eight years later. From then until 1948, South Africa's Afrikaner minority, in league with the country's even smaller English-speaking white minority, developed a system that severely limited the rights of the nonwhite majority.

From 1948 to 1994 the National Party, representing Afrikaner concerns, was in power. It immediately began to make legally absolute the country's segregation in the name of apartheid—separateness— policy. In 1960 the party severed the political knot with Britain. The two econo-

mies continued to be tightly connected, however, with the British-descended minority dominating South Africa's industrial and financial sectors.

The succeeding thirty years saw an increasingly fierce struggle between the government—which tried to control the black majority as a cheap labor force and to keep them in zones accounting for just 13 percent of the land—and the AFRICAN NATIONAL CONGRESS (ANC), the leading black nationalist movement. The ANC's triumph was eventually assured with the release in 1990 of its leader Nelson Mandela, who had been jailed on political charges since 1961. He was elected president in 1994.

Propaganda activities during these years fell under three headings: the Afrikaners' apartheid doctrine; the defense of apartheid on geopolitical grounds; and the national and international resistance to apartheid.

APARTHEID DOCTRINE Apartheid was defined as the strict segregation of Europeans and Africans, those of Indian descent, and of mixed descent. In practical terms the policy meant the demolition of whole African neighborhoods and the forcible relocation of populations to places the regime judged suitable. These might be in new cities such as Soweto, to supply labor to Johannesburg, the financial center, or they might be remote rural locations, where there was no economic base. Families were often separated for nearly the whole year, with only one parent permitted to work in a town.

The original rationale behind the apartheid policy was that the Afrikaners were divinely appointed to rule southern Africa, that Africans were incapable of self-

Young South Africans carry campaign posters during their nation's first fully democratic national election in early 1994. (AP/Wide World Photos)

rule, and that any racial mixing, whether in public buildings, the school system, or through marriage was against God's will and certain to destroy the country. The British, both as colonial overlords and as representatives of British interests, were seen as a nuisance.

Both the inherited residential segregation and its apartheid forms went through various name changes. What had been the Native Reserves under the British became "homelands" and then later "Bantustans," supposedly separate and independent republics based upon traditional tribal identities, such as Xhosa and Zulu. In reality, urbanization had long meant the decline of those identities, and their attempted reinstitution was designed to encourage divisiveness among the African majority. Forced relocation was titled "resettlement" and segregation was named "separate development."

Biological accounts of racial inequality were common in apartheid reasoning, but equally important were the notion of the Afrikaners as a (Calvinist) Christian nation and the ideology of national cultural identity as an absolute, unchanging force. Following the end of Nazi GERMANY, those who generated apartheid propaganda began to deemphasize biological arguments in favor of cultural ones, but the substance of life did not change in the country.

School textbooks massively propagated apartheid arguments, as did radio broadcasting. The English-language press in some instances challenged the system's enforcement, but it is important to note that a consensus on racial subordination overrode the friction between the British and Afrikaner communities. Apartheid bent in other ways, too: The small Chinese minority was defined as nonwhite, but Japanese diplomats and businessmen were given the status of "honorary whites."

GEOPOLITICAL DEFENSES OF APARTHEID   In the COLD WAR era, the antiquated miasma of claiming the Afrikaners' divine vocation was something of an embarrassment outside traditional Afrikaner circles. Similarly, to stress the importance of South Africa's gold mines ran the risk of seeming merely greedy, not least given the notoriously bad working conditions for African miners. In any case gold's role as an international currency-stabilizing factor was abstract. The Soviet system and its putative expansionist intention, provided a more concrete motivation, however.

In this way, the importance of the Cape, especially for Europe's oil routes following the 1967 closure of the Suez Canal, was emphasized to protect South Africa's internal policies. The specter was repeatedly raised as to the disaster that would ensue if the ANC, backed by Moscow, established control of South Africa, whereby the Soviets would gain the capacity to hold Europe's oil to ransom. With this argument the United States, Great Britain, West Germany, France, Japan, and other leading nations were able to justify temporizing with the apartheid regime, complaining about its policies in public but continuing to work actively with its economy.

On this basis the regime was also able to intervene militarily in neighboring states, notably Angola and Mozambique, both directly and through support of guerrilla movements. It was claimed that these nations, following their independence in 1975, had Marxist governments sympathetic to Moscow. The Cold

War dynamic was able to subsume the fact that these nations had no military capacity against South Africa, that they harbored home bases for the ANC, and that they represented alternative models to apartheid.

By the 1980's, with militant resistance gaining ground within South African urban areas, another theme—not new, but massively refurbished—became important in apartheid propaganda: So-called black-on-black violence was given intensive publicity as a way of propagating the inevitable menace of a South Africa under African control.

Violence by blacks against other blacks certainly did occur, but it took a variety of forms. One common form was in confrontations between migrant workers and settled workers, situations that historically arise from competition for scarce jobs. However, these and other clashes were quite often sponsored or exacerbated by the apartheid regime's extensive financial support for and prompting of violence by the Inkatha, a political organization with a mainly rural Zulu base, which maintained that support through a combination of welfare handouts and brutal sanctions against those who defied it. The Truth and Reconciliation Commission hearings in the mid-1990's established many of the sordid facts behind the government's propaganda claims that blacks were prone to violence and could not be trusted to govern themselves or others.

RESISTANCE PROPAGANDA The propaganda disseminated by black resistance groups went through two major phases. The ANC, which was founded in 1912 and whose membership was open to all South Africans, placed a strong emphasis on nontribalism and nondiscrimination. For its first five decades the organization campaigned against segregation, the pass-laws, and other injustices consistently meted out to nonwhite people, including the violent repression of their political opposition. Its appeal was always to the humane conscience.

Following the apartheid regime's departure from its British political connection in 1960, however, and the economic and military support that continued to be afforded the regime by the major powers, the ANC strategy changed sharply. The organization now addressed itself to exposing events in South Africa to an international audience, with the aim of turning the regime into a pariah on the world stage. It particularly set itself the task of forging alliances with sympathetic governments (including the U.S.S.R., Scandinavia, and others), with labor unions and solidarity groups, and in the UNITED NATIONS. Over time the ANC succeeded in establishing more diplomatic missions around the world than the South African regime had embassies.

A further tactic, and one with extraordinary resonance among the white minority inside South Africa, was to lobby for the cancellation of sporting links and contests with the rest of the world. SPORTS are enormously popular in South Africa, and white sportsmen and women often scored considerable success in international tournaments and in the OLYMPIC GAMES. To be cut off from these events was to sense the condemnation of the rest of the world in a way that was otherwise totally muted in the comfortable provincial isolation of white life in South Africa. Tennis, rugby football, cricket, and golf, were part of daily life, whereas no comparable impact resulted to the white minority from the arms sanctions that only gradually took effect, the oil sanctions the country efficiently evaded, or the disinvestment agitation in firms and universities overseas. The total impact of these ruptured links only became fully evident once they were restored after Mandela's release. The sense, especially among young white people, of rejoining the world community and being able when traveling overseas to say they were South African without shame or anxiety, was palpable.

The ANC's long friendship with Moscow, and the important role the South African Communist Party had played for decades within the ANC, was a formidable propaganda issue. To convince world business opinion that the ANC was not planning to put everything in sight under state ownership, it undertook extensive contacts with both South African and international executives throughout the 1980's, and in fact underwent a sharp conversion to neoliberal economic policies in the early 1990's. Whether this turn boded well for South Africa's many millions of dispossessed citizens was a matter of considerable debate within ANC ranks, but the conversion was of great propaganda importance for luring foreign investment into the country.

■ **South Africa: History at a Glance**

Year	Event
1652	The Dutch establish a trading station and settlement. These settlers, also known as Boers, speak a Dutch dialect that later becomes known as Afrikaans.
1799	The first of many frontier wars breaks out between Boer farmers and Xhosa-speaking Africans, who are losing their land to the settlers on the eastern frontier.
1814	The Congress of Vienna awards Great Britain the territory around the Cape of Good Hope.
1834	The British Empire abolishes slavery.
1835	The Boers begin the "Great Trek" north, away from the costal territory under British control. The Boers occupy territory that later becomes the South African Republic and the Orange Free State.
1867	Diamonds are discovered at Kimberley.
1886	Gold is discovered in the Transvaal; the economy booms, bringing immigrants and development; tensions continue between Afrikaners and other (mostly British) white settlers.
1899-1902	Great Britain defeats the Boer republics in the South African (Boer) War.
1910	The Union of South Africa is created. Boers remain influential in the country's government.
1912	The African National Congress (ANC) is formed as the South African Native National Congress.
1945	South Africa joins the United Nations but refuses to sign the Universal Declaration of Human Rights.
1948	The National Party takes power and begins the apartheid system—the policy of rigid segregation, racial classification, white supremacy, and brutal police enforcement.
1956	Nelson Mandela and other African leaders are tried for treason.
1959	The militant Pan African Congress (PAC) separates from the ANC. The government bans both.
1964	Mandela is sentenced to life in prison.
1989	Frederick de Klerk becomes president. He legalizes the ANC and releases Mandela.
1991	Apartheid laws begin to be repealed.
1994	Nelson Mandela is elected president of South Africa in the first all-race national elections.

SUGGESTED READINGS:

Chan, Stephen, ed. *Exporting Apartheid: Foreign Policies in Southern Africa, 1978-1988.* New York: St Martin's Press, 1990.

Downing, John. "U.S. Media Discourse on South Africa: The Development of a Situation Model." *Discourse and Society* 1, no. 1 (1990): 39-60.

Dubow, Saul. "Afrikaner Nationalism, Apartheid, and the Conceptualization of 'Race.'" *Journal of African History* 33 (1992): 209-237.

Evans, Graham. "South Africa in Remission: The Foreign Policy of an Altered State." *Journal of Modern African Studies* 34, no. 2 (June, 1995): 249-269.

Grundy, Kenneth W. *South Africa: Domestic Crisis and Global Challenge.* Boulder, Colo.: Westview Press, 1991.

Thompson, Leonard. *The Political Mythology of Apartheid.* New Haven, Conn.: Yale University Press, 1985.

— *John D. H. Downing*

■ South African War

1899-1902: War between Great Britain and South African Boer republics

In the South African, or Anglo-Boer War, each side was convinced of its own divine mission, and each used domestic and foreign propaganda to portray the war as a contest of good against evil. In practical terms the Boer republics needed allies in an anti-British coalition such as the one that had brought success to the American Revolution of 1776, and the British needed to prevent such a coalition.

BACKGROUND In self-defining books, pamphlets, and feature articles Boer propaganda told the story of religiously devout Dutch farmers—Boers—who had settled in Cape of Good Hope Colony since 1652 and been under British rule since 1806. Harassed by the British government, law, language, missionaries, and "native policy," approximately eight thousand Boers in the 1830's made the "Great Trek" into the African interior, where they defeated the Ndebele and the Zulus and founded Orange Free State and the South African Republic, or Transvaal. British "suzerainty" claims over the emigrants were blunted when the Boers defeated a British army at Majuba in 1881, which provided the climax of the heroic saga of the Boer people.

British propaganda, on the other hand, depicted Great Britain's imperial policy as a mission of world civilization, which had become sharply focused by the 1886 discovery of a major gold field in the Transvaal. This produced an influx of outsiders—uitlanders—on whom the Transvaal president, "Oom" Paul Kruger, imposed heavy taxes and virtual exclusion from voting rights. The mining tycoon and Cape Colony premier Cecil Rhodes received some encouragement from London's Conservative government when he financed propaganda and agitation urging British intervention on behalf of the uitlander victims of "Krugerdom," which he portrayed as a nightmare tyranny of uncouth, unwashed, and intolerant fanatics.

However, Rhodes's attempted putsch, the 1895 Jameson Raid, was a fiasco. Anglo-Boer negotiations over suzerainty, military preparations, and propaganda efforts ensued. Finally, in October of 1899, the Boer republics presented an ultimatum for demilitarizing the frontiers, followed by declarations of war. This gave Great Britain the important propaganda advantage of being the "victim of aggression," entitled to claim that the enemy started the conflict.

HOME FRONTS Initial Boer successes rallied the British public to their government's side. Tory Party organizations, the Imperial South African Association, and the South African Vigilance Committee held public meetings and distributed pamphlets, and most of the London press supported the war in varying degrees. Rudyard KIPLING, Arthur Conan Doyle, H. Rider Haggard, and G. A. Henty wrote or spoke for the cause. Most of the clergy justified the war and the public schools were patriotic and glorified the military adventure. Consumer goods became pro-war propaganda by means of cigarette cards and decorative containers for such items as tobacco, tea, biscuits, cocoa, and soap. Music halls presented "jingo songs" and patriotic sketches, as well as featuring "war films"—brief footage of parades or embarkations, NEWSREELS by Joe Rosenthal, and propaganda reenactments or skits produced by R. W. Paul and Cecil Hepworth. British left-wing Liberals who opposed imperialism were effective propagandists for the Boer cause, however. J. A. Hobson, W. T. Stead, David Lloyd George, Keir Hardie, and John Burns, aided by the South African Conciliation Committee, and the Stop the War Committee, criticized the war. The *Morning Leader* was London's chief anti-war newspaper. On the whole, however, British and Dominion public opinion supported the war effort. As for the Boers, their simpler domestic propaganda operated through the press, the pulpits of the Calvinist Dutch Reformed churches, and local assemblies. Theirs was an organized society, with a strong ethnic identity, but there were internal divisions between the older, ultra-conservative, flat-earth "Doppers" who led the Transvaal and the younger, more educated, and more liberal majority of Boers.

INTERNATIONAL FRONT The Boers were the sentimental favorites of world opinion, but because of British control of telegraph cable transmissions the war news came exclusively from or via British sources. Indeed, for the first weeks of the war, E. E. Easton of *Harper's* was the only foreign correspondent in the Boer republics, whereas scores of reporters were with the British army. The Boers maintained a European headquarters in Brussels, where the Dutch-educated William J. Leyds served as chief diplomat, purchasing agent, and propagandist and used a local paper, *Le petit Bleu*, to publish stridently pro-Boer articles, which were picked up by Europe's many anti-British newspapers. Montagu White was Leyds's subordinate counterpart in the United States, where the *New York World* was the most consistently pro-Boer of the major American dailies. Boer propaganda tended to be naïve, was too infrequent to be effective, and remained insufficiently connected to policy and circumstances. Initially Leyds and White emphasized that the Boers could win without foreign help, but when the Boers began to lose ground they appealed for foreign intervention on moral grounds. In the United States British propaganda reminded Americans of British support during the SPANISH-AMERICAN WAR and the war in the PHILIPPINES, exaggerated the importance of

British concessions on Panama Canal rights, promised harmony and prosperity for all races in a future British South Africa, and emphasized that a Boer victory would not advance American interests. Not surprisingly, British orders for war material and loans from the United States helped their propaganda cause in that country, and no American financier was prepared to try marketing Boer republic war bonds. Despite the largely pro-Boer sentiments of the public, press, and Congress, the business community and the foreign policies of presidents William McKinley and Theodore Roosevelt were consistently pro-British. The vital target of Boer propaganda should have been the Cape Colony Boers, who were more numerous than the total Dutch population in the rest of southern Africa. Without the active rebellion against Britain of these populations, however, the Boer republics could not but lose the war.

Overall, the propaganda of each side in the Boer War held its own on the home front. Boer propaganda did not damage British morale because it did not reach British readers. British propaganda success with the Boers simply followed military victories. Internationally the British cause was unpopular, but the Boers failed to gain allies. As the young Winston CHURCHILL said of the Boers, "[N]o people in the world received so much verbal sympathy, and so little support." Ironically, the defeated Boers later shaped the Union of South Africa according to their own racist notions.

SUGGESTED READINGS:

Galbraith, John S. "The Pamphlet Campaign on the Boer War." *Journal of Modern History* 24 (June, 1952): 111-126.

Koss, Stephen. *The Pro-Boers.* Chicago: University of Chicago Press, 1973.

MacKenzie, John M. *Propaganda and Empire.* Dover, New Hampshire: Manchester University Press, 1984.

Richards, Jeffrey, ed. *Imperialism and Juvenile Literature.* New York: Manchester University Press, 1989.

— *K. Fred Gillum*

■ South America

Continent containing eleven sovereign nations

Much of South American history has involved appeals by political and social groups for support by other groups. Although the same is true of many places, what is unusual about South America is the frequency with which such propaganda was used to advocate illegal uses of power. Conservative groups used propaganda to encourage resistance to change; reform and revolutionary movements used propaganda to try to mobilize mass support for change. Perhaps one reason for the heavy use of propaganda was the low literacy rate in many South American countries. Another reason, suggested by works such as Samuel Huntington's *Political Order in Changing Societies* (1968), was the lack of political institutions strong enough to channel the demands of a mobilizing population.

CONSERVATIVE PROPAGANDA During the 1960's military groups took power in many South American countries. Albert Stepan's *The Military in Politics* (1971) describes how a form of propaganda contributed to this change. In Brazil, Peru,

Uruguay, and Chile, the military leadership became convinced that its duty to maintain national security required it to take the reins of political power. The civilian political leadership, they convinced themselves, was too corrupt or inept to be able to maintain order. Curiously, these coups d'état were conducted not in the name of destroying DEMOCRACY but to help society retain it. In 1956, for example, the Argentinean military banned the Peronist party. It did so through the Board for the Defense of Democracy by declaring that party "nondemocratic." The Brazilian military was particularly scrupulous in maintaining the trappings of democratic institutions while in power. The military used propaganda both to convince itself that it must take power and to try to convince the public that military rule was in its best interest.

Stepan also describes the maneuvering of Brazilian elites to persuade the military to intervene. Through newspaper articles they challenged the military to perform its "duty" by removing the sitting president. These articles emphasized the impending crisis situation that was developing in the country (in the opinion of the members of the social elite). Similarly, elites in Chile called for a military intervention against President Salvador Allende in 1973. As discussed in Arturo Valenzuela's *The Breakdown of Democratic Regimes: Chile* (1978), political groups preferred polarizing the political situation through one-sided attacks on each other to compromising. The conservative-controlled media cultivated a sense of unease among the population by sensationalizing violent incidents and economic troubles. This propaganda implied that the Allende government should be removed. Instigating

this tendency, perhaps, was the national myth-as-propaganda that Chile had nothing to fear from a possible military intervention. The result was the overthrow of President Allende and the ensuing rule of General Augusto Pinochet. As in Brazil, the military did not quickly return power to civilians. Through the use of propaganda, civilian leaders helped to encourage the military to intervene.

Once in power the military governments used propaganda to try to maintain their rule. Enemies of the country were identified and dealt with (the severity of the punishment varied from state to state). In Argentina, expression was censored under an overriding fear of PERONISM. Artists and students were linked to real urban guerrilla movements, cultivating an atmosphere of suspicion. Many members of these movements simply disappeared, never to be seen alive again. Later in their time in office, the Argentine military used nationalist propaganda to justify its actions in the FALKLAND ISLANDS WAR.

REFORM AND REVOLUTIONARY PROPAGANDA Conservative groups held no monopoly on the use of propaganda in South America. In Chile, the Allende government engaged in its own propaganda. It staged rallies and marches designed both to energize its supporters and to try to persuade other citizens that support for the socialist government continued to be strong. Allende also invoked nationalism, directed especially against foreign-owned (often American) corporations. Where these corporations were not nationalized, their activities were more regulated. Ultimately, in Allende's case, the socialist propaganda was not enough to overcome the government's own economic failings and the better-organized propaganda of the anti-Allende groups.

Some governments and candidates relied heavily on propaganda appeals to generate support among labor and agrarian groups. Populist leaders like Juan Perón were successful in using such propaganda to gain power. Brazil's João Goulart also used leftist artists to encourage the unionization of groups such as rural laborers and the enlisted ranks of the military. By some standards, the most successful of such populist movements was Bolivia's National Revolutionary Movement (MNR), which ruled from 1952 to 1964. Even after the MNR was overthrown, military leaders continued to follow some populist policies, which may have helped thwart Ché Guevara's rebel groups during that period. Peru's military regime from 1968 to 1975 also appealed, under Juan Velasco Alvarado, to the same groups. His government appealed to class interests and to nationalism to try to establish support. Peru nationalized several American corporations, including ITT and Chase Manhattan Bank. With the authority that other left-wing governments lacked, Peru's generals also censored journalists and artists who favored the older elite. Other charismatic leaders were able to build vehicles for challenging the political establishment without acquiring the power needed to implement change.

The violent left also uses propaganda to advance its goals. The foremost example is the Sendero Luminoso, or SHINING PATH, of Peru. This group used appeals both to socialist equality and to Incan heritage to become, at one time, one of the most successful guerrilla movements in South America. Other such movements, using propaganda tools to one extent or another, include several Colombian organizations in the 1970's and 1980's, Ché Guevara's movement in Bolivia in the 1960's, and the Argentine and Uruguayan urban revolutionaries of the 1960's and 1970's.

SOCIAL PROPAGANDA Especially during the wave of authoritarianism in the 1960's, artists tended to enlist themselves with the left wing politically. A number of South American writers (along with those from other regions) promoted the model of Fidel Castro's Cuba. Films such as Argentina's *The Hour of the Furnaces* and *State of Siege* presented socialism and guerrilla resistance in a positive light. It is perhaps not without reason, then, that the Argentine juntas that followed were very suspicious of the arts. They attempted to counter these influences through heavy censorship and, frequently, by simply eliminating artists and members of other "suspect" groups. Censorship was also common in earlier governments, including Getûlio Vargas' semi-fascist Estado Nôvo in Brazil in the 1930's and early 1940's.

Propaganda is also among the weapons of South American drug traffickers. As discussed in Rensselaer Lee's *The White Labyrinth* (1989), the *narcotraficantes* use their wealth to try to win public support. Drug traffickers, perhaps most notably Pablo Escobar in Medellín, Colombia, contributed heavily to cities and towns in Colombia, Bolivia, and elsewhere in the Andean region. With the profits from their business, they built sports facilities, schools, clinics, and churches. Other drug kingpins have operated soccer teams, offered scholarships, and contributed to disaster relief. They also encourage national authorities to overlook their line of work by emphasizing their opposition to revolutionary groups. Overall, the *narcotraficantes* attempt to promote the view that coca and cocaine are assets to their countries and appeal to nationalism by suggesting that the United States is once again trying to dominate the region. This propaganda is complemented by threats of violence and offers of monetary award to officials in positions to thwart or advance their goals.

The ROMAN CATHOLIC CHURCH has been involved in propaganda of both a conservative and a reformist direction, some of which is described by Werner Levi in *From Alms to Liberation* (1989). Traditionally, the Church advocated acceptance of the existing social order; this policy can be seen as propaganda that would counter attempts to mobilize the agrarian and urban labor classes. In its reluctance to speak out, the Church in Brazil and Argentina can be seen as a defender of the military regimes of the 1960's and 1970's. At the same time, however, beneath the formal structure of the Church, individual priests began to advocate "liberation theology." This creed interprets the Christian message as one of social equality rather than acceptance of an unjust existing order. This message was most influential in Brazil and in Central America.

SUGGESTED READINGS:

Munoz, Heraldo, and Joseph S. Tulchin, eds. *Latin American Nations in World Politics*. 2d ed. Boulder, Colo.: Westview Press, 1996. A current look at Latin American foreign relations.

Oxford Analytica. *Latin America in Perspective.* Boston: Houghton Mifflin, 1991. One of the few textbook-style overviews of Latin America that provides some discussion of subjects related to political persuasion and cultural issues.

Stepan, Alfred. *The Military in Politics: Changing Patterns in Brazil.* Princeton, N.J.: Princeton University Press, 1971. The classic explanation of the interplay between populism, elites, and the military in Brazil.

Wiarda, Howard J. *Latin American Politics: A New World of Possibility*. Belmont, Calif.: Wadsworth Publishing, 1995. Part of the New Horizons in Comparative Politics series.

Wiarda, Howard J., and Harvey F. Kline, eds. *Latin American Politics and Development*. 4th ed. Boulder, Colo.: Westview Press, 1996. Originally published in 1979, then revised in 1985 and 1990, this standard text has again been updated for the 4th edition.

— *Thomas S. Mowle*

■ Spain

Following the end of the Spanish civil war (1936-1939) Spain was ruled by the dictator Francisco Franco

If the SPANISH CIVIL WAR of 1936-1939 had been only a contest in propaganda, the republic, with the literary and artistic talents of its democratic and communist friends at home and abroad, should have won easily. Instead, decisive military help from Fascist Italy and Nazi Germany helped Falangist-nationalist rebels win the war. Their leader—el Caudillo, Generalissimo Francisco FRANCO—became Spain's dictator, and under his rule nationalist propaganda, organized and developed during the war, dominated the Spanish media until 1975. Following the war's end on April 1, 1939, nationalist propaganda emphasized reconstruction and reconciliation. Posters of the period showed willing workers and playful children, an ironic contrast to the harsh reprisals actually taking place. Spain, exhausted by the war, faced the desperate need to import food, petroleum, and manufactured goods from France, Great Britain, and the United States, all increasingly antifascist.

Spain's poverty kept her neutral in World War II, although her internal propaganda remained more or less pro-Axis powers. Franco was shocked by the Russo-German attack on Catholic Poland in 1939, however, and Spanish propaganda cheered Finland's resistance to Soviet aggression in 1939-1940. After Germany defeated France in 1940, Spanish policy shifted from "neutrality" to pro-Axis "non-belligerence." Adolf HITLER pressed Franco to join in an attack on British Gibraltar, but Franco asked for more foodstuffs, war material, and African territory than Hitler would or could supply. Franco settled for guarding against the remote possibility of a British invasion of Spain. Spain did support the German invasion of Russia in June of 1941 not only with propaganda but also with a division of Falangist "volunteers." However, following Pearl Harbor, Spanish propaganda discovered a "historic friendship" with America. After the Allied North Africa landings in November, 1942, and Germany's defeat at Stalingrad, Spain's propagandists devised a "three wars" attitude—pro-American against Japan, pro-Axis against Communist Russia, and neutral and promoting a negotiated peace in Western Europe. V-E Day was curiously hailed in the Spanish press as a victory for Franco, for neutrality, and for Spain's future as an anticommunist bastion.

From 1945 through 1947, however, proposals for removing Franco as a notorious fascist were considered by the great powers, discussed at the UNITED NATIONS, publicized by artists and intellectuals, and promoted by Soviet-bloc propaganda. Migrant workers, tourists, foreign radio broadcasts, and Hollywood films spread the news and views of a world hostile to Franco, and foreign boycotts became an economic problem. Franco responded with his own public relations campaign, depicting Spain as an "organic democracy" under a "monarchical" constitution that had come into effect in 1947, with himself as regent for life.

Spain's "independent" press was well shackled. The government exercised censorship prior to publication, and government agencies and the Falange Party generated propaganda that newspapers were required to print at length. Since the government controlled the supply of newsprint as well as the supply of news, it in effect also controlled the amount of advertising space each paper could sell. Radio was similarly an instrument of propaganda under rules of censorship. Spanish motion pictures—about fifty a year—were privately produced under close state control. *Raza* (1940), written by Franco himself, was the most propagandistic of the films on the civil war "crusade," and from 1947 to 1951 the CIFESA studio produced several Francoist historical epics. The usual fare, however, was light entertainment, escapist romances, and soap-opera problems, often solved by the village priest and all in the wholesome environment of a good Spanish society.

The morality of the Catholic faith was central to Francoism. The Roman Catholic church was state-supported, and religious instruction was required in public as well as in church schools. Public worship, marriage, and family law followed Catholic norms. Church propaganda was usually uncensored, allowing open criticism of the regime by the progressive Opus Dei movement, and later by Pope John XXIII and his successors.

Spanish schools glorified the ideal of a conservative and unified Spain under Franco, but university students often became radicalized, the increasingly urban population became less conservative, and a number of separatist regions actively opposed centralization. Yet schools, the Church, radio, films, and television had measurable success in Franco's campaign to promote Castilian over local dialects as the national language. Economically progressive Catalonia, a civil war republican stronghold, employed a revived Romance tongue, Catalan, as a vehicle for separatist nationalism, and the Basque provinces had since ancient times preserved a unique language and literature. Yet, here as elsewhere, the usage of Castilian increased, especially among the young.

The "Hispanidad" cultural campaign aimed at Latin America brought much-needed economic support from the right-wing regime of Juan Peron's Argentina (*see* PERONISM). Eva PERON's 1947 visit to Spain was a moderate propaganda success, as was Franco's 1949 visit to Portugal. By the 1950's the COLD WAR and the KOREAN WAR made Franco marginally more acceptable to the West. In 1953 the Vatican concordat occurred, as well as an alliance with the United States. Spain joined the United Nations in 1955 and later received informal visits by Presidents Dwight D. Eisenhower (in 1959), Richard M. NIXON (in 1970), and Gerald Ford (in 1975). Falangism, downgraded in the 1950's, nearly expired in the 1960's, and increasingly propaganda presented Franco as a kindly grandfather, still conservative but tolerant of diversity. Spanish novels and films indulged in critical symbolism—Spain as an oppressive mother, the regime as a harsh father, and Spanish youth prone to senseless acts of destructive violence. By the 1970's political interest focused increasingly on Franco's designated monarchical successor, Prince Juan Carlos de Borbon y Borbon.

After Franco's death in 1975, the new king, in 1977, presided over free elections, in 1980 agreed to provincial autonomy for Catalonia, the Basques, and other regions, and in 1981 thwarted a right-wing coup. The failure of neo-Falangism and the success of Juan Carlos in defending liberal democracy gained quick foreign approval. Inbound tourism flourished, and Spain joined the North Atlantic Treaty Organization (NATO) and was visited by Pope John Paul II in 1982. In 1986 the country entered the European Union (EU) and in 1992 Spain hosted the 1992 summer OLYMPIC GAMES in Barcelona. The end of international ostracism coincided with an end to the repressive censorship and overt propaganda of the Franco era.

SUGGESTED READINGS:

Gunther, Richard, G. Sani, and G. Shabad. *Spain After Franco*. Berkeley: University of California Press, 1988.

Higginbotham, Virginia. *Spanish Film Under Franco*. Austin: University of Texas Press, 1988.

Payne, Stanley. *The Franco Regime*. Madison: University of Wisconsin Press, 1987.

Snyder, Louis. *Global Mininationalism.* Westport, Conn.: Greenwood Press, 1982.

— *K. Fred Gillum*

■ Spanish-American War

1898: Conflict in which the United States defeated Spain and gained control of its major colonial possessions

When William Randolph HEARST sent Frederic Remington to CUBA to draw images on the situation there for publication in the New York *Journal,* Hearst is said to have cabled the artist "you'll furnish the pictures, I'll furnish the war." Many have claimed that the American yellow press played a major part in bringing about war. In early May of 1898 Hearst printed on the front page of the *Journal* "How do you like the *Journal*'s War?"

Whatever the role of American YELLOW JOURNALISM, the U.S. intervention in the conflict between Cuban insurgents and Spanish colonial forces, which had been going on since 1868, also had origins in the social unrest and economic dislocation that accompanied the country's transformation to an urban industrial society. Many Americans found the opportunity tempting to project their anxieties and frustrations outward, and Cuba seemed to offer the opportunity for a reaffirmation of America's destiny. At the same time it gave many the feeling that they were helping a suppressed people against an oppressive European monarchy.

In 1895, when fighting between insurgents and Spanish colonial forces broke out on the Cuban island, Cuban nationalists in the United States, calling themselves the Cuban junta, began to raise money for their cause and to disseminate information to the press to gain support for their cause.

Joseph Pulitzer and Hearst took up the news from Cuba in their competition for readers and advertising. Nothing was to sensational or outrageous to print, and especially atrocities, whether true or not, became favored news items. Pulitzer's *World* carried lines such as "blood on the roadsides, blood on the fields, blood on the doorsteps, blood, blood, blood!"

An early target of American yellow press propaganda was the commander of the Spanish forces on Cuba, General Valeriano Weyler y Nicolau. On the day Weyler arrived in Havana, Hearst dropped the price of his newspaper to one cent. Weyler's *reconcentrado* policy, designed to separate peaceful Cubans from insurgents by concentrating the former in guarded settlements, provoked violent incidents. Pulitzer's and Hearst's two newspapers began to refer to the general as "Butcher" Weyler.

Both newspapers used stories about the mistreatment, abuse, rape, or violence against women as an especially useful tool in their propaganda. Hearst used Evangelina Cosio y Cisneros, the seventeen-year-old niece of the first president of a provisional Cuban government, to galvanize public opinion. The *Journal,* which led the American public to believe with titillating stories that she was in immediate danger, characterized her as the "Cuban Joan of Arc" and, somewhat hastily, the "Cuban Girl Martyr." When Hearst decided to engineer a prison break, the incident became a crucial episode in preparing the American public for war with Spain. Upon her arrival in New York, Hearst's tabloid quoted Evangelina Cisneros as wishing to become an American citizen. The press presented the Cisneros incident as a metaphor for the way the United States should rescue Cuba from Spanish fangs.

The major event associated with the war and its propaganda was the explosion of the battleship *Maine.* While on a goodwill mission to Cuba, the *Maine* suddenly exploded on the night of February 15, 1898. Before an inquiry into the cause for that explosion had begun, the *World* suggested that a mine or a torpedo had been the cause. Three days later the *Journal* reported that "the whole country thrills with the war fever." On April 19, 1898, Congress responded with a joint war resolution.

For the U.S. Navy, the explosion of the *Maine* and its causes were a question of prestige. The *Maine* belonged to the first generation of new, coal-powered ships. A spontaneous-combustion fire, caused by coal dust, could easily spread to the ammunition magazine and result in an explosion. To reveal the faulty design of the *Maine* during an inquiry might have endangered the continuation of the shipbuilding program of the "new navy."

The war events themselves provided less opportunity for journalistic excesses, in part, because the U.S. commanders, weary of the press, instituted strict CENSORSHIP.

The Spanish-American War witnessed the emergence of FILM as a new medium of wartime propaganda. After the sinking of the *Maine*, Albert E. Smith and J. Stuart Blackton, the founders of Vitagraph, produced a four-minute film. The first minute consisted of a Spanish flag which was being torn off a flagpole and replaced by an American flag. The second segment, about three minutes in length, showed a funeral parade for the victims of the *Maine* at Ar-

INFORMATION WANTED.

UNCLE SAM—"Now that I've got it, what am I going to do with it?"

The U.S. victory over Spain in the Spanish-American War left the United States in control of the Philippine Islands. Critics, such as the cartoonist who drew this magazine cover, immediately posed the question of what the United States intended to do with its new possession. (*Library of Congress*)

lington cemetery. The film was a tremendous success with cinema audiences.

That "splendid little war," and the events that led to it, represented a significant occasion when the press intervened propagandistically in American foreign policy. Moreover, the use of film as a tool of information opened a new chapter in journalism and propaganda.

SUGGESTED READINGS:

Brands, Harry. *The Reckless Decade: America in the 1890's.* New York: St. Martin's Press, 1995.

Brown, Charles H. *The Correspondents' War:*

Journalism in the Spanish-American War. New York: Charles Scribner's Sons, 1967.

Juergens, George. *Joseph Pulitzer and The New York World.* Princeton, N.J.: Princeton University Press, 1966.

Milton, Joyce. *The Yellow Kids: Foreign Correspondents in the Heyday of Yellow Journalism.* New York: Harper & Row, 1989.

Mugridge, Ian. *The View from Xanadu: William Randolph Hearst and United States Foreign Policy.* Montreal: McGill-Queens University Press, 1995.

Swanberg, W. A. *Citizen Hearst: A Biography of William Randolph Hearst.* New York: Charles Scribner's Sons, 1961.

_____. *Pulitzer.* New York: Charles Scribner's Sons, 1967.

— *Thomas Winter*

■ Spanish civil war

1936-1939: Conflict between Spain's liberal-socialist government and right-wing military elements

The Spanish civil war began on July 17, 1936, when the country's army launched a rebellion against SPAIN's Republican government. As the insurgents attacked major cities, Spain was quickly divided into Republican and Nationalist zones. On October 1 the Nationalists proclaimed General Francisco FRANCO *generalisimo* and head of state, granting him both military and political rule. Propaganda posters (*see* POSTER ART) immediately went up all over Nationalist Spain proclaiming the virtues of "one state, one country, one chief." The insurgents were backed by the Falange Española, a fascist political party composed of property owners, monarchists, and ROMAN CATHOLIC CHURCH hi-

erarchy. They were supported by Italy's Benito MUSSOLINI and Germany's Adolf HITLER, though Italy and Germany technically remained neutral during the war, as did France, Great Britain, and the United States.

The Republican government, formed by a coalition of liberals, socialists, communists, followers of Leon Trotsky or V. I. LENIN, Spanish separatists, anarchists, and syndicalists, was supported in the war by the COMINTERN and sent supplies and arms by RUSSIA. Though the war began as a conflict over long-standing Spanish agrarian, social, religious, and political issues, it captured worldwide attention, symbolizing for many the battle between FASCISM and DEMOCRACY (or, for some, fascism and communism). Widely viewed now as a testing ground for World War II, the conflict lasted thirty-two months, ending in Franco's victory in March of 1939.

FASCIST PROPAGANDA The Nationalists set out to demonize the Republicans and claim Spain as their own with bulletins such as this from General Emilio Mola on July 24, 1936: "Spaniards! . . . The Government which was the wretched bastard of liberal and Socialist concubinage is dead, killed by our valiant army. Spain, the true Spain, has laid the dragon low. . . . [I]t will not be long before two banners, the sacred emblem of the Cross, and our own glorious flag—are waving together in Madrid."

Franco began early propaganda efforts by labeling the entire Republican side "communist," a tactic effective in gaining needed military support from Mussolini and Hitler. He continually cited the communist menace in his wartime propaganda, portraying himself as a hero fighting to rid Spain of communism. Anyone

Editorial cartoon by Willard Combs summarizing the cost of the Spanish civil war. (*Library of Congress*)

he considered "anti-Spain" was called "red." Franco denounced the intervention of the "Russian wolves" even before the Soviets lent military aid to the Republicans.

One of Franco's chief propagandists, General Gonzalo Queipo de Llano, "the radio general," vowed over the airwaves to wipe out the *canalla marxista* (Marxist rabble). Queipo, listened to intently every evening by Republicans and Nationalists alike, was notorious in his disregard for truth, attempting to rewrite history even as it happened. He denied that the Nationalist bombing of Guernica (April 26, 1937) had occurred at all, saying that the fire came from below and was the work of "Asturian dynamiters, employed by the Marxists, in order afterward to attribute the crime to us."

In Italy, Mussolini was determined to prevent events in Spain from creating unrest, and he ordered the press to restrict war coverage to short, simple pieces with no commentary or photographs. A few weeks into the conflict, Italian newspapers, controlled by Mussolini, began portraying the war as a fascist struggle against communism. In 1937 Mussolini reorganized his Ministry of Culture, whose purpose was to export fascist ideology, into a new Center of Anti-Communist Studies.

Despite these propaganda efforts, Italian intervention in Spain was unpopular with most Italians, and Mussolini ordered measures to punish anyone overheard making a pro-Republican remark or writing phrases such as "Viva la Spagna" on the walls of public buildings. Penalties for such dissent included banishment to a remote village.

In Germany, Hitler used the war in Spain to his advantage as he worked to create the Axis alliance. Like Franco, Hitler used strong anticommunist rhetoric as a tactical measure to divide his enemies and to solidify alliances. Propaganda minister Joseph GOEBBELS developed a joint German Italian stand against the danger of "bolshevism" in Spain. Hitler supported Spain in the interest of his own larger vision, his "New Order," not in the interest of the Spanish people.

REPUBLICAN PROPAGANDA The most famous Republican propagandist of the war, Dolores Ibarruri, "La Pasionaria," broadcast radio speeches. In her first speech she urged uncompromising resistance, telling women to fight with knives and burning oil. She ended with the famous declaration, "It is better to die on your feet than to live on your knees! *No pasaran!*" That last phrase, meaning "they shall not pass," became the battle cry of the loyalists.

Republicans were united in their effort to fight fascism by seeking international aid. A bulletin sent out early in the war read, in part, "Workers and anti-Fascists of all lands! We the workers of Spain are poor but we are pursuing a noble ideal. Our fight is your fight. . . . Come to our aid!" The Republican side was weakened from the beginning, however, by bitter arguments over "revolution versus war"— that is, whether the struggle for land and industry reforms, or the war itself, should be the focus.

For the communists and right-wing socialists, who believed in war before revolution, the chief propaganda tactic was a recruitment of volunteer soldiers, the Comintern-inspired International Brigades. The forty thousand volunteers, many not communist or socialist themselves, came from more than sixty nations, including fascist and democratic countries, and gained worldwide attention for volunteering in this foreign war to fight fascism.

Spanish communists hung posters of Soviet dictator Joseph Stalin throughout Republican Spain. This action angered the anarcho-syndicalists, who, though loyalists, distrusted the Soviets. In all their posters and pamphlets they called for a revolution of Spanish peasants and workers—namely, for the seizure and collectivization of property. The internecine battles among the loyalist factions never saw resolution, and many scholars attribute their defeat to this lack of unity of vision.

LITERARY PROPAGANDA In 1937 the French novelist André Malraux and the German novelist Thomas Mann published articles in the United States urging American writers to take up the loyalist cause in Spain. Both argued that politics, once considered beneath the dignity of the artist, must now be every writer's concern. Ernest Hemingway followed with an article denouncing writers who avoided the Spanish War, calling fascism "a lie told by bullies." Writer Van Wyck Brooks published a statement signed by ninety-eight American writers urging others to take up the pen and fight fascism in Spain.

Writers did respond, to these and other pleas, with an outpouring of poetry, stories, novels, and journalism, often highly partisan. Some wrote from a fascist perspective, but most intellectuals took a loyalist stand—Spain was seen by many newly politicized writers as "the last great cause."

Propagandist in intent and style, most of this literature tended to slant historical events, romanticize battle, trot out political rhetoric, moralize blatantly, and make demons of fascists and saints of loyalists. Upton SINCLAIR sentimentalized idealism and glorified war in his hastily written novel *No Pasaran!* (1937); John Dos Passos created cardboard stereotypes—innocent American idealists and cruel communists and fascists—in his novel *Adventures of a Young Man* (1938); Ernest Hemingway

created a near-caricature of a political convert in his play *The Fifth Column* (1937); and writers Lillian Hellman, Dorothy Parker, Hemingway, and Dos Passos helped produce a straight propaganda film, *The Spanish Earth* (1938). Hemingway did subsequently write well about the war in the novel *For Whom the Bell Tolls* (1941), as did a handful of other American and European writers.

AFTER THE WAR Franco began "modernizing" official Spanish history immediately after the war, portraying the conflict as a religious crusade. The "History of the Crusade," published in weekly installments, glorified the fascist heroes and portrayed the defeated Republicans as the barbaric, irreligious puppets of communism. Franco closed the national archives and exiled prewar historians. Spain's new "historians" were policemen, fascist soldiers, priests, and government propagandists.

A kind of propaganda also continued on the loyalist side with the publication of numerous interpretative histories of the war by exiled Republicans. These continued the arguments over whether Soviet intervention caused the Republicans' defeat or actually allowed the Republic to hold out as long as it did against the far greater resources of Franco's army and allies.

Though postwar propaganda could not alter Spain's political fate, political arguments about the Spanish civil war raged on through Franco's reign and have continued well beyond Franco's death in 1975. The Spanish civil war excited passions and engaged intellects in the 1930's, and that interest has not diminished over time.

SUGGESTED READINGS:

Aycock, Wendell, and Janet Perez, eds. *The Spanish Civil War in Literature.* Lubbock: Texas Tech University Press, 1990. Essayists discuss the literature of the war within a comparative and interdisciplinary framework.

Bolloten, Burnett. *The Spanish Revolution.* Chapel Hill: University of North Carolina Press, 1979. Harsh and fascinating exposé of the communist role in the war, previously published as *The Grand Camouflage.*

Muste, John M. *Say That We Saw Spain Die: Literary Consequences of the Spanish Civil War.* Seattle: University of Washington, 1966. Literary criticism in which the author considers the political passions that sent so many writers to Spain, and their subsequent disillusionment.

Preston, Paul, ed. *Revolution and War in Spain.* New York: Methuen, 1984. Twelve international scholars examine the complicated factors and multiple conflicts that make this war so fascinating and difficult to simplify.

Sperber, Murray A., ed. *And I Remember Spain: A Spanish Civil War Anthology.* New York: Macmillan, 1974. Short selections from the main writers on the Spanish conflict, mostly nonfiction.

Thomas, Hugh. *The Spanish Civil War, 1931-1939.* 3d ed. Harmondsworth, England: Penguin, 1977. Highly respected and readable narrative account of the origins and events of the conflict.

Wyden, Peter. *The Passionate War: The Narrative History of the Spanish Civil War.* New York: Simon & Schuster, 1983. The author weaves hundreds of interviews, documents, and memoirs into a compelling narrative of Spain's civil war years.

— Jan Hill Allister

■ Spin doctors

A slang term that became a regular part of the American political vocabulary during the 1980's, a "spin doctor" is an expert at explaining away or reshaping potentially embarrassing or damaging information associated with a political office holder or a candidate for public office (*see* POLITICAL CAMPAIGNING). The term may also describe an expert at organizing publicity for the views or proposed policies of candidates for public office so as to make them attractive or at least palatable to as wide a range of potential voters as possible. In both variations on the theme the spin doctor is a manipulator and, potentially, a misrepresenter of factual information (*see* DISINFORMATION; DISTORTION; DOUBLESPEAK; and PROPAGANDISTS).

■ Sports

Governments often use sports to promote national interests

Sports and politics have had a long, intertwined, and problematic relationship. Governments and politicians have often used sports as a propaganda tool to promote national interests by influencing people's thinking and emotions. The most notorious examples of government use of sport for propaganda purposes occur at the international level. Many governments "control" their citizens who compete internationally. Most have government agencies responsible both for funding and for organizing national teams, and the national media is directed, subtly or overtly, to publicize and promote athletic successes.

USE OF INTERNATIONAL SPORT It has generally been assumed that international sport, by bringing athletes together from differing political ideologies and economic systems, can help promote world peace and encourage friendship between participating nations and governments. Although this has not usually been the case, international sports events nevertheless furnish opportunities for governments to espouse this ideal and manipulate public thinking at home and abroad. Many countries, however, and especially the superpowers, rarely place international understanding ahead of their own interests and their leaders' egos. Instead they use international competitions to promote their country's image.

The Berlin Olympic Games, where the mere fact of participation grants a country international respectability and legitimacy, provide the most visible forum for government propaganda through sport. This is primarily due to the extensive international interest in and media exposure of the Olympics. Adolf Hitler maximized the political potential of the event in 1936, when he used the Olympic Games to show the world the efficiency and cultural aesthetics of the Nazi regime.

Other prestigious international competitions include the African Games, the Asian Games, the British Commonwealth Games, the Pan Am Games, and the World University Games. In all such events governments try to exploit the symbolism of their country's uniforms and the number of medals their athletes win, which are presented as indicative of national strength. All athletic victories are celebrated with the playing of the athletes' national ANTHEMS and the flying of their countrys' flags.

After heavyweight boxing champion Cassius Clay announced he had joined the Nation of Islam and changed his name to Muhammad Ali, he was frequently vilified as a propagandist for black and radical causes. (AP/Wide World Photos)

SPORT DOMINATION THROUGH EXCESSIVE EMPHASIS When American teams have done poorly in international competition, politicians have chosen not to extol the virtues of that competition. When Soviet athletes scored numerous victories in international competition, the government claimed that this proved the superiority of socialism to capitalism. Sport superiority became immensely important to Soviet propaganda, and as a result the Soviet Union and many other former members of the East bloc were led to place excessive emphasis on their sport programs. East GERMANY, or the German Democratic Republic (GDR), was strongly committed to using its athletes to promote both its own image and that of international communism. Following its success at the 1968 Olympic Games, the first in which it participated as an independent nation, the GDR quickly gained international recognition as a sports superpower. With a population less than one-tenth that of the United States or of the Soviet Union, East Germany had disproportionately high medal counts. This achievement came at a high cost for its athletes, however.

The GDR set up a sport system that in many ways duplicated that of the Soviet Union. Young children who showed athletic promise were segregated and placed into special schools and training programs. There, with the use of advanced scientific training techniques and apparatus, the children were developed into international sport champions. Only after the fall of the Berlin Wall in 1989 did the information become public that the training regimen had included widespread use of steroids and other performance-enhancing drugs. Not only were these athletes deprived of a normal childhood, many of them developed severe and lasting physical and mental problems associated with their government-sponsored drug use.

Fidel CASTRO's CUBA is another government that has gone to excessive lengths in sport to gain international respect. Following the 1959 revolution Castro wanted to show the world that the upheavals, despite bringing much economic hardship to the people, had not disrupted Cuba's political and social stability. The country gained international respect as a result of its athletes' successes, primarily in the Olympic Games. In this case, however, the government's use of sport programs as a propaganda tool also resulted in severe political damage from the political defections of highly visible and accomplished baseball players and boxers. Here sports provided an effective means for athletes to express opposition to their country's political policies.

THE SPORTING IMAGE Sports have also often been used as a propaganda tool at the local and personal level. From the time of George Washington, who supposedly threw a silver dollar across the Potomac, the image of the politician as an athlete has been hammered home to the public. Being a sport participant or fan makes the politician seem like one of the people. Politicians benefit from portraying themselves as athletes—examples include Fidel Castro pitching, Richard Nixon calling a play, and Bill Clinton jogging—and publicists continue to keep that kind of image before the voters (see POLITICAL CAMPAIGNING). In many ways, projecting an image as a friend of sport can be just as important as projecting a sporting image. Many politicians have actively sought to associate themselves with athletes and sports teams in their efforts to be considered worthy of election. Political futures can hinge on whether or not a professional sport franchise decides to leave a city or stay, for which reason politicians often intervene with or hold out promises to franchise owners. In doing so, the politicians, while projecting the image of someone saving a community's image, may seriously injure a local economy.

The relationship between sport and politics is an old one, dating back to the use of sport by Greek city-states to demonstrate the superiority of one state over the other. Throughout history, until the present time, that relationship continues to exist as governments use sports to influence the thinking and emotions of the people of the world.

SUGGESTED READINGS:

Guttman, Allen. *The Olympics: A History of the Modern Games.* Urbana: University of Illinois Press, 1992.

Hoberman, John M. *Sport and Political Ideology.* Austin: University of Texas Press, 1984.

Lilley, Jeffrey. "Russian Revolution." *Sports Illustrated,* January 10, 1994, 56-61.

Mandel, Richard. *The Nazi Olympics.* New York: Macmillan, 1971.

Vogler, Conrad, and Stephen Schwartz. *The Sociology of Sport: An Introduction.* Englewood Cliffs, N.J.: Prentice-Hall, 1993.

— *Stephen Schwartz*

■ Stalin, Joseph

December 9 (December 21, old style), 1879, in Gori, Georgia, Russia—March 5, 1953, in Moscow, U.S.S.R.: General secretary of the Communist Party and premier of the Soviet Union

For approximately three decades, following the death of V. I. LENIN in 1924, Joseph Stalin dominated the Soviet Union through the strict control exerted by the nation's Communist Party. The party used propaganda extensively to justify its monopoly of power, praise Stalin, and denounce individuals and groups it opposed.

Stalin's limited educational background hindered his initial skills in understanding the theoretical basis and scope of propaganda and other categories of abstract knowledge. His calculating mind and driving ambition, however, enriched by astute observations of Russia's political and social conditions, gradually provided him with the ability to develop an extraordinarily powerful dictatorship.

Appointed in 1922 to the newly created position of general secretary of the Communist Party, Stalin's responsibilities included recruitment of new members and supervision of membership files. This provided numerous opportunities to use propaganda techniques demanding that party members unquestionably accept the party's leadership, policies, and practices. Stalin also had the authority to punish party members for violations of party discipline. Such enforced conformity in the monolithic Soviet state was justified by the propagandistic theme of the need for national unity and the maintenance of sufficient strength to withstand those seeking the defeat of communism.

With Lenin's death in 1924 the struggle between Stalin and Leon TROTSKY for the political succession quickly escalated. Stalin used his administrative authority and extensive party connections to isolate Trotsky and his supporters, and he emerged victorious as the next Soviet leader. For the remainder of the Stalin era, official propaganda always portrayed Trotsky in negative terms as a renegade and an enemy of the Soviet state. His later murder in Mexico at the hands of a Stalinist agent showed the extent of Stalin's ambition to create a system in which his authority and leadership were never seriously jeopardized.

After Germany attacked the Soviet Union, Jack L. Warner made *Mission to Moscow* (1943) to present the Soviets as reliable allies, with Walter Huston (left) as U.S. ambassador Joseph E. Davies and Manart Kippen (right) as a warm-hearted Joseph Stalin; Stalin's postwar behavior made Warner later regret making the film. (*Museum of Modern Art, Film Stills Archive*)

Propaganda was used not only to defend communist and Stalinist political orthodoxy but also to dominate public education and culture. The educational curriculum emphasized the positive aspects of communist rule. Motion pictures of the Stalin era portrayed the Communists' break with Russia's past and the creation of a progressive future for the nation in glowing terms. Special AGIT-PROP teams traveled across the country, reaching even the most isolated regions, to spread propaganda about life under the communist system. Other government agencies, including the state-owned press and radio, made similar efforts. Although an ineffective speaker whose speeches rarely moved Soviet audiences, Stalin's directing hand could be found behind all these propagandistic efforts.

PROPAGANDA AS MANIPULATION The suppression of intellectual freedom and independent thought can be illustrated in the creation of the Union of Soviet Writers in the early 1930's. The organization was assigned the task of promoting the party's policies and objectives, including the ruthless and destructive collectivization of Soviet agriculture and the rapid industrialization undertaken in the five-year plans. Writers were expected to emphasize the positive advances, rather than the negative consequences, of these wrenching social and economic changes. As Stalin succinctly stated: "The writer is an engineer of the human soul." The theory of SOCIALIST REALISM appeared at this time to define and promote the new direction of Soviet propaganda.

The historical record of the communist era also suffered at the hands of Soviet propagandists. Stalin's role in the communist movement, including the 1917 revolution, was magnified in new or revised histories of the period. Soviet art showed Stalin standing next to Lenin, seeking to portray the physical connection and ideological transfer of the mantle of power from one leader to the next. By the end of Stalin's life, many statues and busts had been erected throughout the country, and banners with his sayings were draped on buildings. City names were changed to honor the nation's leader, among them Stalingrad, best known as the site of a crucial battle in World War II, Stalinabad, Stalinsk, and Stalinogorsk.

Poems and other publications eulogized Stalin as the most heroic of leaders, serving the people and defending them against evil opponents at home and abroad. Young children sang of their love for the great leader, and youth dedicated their lives to him. What came to be later known as the "cult of personality" reached full development during Stalin's tenure, and propaganda played a crucial role in this effort.

Despite using the full range of propaganda techniques to glorify his rule, Stalin's suspicion of real or imagined opponents never disappeared. This paranoia led to a series of massive purges, especially during the 1930's. Huge numbers of Soviet citizens—including major figures in the economy, military, cultural realm, and even the Communist Party—were arrested. Some of the major figures appeared in crude show trials in which the sentence of death by shooting was a foregone conclusion. The great majority of those arrested were sent to prison or labor camps. Several million, conservatively, were executed or died from mistreatment. The Soviet media, following the rules of party censorship and propaganda under Stalin's dictatorship, denied the massive scope of the purges.

SUGGESTED READINGS:

Conquest, Robert. *Stalin: Breaker of Nations.* New York: Viking Press, 1991.

Fitzpatrick, Sheila, ed. *Cultural Revolution in Russia, 1928-1931.* Bloomington: Indiana University Press, 1984.

Hingley, Ronald. *Joseph Stalin: Man and Legend.* New York: Smithmark, 1994.

Honchalovsky, Andrei, and Alexander Lipkov. *The Inner Circle: An Inside View of Soviet Life Under Stalin.* Translated by Jamey Gambrell. New York: Newmarket Press, 1991.

Marsh, Rosalind. *Images of Dictatorship: Portraits of Stalin in Literature.* London: Routledge, 1989.

— *Taylor Stults*

■ Stars and Stripes

Newspaper published for U.S. troops during the two world wars

Stars and Stripes started in WORLD WAR I as an eight-page paper on February 8, 1918, for the American Expeditionary Forces (AEF) in France and continued publication until June, 1919. It evolved from the pleas of almost two million American soldiers for reliable news from home.

The newspaper supported itself by subscriptions and advertisements. Its editor was Harold Ross, later of *The New Yorker*. Originally a soldiers' newspaper, it eventually was dominated by upper-level officers, who controlled and even censored its contents but saw the paper as an opportunity to publish information about military decorum and orders and to keep morale high among the troops. The stories tried to present a favorable view of U.S. war efforts, but its quality writing made it more than a propaganda tool. It disseminated useful information on subjects as varied as baseball, hygiene, and politics, and doughboy doggerel on the difficulties of living in a foreign culture and on the officer-soldier relationship. *Stars and Stripes* was an excellent morale booster that made American soldiers feel closer to home. A weekly *Stars and Stripes*, edited in Washington, D.C., was published for a few years after the armistice.

During World War II, the name was revived to denote a dozen publications for military units worldwide, all different from their World War I predecessor. None paralleled the eminence of the first *Stars and Stripes*. Army Chief of Staff George C. Marshall considered a publication along the lines of the first one essential to troop morale and considered it a way to counter other potential military newspapers that might be critical of the Roosevelt administration. *Stars and Stripes* started publication in April, 1942, in London and in seven months was publishing daily editions. There were approximately thirty editions by 1945 and an estimated circulation of one million. The paper carried wire service news, features, pinups, cartoons, and a controversial complaints col-

umn of soldiers' gripes and comments about their Army life. It was subsidized by the Army and by the sale of subscriptions. When the war ended *Stars and Stripes* continued its service to the military personnel posted to the occupations in Germany and Japan, where it was popular and a good morale booster.

Eventually publication became restricted to European and Pacific-Command editions, where the paper is the responsibility of the individual commands that publish it. The Department of Defense provides a small subsidy, but the rest of the money is raised through subscriptions and bookstore operations.

— Martin J. Manning

■ Statistics

Quantitative information whose manipulation can be used to persuade

PROPAGANDISTS often use numerical data to try to make their arguments appear to be based on objective and scientific information. Sometimes these are easy to calculate and to verify. A business firm may try to cultivate good will by reporting the number of people it employs and the amount of wages it pays. A community chamber of commerce may try to attract new business by citing its recent population growth.

AVERAGES AND AGGREGATES Many types of numerical data are not as simple and verifiable. A chamber of commerce may boast, for example, that average incomes in the community are high and growing, but there are several types of averages. The arithmetic mean is calculated by adding up the total income of the entire community and then dividing by the number of people in the community; alternatively the total could be divided by the number of families. Moreover, the mean might be raised considerably by the presence of a small number of people with very large incomes. It might therefore be more reasonable to refer to the median, which is the figure between which half the incomes are higher, the other half lower. The median is usually lower than the mean. A chamber of commerce would probably choose the average that presents its community to best advantage.

Political and ideological propaganda often involve the use of numerical data that are the result of aggregation. Data on national output and national income are not directly observable but instead constructed by complex aggregations. Gross domestic product (GDP), often used to represent national output, is carefully constructed to remove double counting. In the former Soviet Union statisticians chose not to make this adjustment, so as to be able to show higher output and growth. To add up the value of output, diverse products and services are added, using market prices. To assess changes in the quantity of output over time, the effect of price changes must be eliminated. Separating price and quantity changes is difficult, especially for services. It may be obvious that the quality of medical care has improved in the course of the twentieth century, but the improvement cannot be definitively determined. Official data probably overstate medical price increases and understate increase in output. Yet the price increases are cited to support government propaganda for a more extensive government medical program.

In the 1980's and 1990's much political discussion in the United States centered on the federal government deficit—the excess of expenditures over revenues—which was assumed, though without much analysis, to be an unsatisfactory situation. What was largely neglected was the fact that there are many plausible ways to calculate the deficit. Some countries, for example, do not include expenditures for capital investment projects; some would not have included the federal payments to bail out the troubled savings and loan institutions.

SURVEYS AND SAMPLES Many of the numerical data cited in propaganda are derived from surveys. Often these survey are limited to a few thousand, or even fewer, respondents who are assumed to be representative of the entire population. Interview surveys can only record what people choose to say; there is no provision for verifying the information. In the case of monthly national unemployment estimates, for example, which are based on a survey of about 60,000 households, there is no reliable indication of how truthful the respondents are. If they say they were available for and looking for work but did not work last month, they are counted as unemployed, but it cannot be determined how hard they looked for work, or how willing they were to accept work that was available. Survey data are also often cited in ADVERTISING propaganda, but there is no indication whether a survey was objective or whether it was repeated until the results matched expectation. The Federal Trade Commission, which administers laws prohibiting false and misleading advertising, may set some boundaries on outright falsehood.

It must be asked whether data that are

collected for only a few thousand people can be representative of a population of 250 million. This question is the subject of the scientific theory of sampling error developed by professional statisticians, who try to determine whether respondents were randomly chosen or whether some SELECTIVITY BIAS can be shown.

The concept of probability is central to scientific statistics. Medical researchers frequently report data generated from rather small samples, which must be tested for their statistical significance. The conviction that cigarette smoking causes lung cancer underlies the heavy antismoking HEALTH propaganda campaigns by government agencies, yet the tobacco industry has produced counterpropaganda. Evidence that smokers have higher rates of lung cancer (and also heart disease) than do nonsmokers is not sufficient by itself but must be corrected for differences in such factors as diet, exercise, income, and ethnic identity.

Government agencies produce propaganda intended to enlarge their appropriations and power. The U.S. Environmental Protection Agency (EPA) has propagandized heavily to claim that cancer is significantly caused by secondary tobacco smoke, chlorinated drinking water, dioxin, dietary pesticide residues, and Superfund sites, but its statistical studies have failed to achieve a reasonable 95-percent level of confidence that the results could not have occurred by mere chance. Indeed, there are often problems of interpretation with the statistical data used in political and ECONOMIC PROPAGANDA.

SUGGESTED READINGS:

Huff, Darrell. *How to Lie with Statistics.* New York: Norton, 1993.

Renner, Tari. *Statistics Unraveled: A Practical Guide to Using Data in Decision Making.* Washington, D.C.: International City Management Association, 1988.

— *Paul B. Trescott*

■ Steinbeck, John

February 27, 1902, in Salinas, California—December 20, 1968, in New York, New York: American author and scriptwriter

John Steinbeck was early made aware of social issues. His father was an accountant and a flour mill manager who was active in local politics and later elected treasurer of California's Monterey County; his mother was a school teacher who encouraged him to read. After graduating from high school in 1919, Steinbeck spent the next several years alternating between studies at Stanford University and various laboring jobs, which instilled in him a strong sense of sympathy for the working class.

Steinbeck's fourth novel, *Tortilla Flat* (1935), the first to earn him the attention of either the public or critics, was named after a Latino slum located near Salinas. In the book Steinbeck portrays the lives of a group of local *paisanos*, Mexicans noted for their poverty and simple lifestyle. Steinbeck next turned his sympathies to the impoverished laborers of the Depression era. The first of these works, *In Dubious Battle* (1936), was prompted by the author's concern over the terrible working conditions of agricultural laborers, and his horror over the often brutal repression of workers in California who attempted to improve their circumstances. This graphic tale of strike organizers in the California fruit industry was praised for its humane portrayal of the working class, and unionists welcomed the publicity. More conservative critics accused Steinbeck of being a communist and even of using his writing to provoke social conflict.

In his next work, the highly acclaimed *Of Mice and Men* (1937), Steinbeck describes two migrant farmworkers searching for the elusive American Dream. That quest is also a subject of *The Grapes of Wrath* (1939), Steinbeck's epic novel about the Joad family and their trek to California in the hope of finding work. Both books had a profound impact on American public opinion and stirred great sympathy for the poor during the Depression. The works' influence was intensified when both were made into major motion pictures. Steinbeck was awarded the Pulitzer Prize for *The Grapes of Wrath*, which is considered to be his best work.

Lee J. Cobb played a resistance leader in the 1943 film adaptation of John Steinbeck's novel *The Moon Is Down*, about the German occupation of a Norwegian village during World War II; playwright Arthur Miller wrote the screenplay. (*Museum of Modern Art, Film Stills Archive*)

STEINBECK DURING WORLD WAR II During the early months of World War II Steinbeck remained uninvolved, for his philosophical leanings led him to believe that the war was both futile and unnecessary. He traveled to Mexico, where he wrote the script for *The Forgotten Village* (1941), a semidocumentary film about Mexican villagers struggling for survival in Baja California. Steinbeck did, however, suggest to Franklin D. ROOSEVELT that the United States and its allies exploit film and radio to provide the world with a rallying cry against Nazi aggression and to counter German propaganda, which he had experienced firsthand on a trip to Latin America. Upon the creation of the new American wartime propaganda agency, the Coordinator of Information (COI, which later became the Office of Strategic Services and then the Central Intelligence Agency), Steinbeck was called to Washington, D.C. He eventually became a staunchly patriotic supporter of the war effort and worked during the war as an unpaid consultant for a number of government bureaucracies involved in the propagation of anti-Nazi information—including COI, the OFFICE OF WAR INFORMATION, and the Air Force.

It was in this role of government service that Steinbeck wrote his two principal works of anti-Nazi propaganda. *The Moon*

Is Down (1942), the story of a small village invaded by Nazis, appeared as both a play and a novella. In this work Steinbeck celebrated the courage of the resistance movements, hoping that it would give encouragement to European freedom fighters. Some critics charged, however, that he portrayed the invaders too sympathetically.

Steinbeck wrote *Bombs Away: The Story of a Bomber Team* (1942) for the Army Air Force. Neither a serious attempt at literature nor an objective effort to analyze the workings of a bomber team, its aim was wholly propagandistic. The book glorified the bomber squads of the Army Air Force and was used primarily for the purposes of Army Air Force recruiting.

THE POSTWAR STEINBECK In the years following the war Steinbeck's literary career began to decline. Although many of his works enjoyed brisk sales, only a handful, including *The Pearl* (1947) and *The Winter of Our Discontent* (1961) achieved much critical success. His script for the film *Viva Zapata!* (1952) earned for Steinbeck his only Academy Award nomination. Some of his other notable postwar works include the novels *Cannery Row* (1945), *The Wayward Bus* (1947), *East of Eden* (1952), and *Travels with Charlie in Search of America* (1962). He was awarded the Nobel Prize in Literature in 1962 despite protest from critics who favored the selection of poet Robert Frost.

Even in Steinbeck's later years he engaged in some political writing. An admirer of the Democratic Party presidential candidate Adlai Stevenson, he worked hard for the 1952 and 1956 campaigns. The author wrote short speeches for Stevenson's supporters and sometimes contributed ideas to Stevenson's own speeches. A collection of the candidate's speeches, sold to finance the campaign, featured a foreword by Steinbeck.

During the Vietnam War Steinbeck traveled to Vietnam to visit his son, who was there on active duty. Steinbeck was one of the few supporters of the conflict from the writing community, and he regularly traveled into combat zones accompanied by the military. Photographs of the author, who had learned how to use an M16 rifle, were widely publicized and drew harsh attacks from many of his former liberal colleagues. He later admitted, however, that he had been mistaken in his support for the war. Steinbeck received the Presidential Medal of Freedom for his years of social engagement.

SUGGESTED READINGS:

Benson, Jackson J. *The True Adventures of John Steinbeck, Writer: A Biography*. New York: Viking Press, 1984.

French, Warren. *John Steinbeck*. Boston: Twayne, 1975.

Parini, Jay. *John Steinbeck: A Biography*. New York: Henry Holt, 1995.

Steinbeck, Elaine, and Robert Wallsten, eds. *Steinbeck: A Life in Letters*. New York: Viking Press, 1975.

Watt, F. W. *Steinbeck*. New York: Chip's Booksellers, 1978.

— *Paul E. Tanner, Jr.*

■ Stereotyping

The process of creating a static, permanent, unvarying form for describing an individual, group, idea, or movement. This may apply to character, mental qualities, or physical characteristics. Such characteristics are usually exaggerated when the point is to attach a negative quality to the stereotype: Jews were represented with hooked noses in anti-Semitic propaganda, and buck-toothed, slant-eyed Japanese populated much United States visual propaganda during WORLD WAR II. Jacques ELLUL has pointed out that stereotyping is a standard element of propaganda during war, when it is used to rouse hate, fear, and paranoia.

■ Stone, Oliver

Born September 15, 1946, in New York, New York: American screenwriter and film director

Few film directors have so blatantly used the cinema to promote personal interpretations of political issues as Oliver Stone. *Platoon* (1986), *Born on the Fourth of July* (1988), *The Doors* (1990), *JFK* (1991), and *Nixon* (1995) established Stone as a historical revisionist of the 1960's. Initially his films represented a cathartic quest for personal identity, but they gradually evolved into political indictments of the arrogant misuse of authority.

As a young man Stone considered himself an outsider, disconnected from the world. He dropped out of Yale University to travel to South Vietnam and Mexico, then joined the Army to fight in Vietnam and received the Bronze Star for Valor. At the age of twenty-one he returned home, only to drift aimlessly and experiment with drugs before entering the film program at New York University.

When *Seizure* (1973), a cheap thriller, failed to establish him, Stone moved to

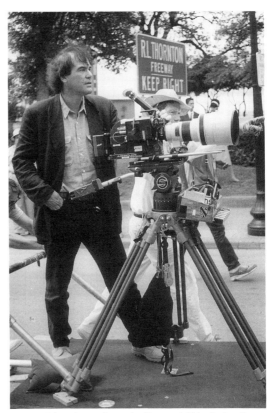

Director Oliver Stone during the filming of *JFK* in Dallas, Texas. (AP/Wide World Photos)

Hollywood in 1976. A turning point came when he was hired to write the screenplay for Billy Hayes' *Midnight Express* (1978). His angry script earned for him the Academy Award for Best Screenplay. The technique of developing a sympathetic antihero fighting for a strong personal cause against the establishment eventually became Stone's prototypic method of developing viewer empathy for the political statements in his films. The second turning point in his career came when he viewed Warren Beatty's *Reds* (1981), about an unorthodox American protagonist, John REED, who defected to Russia. Stone concluded that a credible filmmaker had to be an idealist making a very personal statement.

Horrified by U.S. intervention in EL SALVADOR, Stone wrote *Salvador* (1986), and after American studios rejected the script, he received backing from Hemdale, a small British company that also let him direct the film. *Salvador* failed financially but garnered critical recognition for its liberal themes and humanity. Having established both his political and artistic foundations, Stone turned next to *Platoon*, his autobiographical portrayal of the VIETNAM WAR, which earned for him four Academy Awards including that for Best Director and Best Picture. The film also defined his cinematic style of drawing the audience into the story by way of voiceovers, loud popular music, hand-held cameras, and staccato editing. Stone, who bombards his viewers' senses to drive home his themes, has described his visceral approach to filmmaking as "wake-up cinema."

When Stone filmed *Born on the Fourth of July* he began to revise known historical events to justify his political viewpoint, and he lost credibility as an interpreter of events when he blatantly altered history and characters to support his conspiracy theories regarding the assassination of President John F. Kennedy in *JFK*. Stone has maintained that his openly propagandistic interpretation of events was morally truthful and that his audiences know that he has taken historical liberties. He has maintained that his dramatic reinterpretation is no different from the reinterpretations of historians. Stone continued his examination of the corruption of power during the 1960's by interpreting President Richard M. NIXON's administration in *Nixon*. Apparently weary of defending his dramatic techniques and interpretations of history, Stone published an annotated *Nixon*, citing the sources of all his claims.

— *Gerald S. Argetsinger*

■ Street oratory

Individuals speaking out on some issue on a street corner, park, or other public place rely on being able to draw a crowd, which they can influence to embrace their own views. The style of street oratory is usually flamboyant and the language emotive (*see* ORATORY and RHETORIC), whereas the subject matter—which may be anything from a call to revolution to a call for sinners to repent—is usually sensational. Hyde Park's "Speakers' Corner" in London is historically the most famous site for street oratory, but the phenomenon can be observed on San Francisco's Union Square, most university campuses, and on a strikers' picket line in front of a factory or workshop.

■ Streicher, Julius

February 12, 1885, in Fleinhausen, Germany—October 16, 1946, in Nuremberg, Germany: German journalist and a leading anti-Semitic propagandist for the Nazi Party

Julius Streicher became known as one of Nazi GERMANY's leading anti-Semitic propagandists. Between 1923 and 1945 he published and edited a weekly newspaper, *Der Stürmer*, which featured articles and cartoons about alleged Jewish sexual or sadistic crimes. His anti-Semitic campaign began in December, 1918, when he joined

The Nazi Party's leading anti-Semitic propagandist, Julius Streicher (right), talks with high party officer Hermann Goering in 1937. (*AP/Wide World Photos*)

the Nuremberg branch of the Society for Protective and Defense Action, which was organized to oppose the "growing power of Bolshevik Jews" in Germany. Streicher's racist speeches drew crowds. The fact that anti-Semitism had a long history in Germany contributed to the success of his Jew-baiting. At the end of World War I many Germans also believed that their country had been "stabbed in the back" or betrayed by Jews and Marxists at home.

Streicher helped form the German Socialist Party in 1920 and argued in a party newspaper that there was a Jewish conspiracy to control the world. This argument stemmed from *The Protocols of the Elders of Zion*, allegedly a record of meetings held by a Zionist Congress plotting the overthrow of capitalism and Christianity. Streicher joined Adolf HITLER's National Socialist movement in 1922, and the next year he marched alongside Hitler in the Munich Beer Hall Putsch, an abortive attempt to seize political power. Hitler rewarded Streicher for his loyalty by making him *Gauleiter* (district party leader) for the province Franconia.

When Hitler came to power in 1933 he appointed Streicher chairman of an anti-Jewish boycott. On the day before the boycott Streicher announced in a radio address: "I do not ask you whether you are Catholic or Protestant, but if you are Christian, then I say to you—Golgotha is still not avenged. . . .The Jew is our eternal enemy." The Nuremberg Laws of 1935, which withdrew German citizenship from persons of "non-German blood" and prohibited sexual relations between Jews and non-Jews, were regarded as a triumph for Streicher. He began calling for the extermination of Jews as early as 1938. A leading article in *Der Stürmer* in September described the Jews as "a parasite, an enemy, an evil-doer, a disseminator of diseases who must be destroyed in the interest of mankind."

During the night of November 9, 1938, in a pogrom known as *Kristallnacht* (Crystal Night), synagogues were burned, Jewish businesses destroyed, and Jews murdered. These atrocities were followed by the Aryanization or expropriation of Jewish property. Streicher forced Franconia's Jews to surrender their property at 10 percent or less of its actual value, and he levied commissions on the sales that went

directly to himself and his cronies. In 1940 a special court found him guilty of profiteering and dismissed him as *Gauleiter,* but he continued to publish *Der Stürmer.* During the next five years he wrote or approved many articles advocating the extermination and annihilation of the Jews. Even after he knew of the mass murder of Jews in the concentration camps, he continued to publish his "propaganda of death." The Nuremberg Tribunal in 1946 found him guilty of crimes against humanity and sentenced him to death by hanging.

— *Harry Caltagirone*

■ Students for a Democratic Society

Activist left-wing organization founded during the 1960's

The campus-based group Students for a Democratic Society (SDS) was founded in 1960 in Chicago. The organization's period of growth and influence began in 1962 and corresponded to the publication of the "Port Huron Statement," the SDS manifesto written by Tom Hayden, at the time a student at the University of Michigan. Hayden declared that the American political system had failed to achieve such fundamental goals as international peace or ending poverty and exploitation. Calling for a "participatory democracy," SDS began a nearly ten-year period of activism on behalf of civil rights, inner-city improvements and employment, and opposition to the Vietnam War.

By 1969, at its height of power, SDS had roughly four hundred branches at campuses across the nation and claimed tens of thousands of members. It had also, however, begun splitting into various labor, pro-Maoist, and revolutionary factions, marking the beginning of the end for SDS. By the mid-1970's Students for a Democratic Society had disappeared from the political scene despite having been the most significant, influential student group in American history.

The foundation of SDS's activism was based in Marxism, revolutionary politics, a belief in the inherent exploitive nature of American institutions, the use of direct action to achieve change, and a commitment to equality. The political organization of SDS paralleled the group's beliefs by having very little formal structure or hierarchy and no permanent leaders. SDS utilized a broad array of propaganda techniques and initiatives. Initially the organization engaged in passive rallies and campus protests but later participated in draft resistance, advocacy for and mobilization of the poor, and active demonstrations. Still later, certain SDS factions advocated direct confrontation, armed struggle, and sabotage.

Throughout its existence one of SDS's main tools was pamphleteering. The group issued declarations and demands, distributed leaflets, and wrote political essays. Present in most SDS literature and oratory was the systematic and selective use of the language of propaganda. Using banners and picket signs proclaiming "student power" and "happiness is student power," their target audience was students. In advocating the "radical restructuring" of American society, SDS publications and speeches were peppered with words such as "dehumanizing" and "victimization" and references to the United States as "Amerika" and "the mother country of imperialism." Universities were

SDS leader Tom Hayden testifying before a hearing of the House Committee on Un-American Activities in late 1968. (*AP/Wide World Photos*)

criticized as "knowledge factories" and "appendages to U.S. corporate capitalism" for catering to industry, government, and the military. Other terms used when describing universities and college education included "bourgeois education," "indoctrination," "diploma mills," and "brainwashed." SDS tactics often relied on the emotional, and their political education project taught campaign techniques.

Not all SDS activities were revolutionary. They advocated peace, engaged in community action on behalf of the disfranchised, assisting the unemployed in urban areas and in Appalachia, and fought for civil rights in the Deep South. It appears that SDS was not only the perpetrator of propaganda but was also the recipient of "Establishment propaganda." While it is safe to say that most SDS activity was peaceful, the organization has repeatedly been described as "militant" and "radical" with a penchant for "vandalism." SDS members were deemed "ideological criminals" and "Nazi storm troopers."

— *Robert P. Watson*

■ Stürmer, Der

1923-1945: Anti-Semitic German tabloid

Der Stürmer (the stormer) was a radically anti-Semitic tabloid edited and published in Nuremberg by Julius STREICHER with the purpose of inflaming Germans against Jews. By the late 1930's the paper sold more than half a million copies weekly and was posted in thousands of display cases throughout Germany. The articles employed short sentences and simple vocabulary to appeal to the German masses. The paper was publicly praised by Adolf HITLER and other top members of the Nazi party. On the front page under the title was the subtitle: "Deutsches Wochenblatt zum Kampfe um die Wahrheit" (German weekly dedicated to the struggle for truth). At the bottom of the page was the notorious motto: "Die Juden sind unser Unglück" (The Jews are our misfortune). The leading article usually began in the left column of the front page, opposite which was featured a large cartoon by Philippe Rupprecht (who used the pseudonym "Fips"), who depicted Jews as short, fat, slouching, unshaven, and sexually perverted creatures with grotesque facial features. To dehumanize Jews, Fips's cartoons portrayed them as vampires, vultures, spiders, toadstools, and germs.

The newspaper's articles about Jews included allegations of international conspiracy, ritual murder, and sex crimes.

The paper denounced the Weimar Republic (*see* GERMANY: 1919-1933) as part of a Jewish conspiracy to control Germany and the world. The Treaty of Versailles, which ended World War I, was presented as part of that Jewish plot as were the Dawes and Young Plans dealing with war reparations. In September, 1938, *Der Stürmer* accused Jews of plotting to start a new world war to destroy National Socialism in Germany. During WORLD WAR II the paper alleged that Great Britain, Russia, and the United States were controlled by Jewish international financiers. A Fips cartoon showing a large sinister face peering through a triangle labeled Washington, London, and Moscow at a world in flames has the caption: "The dream of the Jew is to rule the world. Therefore he throws it into murder and horror, to build his throne in chaos."

By quoting passages of Jewish religious writings out of context, *Der Stürmer* alleged that JUDAISM permitted, even commanded, all kinds of crime against Gentiles, including rape, theft, and murder. Reviving medieval legends of Jewish ritual murder, the paper charged that Jews slaughtered Christians to secure blood for their religious rituals and that German children who disappeared prior to the Jewish Passover season were victims of terrifying Jewish crime. In May, 1939, a special edition on ritual murder appeared, which featured gruesome illustrations. A caption beneath one picture reads: "At the Passover Meal. The wine and Matzoh, unleavened bread, contains non-Jewish blood. The Jew prays before the meal. He prays for death to all non-Jews."

Der Stürmer also published sensational stories of Jewish sexual crimes and suggested that such crimes were happening throughout Germany. In 1926, for example, the paper covered the trial of Louis Schloss, who was convicted of committing sadistic acts against German women. For years afterward it repeated details of the Schloss trial and claimed that many similar cases remained concealed. Alleging that Jews sought to defile German women to destroy the country's racial purity, the paper called for the death penalty for racial defilement. Its campaign for anti-Semitic legislation led to the Nuremberg Laws of 1935 outlawing sexual relations between Jews and Gentiles. After the start of war in September, 1939, the paper frequently called for the extermination and annihilation of all Jews.

— *Harry Caltagirone*

■ Subliminal message

A communication aimed at the subconscious, as opposed to the conscious mind or memory, may be contained within a message on a related subject aimed at the conscious mind, or it may be within a communication having nothing to do with the message itself. The phenomenon may function as propaganda when a television advertisement for an expensive automobile explains the machine's physical beauty, mechanical reliability, and ease of handling in words and pictures—this is the message addressed to the conscious mind of the viewer—while the subliminal message lies in the fact that the information is delivered through the medium of an attractive film star, a sexy model, or against the backdrop of an elegant manor house on an estate. That message implies that buying the car will permit the viewer entry into the world of sexy women and expensive homes. (*See also* MIND CONTROL; SENSORY PERCEPTION MANIPULATION; and UNCONSCIOUS BIAS.)

■ Suez crisis

1956: International crisis that arose after Egypt nationalized the Suez Canal

The Suez crisis began in the summer of 1956 when Egyptian President Gamal Abdel NASSER (*see* EGYPT), reacting to an American decision not to finance his Aswan Dam project, nationalized the Suez Canal Company. The British and French feared that Nasser's PAN-ARABISM threatened their interests in the region, and the Israelis were dismayed by Nasser's support of Palestinian rebels. On October 24, therefore, Great Britain, France, and Israel secretly agreed to a coordinated invasion and launched an attack on Egypt the following week. From a military perspective, the invasion was quite successful, but world opinion sympathized with Egypt as a victim of aggression. The United States, fearing intervention in the crisis by the former Soviet Union, strongly condemned the venture and applied economic sanctions. The British and the French, humiliated, withdrew from the canal on December 22, and Israeli troops gave up their advance positions on March 8, 1957. Nasser emerged from the crisis as an Arab hero, and the fiasco almost ended French-British influence in the Middle East.

NASSER'S REVOLUTIONARY PROPAGANDA
Nasser was adept at rousing the emotions of his hearers, and he had ambitious goals for exporting his anti-Western, anti-Israeli, pan-Arab, and socialist messages. In his book *The Philosophy of the Revolution* (1955) he portrayed himself as leader of what he termed the Three Circles: the Arab world, the Islamic world, and the African continent. Although Egyptians cared little about expansionism, they enthusiastically supported other elements of his ideology. When Nasser nationalized the Suez Canal, huge crowds in Cairo celebrated the event as a realization of an old dream. He used the occasion to denounce British and American imperialism, and the enthusiastic response demonstrated that he knew how to exploit historical resentments and to use symbols that tapped into Egyptian aspirations for national renewal.

There was at this time little significant domestic criticism in Egypt, for by 1956 Nasser had taken firm control over the country's mass media. Before he came to power in 1952 Egypt had allowed rival political parties and a pluralistic system of relatively uncensored newspapers. Nasser's regime, however, soon closed down uncooperative publishing houses and silenced or jailed dissident journalists. The 1955 Press Law authorized the Egyptian News Syndicate to censor news reports and to purge critical journalists. The regime published its own magazines and newspapers, the most important being *The Republic*, which was edited by Anwar Sadat. The establishment of a single political party, the National Union, further restricted pluralism and dissent in the country.

Nasser's administration excelled in its use of RADIO. By 1956 even the poorest Egyptian peasants owned small radio receivers, and many listened regularly to the "Voice of the Arabs" over Radio Cairo, the most influential program of the Middle East. Recognizing this, British bombers did their best, but failed, to destroy the transmitters. Radio Cairo provided more than news and speeches: Its broadcasts included interviews, plays, songs, and music designed to promote nationalistic fervor. Many patriotic songs became immensely popular in 1956. The song "Allahu Akbar," which focused on Egypt's determination to defeat the aggressors with God's help, became so popular that it has been called "the Marseillaise of the Arab world."

DEFENDING THE INVASION Both the British and the French governments faced strong domestic criticisms from opposition political parties, as well as from their news media. Although narrow majorities in both countries endorsed the invasion as long as it appeared to be successful, few British or French citizens were convinced that vital interests were at stake. In debates at the UNITED NATIONS it was impossible for the British and French to prevail. The two allies could possibly have used greater skill in their propaganda techniques, but an insurmountable problem was the fact that the invasion appeared to conform to a common perception of imperialism as being the oppression of a weak country by a powerful one. This perception reigned not only in developing countries such as India but also in industrial countries, including in the United States.

To many observers British attempts to justify the invasion distorted reality. Prime Minister Anthony Eden denounced Nasser as a totalitarian dictator and asserted that Nasser's pan-Arab movement was comparable to Adolf HITLER's expansionism, that *The Philosophy of the Revolution* was comparable to *Mein Kampf,* and that appeasing Nasser would have the same consequences as the appeasement of Hitler had had in the 1930's. Such an extreme comparison was persuasive to only a relatively small audience. Likewise, British radio broadcasts from Cyprus into Egypt were generally ineffective. Egyptian listeners tended to distrust programs called the "Voice of Britain," and the programming was too often based on limited knowledge about Egyptian affairs and Egyptian culture; it was, moreover, hampered by the inability to find respected Arab speakers willing to participate in the project. The British were also unsuccessful in their use of "aero-psychological warfare," in which they dropped more than one million leaflets. Ironically, while the leaflets were not taken seriously by most Egyptians, they did save some lives by providing warnings about where bombing raids would take place.

Israel's situation was quite different from that of her two allies. The Israeli public was highly predisposed to believe that a preemptive strike against Egypt was necessary for national survival. Based on memories of the Holocaust and of Arab attacks on Israel in 1948, the UNCONSCIOUS BIAS of most Israeli citizens was to view Nasser's anti-Zionism as resembling Hitler's program for a final solution. Palestinian *fedayeen* raids against Israeli citizens were a reality of their experience, not an invention of propaganda. Given this situation, Israeli leaders had little reason to be concerned about the small number of journalists who attacked their decision to use force. In fact, the Israeli government found that it had been easier to defend the invasion than to defend its withdrawal in 1957.

SUGGESTED READINGS:

Almaney, Adnan. "Government Control of the Press in the United Arab Republic, 1952-1970." *Journalism Quarterly* 49, no. 2 (Summer, 1972): 340-348.

Cooper, Chester. *The Lion's Last Roar: Suez, 1956.* New York: Harper & Row, 1978.

Haykal, Muhammed Hasanayn. *Cutting the Lion's Tail: Suez Through Egyptian Eyes.* New York: Arbor Books, 1987.

Nasser, Munir. *Press, Politics, and Power: Egypt's Heikal and Al-Ahram.* Ames: Iowa State University Press, 1979.

Thomas, Hugh. *The Suez Affair.* London: Weidenfeld & Nicolson, 1986.

— *Thomas T. Lewis*

■ Sukarno

June 6, 1901, in Surabaya, East Java—June 21, 1970, in Djakarta, Indonesia: Leader of the anticolonial movement in Indonesia and head of the country until 1967

During the 1920's, while he was a university student, Sukarno was involved in the Indonesian Youth Movement against Dutch rule in INDONESIA. In 1928 he was one of the founders of the Indonesian National Party (PIN). As a result of his anticolonial activities, Sukarno was jailed by Dutch authorities in 1933. He was released by the Japanese, with whom he agreed to cooperate, after they gained control of Indonesia in 1942. Following Japan's defeat in 1945 Sukarno proclaimed Indonesian independence on August 17, 1945. This was done to prevent the Nether-

Sukarno exhorts workers to support Indonesia's "crush Malaysia" campaign during a May Day address in 1964. (*AP/Wide World Photos*)

lands from reasserting its dominance after the war, but independence was not officially recognized until December 27, 1949.

Sukarno was never happy with the Dutch legacy of parliamentary DEMOCRACY. In 1959 he introduced what he termed "guided democracy" for Indonesia, emphasizing that in this form of democracy freedom from want was more important than freedom of speech. This "guided democracy," a form of personal but not totalitarian rule (see TOTALITARIANISM), was to be the means by which Indonesia achieved a just and prosperous society. Although Sukarno read, and was clearly influenced by, the writings of MAO ZEDONG, he insisted that he was not embracing communism, and he tolerated capitalists as long as they supported his regime. The propaganda methods by which Sukarno persuaded Indonesians to support his personal rule relied heavily upon his gift for ORATORY and his ability to assign all Indonesian problems to previous Dutch misrule. Sukarno was well-aware of his CHARISMATIC LEADERSHIP and his ability to hold an audience spellbound. He once said that if he told the people to "eat stone" they would. In the late 1950's Sukarno began to introduce SLOGANS such as "Revolution, Indonesian Socialism, National Guidance," which he encouraged crowds to repeat again and again. The slogans became a major aspect of every speech he gave from the late 1950's through 1964. When, in 1962, he carried out CENSORSHIP of the press, banned most political organizations, and restricted public meetings, little opposition was raised. Those who opposed Sukarno's rule were constantly frustrated by his ability to control PUBLIC OPINION.

Neither the United States nor the Soviet Union had a clear perception of Sukarno's position on most matters critical to their interests, for the Indonesian leader deliberately kept both superpowers off balance with his showmanship and DOUBLESPEAK. In 1964 he seemed to be moving toward creating a Peking-Djakarta alliance. When a Communist coup was attempted in 1965, he was suspected of being complicit, and the Indonesian army reacted by removing all of Sukarno's supporters from their government offices. In 1967 General Suharto assumed Sukarno's powers. Fearful of his influence over the people, Suharto kept his predecessor under house arrest until his death three years later.

— *Ronald K. Huch*

■ Surgeon general

Head of Public Health Service in the U.S. Department of Health and Human Services

The U.S. surgeon general directs the operations of the U.S. Public Health Service, the agency that distributes HEALTH propaganda in the United States. The office has its origins in the Marine Hospital Fund, which was established in 1798 to provide health services for sailors. In 1871 Congress created the office of supervising surgeon to direct operations; in 1902 the position's title was changed to surgeon general. With the passage of the 1912 Public Health Service Act, the surgeon general became responsible for directing the federal government's attempts to combat the spread of disease in the United States.

Prominent among efforts at disease prevention were educational programs directed at the public, as well as posters, pamphlets, films, and reports. Surgeon General Thomas Parran, who held the office from 1936 to 1948, participated in these publicity activities; in 1937 he published *Shadow on the Land*, in which he warned of the dangers of venereal disease. However, it was not until 1964, when Surgeon General Luther Terry published a report linking cigarette smoking to cancer, that the position of surgeon general gained national attention.

As of that time the surgeon general's office became associated with antismoking campaigns; William Stuart, who was surgeon general from 1965 to 1969, held many press conferences and testified before Congress about the dangers of smoking. In the following years several more reports about the health effects of smoking were released to considerable press attention. The new prominence of the office, accompanied by an increasing budget during the 1960's and early 1970's, led to even greater activism. Surgeon General Julius Richmond, who served from 1976 to 1981, used his office to promote disease prevention and improved health. A 1979 report entitled *Healthy People* advocated positive health habits, including exercise, and contributed to a growing awareness of health in the United States.

When President Ronald REAGAN in 1981 appointed C. Everett Koop as surgeon general he may not have anticipated Koop's outspokenness on such issues as acquired immunodeficiency syndrome (AIDS). Arguing that he was responsible for public health, Koop ignored moral controversies in advocating increased sex education in public schools and the distribution of condoms to prevent the spread of the AIDS virus. Although his stance earned him the wrath of some conservative organizations, Koop quickly became an influential and popular figure. Unlike many earlier surgeons general, Koop chose to wear the official military-style uniform of his office, which gave him a striking and authoritative air. The increased attention given to the office of surgeon general led to its being used by both liberals and conservatives to advance their causes. President Bill Clinton's nomination of Henry Foster to the position in 1993 failed because Foster had at one time performed abortions. With that, it became clear that the surgeon general was no longer an agent for the dissemination of propaganda in the interests of public health but that the office itself has become a component in propaganda battles over the government's role in such areas as sexuality and abortion.

— *Thomas Clarkin*

■ Symbolic fiction

Any story, whatever the form or medium of its narration, has a didactic purpose. That purpose may involve doctrines, precepts, principles, morality, and rules of behavior. The symbolic element may be the use of specific SYMBOLS (metaphors that have become conventional representations of things other than themselves) to make didactic points within the story, or the story itself may be a symbol. In Aesop's fables, for example, each character is a symbol of good, evil, or innocence; in Ayn Rand's novel *We the Living* (1936), the story itself of ordinary Russian people struggling in their everyday lives against the dehumanizing effects of Bolshevism is symbolic of an indomitable spirit; and in Jean Renoir's film *Les Marseillaise,* the fictitious account of revolutionary soldiers from Marseille in 1789-1790 combines with the character Bombier, who represents the common people of France, to symbolize the struggle of a people against tyranny.

■ Symbols

Images, emblems, signs, and slogans serving as links between the intellectual and emotional dimensions of the mind

The use of symbols in propaganda is a form of emotional shorthand through which the recipient is able to recapitulate instantly all previous knowledge, experiences, and feelings that have been attached to a symbol. As the message becomes more familiar, the symbol becomes the only link necessary to reinforce the purpose of the wielders of the image.

The importance of symbols can be seen in the laws that have been enacted by many nations to protect the production, design, and display of national symbols. In the United States the appropriate respect or allowable disrespect accorded the flag has been debated at length. The general study of shapes and their affective meanings, used chiefly in ADVERTISING, is called semiotics.

DEFINITIONS Symbols are shapes or forms that are imbued with multiple ideas and concepts, both intellectual and emotional. A symbol embodies the cultural MYTHS of the group it serves to represent.

Cultural myths can be described as the complex of inner beliefs and values that form the reality of an individual or the group. When a symbol is displayed, it produces a conditioned reflex, as described by Jacques ELLUL in *Propaganda: The Formation of Men's Attitudes,* 1973. A conditioned reflex is a predictable emotional response that occurs without conscious intent on the part of the individual. The inexplicable lump in the throat that a patriotic American feels at the raising of the American flag, or an automatic feeling of hostility toward a display of a communist country's flag are conditioned reflexes. For propaganda purposes, symbols can be classified as symbols of identification, integration, and agitation; symbols sometimes fulfill all three purposes. Symbols of identification label people and groups; symbols of integration have as their goal the assimilation of more members to the group or the encouragement of others to change behavior in the group's direction, and symbols of agitation urge people on to action.

Symbols are the most direct link to mental stereotypes, and since STEREOTYPING represents common group perceptions, symbols may be used to communicate with large groups of people based on their commonly held beliefs and values. The massed display of symbols has been a technique commonly used in propaganda, as it is easier to overwhelm the senses with symbols than with words. Political conventions in the United States overflow with red, white, and blue flag symbols, as do American parades, fairs, and rodeos.

PRIMARY PROPAGANDA SYMBOLS The most effective symbols combine a contemporary message with an evocation of a person's cultural, racial, and national history. Such symbols as the cross, the five-pointed star as used by the United States, the six-pointed Star of David, and the swastika all serve this multiple purpose. Other effective symbols, such as the crossed hammer and sickle, were crafted specifically to serve the communist movement, but they lost their power to persuade as the movement began to languish.

The cross is perhaps the most powerful of symbols traditionally used in propaganda. It is a perfect symbol of crucifixion and resurrection, and the ROMAN CATHO-LIC CHURCH used the cross as the means of propagating the faith throughout the world, overcoming language barriers with it and allowing it to endure for millennia.

The five-pointed star is traditionally ascribed to the five points on the human body and its five senses; as an American political symbol, the star asserts the preeminence of the people within the nation. It is the primary symbol on the American flag.

The Star of David, emblematic of the nation of Israel (see ZIONISM), is the traditional seal of Solomon, with very early historical roots. Its form of two interlaced triangles has remained virtually unchanged through the centuries.

The swastika, like the cross, is a primordial sun image known throughout the world. Its employment by the German Third Reich was a dynamic choice, because the symbol was at once an early symbol of identification by the northern European peoples and a symbol of an aggressive political program (see GERMANY: 1933-1945). Despite postwar attempts to degrade the symbol, it is enduring in all its forms.

The hammer and sickle depicted the workers' communist movement, and it was the symbol of the Soviet Union from 1918 to 1991 (see RUSSIA: 1918-1953 and RUSSIA: 1918-1991). With the demise of the Soviet system, the symbol rapidly declined in use and significance, as it did not have the primal racial and cultural roots of some other symbols.

SYMBOLIC ANIMALS, LEADERS, AND FLAGS
The use of animals as mascots for school sports teams mirrors the power that people have bestowed on animal images throughout history (see SPORTS). The eagle has stood for spirit, power, and empire since Egyptian times and has been the symbolic image of many cultures, including Rome, Germany, and the United States of America. Labeled a national symbol, the bald eagle's survival is seen as linked to the survival of the nation. As other examples of animal symbols, the Russian bear and the British lion are traditional national symbols that are recognized worldwide.

Political parties have also been labeled with animal images, such as the Democrat donkey (see DEMOCRATIC PARTY) and the Republican elephant (see REPUBLICAN PARTY). Here the animals have less obvious meanings as symbols, and their use relies on shared understanding of the associations between the animal and the party.

Images of leaders, from the photograph of a current U.S. president on the wall in a federal government office to a poster of a leader such as Chairman MAO ZEDONG or Adolf HITLER, are meant to communicate a complete ideology in a single image. The marketing of popular MUSIC idols proceeds under the same method. When people elevate a leader or

Hardline communists hold the flags of the Liberal Democratic Party (left) and the former Soviet Union (right) while watching fires that erupted during confrontations with Moscow police in October, 1993. (*AP/Wide World Photos*)

a film or music star through adulation, the mere appearance of this icon has the effect of a symbol.

Flags, although some seem simple in appearance, are precisely and intricately designed to signify a nation's roots, composition, and mission. The flag could be called the ultimate national symbol storage unit. Virtually every governmental official or politician who speaks to the public has a flag at his or her side during speeches and interviews.

The American flag, with its red and white stripes in the number of the original thirteen colonies and the blue canton with white five-pointed stars numbering fifty, the number of states of the union, is an image seen daily by U.S. residents. Its display links intellectual ideas about the United States of America to the complex of feelings carried by Americans. Most major events in the United States are preceded by a display of the flag, thus perpetuating the reactions it is intended to stimulate. Its impact on Americans can be heightened when it is seen displayed outside the U.S. borders, such as at an American embassy.

Some flags outlive their nations. The crossed "stars and bars" of the Confederate States of America, for example, although it provokes controversy, continues to be displayed publicly and is flown unofficially throughout the South on a daily basis as a symbol of a way of life that was riven by the Civil War (*see* CONFEDERATE FLAG).

SLOGANS SLOGANS have a short life but are symbolic in their own right. "Liberty, equality, fraternity," "Workers of the world unite," "Don't tread on me," and "Freedom and bread" were all symbols in their time, but most slogans are not as durable as primary symbols in advancing a message. Slogans are primarily rallying cries for adherents of a group rather than symbols of that group. Such American slogans as "Remember Pearl Harbor" and "We shall overcome" generated high propaganda value at critical times. Word messages must be crafted to fit specific times and circumstances, whereas primary symbols transcend those limitations.

SUGGESTED READINGS:

Cirlot, J. E. *A Dictionary of Symbols.* New York: Philosophical Library, 1962. A catalog of symbols with elaborate discussions of their meanings and implications.

Crampton, W. G. *The Complete Guide to Flags.* New York: Gallery Books, 1989. An illustrated guide to flags of all kinds.

Doob, Leonard W. *Propaganda: Its Psychology and Technique.* New York: Henry Holt, 1939. Explication of attitudes and stereotypes that make propaganda effective.

Frutiger, Adrian. *Signs and Symbols: Their Design and Meaning.* New York: Van Nostrand Reinhold, 1989. Basic shapes and their relation to human memory and feelings, with discussion of the difference between sign and symbol.

Jackall, Robert, ed. *Propaganda.* New York: New York State University Press, 1995. Essays on propaganda including a condensation of its religious roots and its emergence as a dominant tool of the technological age.

Lippman, Walter. *Public Opinion.* New York: Macmillan, 1941. A standard work on public opinion and its development, including discussion of stereotypes.

— *Frank Thayer*

■ Syria

Middle East Islamic Nation whose government has tended to take strong pan-Arabist stands

After World War I the LEAGUE OF NATIONS awarded control of Syria, which at that time included Lebanon, to FRANCE. Syrians disliking French control attempted to stir resistance by describing the situation as a latter-day renewal of the medieval crusades. The French subsequently partitioned Syria, focusing their control in the western region, Lebanon, which developed a Christian majority. In the mostly eastern, Muslim region of Syria, France followed a policy of divide and rule, using propaganda to exploit religious and territorial or tribal differences.

On April 17, 1946, Syria became fully independent, although the country was politically weak and disunited. Syria had no significant oil reserves, and French actions had removed from Syrian control the ports needed for economic development. However, creation of the state of ISRAEL in 1948 and the beginnings of the

COLD WAR at about the same time enabled Syria to become a "power broker" in the Middle East, building itself economically and politically through effective management of propaganda. Defiance of Western and pro-Israel policies became a basis for national identity. Through support for Arab nationalism, and through pursuing an independent political course, Syria became a standard of virtue for many in the Arab world. Economic assistance and military hardware were the rewards Syria received from its patron, the former Soviet Union (*see* RUSSIA: 1953-1991), for providing a base for Soviet influence in the Middle East.

Throughout the 1950's and early 1960's Syria's struggle with EGYPT for Arab leadership and Soviet patronage were the primary focus of Syrian propaganda, as various factions sought control of the government. In 1966 the Ba'thist party seized control in a coup. Under the leadership of Hafez al-Assad, the Ba'athist defense minister who came to power November 13, 1970, the Ba'thist economic philosophy of socialism, and its aggressively anti-Israel politics were effectively used. Assad continued to promote Soviet propaganda in the Middle East, thereby continuing to receive economic and military rewards. The SIX-DAY WAR of 1967 provided an excellent propaganda tool

for Assad, who began sheltering Palestinian resistance movements and portraying Syria as the locus of Arab and Muslim resistance to Israel and as the principal supporter of the Palestinian cause. Substantial aid flowed from oil-rich Arab countries to Syria on behalf of the Palestinian cause, enhancing Syria's economy.

Internally, a firm military rule discouraged any who might challenge Assad's regime, while strict censorship limited the flow of information and ideas. Assad developed a personality cult focused on himself. The Camp David Accords were a propaganda bonanza for Assad: Egypt's peace with Israel left Syria as the most prominent country in the Middle East supporting the Palestinian cause. Iran's fall from favor among Western and Arab nations due to the Islamic Revolution of 1979 and Iraq's fall from favor with the Persian GULF WAR of 1990-1991 further promoted Syrian leadership in the region and internationally. However, the dissolution of the Soviet Union at the end of 1991, Syria's alleged role in international terrorism, and Israeli agreements with various Arab states and the Palestinians have challenged Syria's continued use of propaganda for economic and political control.

— *Richard A. Bennett*

T

■ Taiwan

East Asian island known under Kuomin-tang (Nationalist Party) rule as the Republic of China (ROC)

A part of CHINA for centuries before the civil war between the Chinese Communists and Nationalists (1927-1949, intermittently), Taiwan had always been considered a frontier area. By the time of the ascendancy of the Qing Dynasty (1644-1912), the island had for some time been a haven for Japanese pirates, Dutch traders, and Ming Dynasty loyalists fleeing the Chinese mainland. By the 1680's Qing forces had established control of the western portion of Taiwan, but settlement was slow and the rugged country to the east remained in the hands of the island's aboriginal peoples until the end of the nineteenth century.

By the mid-nineteenth century, Taiwan's strategic position along major shipping routes, its potential as a coaling station, and its camphor resources made it a potential target for outside interests. Following a Japanese raid on the island in 1874, the Chinese redoubled their efforts to strengthen and modernize the island's infrastructure through the 1880's. Following the disastrous Sino-Japanese War of 1894-1895, Taiwan was ceded to JAPAN by the Treaty of Shimoneseki and would remain part of the Japanese empire for fifty years.

THE UNITED STATES AND TWO CHINAS It had been expected that a strong Republic of China under Nationalist Party rule would replace Japan as the principal East Asian power. Nationalist leader Chiang Kai-shek had participated in the 1943 Cairo Conference, and it was understood that Chinese territory under Japanese occupation would revert to China. Taiwan was thus absorbed into the ROC at the end of the war, but resentment directed at mainland administrators who, in turn, mistrusted the islanders as "collaborators" with the Japanese resulted in repression and bloodshed. This only intensified as the civil war, renewed in 1946, forced ROC mainlanders to flee to the island and try to turn it into a last redoubt against the advancing communists.

By the time MAO ZEDONG proclaimed the People's Republic of China (PRC) on October 1, 1949, the United States had written off the Nationalists as unsupportable and expected that Taiwan (or Formosa, as it was more commonly known), placed conspicuously outside America's defense perimeter, would soon fall as well. Massive Chinese communist participation in the KOREAN WAR in the fall of 1950, however, persuaded American planners that Taiwan was an integral part of the West's strategy of containment. Chiang Kai-shek's pleas for renewed U.S. aid were answered and the American Seventh Fleet was sent to patrol the Taiwan Straits. By 1953 the administration of Dwight D. Ei-

After being forced to move his Nationalist regime to Taiwan, Chiang Kai-shek built up his military forces in the hope of reconquering mainland China; here he inspects army troops in 1952. (*National Archives*)

senhower, as part of its new strategy of rolling back communism, raised the possibility of unleashing Chiang's revitalized forces in a Nationalist invasion of the mainland.

Through the COLD WAR of the 1950's and 1960's the United States and Taiwan each maneuvered to use each other to best advantage against the People's Republic of China and the communist world in general. Through three successive Taiwan Straits crises, in 1954, 1958 and 1962, the Nationalists attempted to use Communist shelling of the Nationalist-held islands of Quemoy and Matsu as a means to provoke a major American action against the mainland. For its part, the United States sought to use the threat of the use of ROC's fully modernized armed forces as a check on PRC adventurism. The position of both Nationalists and Communists during the leadership of Chiang Kai-shek and his son Chiang Ching-kuo remained consistent: There is but one China and Taiwan is part of it.

CHANGING PLACES The winding down of the VIETNAM WAR in the early 1970's and the abrupt change in the American position toward the People's Republic had a profound impact on Taiwan's international status. The administration of

Richard M. NIXON, sensing that recent Chinese-Soviet animosity provided an opportunity for overtures toward the People's Republic, stunned the world with the president's 1972 visit to the mainland. In the accompanying Shanghai Communique both sides pledged mutual diplomatic recognition, with the United States no longer standing in the way of PRC admission to the UNITED NATIONS (UN). For Taiwan this meant the downgrading of its diplomatic status in the United States and the ultimate loss of the seat on the UN Security Council, which it had retained since 1949. Although the ROC received repeated assurances that its security would not be compromised by the new arrangements, Taiwan entered the 1980's with little diplomatic support and in a clearly subordinate position to the PRC.

The 1980's and 1990's were marked by an unprecedented economic boom on the island, a dramatic improvement in relations with the mainland—with an equally dramatic reversal of that trend in the wake of the TIANANMEN SQUARE DEMONSTRATIONS—and a pronounced liberalization of the ROC's political environment. To a certain extent, these events are interrelated: American aid and land reform in the 1950's and 1960's had already provided a solid base for a government-directed export economy. By the 1980's, following the lead of Japan, Taiwan became a leading exporter of consumer items, with the United States as its largest customer. The 1980's also saw the PRC attempting to modernize its economy, and Taiwan's investors increasingly saw the mainland as an attractive market. As the island's economic fortunes climbed and the old guard of Nationalists died off, opposition parties and independence movements grew in an atmosphere of slowly increasing toleration. In 1991 the first elections were held for positions in the Legislative Yuan and for the presidency.

PROPAGANDA ON TAIWAN Much of the propaganda effort of the Republic of China since 1949, especially the propaganda effort directed at the United States, has necessarily been in reaction to events on the mainland. Throughout WORLD WAR II, Chiang Kai-shek, often through the efforts of his Christian, American-educated wife, Soong Mei-ling, sought to paint a picture of China as fighting a heroic, lonely battle against Japanese barbarism. Madame Chiang was influential in the United States and had the continual support of Henry Luce, publisher of *Time* magazine, and members of what would later be known as the China Lobby.

Nationalist propagandists would continue this effort through the late 1940's, this time with Chinese communism as the enemy. The expulsion of the Nationalists from the mainland and the efforts of the Congressional China Lobby precipitated a lengthy inquiry into the question of who lost China, which coincided with the hunt for communists in the early 1950's. By the mid-1950's, Nationalist domestic and international propaganda was increasingly in the hands of Chiang Kai-shek's son, Chiang Ching-kuo, from his position as head of the party's political department.

In the Nationalists' ideology, Mao Zedong and the Chinese Communists were not merely bandits but the usurpers of the mantle of Sun Yat-sen, the founder of both the Chinese Republic and the Kuomintang. At the heart of Nationalist political theory was Sun's concept of *San*

Min Chu I, the Three Principles of the People: Sovereignty, Democracy, and the People's Livelihood. Sun had also considered that since the Chinese people had no familiarity with representative government, they would have to undergo a period of "tutelage" under one-party rule. This was the official position on Taiwan, which, because the leadership also considered the civil war to still be in effect, had placed the island under martial law.

As the 1960's progressed, Nationalist propaganda continued its uncompromising stand that it was the sole legitimate Chinese government, but now with the added claim that it was also the conservator of Chinese culture and civilization. The Nationalists had shipped the bulk of the treasures from Beijing's Palace Museum to Taiwan by 1949, and since American students and academics were barred from traveling to the PRC until the 1970's, ROC institutions remained the only source for research and training in Chinese disciplines. American foundations contributed heavily to Taiwan's research facilities and the destruction of art objects during the Cultural Revolution on the mainland assured the island's cultural pre-eminence. Additionally, a government-sponsored Cultural Renaissance Movement sought to refashion social mores at home along more traditional lines as a middle way between the excesses of collectivism and individualism.

More convert means were also employed. Government lobbyists in the United States sought to keep a political presence through the remnants of the China Lobby and the Committee of One Million Against the Admission of Communist China to the UN. Following American recognition of the PRC in 1979, increased surveillance and intelligence gathering was conducted in the United States by ROC operatives. Since 1949 as well, the Consolidated Chinese Benevolent Associations in the U.S. have proved a solid base of ROC support.

The 1980's and 1990's have seen propaganda efforts centered around creating an image of Taiwan as stable, prosperous, and moderate in comparison to the irregularities of communist rule on the mainland. Since the Tenth Kuomintang Congress in 1969, official emphasis has been placed on creating a model of economic dynamism on the island before reconquering the mainland as a means to show the efficacy of Sun's three principles in practice. In an effort to circumvent criticism of the island's one-party rule, particular emphasis has also been placed on publicizing the gradual liberalization of the political system, the vibrancy of the electorate, and the growing diversity of opposition parties.

SUGGESTED READINGS:

Fairbank, John King, and Edwin O. Reischauer. *China: Tradition and Transformation.* Boston: Houghton Mifflin, 1989.

Gibert, Stephen P., and William M. Carpenter, eds. *America and Island China: A Documentary History.* Lanham, Md.: University Press of America, 1989.

Kaplan, David E. *Fires of the Dragon.* New York: Atheneum, 1992.

Kau, Michael Y. M. *Taiwan: Beyond the Economic Miracle.* Armonk, N.Y.: M. E. Sharpe, 1992.

Lee, Lai To. *The Reunification of China: PRC-Taiwan Relations in Flux.* New York: Praeger, 1991.

Tucker, Nancy Bernkopf. *Taiwan, Hong Kong, and the United States, 1945-1992.* New York: Twayne, 1994.

— *Charles A. Desnoyers*

■ Talk shows

Radio and television programs built around interviews and audience participation in discussions

Talk shows have long been a staple of broadcast programming. These shows began on radio and were easily adapted to television. Magazine formats are the most common type of talk show. Magazine format programs resemble a print magazine in that they cover a variety of topics and issues. The *Today* program and *Good Morning, America* are examples of magazine talk shows.

ORIGINS OF THE TALK SHOW Radio talk shows were common features on early broadcasts. All three networks used talk shows to fill time on their programming schedules. Early talk shows included *Dental Talk, The Criminal Court,* and *My Greatest Flying Thrill,* a children's program. Later, when television became America's favorite entertainment pastime, radio talk show programs made easy transitions to television. One of the first morning talk shows on network television was the *Dave Garroway Show,* the forerunner of *Today.*

Talk shows are common on radio, television, and cable outlets. They are popular with station managers and program producers because they are inexpensive to produce, especially when compared with other programming fare. They are popular also because these programs cover a variety of topics, including news, sports, health, finance, and car and home repairs. Moreover, call-in talk shows encourage audience participation, giving those who call, as well as listeners, the impression that everyone can participate in a public debate on issues of importance to the community.

FEATURES OF TALK SHOW PROPAGANDA Talk shows may be classified as propaganda vehicles when they express and advocate (either blatantly or subtly) social or political ideas. Radio talk shows such as those hosted by Rush LIMBAUGH, G. Gordon Liddy, and Armstrong Williams, are fundamentally political and attempt to influence the politics and beliefs of listeners. Although discussion of politics is not propaganda, these programs go far beyond simple discussion: The information they provide is not straightforward but is one-sided and is intended to lead and manipulate listeners.

Social propaganda is created to influence social behavior. Talk shows that discuss issues such as welfare reform, abortion rights (*see* ABORTION DEBATE), animal rights, public health, and education frequently intend to influence social behavior. Among such programs are the talk shows of Oprah Winfrey, Sally Jessy Raphael, Geraldo Rivera, and Ricki Lake. Talk shows, regardless of format and intent, are forms of cultural propaganda. Indeed, even talk shows that do not push political agendas subtly promote values associated with American culture.

Regardless of format or broadcast outlet, talk shows seek to influence the emotions, thoughts, and sometimes the actions of a group or the public at large through careful selection and manipulation of information. Partisan political talk shows attempt to persuade audiences to accept one political viewpoint over others. Topics, questions, and viewer comments are all carefully selected and assembled to evoke the desired responses. Talk shows select, arrange, and deliver information to elicit desired public responses.

Talk shows are a form of manipulation in which powerful broadcast and cable network executives exert their power. This manipulation is achieved through the choice of certain hosts, audiences, and topics. Talk shows also promote an illusion of inclusiveness, promoting the idea that they are part of the public debate. As many forms of entertainment do, talk shows construct, or reconstruct, reality. Although some talk shows purport to offer news, in actuality they provide entertainment, mixed with carefully selected bits of news, creating a form of "infotainment."

SUGGESTED READINGS:

Kurtz, Howard. *Hot Air: All Talk, All The Time.* New York: Random House, 1996.

Levin, Murray B. *Talk Radio and the American Dream.* Lexington, Mass.: D. C. Heath, 1987.

Lewis, Tom. *Empire of the Air: The Men Who Made Radio.* New York: Harper Perennial, 1993.

Munson, Wayne. *All Talk: The Talkshow in Media Culture.* Philadelphia: Temple University Press, 1993.

Priest, Patricia Joyner. *Public Intimacies: Talk Show Participants and Tell-All TV.* Cresskill, N.J.: Hampton Press, 1995.

— *Gilbert A. Williams*

■ TASS

Official Soviet Union news agency

Telegrafnoe Agentstvo Sovetskovo Soiuza (telegraph agency of the Soviet Union), TASS was established on July 10, 1925, by the presidium of the Central Executive Committee of the U.S.S.R., as the official news agency of the Soviet Union. The agency replaced the Russian Telegraph Agency (ROSTA), which had been formed by the Bolsheviks soon after the Russian Revolution of 1917.

From its headquarters in Moscow, TASS provided regional, national, and foreign news to national media, as well as to each Soviet state's local news agency. The job of TASS was to portray national and international news and events from the Marxist-Leninist perspective, as well as providing information and propaganda for domestic and international consumption. TASS was a tool for bringing outside information into the Soviet Union, but it was also the official mouthpiece of the Soviet establishment.

During the COLD WAR the Soviet Union and the United States perceived propaganda differently. From the Marxist-Leninist perspective, the role of the media was to help move the revolution (and society) forward, theoretically to the final stage of communism. In that sense, only information perceived as helping to achieve that goal was considered important news, whereas events that did not fit the purpose were not considered news.

DISINFORMATION was one of the tools used by TASS. Such measures included efforts to influence policies of other governments, undermine confidence in a country's leaders or institutions, and disrupt relations between countries. Disinformation was practiced using both officially sanctioned and clandestine means. It was often reported that a number of TASS correspondents overseas worked as intelligence officers on behalf of the Soviet State Security Committee (KGB).

TASS provided both wire copy and photo service to about 1,200 clients in 115 countries, using seven languages. Its 1,300

Luis Valdez, founder of the "peasant theater," by a poster for his play *Zoot Suit* in 1979. (*AP/Wide World Photos*)

reporters, editors, and photographers included correspondents in more than 120 nations. TASS distributed news, commentaries, official government materials, reports on official visits and meetings within the Soviet Union, and Soviet government appointments. It was considered among the world's five largest news agencies, but it was not accepted as a reliable member of that group because it was a government-controlled and state-financed news agency. TASS nevertheless operated as a world agency and made its service available, free of charge, to media and news agencies in many parts of the world. It was primarily used in Eastern Europe and certain Third World nations that had ties to the Soviet Union.

Under communist rule, all Soviet republics had their own news agencies, which were affiliated with TASS. TASS lost its affiliate news agencies in the Soviet republics when they became independent states after the dissolution of the Soviet Union in 1991. In December, 1991, the Russian Supreme Soviet abolished censorship for the first time in Russian history and gave people the right to read any publications they desired. Some media organizations, however, including TASS, remained under state political and financial control, though they attempted to be more objective and professional. In February, 1992, TASS merged with the Russian Informational Telegraph Agency and its name was changed to ITAR-TASS.

— *Thimios Zaharopoulos*

■ Teatro Campesino

Traveling theater troupe founded by Luis Valdez to help support the farmworkers' movement during the 1960's

Teatro Campesino, the farmworkers' theater, was born out of the grape-pickers' strike and boycott that began in September, 1965, in Delano, California. Valdez, a graduate of San Jose State University, had had some experience with the San Francisco Mime Troupe. He invited Chicano farmworkers in Delano to an organizational meeting on November 2, 1965. Although Valdez spearheaded the group, all performers participated in the creation of the *actos*, or brief skits, used to convey the message of the troupe: United the farmworkers must persist, and if they did they would win the strike, which called for the recognition of the National Farm Workers

Association (NFWA). Under the guidance of the revered leader César Chávez this group gained international recognition and increasing power as the United Farm Workers (UFW), for which Teatro Campesino provided entertainment and effective social propaganda from 1965 through 1967.

Valdez brought the theater to the people, and the people participated in the creation of theater, which was often performed on the back of flat-bed trucks before workers in the fields. Teatro Campesino accompanied the farm workers' march from Delano to Sacramento in the spring of 1966, and it toured the San Joaquin Valley, rallying workers to the cause of *la huelga*, the strike.

Like Italian *commedia dell'arte*, the group's *actos* drew on stock characters again and again, in varying skits, to communicate the status and needs of the strike. These included *esquiroles* (scabs), *contratistas* (contractors), *patroncitos* (growers), and *huelgistas* (strikers). As propaganda, the *actos* served an important function for a community of agricultural laborers who often lacked formal education and would not have responded well to lengthy written texts or wordy lectures. Like the morality plays of medieval Europe, the *actos* helped a community reinforce its values, its desires, and its identity. In 1971 Valdez described the *actos* as a variant of AGITPROP (a theatrical style associated with the former Soviet Union), but he also emphasized the troupe's strong heritage from Mexican folk culture. As early as January, 1966, Valdez explained the Teatro Campesino as "somewhere between [Bertolt] Brecht and Cantinflas." The troupe drew on the German playwright's commitment to social

realism and theater as propaganda for the working people at the same time it also drew on Mexican comedy's use of the *pelado* (underdog) in the Mexican *carpa* (tent performance) tradition.

The early flat-bed performances used no scenery, scripts, or curtains; props were used sparingly and signs were hung around characters' necks to identify them. After two years of working with the UFW, the troupe in 1967 moved to Del Rey, California, where it broadened its focus to larger cultural issues such as U.S. imperialism, racism, and immigrants' "selling out" to the dominant culture. By 1969, when it relocated to Fresno, Teatro Campesino had become the model for many other Chicano theater groups that had sprung up under its influence. In 1971 the troupe relocated again to San Juan Bautista, and although its use of *actos* gave way to a variety of other plays, musicals, a Broadway show, and Public Broadcasting System specials, the distinctive propaganda skit, the *acto*, remains the classic symbol of the Teatro Campesino.

— *Scot M. Guenter*

■ Technology

Propagandists use a variety of technologies to communicate a controlled vision of reality to a mass audience

Communication technologies, from Johannes Gutenberg's introduction of moveable type to the latest computer-based INFORMATION systems, have offered those who own and use the MEDIA the ability to control the nature and content of what is seen and heard. Sophisticated technology, from TELEVISION to computers, increases the availability of information even as it transmits misleading and manipulated messages aimed at eliciting desired responses.

THE NATURE OF TECHNOLOGY Technology by definition includes both the devices and the technique associated with MASS COMMUNICATIONS. Technology consists of much more than devices or objects such as the printing press, camera, television receiver, and computer. Analysis of the relationship of technology and propaganda must consider both the development of the devices and the evolution of their use. The films of Leni RIEFENSTAHL extolling the Third Reich (*see* GERMANY: 1933-1945 and Joseph GOEBBELS) are a powerful example of the ability of FILM to influence public perception through the use of camera and editing techniques.

Of particular significance to the relationship of technology and propaganda are the differing points of view regarding which factors dominate. Marshall McLUHAN's famous phrase "The medium is the message," in *Understanding Media: The Extensions of Man* (1964), gives primacy to technology itself. Raymond Williams' analysis in *Television: Technology and Cultural Form* (1974) argues for the important, if not formative, role of culture. Part of this disagreement centers on whether society is active or passive in relationship to the potential power of technology. Jacques ELLUL's analysis in his *La Technique: Ou, L'Enjou du siècle* (1954; *The Technological Society,* 1964) stresses additional factors in the nature and potential of technology as being particularly relevant to the centralizing tendency of technology. Technological systems, both in concept and in physical structure, increase the control of informa-

tion design and flow. Networking as a thought process and structure—particularly associated with electronic media—promotes the notion of both belonging and dependency.

Beyond such theoretical discussions, technological devices and techniques are integral to the creation, transmission, and reception of information. Changes in technological devices and shifts in types of media alter the creation, reproduction, and distribution patterns of information. A major consequence of such changes pertains to the knowledge required by the initiator and receiver of the media. For example, text-based media require reading skills on the part of the reader, whereas images can generally gain recognition without any specialized training on the part of the viewer.

One cultural factor that influences the effectiveness of technology as a propaganda tool is the culture's general attitude toward a given medium. Elements that promote or limit acceptance include the language used to describe devices or processes. Patterns of reception influence whether the interpretation occurs in isolation or in a group setting: Reading is usually private, while films are often a shared experience.

The convergence of communication technologies has magnified the potential power of media. The combining, at various historical stages, of text, images, and sound, as well as the addition of qualities such as color and motion, have increased the options for those creating propaganda. Some theorists contend that increased sophistication in equipment and technique has enabled the producer to overwhelm the senses so that desired effects, especially emotional reactions, are experienced by many viewers.

THE PERCEPTION OF REALITY Propaganda by definition attempts to control or influence the meanings attached to experiences or information. The more an individual is passive in relation to the methods of the conveyed media, the greater the potential for influence. For example, ADVERTISING photography can use lighting, filters, or a particular type of focus to project an interpretation of "softness." If the desired interpretation is accepted, even at a subconscious level, then a meaning has been established.

The visual image represents the epitome of artifice perceived as reality. As image reproduction in print, film, and electronic media improved, a transition occurred in which viewers suspended belief and accepted two-dimensional images, usually composed of dots, as accurate representations of reality. The consequences for perceived truth are profound. The addition of sound, motion, and color to photographic and electronic technology during the twentieth century has increased acceptance of media as reality (*see* PHOTOGRAPHY AND PHOTOJOURNALISM).

Walter J. Ong's 1982 study of language as technology and of the shift from oral to visual (print) language demonstrates the profound significance of such transformations. Being a "literate" person has for many centuries been a class privilege that was often jealously guarded. In nineteenth century Britain taxes on NEWSPAPERS and newspaper advertising, known as "taxes on knowledge," were an attempt to keep cheap sources of news and ideas away from the lower classes for the reason that those who possess knowledge of the technology can claim ownership of the meaning of events.

PRINTING Gutenberg's development of moveable type in the fifteenth century established the base point for referencing later changes in information technology. Very low literacy rates inhibited the social dimension of the printing revolution. Nonetheless, the printed text in various forms was particularly significant in promoting the changes associated with the Protestant Reformation. An estimated one million copies of Martin Luther's translation of the Bible were printed in the first hundred years of its existence.

Typography is central to print media. Typography captures much of the essence of the spoken word. The style and size of the reproduced letters contain several layers of meaning. Similar to the spoken word, a sense of volume and tone can be achieved through size, style (bold or italic), and font. Another important element is the ability to either construct or deconstruct the language through placement and through the mixing of fonts and styles. Newspapers gradually adopted new standards for typography and design. By the late nineteenth century the use of large type and multiple-column groupings had become common. Some of these innovations were dependent on changes in typesetting technology. By condensing the content of an article in a headline, the editor/propagandist could reduce complex issues to simplistic abstractions.

The central development of print media was the ability to reproduce words more and more quickly. Hand-set type had a limit of about one line per minute. The linotype machine in 1885 immediately increased production to five lines a minute. The computerized processes which have emerged since the 1960's have continued to expand production rapidly.

Another key ingredient for increased volume in reproduction has been ongoing improvements in the printing press. The first steam-powered press, patented in 1813, achieved a fourfold speed increase over hand presses. Developments in the 1870's and 1880's, including the web (a continuous role of paper), facilitated the rise of the mass-circulation newspapers in urban centers. These papers, taking advantage of the production of cheap paper, became known for sensationalism under the name YELLOW JOURNALISM. The telegraph, both in Europe and the United States, allowed masses of people to hear news of far-off places immediately; this access to immediate information led readers to feel connected to events occurring outside their immediate experience.

PHOTOGRAPHY AND FILM The cliché "seeing is believing" demonstrates the power of images. The early photographs known as daguerreotypes, invented in France in 1837, initiated the rapid rise in the popularity of the camera as a way to reproduce visual experiences. The development of stereographic photography in the 1850's further enhanced the public perception that the images were realistic.

Photography had a profound influence on the print media. Woodcuts, often based on photographs, projected an impression that the artist was present at the scene. Photoengraving techniques had emerged by the 1880's, and the development of the half-tone process by 1900 further enhanced the role of images in publications for news and advertisements. Photojournalists utilized smaller cameras with improved lenses and film to create images that have served as icons of the Great Depression and World War II. The seeming simplicity and candor of such images conveyed emotion-laden content.

Beginning with Eadweard Muybridge's study of motion in the 1870's, the motion picture enabled the reconstruction of reality. Images were reassembled and moved in sequence in front of the viewer, creating an illusion of motion that was perceived as reality. Early news film, in fact, were known as actualities. In the 1960's the use of hand-held camera equipment gave rise to the technique known as cinema verité. Sound and color were vital aspects of the technological enhancement of film. The addition of sound in 1927 provided a sensation which more realistically approximated viewers' normal experience. Color tinting occurred in both photography and film from early days. The development of improved coloration through Technicolor in the 1930's, coupled with the emergence of the wide screen in the 1950's, enhanced the sensory experience.

A primary limitation of film technology occurred in the viewing. Projecting films required the physical delivery of the film to the site of the projection equipment and the willingness of people to congregate in a specified location at a designated time. Flexibility and ease of delivery were limited, owing to the physical nature of the medium. Electronic media overcame some of these limitations.

RADIO AND TELEVISION Electronic media offered additional advantages to the propagandist. One of RADIO's primary attractions was the broad area that could be covered by the electronic signal. The speed of electronic broadcasting provided a nearly instantaneous connection with listeners, affording the notion of "live" reception and thus the illusion that the recipient was actually witnessing the event.

A primary limitation of electronic media, unlike print media, was that the recipient had to possess a receiver (*see* GERMANY: 1933-1945 and Joseph GOEBBELS). Once ownership was pervasive, the perception that information was free heightened the persuasive potential of the medium. The development of portable receivers with battery operation and the significantly lower energy requirements of transistor, which emerged in the 1950's, resulted in radios becoming almost ubiquitous. A major advantage of electronic media was the ability to leapfrog boundaries that could block distribution of more tangible media. Radio was a significant propaganda tool during WORLD WAR II and the COLD WAR; it was used in efforts to influence the citizenry of an enemy country or of occupied nations (*see* VOICE OF AMERICA and RADIO LIBERTY). Mobile broadcasting units used by guerrillas could be easily moved to avoid detection and capture.

Both radio and television followed technology's tendency of centralized control in ownership and distribution. The systematic nature of the technological organization and equipment was demonstrated in the creation of large networks, resulting in a unified delivery and ultimately in standardized content. National programming, and even the international sharing of equipment and product, redefined the notion of community.

The first operational television was developed in England in 1926. Standardization of the technology in the United States was established in 1941. By the late 1950's the vast majority of U.S. homes possessed at least one television. Cable delivery systems were pioneered in the late 1940's to reach small and isolated communities.

The addition of color to the television picture was commonplace by the late 1960's, and the use of videotape recording and playback by the television industry changed the quality of the image and, more important, increased the speed with which visual information could be transmitted in the 1960's and 1970's. News programming became much more visual. Satellite transmission redefined transmission and reception beginning in the 1960's and expanding transmission to locations not reachable by direct transmission or cable. The notion of the "global village" was born.

The primary power of television rests with the visual nature of the information and with the fact that viewing takes place in the home. The apparent naturalness of the appliance, once established in the home and in daily routine, adds to the potential disarming of the viewer. The viewing of events is a shared experience, but one shared in isolation. The integration of the message by the individual is frequently accomplished before the contrary views that might be expressed by others can be expressed or heard.

COMPUTER TECHNOLOGY Computer-assisted media builds upon the techniques of earlier communication systems while increasing the capacity to manipulate information. The growth of computer networks has facilitated the distribution of information. The ease of combining sound, text, and images empowers the propagandist. The term "multimedia," associated with computer systems, reflects the convergence of multiple technologies that have been given entertainment, education, and business applications. The potential for interactive communication increases the likelihood of feedback to the creator; this feedback can be assessed to enable more specific matching of the message to the targeted recipient. Broadcasting, an indiscriminate strategy, can be replaced by "narrowcasting," which targets recipients based on predetermined criteria.

Digital technology makes possible the manipulation of media of all types, and sophisticated use of visual images can be coordinated with sound and text. The ease of altering documents and creating new images has increasingly blurred the distinctions between artificial and real. The ability to store and manipulate information on electronic databases is a major asset to those seeking to promote particular views of events, policies, or products. Records of official documents, financial transactions, and other data create the potential to assemble profiles of individuals that can be arranged in groups for targeting.

Hypertext markings—electronic links within documents that act as enriched headlines—attempt to lead those seeking information (text and visual) along predetermined paths. This structure offers associations within the presented information; networks have been replaced by the Internet. Search tools on the Internet can similarly be exploited to connect individuals interested in established key words or phrases to connect individuals with groups of particular persuasions.

Electronic information can be tailored to address the preferences of the reader more easily than ever before. Thus electronic formats of news or information discussions can be limited to reinforce existing interpretations or to limit the scope of information that might otherwise offer contrary or alternative views that could challenge established interpretations. Computer technology offers a plethora of techniques and strategies to the propagandist.

SUGGESTED READINGS:

Coombs, James E., and Sara T. Coombs. *Film Propaganda and American Politics.* New York: Garland, 1994. Comprehensive overview of film propaganda in the twentieth century.

Eisenstein, Elizabeth L. *The Printing Press as an Agent of Change.* 2 vols. New York: Cambridge University Press, 1979. Useful concepts and analysis about the cultural consequences of the introduction of movable type in early modern Europe.

Ellul, Jacques. *The Technological Society.* Translation. New York: Vintage Books, 1964. Major contribution to the analysis of the interaction between technology and society by a primary theorist about propaganda.

Lubar, Steven. *Infoculture: The Smithsonian Book of Information Age Inventions.* New York: Houghton Mifflin, 1993. Comprehensive overview of the modern history of communication technologies.

McLuhan, Marshall. *Understanding Media.* New York: Signet Books, 1964. Classic book which popularized the often quoted phrase, "The medium is the message."

Mitchell, William J. *The Reconfigured Eye: Visual Truth in the Post-Photographic Era.* Cambridge, Mass.: MIT Press, 1992. Examines the design and meaning of images in the light of digital technology.

Ong, Walter J. *Orality and Literacy: The Technologizing of the Word.* New York: Routledge, 1982. Pioneering theoretical examination of the most fundamental communication technology shift with many implications for low and high technology comparisons.

Trachtenberg, Alan. *Reading American Photographs: Images as History.* New York: Hill and Wang, 1989. Insightful analysis that places photography in its social context; covers 1839 to 1938.

Williams, Raymond. *Television: Technology and Cultural Form.* Hanover, N.H.: Wesleyan University Press, 1974. Thought-provoking analysis by a major cultural theorist regarding the interplay between television technology and cultural contexts.

Williamson, Judith. *Decoding Advertisements: Ideology and Meaning in Advertising.* New York: Marion Boyars, 1978, 1984. Essential source for anyone serious about deciphering visual media.

— Daniel J. Doyle

■ Telethon

A telethon is a fund-raising broadcast over television that may go on without interruption for as long as a weekend. One of the best-known such events is the annual fund-raiser telethon presided over by Jerry Lewis to raise money to fund research on muscular dystrophy. In this example, one or more television networks and their affiliates carry the telethon, which moves back and forth at regular intervals between the national studios and those of various local stations. The content of the Lewis telethons includes talk, musical entertainment, and interviews with children afflicted with the disease (*see* MASS COMMUNICATIONS, MASS PSYCHOLOGY, and PROPAGANDA CHANNELS).

■ Television

Electronic audiovisual broadcast medium that, in addition to providing entertainment, influences human thought and behavior through subtle means of suggestion

Propaganda is the persistent endeavor to manipulate the attitudes and opinions of groups of people to persuade them into internalizing and adopting the point of view communicated. Although propaganda need not be pernicious, it becomes so when the results are not in the interests of the individuals being addressed; when the methods of persuasion are questionable; when the presentation promotes unrealistic illusions; when the methods of inducement permit no argument; when free will or free choice is denied; and when the recipients are unaware that they are being influenced.

The average American watches television for nearly thirty hours every week, making it the most pervasive mind-structuring instrument ever evolved by civilization. As a propaganda tool, television is double-edged because the nature of the medium itself imprints subconscious messages on the viewers' minds while commercials overtly strive to control purchasing patterns.

PROGRAMMING AS PROPAGANDA Because television is primarily a two-dimensional visual medium with severe sensory limitations, the viewers' interest can be maintained only by televising a distorted and artificial reality. By choosing action over content, depicting strong emotions rather than subtle ones, and portraying an idealized pseudoenvironment, television selectively tells people where to look and what is worth looking at. That selectivity is the beginning of propaganda.

Each genre of commercial television programming—whether it is soap opera, situation comedy, news, sports, or music video—is imbued with subtle elements that can influence the viewer's mind. Soap operas have convoluted plots characterized by infidelity, greed, avarice, and unstable relationships, yet the central characters are inevitably depicted as financially and professionally successful, so-

cially prominent, attractive people. Because viewers identify with these characters, they can be influenced to supplant traditional values with valueless imprints.

TELEVISION NEWS, supposedly an impartial recounting of the day's most important events, is controlled by two constraints: time and the visual nature of the medium. News items selected for broadcast must present a strong visual impact, and they must be condensable into one or two minutes. Important but complicated stories lacking visual impact are often ig-

Television and Radio Sets in Selected Countries in 1995

Country	Persons per Radio	Persons per Television	Country	Persons per Radio	Persons per Television
Afghanistan	4.0	203.0	Iraq	5.5	19.0
Algeria	7.7	14.0	Israel	2.2	4.1
Argentina	1.6	4.7	Italy	3.9	3.4
Australia	0.9	2.2	Japan	1.3	1.2
Austria	1.7	2.9	Kuwait	1.4	1.8
Brazil	2.6	5.2	Lebanon	1.3	2.6
Cambodia	9.0	133.0	Libya	5.0	10.1
Canada	1.3	1.6	Mexico	5.5	6.7
China	5.4	32.0	Nicaragua	4.7	20.0
Cuba	5.1	5.5	Pakistan	13.0	62.0
Dominican Republic	6.7	11.0	Panama	5.6	12.0
Egypt	4.0	11.0	Philippines	17.0	9.5
El Salvador	2.9	11.0	Portugal	4.0	5.6
Ethiopia	17.0	518.0	Saudi Arabia	3.5	3.9
France	1.2	2.0	Somalia	16.0	?
Germany	2.3	2.5	South Africa	4.1	12.0
Guatemala	25.0	21.0	Soviet Union[1]	1.7	2.7
Haiti	2.1	255.0	Spain	3.1	2.3
Honduras	2.9	32.0	Syria	4.5	19.0
India	16.0	45.0	United States	0.5	1.2
Indonesia	8.5	17.0	Vietnam	8.8	28.0
Iran	5.0	26.0			

[1]Prior to 1992

nored, regardless of their merit. A story about a county that pays teachers to tutor potential drop-outs after school is not aired because a clip about students rioting in a school cafeteria provides a greater visual impact.

Programming also falls victim to the constraints of time and visual images, resulting in shallow programs characterized by underdeveloped plots and an emphasis on action. Fast-paced, riveting scenes relate the story while undercutting a thoughtful development of the plot and sacrificing the depiction of subtle human emotions.

Because of commercial television's rating system, producers and script writers must compete to procure and maintain a satisfied audience. Violence, sex, and fast-paced action attract the largest audience, so the studios continue to emphasize such programming. If one station previews a show with burning buildings, bloody gang fights, and seductive heroines, other studios must follow suit or lose their share of the audience. By viewing predominantly negative human behavior, many viewers have become reconditioned to accept this as reality. Thus the average American tends to believe that promiscuity is natural and that the world is a far more dangerous place than it actually is.

COMMERCIALS Television not only delivers programs to the viewer home, it also delivers the viewer's mind to the sponsors. Commercial broadcasting is the result of, and dependent upon, paid ADVERTISING designed to modify and control buying habits. A typical American is subjected to almost 38,000 television commercials yearly. These paid messages are characterized by short catchy phrases and high-impact visual images carefully engineered to provide a strong mental imprint in thirty seconds.

Consumers, faced with an often bewildering array of products and choices, often make selections on the strength and repetition of advertising images they have been exposed to. Commercials are regulated to prevent outright fraud, but they can misrepresent reality by the clever manipulation of duplistic images. The messages promote not only the purchase of a particular product but an unrealistic, ideal lifestyle or cultural image.

Viewers are drawn to identify with characters in thirty-second minidramas and to believe that a particular lifestyle is attainable simply by possessing certain products. Human needs are not necessarily equivalent to the advertiser's need to sell products, however, and by subtle but persistent persuasion advertising can separate humans from their true inner needs and urge them to believe that happiness is achieved through commodities.

The unreal pseudoworld of advertising succeeds on television only because the medium itself creates a mental environment in which the real and the fictional merge into an undifferentiated mass of entertaining images and sound bites. Because commercials are completely devoid of inherent interest, advertisers must rely on technical tricks and highly entertaining but subtly persuasive images to undermine the reasoning centers of the mind.

PERNICIOUS ASPECTS OF TELEVISION PROPAGANDA Most Americans believe that television exerts no control on their lives, that it is merely a conduit for information and entertainment. Television persuades by mediating human experience and implanting an artificial reality. With sufficient viewing, humans lose the ability to distinguish reality from fantasy and the world becomes that which is projected on the television screen. Television is an ideal tool for propaganda because, by confining human experience into one narrow and well-defined channel and retraining minds into passivity, prearranged experiences and ideas can be easily implanted. Human minds can be recast to conform to the values and worldviews of sponsors, producers, and scripwriters.

It is in the interest of network television producers to air shows that will attract as large a share of the potential audience as possible. If the ratings indicate that a show is popular, more and wealthier sponsors will pay to have their product advertised. Viewers' purchasing patterns are then influenced by the strength and repetition of the commercials, leading to greater profits for the sponsoring company. Although television was not conceived as an instrument for mind control, a vicious cycle has evolved. In order to attract the greatest audience and to keep the audience tuned in to an inherently boring and sensorially limited medium, shows must emphasize action, violence, and sex to the detriment of plot and critical reasoning. The audience desires shows that titillate and entertain them, the producers want to attract sponsors, who in turn expect a large share of the potential viewing audience. Thus, a vortex of decline is created as the limits of decency and propriety are constantly being stretched and tested. This type of self-sustaining propaganda promulgates negative situations and undesirable human characteristics, while simultaneously appeasing television's overwhelming need to keep people tuned in.

Television messages, both the overt messages of commercials and the covert images from programming, enter the mind and create changes from within. By dulling sensibility and diluting connections with the external world, television can bend the mind to the programmed imagery. Moreover, the experience of watching television can be addictive, making it difficult to escape from its mind-altering influence. The flickering light from a television screen can evade conscious control and implant messages. When thinking processes are disabled, the viewer's ability to discriminate and critically analyze incoming messages is lost, allowing the mind to fill with the thoughts of others.

By alienating human beings from conscious control of their minds, television programs can fuel the societal conditions that lead to aggression. Within the constraints of a televised drama it is almost impossible to depict a character's inner struggle; characters move rapidly and directly from conflict to visible resolution, bypassing any attempt to apply critical thinking and logical problem-solving skills. Action and simplistic solutions to complex problems thus become the model for decision making.

In the late twentieth century industrialized United States, television viewing is a routine and intrinsic part of life. It is a source of entertainment easily and readily available to almost every sector of society, but its powerful direct influence on millions of lives is being used to redesign human minds into a channeled, artificial form that meshes into the artificial environment projected onto the screen. As an ubiquitous and insidious form of pernicious propaganda, television is an unknowing and uncaring accomplice to the creation of societal conditions that lead to autocracy. Television not only creates the appropriate mental patterns for passively accepting authority without questioning its legitimacy, it simultaneously dulls the awareness that this is occurring. The challenge facing society is to find an intelligent means of mitigating the negative aspects of television viewing and to integrate it with democracy, independent thought, and creativity.

SUGGESTED READINGS:

Condry, J. *The Psychology of Television.* Hillsdale, N.J.: Lawrence Erlbaum, 1989. Evidence supporting the addictive nature of television is reviewed, as are arguments concerning its mind-controlling influence.

McKibben, Bill. *Age of Missing Information.* New York: Penguin Books, 1992. This insightful book persuasively argues that the vast amounts of information provided by television imparts neither knowledge nor understanding.

Mander, Gerry. *Four Arguments for the Elimination of Television.* New York: William Morrow, 1978. Charges that television mediates experience, replaces human images with artificial ones, and operates against sensory experience.

Postman, Neil. *Amusing Ourselves to Death.* New York: Penguin Books, 1985. Exposes the detrimental effects of television upon modern society and claims that Americans raised in the age of information are less well informed than their ancestors were.

Pratkanis, A., and E. Aronson. *Age of Propaganda: The Everyday Use and Abuse of Persuasion.* New York: Freeman, 1992. Details the means by which American beliefs, preferences, and choices are being influenced by the mass media.

— *George R. Plitnik*

■ Television news

Regular and special news programs broadcast on television

Propaganda can be either explicitly stated or merely suggested and implied. Television news employs both forms, but because of the nature of the medium it excels at hidden propaganda. The visual component of television, its seemingly instantaneous presentation, and the broad distribution of television news contribute to the public's preference for news presentation on television. Network and local news, documentaries, and special broadcasts promote the perception that those who are viewing are becoming informed citizens. Yet the patchwork of major and trivial topics, advertisements, and other elements creates a homogenized package with predetermined meaning.

FRAMING A VISION The dominance of television news and its strength as an agent of propaganda stems largely from the nature of the TECHNOLOGY. Through the use of photographs, video clips, and remote transmission, television has built upon techniques established by photojournalism and NEWSREELS. Visual content prevails in such phrases and symbols as "Eyewitness News" or the "eye" of the Columbia Broadcasting System (CBS) logo.

The images of television news influence the audience with a variety of hidden meanings. People tend to judge critically what they hear or read, but they are less likely to do so with what they see. The visual is evaluated as to whether it is pleasant or not rather than whether it is truthful or relevant. Furthermore, the camera

Journalist Edward R. Murrow was one of the most important forces in the development of television news in the United States during the 1950's. (*AP/Wide World Photos*)

can easily frame the mind's eye because it can set the boundaries. The camera's control of vision has the potential to shape meaning through focusing on selected elements and eliminating others. Mere inclusion of images implies significance. At times the television reporter enters the image. If trust has previously been established with the viewer, the presented image gains a personal dimension.

Many events and issues demonstrate the potential power of television news. The Vietnam War, often characterized as the first "television war," and the broadcasts on the night the air bombardment in the Persian Gulf War began, gave viewers the perception of being present as the events were occurring. Most viewers did not ask whether what was seen was reality. Images, augmented by verbal characterizations, led the audience to the intended interpretations.

In the United States television news production is primarily a component of commercial enterprises. The major networks, cable companies, and local channels exist as business ventures. News attracts viewers and thus sells advertising, which is the primary revenue source. News also helps meet Federal Communication Commission requirements for a minimum of community programming. Through regular news programs a station or network can establish both an identity for itself and a bond between the viewers and the media enterprise. Local stations use news to define their community, which reflects the area reached by the broadcast or cable signal. News also enables a television station to promote other programs and encourage viewers to continue watching. Television news is part of a social system that the chosen news content firmly supports.

The limitations and biases of television news are shared with those of NEWSPAPERS and RADIO. The subjective preferences and political inclinations of the various members of the production staffs help shape the production. Even without accompanying narration, the placement of camera and range of focus, as well as the broadcast time within the overall programming influence the ways in which the viewer may interpret meaning. The selection of experts also shapes the message. Some of the biases underlying a presentation may be obvious, but many others are quite subtle.

MEDIATING THE WORLD To be judged as successful, news programs require that the product attract, retain, and please the viewer. The formula for regular television programming, whether network or local, serves to meet these competing requirements. News broadcasts employ the structure borrowed from newspapers. Unlike newspapers, however, where readers can choose their own path through the product, television news is linear and requires the viewer to accept the predetermined sequence. Segments are presented in a sequence that moves the viewer through events so as to elicit an emotional rhythm beginning with anxiety, moving to security, and ending with comfort or happiness. Simply stated, the "bad" exists in the outer world or community, but the program ends by stressing something "good." Through a careful sequencing of elements, news production mediates the external world, and the program interprets the unknown or unfamiliar. Mediation usually entails mitigating or eliminating what is potentially harmful. One of the great advantages in this process is the opportunity to define what is potentially harmful. The program anchor serves as the central point in this process of presenting and interpreting events by being the one who introduces or announces information and provides transitions to segments. Anchors occasionally interact with other staff in what is often a scripted set of questions and answers, and they offer a sense of security—all is or will be well.

Network and local programming, along with newspapers and radio, contribute to defining what individuals, groups, and even a nation considers to be "news." Repeated scenes or treatment of certain topics contribute to shared perceptions. Wars or crimes acknowledged by visual reports come to be perceived as crises or tragedies, while problems the viewer has not seen are ignored.

The juxtaposition of stories is an essential part of the mediation process. Shocking news such as recent crime may be followed by unrelated stories of apprehension of alleged criminals or stories of convictions at court. The viewer is likely to infer that what has occurred today will later follow in a similar pattern. The program encourages this expectation with the implication that the reporters will "stay on top of the story." Local viewers are sometimes encouraged to call in or send videotape. Analysis and evaluation are suspended, and all become part of the "team." The presentation confirms that the established system maintains order.

The interspersion of news segments with advertisements is a further part of the mediation process. As in other media, news stories may be interwoven with unrelated even contradictory ads. Thus a story on hunger or homelessness may shortly be followed with a commercial for food or clothing. This apparent contradiction is usually ignored except in times of major crisis when the station or more often the advertisers suspend the commercials for a time in fear of viewer criticism. So-called documentaries employ music in ways that contribute to this mediation, for music packages an additional emotional layer for the viewer.

The transition from anxiety to calm or happiness varies in different formulas. Local programming moves from traditionally defined news to features such as weather, sports, consumer or medical reports, and an upbeat human-interest story that normally ends a broadcast. These non-news segments coupled with the ads complete the process of demonstrating that the external world, which was potentially threatening, has been pacified. Viewers' lives can go on as before.

BLURRING DISTINCTIONS The lines that distinguish between news and entertainment have been increasingly blurred. In addition to regular news programs, news departments produce an increasing variety of programs, including what initially were called documentaries and such "special" broadcasts and magazine features as *60 Minutes.* Some characterize these kinds of programs as "soft news."

Another format, the interview program, has been popular for news departments since the early success of *Meet the Press,* wherein print and television reporters interview so-called newsmakers—elected and government officials. Part of the initial purpose was to heighten the importance of the reporter (first by gaining legitimacy from association with print journalists) and to obtain statements that might later be used in the news or become news through being important or controversial. Eventually reporters themselves became celebrities, and some programs have emerged in which reporters query themselves. This assumption that the reporter is the expert is also exhibited in regular news programs, in which anchors question reporters in the field. The promotion of television staff, especially anchors, to celebrity status enhances for some viewers the weight of the statements made.

Special events in particular demonstrate the power of television news productions. The preemption of a regular routine convinces many that the topic is of great importance. Continued coverage verifies significance and conveys a sense of "history in the making." The CBS journalist Edward R. Murrow fostered a legitimacy of early television news through the *You Are There* series, which alleged to reenact historical events with a reporter commenting and even interviewing historical figures.

The blurring of news types and the inclusion of entertainment-style features, which infuse all forms of news productions, further cloud the viewer's comprehension. The framing of images, mediated through a formulaic sequence, and the packaging of news productions complicate evaluation of imbedded meanings, and viewers are often unaware of the manipulation of their points of view.

SUGGESTED READINGS:

Altheide, David L. *Creating Reality: How TV News Distorts Events.* Beverly Hills, Calif.: Sage Publications, 1976.

Dayan, Daniel, and Elihu Katz. *Media Events: The Live Broadcasting of History.* Cambridge, Mass.: Harvard University Press, 1992.

Dobkin, Bethami A. *Tales of Terror: Television News and the Construction of the Terrorist Threat.* New York: Praeger, 1992.

Donovan, Robert J., and Ray Scherer. *Unsilent Revolution: Television News and American Public Life.* New York: Cambridge University Press, 1992.

Kellner, Douglas. *The Persian Gulf TV War.* Boulder, Colo.: Westview Press, 1992.

Rapping, Elyane. *The Looking Glass World of Nonfiction TV.* Boston: South End Press, 1987.

Spragens, William C. *Electronic Magazines: Soft News Programs on Network Television.* Westport, Conn.: Praeger, 1995.

— *Daniel J. Doyle*

■ Temperance movements

Organized efforts in the United States to suppress the consumption of alcoholic beverages

Movements advocating temperance reform prior to the onset of the PROHIBITION ERA in 1919 succeeded or failed according to the extent of their persuasive power. Temperance propaganda remained significant but less so after Prohibition's repeal in 1933.

BACKGROUND An early example of temperance propaganda was authored in 1785 by Benjamin Rush, a signer of the Declaration of Independence and the first prominent American to speak out against the lethal effects of distilled beverages. In *An Inquiry into the Effects of Ardent Spirits on the Human Mind and Body*, Rush emphasized the addictive qualities of alcohol and urged "personal abstinence" and social pressure against drunkenness. He stated that four thousand deaths annually were caused by the use of distilled liquor. Approximately 200,000 copies of Rush's work were distributed nationally during the first three decades of the nineteenth century.

Despite Rush's effort to introduce a scientific approach to understanding the effects of alcohol, temperance movements throughout the nineteenth century, and well into the twentieth, were crusades directed at both moderate and heavy drinkers who, as sinners, required conversion back to the purity of a non-alcoholic state. Propaganda touting the movements was generally emotional and sensational in content. Methods of propaganda included articles, stories, poems, plays, songs, and novels. Pamphlets and books were published, surveys were taken, and saloons were attacked by ax-wielding reformers. Parades, demonstrations, meetings, and conventions were held. Pressure groups were organized within political parties, and new parties were formed to run their own candidates on an anti-alcohol ticket.

Passage of the Eighteenth Amendment of the Constitution in 1919, which outlawed the manufacture, sale, and transportation of intoxicating liquors, was the high point of the American temperance crusade. Even though Prohibition was repealed in 1933, American temperance reform continued to follow a consistent pattern of coercion. The most prominent movements included the Women's Christian Temperance Union (WCTU), the Anti-Saloon League (ASL), Alcoholics Anonymous, and the Yale Center of Alcoholic Studies.

THE WCTU AND THE ASL The WCTU was a successful nineteenth century temperance movement. Established in 1874 and the undisputed leader in temperance reform throughout the remainder of the century, the WCTU was a middle-class movement dedicated to closing saloons and promoting morality. Combining prohibition and women's rights, it argued that mothers and wives understood better than anyone else the costs of intemperance. Frances E. C. Willard became its

dedicated leader. She stressed "home protection," or the preservation of the family, as the bedrock of society. The WCTU published the monthly *Union Signal* and a periodical dedicated to American youth, the *Young Crusader*, along with numerous books, pamphlets, and leaflets. The Frances E. Willard Memorial Library for Alcohol Research in Evanston, Illinois, became one of the largest libraries of its kind in the world. The WCTU lost its primary place in temperance reform when it split over the issue of continuing as a single-issue pressure group or whether to ally itself with other social reform efforts, such as labor and POPULISM.

The ASL was established in 1895 at almost the same time that the WCTU was starting to decline. Calling itself "the church in action," the ASL relied heavily on Protestant church congregations serving as ASL affiliates. Between 1905 and 1915, forty thousand churches cooperated with the ASL. League representatives gained support by speaking from the pulpit at least once each month in affiliated churches. The ASL also established a publishing house that printed 250 million pages of antialcohol literature during its first three years. An annual *Yearbook* was published, identifying dry counties in white and wet counties in black on maps of the United States. The ASL was virtually a political machine, supporting political candidates and parties that favored prohibition. Its efforts were paramount in the passage of the constitutional amendment officially establishing Prohibition in the United States.

ALCOHOLICS ANONYMOUS AND THE YALE CENTER Alcoholics Anonymous (AA) was founded by William G. Wilson and Dr.

Robert H. Smith in 1935, shortly after the repeal of Prohibition. Each had been heavy drinkers. AA followed a formula stressing simplicity, candor, and anonymity. It recognized alcoholism as a disease that could be controlled but not cured. AA's approach is described in *Alcoholics Anonymous*, "the Big Book." Published in 1939, it contains twelve critical steps to be followed in recovery from alcoholism. Millions of copies were sold. Much of AA's success has been based on confidentiality among its members, who are identified by first name only. In 1988 there were more than eighty-five thousand AA groups worldwide. AA has been an example of a temperance movement that has succeeded in part because of its propaganda output, but even more because of the conditions of belonging to AA, including anonymity. Alcoholics Anonymous has also avoided divisive political issues; it neither supports nor opposes such causes as laws restricting the sale of alcohol.

The Yale Center of Alcohol Studies was another successful temperance effort. It was established by Dr. Elvin M. Jellinek shortly after his arrival at Yale University in 1939. Although the center's purpose was alcohol research and education, it also became a superb propaganda machine through the publicity efforts of Jellinek and Marty Mann. A former heavy drinker herself, Mann was an effective and popular speaker who traveled throughout the United States delivering an average of two hundred speeches a year. She stressed a scientific rather than a moral message. Harking back to Dr. Rush, alcoholism increasingly was defined and accepted as a disease rather than an example of moral degeneracy. Mann was the founder (in 1944) and executive director

of the National Committee for Education on Alcoholism (NCEA). It published literature on alcohol and alcohol abuse and was effective in organizing affiliates throughout the country. With some reservations, both AA and the WCTU supported the disease concept; eventually the American Medical Association accepted alcoholism as a condition requiring treatment, not punishment. Alcoholism became viewed as a public health problem as Mann won over both the press and the public. By the early 1960's nearly two-thirds of those responding to a survey on alcoholism agreed that it was a disease; twenty years earlier the fraction had been only one-fifth.

From these efforts grew a more coercive approach through intervention. Governments at the federal, state, and local levels became more heavily involved with the prevention and treatment of alcoholism. Private industry inaugurated occupational alcoholism programs and became convinced that employee drinking problems should be identified and addressed by human resource programs. Family, job, and citizens' rights encroached upon individual privacy rights. Propaganda through creative persuasive techniques by the media, literature, plays, films, and organizations such as MOTHERS AGAINST DRUNK DRIVING (MADD) became effective in fighting alcoholism and the damaging and dangerous behavior it encouraged. During the last two decades of the twentieth century, however, the more private hands-on, direct interventionist approach became the treatment of choice.

SUGGESTED READINGS:

Aaron, Paul, and David Musto. "Temperance and Prohibition in America: A Historical

Overview." In *Alcohol and Public Policy: Beyond the Shadows of Prohibition*, edited by Mark H. Moore and Dean R. Gerstein. Washington, D.C.: National Academy Press, 1981.

Blocker, Jack S., Jr. *American Temperance Movements: Cycles of Reform.* Boston: Twayne, 1989.

Gusfield, Joseph R. *Symbolic Crusade: Status Politics and the American Temperance Movement.* Urbana: University of Illinois Press, 1963.

Kurtz, Ernest. *Not-God.* Center City, Minn.: Hazelden, 1979.

Lender, Mark E. *Dictionary of American Temperance Biography.* Westport, Conn.: Greenwood Press, 1984.

— *John Quinn Imholte*

■ Terrorism and violence

Violence and threats of violence used to advance or call attention to social or political causes

Terrorists commit bombings, kidnappings, hijackings, murders, maimings, and other violent acts to communicate their message to major decision makers and the general public. Organizations that use terrorism hope to influence world opinion, those opposed to their goals, the social class or people for which they claim to fight, the national government opposed to them, rival political movements, and existing and potential group members and sympathizers.

Terrorists perpetrate atrocities to generate media coverage for their cause when other forms of persuasion have failed or fallen short of expectations. In effect, terrorists hijack the media to achieve their ends, which may include trying to overthrow the state or to alter national boundaries. They also resort to violence to demoralize their enemies, to provoke the state to adopt repressive countermeasures, to demonstrate their movement's strengths, to gain public sympathy for their cause, and to create fear and chaos.

For terrorists, television, newspapers, and the other news media are the conduits to their target audiences. Their acts are carefully choreographed to attract media attention, and they try to manipulate the media to tell their stories, publicize their grievances, and air their aspirations. The nature of the terrorist act—its atrocity, its location and the identity of its victims—can serve to enhance the power of the message. Terrorists often use the "confessions" of hostages and interviews with them to amplify their message, and they rely on the plight of the families and relatives of hostages and victims to move their audiences. Sometimes terrorists attempt to win favorable publicity by releasing hostages.

The idea behind violent acts is to prove that anyone can at any time become the victim of terrorism and that even the most powerful government is unable to prevent such attacks against its citizens. Terrorists use terror to combat the popularity of institutions and to circumvent superior military and economic strength. Through fear and violence they hope to compel a state to comply with their demands.

THE THEATERS OF TERROR Terrorists combine their ability to manipulate the media with the advantages of shock, surprise, and secrecy. They rely on the fact that terror is powerful theater and thus ideal material for news media. The terrorist kidnapping, for example, of Patricia Hearst, the teenage daughter of William Ran-

One of the "Black September" commandos who took eleven members of the Israeli Olympic team hostage in Munich's Olympic Village in 1972. (*AP/Wide World Photos*)

dolph HEARST, illustrates how terrorists proceed. In February, 1974, the twelve-member Symbionese Liberation Army (SLA) seized Hearst and threatened to kill her if the media did not publish their manifestos. The Hearst newspaper in San Francisco—the *San Francisco Examiner*—thereupon published the terrorists' press releases and manifestos. Other newspapers and magazines covered the story as well, and the SLA and Hearst were featured on the cover of *Newsweek* seven times.

Terrorist acts are often symbolic and must be explained by the terrorists to be generally understood. It is because a newsworthy tragedy allows them the op-portunity to issue statements telling their story that terrorists claim responsibility for atrocities. Publication of their documents allows then to publish their stories without the intervention of censorship or interpretation. Putting the right spin on the act is important because the victims are often not the actual target of the terrorist but simply a means to an end.

Terrorist groups may change how they use the media over time. Initially terrorists often commit violent acts to secure media coverage to gain recognition, draw attention to their demands, and build credibility. However, a continued use of violent acts limits the ability of a group to present its case. To move from armed struggle to rational debate over broader social and political issues requires a shift from violent acts to more reasoned rhetorics.

Bomb throwing, hijacking, hostage-taking, and other acts of violence can be an effective tool for terrorists. Media coverage of terrorism has, in some cases, made the public familiar with the causes of terrorists, which may include the wrongs committed against a people by a regime. News about terrorist actions can have an especially potent influence on the public agenda in the United States, especially if the government supports the regime under assault. The individuals responsible for the long hostage crisis in Tehran, IRAN, achieved one of their most important goals by exposing the information about the shah's oppressive regime and its ties to the U.S. government.

The cause of the Palestinians was dramatized worldwide with the deadly attack of the "Black September" group on the Israeli team at the 1972 Munich OLYMPIC GAMES, an event that marked the beginning of a long process toward the eventual recognition of Yasser ARAFAT and the PALESTINE LIBERATION ORGANIZATION (PLO) as legitimate political players by countries such as the United States. In this case terrorism was able to bring the movement to the point where other channels of communication became available.

Terrorists' media successes do not automatically assure that public opinion will be swayed their way or that public policy will be changed. The deadly nature of some terrorist acts can sow the seeds of the terrorist group's own destruction, and supporters and sympathizers may turn on the groups that kill and maim innocent victims.

Terrorists use violence to dramatize their grievances and goals. They resort to bullets and bombs when they fail to win, or lack the patience to try to win, attention in other ways. To them, as to the rest of the world, terrorism speaks louder than words.

SUGGESTED READINGS:

Alexander, Yonah, and Robert G. Picard, eds. *In the Camera's Eye—News Coverage of Terrorist Events.* Washington, D.C.: Pergamon-Brassey's, 1991.

Nacos, Bridgette L. *Terrorism and the Media: From the Iran Hostage Crisis to the World Trade Center Bombing.* New York: Columbia University Press, 1994.

Paletz, David L., and Alex P. Schmid. *Terrorism and the Media.* Newbury Park, Calif.: Sage Publications, 1992.

Schmid, Alex P., and Janny de Graaf. *Violence as Communication—Insurgent Terrorism and the Western News Media.* Beverly Hills, Calif.: Sage Publications, 1982.

Weimann, Gabriel, and Conrad Winn. *The Theater of Terror—Mass Media and International Terrorism.* New York: Longman, 1994.

Wright, Joanne. *Terrorist Propaganda: The Red Army Faction and the Provisional IRA, 1968-1986.* New York: St. Martin's Press, 1990.

— *Fred Buchstein*

■ Theater and drama

Plays and improvised performance have been used throughout history as propaganda tools

Whether a work of theater is considered propaganda depends often on the perspective of the audience or critics. The drama critic Eric Bentley attempts to put this fact in perspective by noting that true propaganda implies "a direct effort at changing history, if, in some cases, only a little bit of history." If a religious work seeks to convert its audience, that is propaganda. On the other hand, conversion may be a by-product of a drama that was not written for the purpose of attaining converts; such a conversion would not automatically cause the work in question to be classified as propaganda. Although some theater groups make no secret of their propagandistic intent, drama categorized as "social" or "protest" drama is sometimes labeled propaganda since its aim, to some, is to convert the viewer to the playwright's or producer's politics.

PROPAGANDA IN AMERICAN HISTORY Early American history is replete with the use of drama as propaganda. Mercy Warren, the sister of James Otis, wrote bitter political satires as a means of harassing the British. Although her plays are deemed of little value artistically, they serve as examples of the use of the genre as propaganda. Often her words made little attempt to disguise her characters, who obviously represented the British leadership of the day. For example, *The Group* (1775), a farce poking fun at England ("Blunderland") featured such characters as Hateall, Spendall, and Humbug, all representative of easily recognizable British figures. Because the play was so narrowly focused, it can be understood only in light of the events of the time. Loyalist views, too, were projected in theater propaganda. H. H. Brackenridge's cleverly written plays belittled colonial efforts, often with little regard for the truth. Anticolonial plays included such works as *The Americans Roused in a Cure for the*

Spleen: Or, Amusement for a Winter's Evening (1774) by Roger de Coverly.

Propaganda drama continued after the American Revolution at a time when most of the artistic theater was imported from Europe. Nationalism was high and was reflected in a number of works, both serious and comedic. One example is David Everett's *Daranzel: Or, The Persian Patriot* (1800), in which the hero leads a fight for freedom that paralleled the Revolution. A number of plays during this era focused on domestic issues such as taxes, the Whiskey Rebellion, education, and the Constitution. They reflected history's perennial attack on politicians in such works as *The Politician Outwitted* (1788), by Samuel Low, which defended the Constitution, and John Murdock's *The Politicians: Or, A State of Things* (1798), a strongly nationalistic work.

The attacks on U.S. ships by Barbary pirates aroused patriotic playwrights such as David Everett. His *Slaves in Barbary* (1817) stirred up Americans' anger. Other playwrights whose work might be termed propaganda for their emphasis on social and political themes were John Murdock, Joseph Croswell, and Susanna H. Rowson.

Harriet Beecher Stowe's 1852 novel *Uncle Tom's Cabin*, which is said to have strongly influenced the antislavery movement, was brought to the stage many times in the 1800's. It was presented at the National Theatre in 1852, and the popularity of the novel brought out large audiences. The *New York Herald* of September 3, 1852, decried its performance, calling it "a crude and aggravated affair." The review continued, "It is a sad blunder; for when our stage shall become the deliberate agent in the cause of abolitionism, with the sanction of the public, and their approbation, the peace and harmony of this Union will soon be ended." Stowe never gave permission for its use on the stage, but that did not stop producers. As time went on, the staged versions became more and more burlesque, failing to impart Stowe's original message.

In the late nineteenth and early twentieth centuries, as American society matured and became more complex, American drama turned to social issues, some of which works might be termed propaganda. Charles H. Hoyt and James Herne took opposite views toward a popular issue, temperance (*see* PROHIBITION ERA), with Hoyt's play *A Temperance Town* (1893) holding that legally enforced prohibition was not good, although temperance was. In the last few years of the eighteenth century dramas protesting labor and economic conditions began to appear. Hamlin Garland's *Under the Wheel* (1880) portrayed realistically the labor conditions of the time. Several plays dealt with strikes: *The Strike* (1887), *The Workingman's Strike* (1881) and Henry C. DeMille's play *The Lost Paradise* (1891), adapted by DeMille from the Ludwig Fulda play *Das verlorene Paradies*. In 1911 Charles Kenyon produced *Kindling*, which stressed the hardships suffered in a strike.

Between the world wars, although acknowledged propaganda still existed, the move in the United States was toward the theater's taking on serious social themes with the emphasis primarily on theater as art. However, the content of much of the drama dictated its use as a vehicle for persuasion and protest—thus it was often viewed as propaganda.

MARXIST INFLUENCES The Marxist Revolution in RUSSIA in 1917 and 1918 (*see* RUSSIA: 1918-1953) spurred theater groups and playwrights throughout the world to espouse the communist cause in their productions. The Russians themselves tried to control theater and drama for propaganda purposes. In the 1920's the genre and doctrine of SOCIALIST REALISM became the bedrock of Soviet drama, art, and literature. It attempted to approach even traditional plays from a social perspective, relating them to the problems of the day. In this way the Communist Party sought to "educate" the masses.

In the 1930's leftist and radical theater groups formed a large part of the U.S. theater community. To these groups the Great Depression signaled the end of capitalism, with communism presenting a logical alternative. Much of the artistically strong drama of that era focused on socialist themes and methods: violent action, conflict, labor and capital, strikes, evictions, and unemployment. The COMMUNIST PARTY in the U.S. established its own theaters in the 1930's and attempted to use other groups such as the Theater Guild and Group Theater for its propaganda. The Worker's Laboratory Theatre (1932-1940), a communist workers' group, tried to destroy what it termed "bourgeois" theater, charging that both its content and its focus on making money limited its social effect.

A noncommunist group, the Labor Stage, was sponsored by the International Ladies' Garment Workers' Union. It attacked many of the country's social ills, using a balance of humor and propaganda. For example, it produced *Pins and Needles* (1937), a revue in which Charles Foster's late nineteenth century heroine (from *Bertha, the Sewing Machine Girl*) is saved by a union man.

The AGITPROP performance (the term is a condensation of agitation and propaganda) was another means of teaching Marxism directly. It advantage was a simplicity of venue, props, and script. It could be performed anywhere. One example is John Bonn's *15 Minute Red Review* (1932), which promoted the Soviet Union and exorted its audience to "fight for the Soviet Union." Many of these works were primitive and lacked artistry.

The Living Newspaper drama, in some ways similar to agitprop, was a contribution of the NEW DEAL's Federal Theater. It used a number of techniques to present facts and progressive views to its audiences, and because it was Federal Theater, its audiences included many working people. For example, in *Triple A Plowed Under* (1936), it used twenty-six scenes to show the progression of the farm depression from World War I to the demise of the Agriculture Adjustment Administration (AAA) when the Supreme Court declared it unconstitutional. Such theater was even applauded by the communists on occasion.

PROTEST AND PROBLEMS A number of lesser playwrights wrote protest plays during the 1920's and 1930's, often supporting Marxist ideology. Among these was the full-length propaganda play *Stevedore* (1934) by George Sklar and Paul Peters, which dealt with racial prejudice and economics. The case of the "Scottsboro boys" was treated in John Wexley's *We Shall Not Die* (1934). *Black Pit* (1935) by Albert Maltz treated the problems of miners, and Irwin Shaw's *Bury the Dead* (1936) was a satire attacking war.

Eric Bentley views propaganda's primary aim as preaching to the unconverted, but he acknowledges that in some cases propaganda reaches out to those already convinced. In the case of Marxism, many authors of the 1930's, while they did not openly profess communism, imparted Marxist philosophy in their works. The party line in many cases seemed to be that because truth exists in progressive philosophy, any good person and right-thinking person would have to accept it.

During this time a number of legitimately artistic playwrights, whether avowedly communist or not, wrote serious plays espousing communist ideals. The noted German dramatist Bertolt BRECHT was one. Many of his plays were based on questionable "facts." Underlying much of his work was the assumption that since these are the "facts," what follows in the drama is a foregone conclusion—a frequent assumption of dramatic propaganda. American dramatist Clifford Odets was also an avowed Marxist, and much of his work reflected his political orientation. He joined the Communist Party in 1934 but left it the following year, claiming that he was "a liberal, not a Communist." His work transcends most propaganda in its dramatic value; in fact, his work during his Marxist period is considered better than of his later period, when he went to Hollywood seeking fame and fortune.

Most notable of Odets' work that is considered agitprop is *Waiting for Lefty* (1935), which was awarded a prize by *New Masses* and *New Theatre* magazines, both leftist publications. Odets' aim was to present problems with which his audience might identify in the hope that they would then support the proposed action of the drama. In *Waiting for Lefty* he uses a minstrel-show technique and a union meeting where a group of taxi drivers wait for Lefty, their leader, before discussing a strike. The play includes five scenes: The first shows the extreme poverty of a taxi driver's family, the second shows a laboratory assistant asked to spy on his supervisors, the third shows a taxi driver prevented by poverty from getting married, the fourth shows a spy at the union meeting, and the fifth shows prejudice against a Jewish physician. When news of Lefty's death is brought to the meeting, the workers make their decision: Strike!

Other playwrights of the era rejected blatant Marxism but, because their works attempted to arouse social concern or provoke protest, they are often considered writers of propaganda. One such was Elmer Rice. Rice was concerned about the increased dehumanization and victimization of humanity in an industrial and increasingly technological era. In *The Adding Machine* (1923) his characters' names are numbers. When Mr. Zero is fired, he kills his boss, then is tried, found guilty, and executed. Heaven does not provide a better existence for Zero, for there he operates a huge adding machine and is sent back to earth. Rice uses such expressionistic techniques as carousel music that grows louder and louder and a revolving stage that moves faster and faster.

CONTEMPORARY THEATER Although a number of lesser dramatic works presented during the VIETNAM WAR might be classified as propaganda, the most notable example of propaganda theater in the 1960's was related to the rise of the United Farm Workers (UFW) unionization movement led by César Chávez. The movement gave a voice to a long-silent and impotent minority, migrant farm workers living in squalid and inhumane conditions. They worked in life-threatening situations and earned a pittance for their labor. At the time of the UFW's agitation, Luis Valdez began his TEATRO CAMPESINO. Chávez allowed Valdez to present his original dramas to farm workers as a means of strengthening the union. In contrast with writers such as John STEINBECK, who wrote about migrant workers from an outside perspective, Valdez had actually been part of an itinerant farm family. Uncomfortable in middle-class city life, he returned to his roots in the Salinas Valley. Valdez sought to develop drama both reflective of and appealing to the farm workers themselves.

The base of the Teatro performance was the *acto*, Valdez' own creation. Performed outdoors, an *acto* included song and dance and used masks. It required few props. Valdez credits such influences as ancient Greek Old Comedy, *commedia dell'arte*, Bertolt Brecht's plays, Japanese ritual theater, and the religious drama of the pre-Hispanic peoples of Latin America. His *actos* detail the lives and hardships of farm workers. The characters—farm worker and owner—are more symbolic than realistic. Valdez's concerns were solely with the campesinos (farm workers) and the *huelga* (strike). The *actos*' narrow target audience and their association with Chávez's desire to strengthen the union through the Teatro clearly validate the classification of this theater as propaganda.

The effectiveness of theater as propaganda has been the subject of some debate. Many would argue that the theater is primarily entertainment and that any "conversion" that occurs as the result of viewing a performance is simply a byproduct. With the exceptions of those works specifically aimed at an audience of workers or "common people," theater is considered the realm of the affluent and the educated, and it often reaffirms the beliefs they already hold. Social drama (as opposed to straight propaganda), being the stuff of human existence, will certainly persist. It should be noted, however, that since the advent of nuclear weapons, much social and protest drama tends to create a mood of pessimism or despair rather than attempting to be effective in presenting a particular view or action and attempting to persuade an audience as to its correctness.

SUGGESTED READINGS:

Bentley, Eric. *The Theatre of Commitment and Other Essays on Drama in Our Society*. New York: Atheneum Press, 1967. Critical discussion of contemporary theater.

————, ed. *The Theory of the Modern Stage: An Introduction to Modern Theatre and Drama*. Baltimore, Md.: Penguin Books, 1968. An introduction to modern theater.

Field, Bradford S., Miriam Gilbert, and Carl H. Klaus, eds. *Stages of Drama: Classical to Contemporary Theater*. New York: St. Martin's Press, 1995. A one-volume collection of forty-one plays, from the Classical Greek period to the present.

Hatch, James V. *Black Theater USA: Forty-five Plays by Black Americans, 1847-1974*. New York: Free Press, 1974. Collection of plays by African Americans.

Krutch, Joseph Wood. *"Modernism" in Modern Drama*. Ithaca, N.Y.: Cornell University Press, 1953. A discussion of the term "modernism" in the work of European dramatists and some American playwrights.

Meserve, Walter J. *An Outline History of American Drama*. Totawa, N.J.: Littlefield, Adams, 1965. Traces the history of American theater to 1965.

Moses, Montrose J., and John Mason Brown, eds. *The American Theatre as Seen by Its Critics, 1752-1932*. New York: Cooper Square, 1967. A compilation of theater reviews.

— *Patricia J. Huhn*

■ Third-party movements

American political parties outside of the two-party system

In the United States third-party movements have periodically coalesced to challenge the traditional two-party system, despite significant obstacles that block their formation. The existing two parties are well organized and well funded, and laws concerning electoral procedures tend to favor the existing parties. Most important, voters tend to support the two-party system. As a result, no third party has captured the presidency. Yet third parties have influenced elections and have forced the two major parties to incorporate some of the goals of third parties into their agendas. The influence of such third parties is in part a result of their use of propaganda techniques to disseminate information and sway voters.

POPULISTS AND PROGRESSIVES Third parties typically form around an issue that the major parties have neglected or are ignoring, and they usually depend upon ambitious and CHARISMATIC LEADERSHIP. The first important third party of the modern era, the Populist Party, which was organized in 1892, called for agrarian reform. Populist speakers such as Mary Elizabeth Lease portrayed their party as that of the poor and working classes, which they contrasted with the industrial might of the Northeast, and they advocated economic reforms that promised to increase the income of farmers and workers. In the 1892 election the Populist Party's presidential candidate, James B. Weaver, received more than one million votes and Populists gained seats in many state legislatures. However, by 1896 the DEMOCRATIC PARTY adopted many of the Populists' reforms, and thereafter the party rapidly declined.

When Theodore Roosevelt, after having served for nearly eight years as president, was unable to capture the 1912 Republican nomination for a third term, he formed the Progressive Party. Popularly known as the Bull Moose Party because Roosevelt declared he felt as "fit as a bull moose," the Progressive Party called for social reform. The photogenic Roosevelt, who was enormously popular with the American public, served as the party's symbol. However, his candidacy split the REPUBLICAN PARTY and sent a Democrat to the White House, and the party collapsed soon thereafter.

American politics witnessed a small number of third parties in the following decades, including the LaFollette Progressives of 1924. Committed to reform efforts, this party failed after the death of its leader, Robert LaFollette, in 1925, but in the 1928 presidential elections the Democratic Party made appeals to LaFollette's constituency by including some of his reforms in its programs. The 1948 States' Rights Party was a splinter group of the Democratic Party because it opposed the party's civil rights plank. However, it was not until 1968 that a third party movement again captured the attention of the nation.

WALLACE AND PEROT The central figure of the American Independent Party (AIP) was George WALLACE, at several times governor of Alabama. Wallace received national attention in 1963 when he stood in a doorway at the University of Alabama to prevent two black students from entering the school. Wallace made a presidential bid in 1964, but it was a small and amateurish attempt that relied on speeches and country-and-western bands. In the ensuing four years Wallace developed his campaign style partly through greater use of effective propaganda. He formed the AIP in 1967, which, like Roosevelt's Bull Moose Party, was primarily a vehicle for the presidential aspirations of one man. However, its existence enabled voters to believe that the Wallace movement was much larger and better organized that it actually was. Wallace, a talented speaker, employed advance staff to drum up support for his public appearances and he seized on controversial issues that were certain to appear on evening news broadcasts. When he discovered that his audiences enjoyed his acerbic responses to hecklers, Wallace made interaction with opponents an important part of his public appearances. These performances gave the appearance that Wallace was a brave man who would stand up to anyone, an impression that appealed to voters who believed that politicians no longer listened to the common man. Playing on fears that the United States might suffer defeat in the VIETNAM WAR, he took a hawkish stance toward the war. He also took advantage of the backlash against the CIVIL RIGHTS MOVEMENT of the 1960's. Wallace did not win the presidency, but he forced the major party candidates to respond to his positions on these issues.

Although Wallace's campaign revitalized interest in third parties, it was not until 1992 that another significant third-party movement appeared with the wealthy Texas businessman H. Ross Perot, who received 19 percent of the popular vote in the presidential election that year. Perot capitalized on an economic issue, deficit reduction, that the major parties had been avoiding. He purchased long segments of television time to present his message to the American people, and he used simple charts and graphs to make his argument. After the 1992 election the major parties made deficit reduction a part of their programs. It was primarily because of improved economic conditions that Perot's 1996 presidential bid was not as successful as the earlier one.

Third-party propaganda strategies have focused on voter concerns for reform in particular policy areas, and they have usually relied on a strong figure to represent their party and its programs. Techniques have tended to resemble those of the major parties, including campaign tours, rallies, and more recently, the use of television news and advertising. Because major parties have typically incorporated third-party issues into their own POLITICAL PLATFORMS, third-party movements rarely meet with long-term success. However, they have influenced the topics and terms of political debate in the United States.

SUGGESTED READINGS:

Canfield, James Lewis. *A Case of Third Party Activism: The George Wallace Campaign Worker and the American Independent Party.* Lanham, Md.: University Press of America, 1984.

Kruschke, Earl R. *Encyclopedia of Third Parties in the United States.* Santa Barbara, Calif.: ABC-Clio, 1991.

Mazmanian, Daniel A. *Third Parties in Presidential Elections.* Washington D.C.: The Brookings Institution, 1974.

Rosenstone. Steven J., Roy L. Behr, and Edward H. Lazarus. *Third Parties in America: Citizen Response to Major Party Failure.* 2d ed. Princeton, N.J.: Princeton University Press, 1996.

— *Thomas Clarkin*

■ Tiananmen Square demonstrations

1989: Chinese protest movement that culminated in a massive demonstration in Beijing's Tiananmen Square, where it was brutally crushed

The protest movement and Tiananmen Square demonstrations of 1989 paradoxically grew out of dislocations caused by the Communist government's reform efforts that began in the late 1970's. Until then CHINA had suffered under a command economy which the ruling Communist Party had directed since coming to power in 1949. The death of the revolutionary leader MAO ZEDONG in 1976 and the ascendancy of Deng Xiaoping shortly thereafter ushered in a modernization movement that allowed for decentralization and privitization of much of the economy and greater freedom for individuals.

People could move about fairly freely within China, could go overseas, and could gain access to foreign cultural concepts. They could also lose jobs, experience the effects of inflation, and complain about corruption in government. Periodically the government would crack down on dissenters—as occurred with the dismantling of Democracy Wall in 1979—or inveigh against evil foreign influences, as in the campaign against "bourgeois liberalism" in the early 1980's. The balancing of the freedom necessary for modernization with the possibility that such freedom might destroy the party's monopoly of power became a continual tightrope walk for the government, a walk that had become perilous by 1989. As the demands for freedom, and for the release of political prisoner and Democracy Wall hero Wei Jingsheng, mounted, the death in April of former party general secretary Hu Yaobang, who had been dismissed for being too soft on democracy demonstrators in 1986 and 1987, sparked the Tiananmen Square demonstrations.

Students and others gathered in the square in part to honor Hu but chiefly to air grievances against the government. At the height of the protest, demonstrators in the square numbered more than a million, and hunger strikers numbered in the thousands. The protest culminated with the appearance on May 30 of the effigy of the Goddess of Democracy, dedicated to the hunger strikers. These direct challenges to the legitimacy of the government resulted in the decision to remove the protestors from the square by military force on June 4.

Those with significant political or ideological stakes in the events surrounding the Tiananmen Square protest sought to put their "spins" on it. Interested parties could not remain silent because the popular demonstrations and brutal reaction were too widely publicized to be ignored. Within China the government branded the protest movement a counterrevolutionary rebellion fomented by the dregs of society linked to foreign elements in Hong Kong, TAIWAN, and the West: The heroic People's Liberation Army overcame these murderous thugs to restore order. The demonstrators' viewpoints varied; some called for a reform of the Communist Party and government, and some called for their ouster. All clearly proclaimed dissatisfaction with the existing state of affairs.

The people and governments of both Hong Kong and Taiwan manifestly sided with the demonstrators, and they provided them with money and equipment as the protests proceeded. In the West, academic discussion soon turned to the deeper causes of the events at Tiananmen Square. Nevertheless, Western scholars have exchanged heated words over documentaries that interpret the protest, principally Ted Koppel's *Tragedy at Tiananmen* (1989), Carma Hinton's *The Gate of Heavenly Peace* (1996), and Michael Apted's *Moving the Mountain* (1994). The Hinton project especially has stirred controversy, as many claim that it deals much too gently with the government's role and much too harshly with the student leaders, especially Chai Ling. Western governments initially roundly denounced Beijing's savage suppression, and the United States gave dissident physicist Fang Lizhi asylum in its embassy there, but the criticisms have faded with time. As a turning point in modern China, the Tiananmen Square demonstrations will continue to provoke passionate commentary.

— *Thomas D. Reins*

■ **Tito, Josip Broz**

May 7, 1892, in Kumrovec, Croatia—May 4, 1980, in Ljubljana, Yugoslavia: Leader of communist Yugoslavia

During his career as a communist careerist and agitator, military commander of the partisan guerilla resistance forces during World War II, and head of state of YUGOSLAVIA from 1945 to his death in 1980, Josip Broz Tito employed propaganda techniques to solidify his position, outmaneuver military and political opponents, resolve economic problems, and establish Yugoslavia as a country bridging the Soviet bloc and the democracies of Western Europe and the United States.

Born to a Croatian peasant family in Austria-Hungary, Josip Broz (who later added the Tito) began his career as an itinerant manual laborer before being recruited into the Austro-Hungarian army. Sent to the Eastern front in World War I, he was wounded in 1915 and taken prisoner to Russia. After the Russian Revolution, Tito joined the Red Guards and the Communist Party.

When he returned to Yugoslavia with his Russian wife, he undertook political activity for the international communist movement. By then Croatia was part of the Kingdom of the Serbs, Croats, and Slovenes, known after 1929 as Yugoslavia.

Tito's political activity, which entailed organizing trade union workers for the Communist International, resulted in his arrest and a prison sentence in 1928. In 1935 Tito was sent to Moscow, where he met Joseph STALIN. By then fascism was on the rise, and Stalin had adopted the peaceful guise of the popular front as a propaganda measure.

Armed with Stalin's new propaganda line of class war and the Soviet Union's championship of small countries against the imperialist West, Tito returned to Yugoslavia in early 1939 to reorganize the Communist Party. As Stalin's protégé, Tito was apprised of Stalin's secret alliance with Adolf HITLER. However, Germany's attack on and occupation of Yugoslavia in April, 1941, followed by the attack on the Soviet Union two months later, caused Tito to reassess how he might use the chaos of war to further his own personal and political goals.

World War II led to civil war in Yugoslavia, as Germany exploited national rivalries to set up a puppet fascist state in Croatia and used latent antagonisms to fracture the country along ethnic lines. Tito took advantage of this situation to seize power as commander of the partisan forces, uniting under the banner of communism the disaffected members of various hostile groups. He also used his very real abilities as a military strategist and a program of DISINFORMATION and slander to convince the Allied forces to support his resistance effort instead of that of his rivals.

After the war Tito's most important propaganda campaigns were directed at Stalin, whom he successfully defied in order to pursue a separate path to communism for Yugoslavia. When the Soviet Union expelled Yugoslavia from the Cominform (see COMINTERM) in 1948, Tito turned to the West for economic assistance and trade, outmaneuvering his former mentor by forming strategic alliances. In his relations with the West Tito is remembered, thanks to his skill at public relations and propaganda, as an advocate of workers' self-management, the diplomacy of nonaligned countries, and as the man who single-handedly changed the image of a monolithic communist movement.

— *Gloria Fulton*

■ Tobacco industry

Producers of such tobacco products as cigarettes rely heavily on both advertisement and propaganda

Six major tobacco companies dominate the U.S. tobacco industry. Each of these companies uses advertisement and propaganda to try to capture a larger market share than that of its competitors. Together they work to improve the public image of the industry and to counter the increasing evidence that tobacco consumption causes significant health risks.

ADVERTISING AND PROMOTION ADVERTISING is the primary method used to increase consumption of tobacco products such as cigarettes. Advertising and other promotional expenditures reached an estimated five billion dollars annually in 1996. Because tests have revealed that smokers can detect little difference between brands, tobacco companies rely on advertising to persuade smokers that their product is preferable to other available brands. Before 1971 cigarette advertisements included television and radio commercials, but the 1970 Public Health Cigarette Smoking Act banned all broadcast advertising of tobacco products. Since 1970 the tobacco industry has turned to other formats to present their products to the public. Cigarette companies make extensive use of magazines, newspapers, and billboards for advertising purposes. The sponsorship of sporting events and music festivals is another effective promotional technique. A cigarette company will sponsor a racing car team, for example, which emblazons both its car and its outfits with the name of the company's product. This practice allows the brand name to be identified with an exciting and popular activity; the brand name also appears on television broadcasts of car races and in interviews with winning drivers. Another promotion offered by a cigarette manufacturer allows its consumers to redeem points earned from cigarette packages for outdoors goods such as backpacks, thus identifying smoking with robust and healthy activities.

Cigarette manufacturers use images that associate smoking with adventure and excitement, or with glamour and sophistication to encourage smokers to use their product. Perhaps the most successful commercial image was that of the Marlboro Man, which the Philip Morris Company introduced in 1954. The Marlboro Man was a rugged cowboy, usually shown engaging in masculine activities such as roping or herding cattle. Marlboro eventually became the best-selling cigarette brand in the nation. Another well-known advertising campaign featured Joe Camel, who was depicted in fashionable suits enjoying such activities as playing pool. Tobacco companies also develop packaging and run ads targeted at specific markets. Several brands have been designed to appeal to women; other advertising campaigns have been aimed at African American and Latino smokers. Critics who charge that some advertising targets young people point to the Joe Camel ads as evidence that the tobacco industry hopes to introduce adolescents to the lifelong habit of smoking. Magazines with a large number of young readers often contain a significant number of cigarette advertisements.

RESPONDING TO HEALTH CONCERNS Since the 1950's the tobacco industry has been forced to respond to mounting evidence that smoking poses a significant health hazard. The industry has responded in two ways. It has engaged in efforts to disprove the reports that smoking is dangerous, and it has undertaken projects to improve the industry's standing in the eyes of the public. To coordinate its efforts, the tobacco industry formed the Tobacco Institute in 1958.

Since 1964 the U.S. SURGEON GENERAL has released several reports that link smoking to illnesses and diseases, among them cancer. Studies by other medical organizations have reached the same conclusions. These findings pose a threat to the tobacco companies, for not only might customers drop off but the industry might be found liable for individual cases of lung cancer or respiratory illnesses. The Tobacco Institute has challenged the findings of each surgeon general's report, claiming that either the study or the conclusions reached are flawed. To influence the public the Tobacco Institute has distributed booklets and conducted advertising campaigns that give the industry's detailed response. The industry also sponsored the Council for Tobacco Research, an organization that conducted an independent study and found no link between smoking and cancer.

When growing health concerns led to antismoking ordinances in several communities and states, the tobacco industry condemned the initiatives as attacks on the rights of smokers. The health issue also generated calls for a total ban on tobacco advertising. One tobacco company responded with an essay contest. Writers were asked to use the First Amendment to defend the tobacco industry's right to advertise. Though opponents countered that there are limitations on commercial speech such as advertising, the industry's position adroitly joined the issue of cigarette advertising with the cherished American right to free speech. The propaganda efforts of the tobacco industry in regard to health issues have been aimed at raising doubts about the accuracy of studies that are critical of smoking and at raising concerns that antismoking initiatives constitute attacks on civil liberties.

The controversy over health issues has tarnished the reputation of the tobacco industry. To improve its public image the industry engages in a variety of public activities, including sponsorship of the arts through grants to dance companies and underwriting museum exhibits. Tobacco companies also donate money to popular charities and nonprofit organizations. One tobacco company gave money to the New York Public Library for a book-cleaning project. An industry organization called the Tobacco Heritage Committee donated $1.2 million to the construction of a Treaty Room at the Department of State. Decorations included carvings of tobacco leaves and blossoms. These responsible, civic-minded activities present an alternative image to that of the tobacco industry as being reckless and irresponsible in its pursuit of profits.

SUGGESTED READINGS:

Carey, John, Gail DeGeorge, and Lori Bongiorno. "Not So Fast." *Business Week* (July 7, 1997): 34.

Kluger, Richard. *Ashes to Ashes: America's Hundred-Year Cigarette War, the Public Health, and the Unabashed Triumph of Philip Morris.* New York: Alfred A. Knopf, 1996.

Myers, William. *The Image Makers: Power and Persuasion on Madison Avenue.* New York: Times Books, 1984.

Whiteside, Thomas. *Selling Death: Cigarette Advertising and Public Health.* New York: Liveright, 1971.

— *Thomas Clarkin*

■ Tokyo Rose and Axis Sally

Tokyo Rose and Axis Sally have become the defining figures of subversive propaganda warfare as practiced by the Japanese and Germans during World War II

Subversive warfare, better known in the United States as psychological warfare, has its roots in ancient Chinese principles of war. The Chinese philosopher Sun Tzu in the fourth century B.C.E. (*See* ART OF WAR, THE) preached that the supreme act of generalship might be defined in terms of absence of battle. To control the enemy with no loss of blood attests to the art of the commander. The zenith of this philosophy may be seen in the war of propaganda waged between 1939 and 1945.

The war of propaganda was initiated by Great Britain when, at the beginning of World War II, the British army began dropping leaflets expounding the validity of the Allied position. By natural progression this war by rhetoric expanded into the realm of radio broadcasting. Propaganda broadcasts, which were controlled by government, sought to undermine the morale of the enemy and encourage soldiers of the warring nations to surrender in the face of insurmountable obstacles or to simply lay down their arms and return home. Legendary among such broadcast programs were those of Tokyo Rose and Axis Sally.

"Tokyo Rose" was the name given to thirteen female announcers who worked

for Radio Tokyo. These women came from various parts of the globe—several were Filipino, and there was an American and a Japanese American—and all aimed their demoralizing rhetoric specifically at U.S. servicemen stationed in the Pacific. The Japanese broadcasts played American music and interspersed the selections with seductive banter. It was the servicemen themselves who coined the nickname "Tokyo Rose" in response to the broadcasts.

The most celebrated Tokyo Rose was Iva Toguri D'Aquino, born in California to Japanese American parents in 1916. She was a graduate of the University of California who had been traveling in Japan when the war broke out. Stranded in Japan, she gained secretarial employment in the overseas bureau of the Japanese Broadcasting Corporation. She was recruited from this job to participate in broadcasting the "Zero Hour," a program of music, chat, and subversive rhetoric. Born, bred, and educated in the United States, she had firsthand knowledge of the cultural and philosophical mores of the society that had nurtured the American servicemen.

After the war D'Aquino was arrested by the American military authorities and imprisoned during a thorough investigation, following which she was released in 1946. Because American public opinion was intensely critical of her release, the U.S. Department of Justice, bowing to political and public pressure, prosecuted her for treason in 1948. This second prosecution resulted in her conviction on charges of treason, for which she was imprisoned from 1949 to 1956. Throughout this period D'Aquino maintained her innocence, claiming that she had been coerced into making the infamous broadcasts. It was not

Mrs. Iva Toguri D'Aquino speaking with reporters in January, 1956, after being released from a federal reformatory, where she had been imprisoned for making treasonous broadcasts as "Tokyo Rose" during World War II. (*AP/Wide World Photos*)

until 1976 when former prosecution witnesses admitted that they had perjured themselves during the earlier trial that this transgression of justice was corrected. In January, 1977, President Gerald Ford issued a formal pardon for D'Aquino and fully restored her U.S. citizenship.

Unlike Tokyo Rose, Axis Sally was a single person, the American Mildred Gillars (1900-1988). Gillars was a college dropout from Ohio Wesleyan College, where she became known for her independence and failure to adhere to the school's rules and regulations. After leaving Wesleyan, Gillars traveled to Germany in the 1920's as a music student. There she was recruited to

do much the same work as Tokyo Rose did in Japan. She is remembered for greeting American troops with such simplistic rhetoric as, "Go home and forget the war!" As in the case of Tokyo Rose, it was the Americans who called her "Axis Sally." After the war Gillars was arrested, convicted of treason, and sentenced to twelve years in a federal penitentiary for women, from which she was paroled in 1961. She then became a teacher in a Roman Catholic convent school in Ohio. In her maturity Gillars returned to Ohio Wesleyan University, where she completed her B.A. in speech in 1973 at the age of seventy-two.

Tokyo Rose and Axis Sally exemplified the benefit of drawing on familiarity when creating a rhetoric of propaganda. Intimate knowledge of the society being targeted for propaganda is of paramount importance. The theories of "war by propaganda" as initially envisioned by the philosopher Sun Tzu were advanced with this basic precept.

— *Murray Henner*

■ Totalitarianism

In the system of government known as totalitarianism the state exercises almost total control over social, political, and economic activity. This system emphasizes the duty of the citizens to the state, represents the state as being an entity separate from and superior to its components, and maintains the state by a combination of propaganda and police terrorism. The organization of the system usually represents an effort to amalgamate political, economic, and social structure into a rigid hierarchy. An official party (Nazi, Fascist, or Communist) is the directing and unifying force in the country, headed by a leader who, often through CHARISMATIC LEADERSHIP, has achieved virtual cult status as the symbol of the ideological basis of the party. Adolf HITLER, Benito MUSSOLINI, and Joseph STALIN are historic examples of totalitarian leaders.

■ Treason

Criminal betrayal of one's country to an enemy

One of the most effective forms of propaganda is the LABELING of people or ideas as treasonous. Because treason, the betrayal of the loyalty owed to a country, evokes strong emotional reactions, charges of treason can be effective in manipulating public opinion.

Accusations of treason became part of American political propaganda early in the nation's history. Members of President John Adams' Federalist Party accused their rivals in Thomas Jefferson's Democratic-Republican Party of sympathizing with revolutionary France. Some Federalists claimed that Jefferson's followers were trying to worm their way into office in order to overthrow the government. In 1798 the Federalists passed the Alien and Sedition Act, which enabled them to arrest and suppress critics of the Adams administration. This proved to be ineffective propaganda, however, since the law's unpopularity helped Jefferson win the presidency in 1800.

In France in 1894 the charge of treason became part of anti-Semitic propaganda surrounding the charge that a Jewish French army captain, Alfred Dreyfus, had sold military secrets to the Germans. When Dreyfus was found guilty of treason (on the basis of questionable evidence), anti-Semitic French newspapers used the conviction to accuse all French Jews of disloyalty to the nation; these writers claimed that the Jews were part of an international group whose loyalties lay not with France but with JUDAISM.

Many prominent French intellectuals, among them Émile Zola and Anatole France, defended Dreyfus, and pro-Dreyfus literature became part of French leftist propaganda. In 1906 Dreyfus was cleared of all charges, but his case remained a divisive issue in French political life. When the Nazis came to power in GERMANY, they took up a similar strategy of SCAPEGOATING the Jews as internationalist traitors to the nation.

Joseph STALIN's show trials in RUSSIA during the early Soviet era may serve as an example of how an individual can use the propaganda of treason to pursue personal power. In 1934 Stalin, then general secretary of the Communist Party, began charging his political rivals with treason. In 1936 two leading communists, Grigory Zinoviev and Lev Kamenev, were accused of treason and of having murdered one of Stalin's rivals who was probably actually killed on Stalin's orders. Zinoviev and Kamenev were shot after a highly publicized trial. In June, 1937, Mikhail Tukhachevsky, Russia's foremost military man, was court-martialed for treason and executed. Other generals and politicians had a similar fate, leaving Stalin as the sole ruler of the nation.

In the United States treason became a favorite propaganda subject for anticommunists. In February, 1950, Republican Senator Joseph McCARTHY of Wisconsin rose to prominence by claiming that 205 communists had infiltrated the U.S. State Department. J. Edgar HOOVER, director of the FEDERAL BUREAU OF INVESTIGATION (FBI), claimed that communist traitors had infiltrated nearly every sphere of American life and that the U.S. COMMUNIST PARTY posed a serious threat as a fifth column within the country. John Stormer, in his influential book, *None Dare Call It Treason* (1964), accused American liberals of betraying the country to the communist conspiracy.

— *Carl L. Bankston III*

■ Triumph of the Will

1935: Pro-Nazi documentary film made by Leni Riefenstahl

GERMANY during the Nazi era engaged in a great deal of highly effective propaganda designed to maintain and build the loyalty of German citizens and to intimidate foreign foes. Leni RIEFENSTAHL's film, *Triumpf des Willen*, or *Triumph of the Will*, is one such example. Commissioned and titled by Adolf HITLER, and overseen by the Nazi propaganda minister Joseph GOEBBELS, the film depicts the 1934 Nazi Party rally in Nuremberg. The film is, however, much more than the documentary of a party rally. Rather, it is an epic propagandistic vision designed to showcase the glories and triumphs of a united German people under the leadership of Hitler.

The prologue highlights the preceding twenty years of German history, including the outbreak of World War I, Germany's humiliation in 1919, and Hitler's ascent to power. The message is that with Hitler in charge, Germany has order, stability, unity, pride, and strength. The prologue ends with Hitler's airplane descending through the clouds to Nuremberg, where the führer is given a rapturous welcome. The effect of this scene is to show Hitler as a god-like savior coming to earth.

The major portion of the film shows speeches by Nazi Party officials, loyalists, and Hitler himself. This is the only major Nazi film about Hitler, and he is portrayed as he wished to be seen: as the savior of the German people.

Much of the film shows elaborate pomp and circumstance of parades of young Germans. The camera shows boots,

Leni Riefenstahl's *Triumph of the Will* celebrated Germany's Third Reich through images such as this Nuremberg rally scene that conveyed the overwhelming power of Adolf Hitler (marching at the center). (*Museum of Modern Art, Film Stills Archive*)

uniforms, happy faces, and mass adulation of Hitler. The cumulative effect of speeches, marches, parades, and night rallies is intended to convey the immense size, strength, unity, and unstoppable future of the Nazi movement and thus to solidify support among the committed, convert the unconverted, and frighten foes abroad.

— *Lisa Langenbach*

■ Trotsky, Leon

October 26, 1879, in Yanovka, Ukraine— August 20, 1940, in Mexico City, Mexico: Russian communist revolutionary

Born Lev Davidovich Bronstein, Trotsky was a member of a Russian farming family who experienced anti-Semitic hostility that became institutionalized under the oppressive regime of Czar Alexander II. Trotsky's association with Marxist revolutionaries began in the 1890's, and he became a supporter of the newly formed Social Democratic Party in 1899. When that party split into Menshevik and Bolshevik factions in 1903, Trotsky maintained ties with the Mensheviks, whose organizational and ideological views he propagated throughout Russia and elsewhere until 1917. In that year he joined the great Bolshevik leader V. I. LENIN in planning the successful October Revolution.

Trotsky's two major contributions to the revolution lay in his tireless advocacy of Marxist principles and his role in organizing the Red Army which, after a three-year civil war (1918-1921) prevailed over counterrevolutionary forces. After Lenin's death in January, 1924, Trotsky and Joseph STALIN began a struggle for power within the Communist Party. When Stalin emerged victorious in 1927 Trotsky sought refuge in Norway before settling in MEXICO. In 1940 he was murdered there by Ramon Mercader, a Stalinist agent.

In the early days of communist Russia, Trotsky's popularity rivaled that of Lenin. He influenced people with his writings and speeches, which were delivered in distant reaches of the country. In 1908 he became editor of the then-Menshevik newspaper *Pravda* (truth), and later he joined the editorial board of *Novy Mir* (New World), which was published in New York City. Trotsky used Marxist SLOGANS to inspire workers to rebel against capitalist exploitation. After his exile he wrote hundreds of political essays that were published in NEWSPAPERS throughout the world. Trotsky's rhetoric adhered closely to Karl Marx's insistence on a worldwide proletariate revolution. Trotsky

therefore strongly objected to Stalin's idea of "communism in one country" and to his totalitarian rule. Trotsky was clearly an effective propagandist for Marxist ideas with the people, but he was outmaneuvered by Stalin's manipulation of the Communist Party.

— *Ronald K. Huch*

■ Truth

Generally truth is considered to be that which is factual, real, and verifiable through the presentation of evidence. Related but variable applications include established principles in law or philosophy, fixed laws in science as in "the law of gravity," and belief systems that rest upon the truth of a particular doctrine as in religion and ideology. Propaganda usually claims that its content is truth, even if it does not necessarily respond to the test of the laws of factual evidence.

■ Turkey

Near Eastern Islamic nation with cultural roots in both Europe and Asia

As the core of the Ottoman Empire, Turkey participated in World War I, which saw the rise of an image of the army, especially the common soldier, or *Mehmedjik*, that was designed to bolster the morale of the military and civilian populations alike. Turkey's differences in religion and ethnicity from its German ally in the war meant that there was no concerted coordination of wartime propaganda between the two nations.

Turkey's attempt to proclaim itself an Islamic power was undermined by the Turks' non-Arab ethnicity. A more sustained pan-Turanian policy designed to unite the Turks in Asia Minor and those in Central Asia helped occasion the AR-MENIAN GENOCIDE. The Ottoman Empire's dissolution led to a nationalist movement led by Mustafa Kemal Ataturk, a general popular among the rank-and-file soldiers. After he consolidated power in 1923, Ataturk systematically overhauled internal perceptions of what sort of nation Turkey was. Previously, Turks had drawn all their national identity from the reigning Osmanli family, which ruled a multinational array of peoples; now they were Turks, and Turks only.

Ataturk claimed that the popular will of the Turkish people had reasserted itself in his person, although he ruled not as a democrat but as a dictator (albeit a mild one). Ataturk abolished Islamic law in Turkey and replaced it with the Swiss Civil Code; he also discouraged traditional dress and advocated the adoption of Western-style manners, mores, and even surnames. Turkey was to be a self-contained, homogeneous nation, part of the West, not of Asia. These attitudes have been reflected in media outlets such as the newspaper *Cumhriyet.* Serious criticism of Ataturk or his policies is still illegal in Turkey, and Ataturk is seen as a semisacred symbol of the Turkish nation itself.

Turkey's indecision in World War II placed it among the ranks of the neutral countries. Turkey, however, did assume a pro-Western posture after the war that helped it attract considerable foreign aid from the United States and its allies during the Cold War. Turkish propaganda abroad faced tough opposition from Armenians, who deeply resented the Turkish effort to suppress discussion of the Armenian genocide. Vigorous debates were waged between Armenian advocates and Turkish government officials, largely in the pages of U.S. newspapers. Greek Americans also denounced the Turkish support of ethnic Turks on Cyprus, especially after Turkey invaded Cyprus in 1974. Turkey also drew criticism for its suppression of Kurdish rebels in southeastern Turkey. The Kurds, according to Turkey, were not a nation; they were merely "mountain Turks." These attitudes were reflected in the Turkish media, which tended to be self-censoring under government pressure.

Although Turkey has been largely democratic after Ataturk's death, the military has occasionally intervened whenever it decides that the state ideology is under threat. These blots on the face of the successful modernization and secularization of Turkey have been largely overlooked by Westerners grateful for Turkey's support in conflicts such as the GULF WAR and its opposition to ISLAMIC FUNDAMENTALISM. The flustered reaction of Western opinion to a government led by the Islamic politician Necmettin Erbakan in 1996 suggested that Turkey's image as a secular society was projected partially for Western benefit.

— *Nicholas Birns*

U

■ Uncle Sam

Unofficial symbol representing the United States of America

The symbol Uncle Sam is typically portrayed as a tall, white-haired, and bearded figure wearing a top hat and a coat with tails and dressed in the stars and stripes of the American flag (*see* SYMBOLS). This image has accompanied various examples of official government propaganda in which Uncle Sam is intended to personify democracy and liberty. In 1917 James Montgomery Flagg first used the image for an army recruiting poster that showed Uncle Sam with his index finger pointing at the viewer; the caption read "I Want You for the U.S. Army." Some versions show him as kind and friendly, others as determined.

The term originated with Samuel Wilson, a beef supplier for the U.S. Army. Born in Arlington, Massachusetts, in 1776, Wilson had run away from home at the age of fourteen to enlist in the Army. After the war he had begun a meat-packing business in Troy, New York, where he established a reputation for being hardworking, trustworthy, and practical. After he was appointed the inspector of provi-

sions for the U.S. Army in New York and New Jersey during the war of 1812, a worker claimed that the stamp used on barrels of meat, "EA-US," referred to the contractor Elbert Anderson and "Uncle" Sam Wilson. The term caught on after the New York press reported the incident, and Uncle Sam came to represent an honest, independent, diligent American. By the end of the war it had come to be used to symbolize not only the government but the character and personality of the nation.

Flagg's image of Uncle Sam has been a respected patriotic symbol for well over a century. The image has been used by the U.S. Army for recruitment purposes since its inception, and in the twentieth century it also became associated with government savings plans, as well as being incorporated by private business. Toward the end of the twentieth century the term also came to be used to reflect PUBLIC OPINION that challenges or criticizes the government and its policies or the economy.

— *Merle Sara Meyers*

■ Uncle Tom's Cabin

1851-1852: Antislavery novel by Harriet Beecher Stowe that rallied abolitionists before the Civil War

In 1850 the U.S. Congress passed the Fugitive Slave Law to facilitate the return of runaway slaves to their owners. Abolitionists condemned the new law and pledged to increase their efforts to end slavery. One abolitionist appalled by the law was Harriet Beecher Stowe, a writer of stories and sketches, and the wife and

James Montgomery Flagg, originator of Uncle Sam, one of the most enduring American propaganda images ever created. (*National Archives*)

daughter of prominent abolitionist clergymen. Early in 1851 Stowe informed her sister that she would oppose the Fugitive Slave Law by writing a novel to illustrate the evils of slavery. In June, 1851, *The National Era* began publishing weekly installments of Stowe's novel, titled *Uncle Tom's Cabin: Or, Life Among the Lowly*. The forty-five chapters ran through April, 1852, and a book version immediately followed.

Stowe's novel follows the fortunes of several slaves from Mr. Shelby's Kentucky plantation, including Uncle Tom, George and Eliza Harris, and the Harrises' son. In the course of narrating their stories, Stowe describes the many atrocities associated with slavery: hard toil, brutal beatings, and the painful separation of slave families.

When it appeared in book form, *Uncle Tom's Cabin* sold 10,000 copies during its first week of publication and 300,000 during its first year. The novel not only became the best-selling American novel of its time, it had an enormous political and social impact. Letters and diaries of the 1850's reveal the reactions of readers who wept as they turned the pages of *Uncle Tom's Cabin.* Northerners who had accepted slavery as part of American life condemned the institution after reading the book. Christian ministers invoked Stowe's novel while delivering antislavery jeremiads from their pulpits. The names of Stowe's characters—"Uncle Tom" and "Simon Legree"—became a part of the American vernacular.

Historians acknowledge that slavery was not the only cause of the American Civil War. Nevertheless, when President Abraham lincoln met Stowe at a White House reception in 1862, he reportedly commented: "So you're the little woman who wrote the book that started this great war!" Moreover, some historians have argued that Stowe's novel played a role in the North's victory. For a time Great Britain considered recognizing the South and providing aid during the war, but Stowe's novel, which was extremely popular in England, helped turn British popular opinion against the South's cause.

For several decades *Uncle Tom's Cabin* was dismissed by literary scholars as a sentimental propaganda piece lacking artistic merit. Twentieth century African American literary critics and scholars found the novel particularly objectionable for its depiction of Uncle Tom as a black man who is subservient in the face of oppression. The African American essayist and fiction writer James Baldwin articulated this sentiment in his 1955 essay titled "Everybody's Protest Novel." Baldwin called *Uncle Tom's Cabin* "a very bad novel," marred by "self-righteous, virtuous sentimentality" and a hero who "has been robbed of his humanity and divested of his sex." The name "Uncle Tom" has become a term of derision for African Americans who react passively to threats to their civil rights.

During the 1970's, however, Stowe's novel gained renewed attention, particularly from feminist scholars. These critics have highlighted such important themes in the novel as Stowe's presentation of the devastating effects of American slavery on African American women, her outcry at the political impotence of white women, and her depiction of the sisterly bonding of women of both races in the face of oppression. As a result of the work of feminist scholars, *Uncle Tom's Cabin* has returned to college course reading lists and has become a topic of discussion at literary conferences and in literary journals.

— *James Tackach*

■ Unconscious bias

This term refers to BIAS of which an individual is unaware, but which finds expression in certain kinds of behavior. Human beings grow up in environments in which beliefs and assumptions are a natural part. These often include bias for or against certain races, religions, or nationalities. Conscious rejection of a bias as a result of becoming more critical may not always carry over into unconscious behavior. A person raised to see Irish people stereotypically might later reject the STEREOTYPING yet continue to enjoy "Irish jokes" that draw upon such LABELING. To do so expresses an unconscious ethnic bias rooted in upbringing. Unconscious bias linked to conscious bias is an important contributor to the effectiveness of propaganda incorporating stereotypes.

■ Union of Democratic Control

British antiwar organization formed during World War I

The Union of Democratic Control (UDC) was organized on August 5, 1914, the day after Great Britain entered World War I. Its members considered themselves builders of peace, and the group was an important organ of opposition to governmental policy in Great Britain during World War I. The group's goals were parliamentary control over foreign policy and the prevention of secret diplomacy; negotiations after the war with Continental democracy to form an international understanding depending on popular parties rather than on governments; and a lasting peace settlement with terms that neither humiliated the defeated nation nor artificially rearranged frontiers that could provide cause for future wars. UDC's membership included such influential intellectuals, publicists, and politicians as

Bertrand Russell, Norman ANGELL, and James Ramsay MacDonald; its founders—Angell, Charles Trevelyan, Arthur Ponsonby, and Basil Davidson—were all eminent politicians. The organization tried to bring together all British opposition to World War I. UDC attracted Radicals, the left wing of the social-reform Liberals, who objected to their party's backing of wartime policies, and members of the Labour Party, who were increasingly attracted to the Union's views as the war progressed. UDC's activities were noticed by the government and had an impact on the War Cabinet. A significant number of Liberals went over to the Labour Party which, in turn, was more ready to accept Liberals and their ideas because of the cooperative Labour-Liberal attack on wartime policy that was led by the UDC and its capable secretary, E. D. Morel, who advocated a "bold and aggressive, almost arrogant" propaganda to make it different from other peace societies. In 1924 nine former UDC members were in the first Labour Cabinet. This and Morel's death that same year effectively ended the UDC's function as Labour's most important source for formulating foreign policy. The union continued to exist for more than four decades, with members such as Harold Wilson in the 1950's, but it never again exerted the same influence.

In the beginning the union's propaganda was pamphlets and leaflets; the leaflets tended to be one or two pages long, with capitalized words used for emphasis and designed to attract the worker. The pamphlets, much longer, were calculated to influence public opinion on the economic consequences of the war and to suggest reform of the foreign-policymaking procedures. UDC expanded its opinion-making activities with public meetings, and in November, 1915, it began a journal, *U.D.C.*, edited by Morel, which became *Foreign Affairs: A Journal of International Understanding* in July, 1919, and ceased publication in 1931.

The interrelationship between domestic politics and foreign policy, which is important to any understanding of the UDC, played a major role in Labour's discontent with the war. The Labour party's foreign policy programs, similar to those of the UDC convinced Radical dissenters and other Liberals to switch their political allegiance. Most of the leaders of the Union of Democratic Control were Liberals when World War I began, and their abandonment of their party was both a cause and a sign of its political demise when the war ended. The union's attitudes toward the war and then toward the peace settlement strongly influenced British public opinion in the interwar period. Had Morel lived, the UDC would probably have tried to reshape attitudes through the 1920's and into the 1930's. The UDC's major success was in fostering the revolutionary changes by which Great Britain adjusted to mass democracy.

— *Martin J. Manning*

■ United Nations

International organization established in San Francisco in 1945 for the purpose of preserving global peace and security

International organizations such as the United Nations (U.N.) are created by governments to facilitate the interaction of states. Unlike governments, such organizations lack sovereignty and must draw on their member states for whatever authority or mandates they have. Dependent as they are on their member states for their budgets and for approval of their operational activities, international organizations are not normally in a position to challenge a member state's sovereignty. Rather, they are intended to serve as impartial venues for international discussion and coordination.

Because the United Nations, too, is subject to these constraints, it might seem that there is little occasion for propaganda while the organization pursues its charter-based and state-mandated functions. The very nature of the United Nations's principles and purposes, however, is rooted in such highly political and often controversial arenas as the maintenance of international peace and security, the promotion of human rights and economic development, the alleviation of poverty, and the pursuit of cultural interchange. Therefore the various U.N. organs, committees, commissions, and related agencies charged with the pursuit of these objectives frequently rely heavily on propaganda techniques.

The U.N. Security Council may take military action against a government that is guilty of aggression, as happened in 1992 when the council authorized the use of "all necessary means" to evict IRAQ's military forces from KUWAIT. Determining aggression is a political exercise, however, and punishing aggression normally involves efforts to convince governments and international PUBLIC OPINION of the errors of the offending parties, so that sufficient support can be built to punish them. The U.N. Security Council, its member states, and the secretary-general

---

Preamble of the United Nations Charter[1]

We the peoples of the United Nations determined to save succeeding generations from the scourge of war, which twice in our lifetime has brought untold sorrow to mankind, and

To reaffirm faith in fundamental human rights, in the dignity and worth of the human person, in the equal rights of men and women and of nations large and small, and

To establish conditions under which justice and respect for the obligations arising from treaties and other sources of international law can be maintained, and

To promote social progress and better standards of life in larger freedom, and for these ends

To practice tolerance and live together in peace with one another as good neighbors, and

To unite our strength to maintain international peace and security, and

To insure, by the acceptance of principles and the institution of methods, that armed force shall not be used, save in the common interest, and

To employ international machinery for the promotion of the economic and social advancement of all peoples, have resolved to combine our efforts to accomplish these aims.

Accordingly, our respective Governments, through representatives assembled in the city of San Francisco, who have exhibited their full powers found to be in good and due form, have agreed to the present Charter of the United Nations and do hereby establish an international organization to be known as the United Nations.

---

[1]Adopted at the San Francisco Conference of 1945.

have engaged in such global propaganda campaigns against the Saddam HUSSEIN regime in IRAQ, the Raul Cedras regime in HAITI, and against the Somali warlord Mohammed Aideed, who was labeled by the United Nations as a war criminal for imputed responsibility in the deaths of U.N. peace-keeping forces in the international campaign to relieve mass starvation in the SOMALIA RELIEF CAMPAIGN.

The human-rights and humanitarian agencies affiliated with the United Nations also engage in propaganda in their efforts to prevent racism, discrimination, and persecution. The U.N. General Assembly, for instance, repeatedly condemned SOUTH AFRICA for its racist policy

of apartheid in resolutions, reports, and recommendations. ISRAEL faced similar condemnations in U.N. bodies when Arab nations joined other Third World nations in declaring ZIONISM to be racist.

Members of the U.N. secretariat and staff tend to support the ideas of cultural relativism, idealism, cosmopolitanism, multilateralism, globalism, and humanitarianism. These philosophical beliefs and political ideologies are pervasive in the speeches, reports, and recommendations that issue from U.N. conferences, the public-relations departments of the United Nations, and affiliated agencies.

The United Nations was established by governments in reaction to the devastation of World War II. Its primary purpose was to maintain the collective security of its member states by preventing war, promoting the use of peaceful means of conflict resolution, and punishing aggression between member states. The United Nations Charter also sought to eradicate the underlying causes of conflict by promoting the development of international law and human rights; by pursuing economic development, self–determination, and decolonization; and by promoting humanitarian assistance and international cultural, scientific, and technical exchanges.

THE EAST-WEST DISPUTE The goal of promoting global peace, prosperity, and co-

operation, however, collided with the realities of an emerging COLD WAR, in ways that frustrated many charter goals. The ideological differences between the U.S.-led capitalist states and the Soviet-led communist states grew increasingly hostile after World War II, as both blocs sought to use the United Nations to advance their political interests and agendas. The outbreak of the KOREAN WAR deepened the rift. Communist states supported the North Korean invasion of South Korea, but the United States and Western governments outnumbered the communist states in the United Nations, and as a result, in its first major collective security initiative, the United Nations condemned the Communist invasion as an il-

Session of the United Nations Security Council in late 1992. (*AP/Wide World Photos*)

legal intervention; the U.N. flag flew over the forces, led by the United States, which were sent to Korea to oppose the invasion. The United States and Western governments used the United Nations as a forum both to oppose communist aggression and to condemn the activities of communist states. The Soviet Union and Eastern bloc countries, in turn, became isolated and criticized the United Nations as being a mere tool of Western imperialist interests.

THE NORTH-SOUTH DISPUTE   Eventually the balance of forces changed in the United Nations. Pursuing one of its other goals, that of self-determination and decolonization, the U.N. General Assembly gradually admitted large numbers of African and Asian countries. These governments used U.N. bodies as a means to accelerate the pace of decolonization and to focus on the economic needs of the newly independent states. Fearing that the East-West dispute would detract from this goal, many of these governments pursued a policy of neutrality or nonalignment in relation to the superpowers and attempted instead to press their own agenda of economic development. The majority of these states, however, adopted socialist-oriented governments, and gradually the influence of the Soviet Union and Communist China increased. There emerged a substantial bloc of Third World states, that, although professedly nonaligned, sympathized with East-bloc ideology and was critical of the Western capitalist nations' dominance of the global economy.

Controlling numerical majorities in the U.N. General Assembly, as well as eventually in the expanded Economic and Social Council, these states used U.N. bodies to condemn South Africa for its apartheid policy, to promote the independence of non-self-governing territories and colonies, and to demand reforms to the international economic order favorable to the needs of developing countries. Many of the resolutions adopted by U.N. bodies to these ends reflected socialist and anti-imperialist rhetoric and were consequently resented and opposed by Western governments, chiefly the United States.

Characteristic of the use of propaganda in U.N. pronouncements was the effort of Arab governments to condemn Israel and promote the Palestinian cause by joining with African and other Third World states and by treating the governments of Israel and South Africa as international pariahs. The Soviet Union encouraged and supported such efforts because they were in line with the U.S.S.R's anti-Western and anticapitalist foreign policy agenda.

The United Nations thus became a forum in which not only East-West disputes but North-South competitions were played out. The propaganda battles between developed Northern and developing Southern countries did not, however, wholly prevent the organization from developing programs and policies that addressed many new international problems. The U.N. General Assembly developed means of coordinating the provision of international emergency humanitarian assistance, even as the Security Council fielded peace-keeping missions to facilitate diplomatic solutions to various conflicts. Yet even these efforts were often marred by ideological contention, and the Soviet Union and Eastern bloc were conspicuously absent from the humanitarian activities of the U.N. High Commis-

United Nations Member States in 1997

The 185 members of the United Nations, with the years in which they became members, as of July, 1997.

Member	Year	Member	Year
Afghanistan	1946	Djibouti	1977
Albania	1955	Dominica	1978
Algeria	1962	Dominican Republic	1945
Andorra	1993	Ecuador	1945
Angola	1976	Egypt	1945
Antigua and Barbuda	1981	El Salvador	1945
Argentina	1945	Equatorial Guinea	1968
Armenia	1992	Eritrea	1993
Australia	1945	Estonia	1991
Austria	1955	Ethiopia	1945
Azerbaijan	1992	Fiji	1970
Bahamas	1973	Finland	1955
Bahrain	1971	France	1945
Bangladesh	1974	Gabon	1960
Barbados	1966	Gambia	1965
Belarus (formerly Byelorussia)	1945	Georgia	1992
Belgium	1945	Germany	1973
Belize	1981	Ghana	1957
Benin	1960	Greece	1945
Bhutan	1971	Grenada	1974
Bolivia	1945	Guatemala	1945
Bosnia and Herzegovina	1992	Guinea	1958
Botswana	1966	Guinea-Bissau	1974
Brazil	1945	Guyana	1966
Brunei Darussalam	1984	Haiti	1945
Bulgaria	1955	Honduras	1945
Burkina Faso	1960	Hungary	1955
Burundi	1962	Iceland	1946
Cambodia	1955	India	1945
Cameroon	1960	Indonesia	1950
Canada	1945	Iran	1945
Cape Verde	1975	Iraq	1945
Central African Republic.	1960	Ireland	1955
Chad	1960	Israel	1949
Chile	1945	Italy	1955
China	1945	Jamaica	1962
Colombia	1945	Japan	1956
Comoros	1975	Jordan	1955
Congo	1960	Kazakhstan	1992
Costa Rica	1945	Kenya	1963
Côte d'Ivoire (Ivory Coast)	1960	Korea, North	1991
Croatia	1992	Korea, South	1991
Cuba	1945	Kuwait	1963
Cyprus	1960	Kyrgyzstan	1992
Czech Republic	1993	Laos	1955
Denmark	1945	Latvia	1991

United Nations Member States in 1997—continued

Member	Year	Member	Year
Lebanon	1945	Saint Kitts and Nevis	1983
Lesotho	1966	Saint Lucia	1979
Liberia	1945	Saint Vincent and the Grenadines	1980
Libya	1955	Samoa	1976
Liechtenstein	1990	San Marino	1992
Lithuania	1991	São Tomé and Principe	1975
Luxembourg	1945	Saudi Arabia	1945
Macedonia	1993	Senegal	1960
Madagascar	1960	Seychelles	1976
Malawi	1964	Sierra Leone	1961
Malaysia	1957	Singapore	1965
Maldives	1965	Slovakia	1993
Mali	1960	Slovenia	1992
Malta	1964	Solomon Islands	1978
Marshall Islands	1991	Somalia	1960
Mauritania	1961	South Africa	1945
Mauritius	1968	Spain	1955
Mexico	1945	Sri Lanka	1955
Micronesia	1991	Sudan	1956
Moldova	1992	Suriname	1975
Monaco	1993	Swaziland	1968
Mongolia	1961	Sweden	1946
Morocco	1956	Syria	1945
Mozambique	1975	Tajikistan	1992
Myanmar (formerly Burma)	1948	Tanzania	1961
Namibia	1990	Thailand	1946
Nepal	1955	Togo	1960
Netherlands	1945	Trinidad and Tobago	1962
New Zealand	1945	Tunisia	1956
Nicaragua	1945	Turkey	1945
Niger	1960	Turkmenistan	1992
Nigeria	1960	Uganda	1962
Norway	1945	Ukraine	1945
Oman	1971	United Arab Emirates	1971
Pakistan	1947	United Kingdom	1945
Palau	1994	United States	1945
Panama	1945	Uruguay	1945
Papua New Guinea	1975	Uzbekistan	1992
Paraguay	1945	Vanuatu	1981
Peru	1945	Venezuela	1945
Philippines	1945	Vietnam	1977
Poland	1945	Yemen	1947
Portugal	1955	Yugoslavia	1945
Qatar	1971	Zaire (Congo)	1960
Romania	1955	Zambia	1964
Russia	1945	Zimbabwe	1980
Rwanda	1962		

Source: U.N. Press Release ORG/1190 (updated July 17, 1997)

sioner for Refugees, which they viewed as representing the interests of Western governments.

BEYOND THE DISPUTES Eventually the Soviet Union, its own economy in shambles, was unable to sustain the competition of the Cold War. Under Mikhail GORBACHEV the country began a process of reforms that led to the dissolution of the union. With that, capitalism emerged as the reigning international economic ideology. In the face of these dramatic changes even the highly contentious North-South debates began to be less combative and propagandistic, and many developing states turned away from socialist experiments and sought to implement capitalist-oriented reforms. In the absence of the competition for allies that was so integral a part of the Cold War, many developing nations feared that economic assistance programs from wealthier Western nations would cease when these no longer brought political gains. Indeed, countries of the former Eastern bloc began to make substantial claims for assistance from the West in U.N. bodies dominated by such Northern developed states as the United States, Germany, Great Britain, Japan, France, and Canada.

SUGGESTED READINGS:

Finkelstein, Lawrence S., ed. *Politics in the United Nations System.* Durham, N.C.: Duke University Press, 1988.

Mingst, Karen, and Margaret Karns. *The United Nations in the Post-Cold War Era.* Boulder, Colo.: Westview Press, 1995.

Stoessinger, John. *The U.N. and the Superpowers.* 4th ed. New York: Random House, 1977.

— *Robert F. Gorman*

■ United Service Organization

Support organization for U.S. troops formed shortly before the United States entered World War II

In October, 1940, representatives of a number of private agencies met in New York City to discuss the providing of social services to American troops in any future military engagements. The services originally envisioned included programs for the recreation, welfare, and spiritual needs of military personnel. The United Service Organization for National Defense, later shortened to the more familiar United Service Organization (USO), was incorporated by six national private organizations: Young Men's Christian Association (YMCA), Young Women's Christian Organization (YWCA), National Catholic Community Service, National Jewish Welfare Board, the Salvation Army, and the Travelers Aid Society. Walter Hoving, the director of the Salvation Army was its first president, and Thomas E. Dewey headed its initial fund-raising drive, which raised more than sixteen million dollars that first year.

In January, 1941, President Franklin D. ROOSEVELT summoned representatives of the USO to Washington, D.C., for a meeting with government officials. He directed that private organizations would handle the on-leave recreation and the government would put up the buildings. On February 4, 1941, the USO was incorporated under the laws of New York State. That October the organization established the camp shows, and in November the first government-built USO club opened in Fayetteville, North Carolina. At least three hundred service centers were set up before the Japanese attack on Pearl Harbor on December 7, 1941. The USO's first honorary chairman was President Roosevelt, who was also one of its first poster boys, with his exhortation that "USO deserves the support of every individual citizen." One of the USO's earliest efforts was Victory Book Day on April 17, 1942, when the USO, the Red Cross, and the American Library Association sponsored a campaign to provide ten million books "for the fighting men" through donations from the American people.

Early funding came from the National War Fund, a philanthropic federation that was established in early 1943 by the president's War Relief Control Board. The USO also planned to provide live entertainment for the troops, both to boost morale and to transfer the burden from small towns near the bases. On October 31, 1941, the USO created Camp Shows, Inc. What started out as the attempt to bring shows to soldiers became the greatest entertainment enterprise in the history of show business. All the major entertainment unions agreed to allow members to waive pay and working requirements to bring live shows to armed forces stationed worldwide. Camp Shows engaged more than seven thousand performers (called "soldiers in greasepaint"), including some of the best-known entertainers of the time, among them Bing Crosby, Gary Cooper, Fred Astaire, and Dinah Shore. BOB HOPE, the entertainer most often associated with the USO, to which he contributed for more than thirty years, undertook his first wartime tour in 1942 to Alaska and to the Aleutians.

During World War II the USO was an integral part of the American war effort. On December 31, 1947, all USO clubs and facilities were closed by President Harry S Truman, but he soon re-activated them for the KOREAN WAR with a memorandum of understanding between the president and the Department of Defense, which recognized the USO as the principal civilian agency for assisting military authorities. In September, 1963, the USO opened its first club in Saigon, Vietnam, and seventeen others were established in that country over the next nine years.

The USO is probably best remembered today for the annual Christmas visits by Hope and his troupe to Vietnam that began in December, 1964, and continued well into the post-Vietnam era; in those later years the show was not always well received by those servicemen who were critical of U.S. military policy. In any case, the real propaganda value of these shows was in their annual broadcast on American television, which included a favorable portrayal of overseas war efforts. As military involvement in Vietnam continued to divide the country, the broadcasts had to be edited to remove the often stinging criticism from servicemen in the audience, which would have presented a contradictory image that the USO and the military did not want. All USO clubs in Vietnam were closed in June, 1972, when the American troops withdrew. Five years later the USO moved its headquarters from New York to Washington, D.C., where it opened as the Bob Hope USO Center and World Headquarters in May, 1985.

On December 20, 1979, President Jimmy Carter signed the USO's newly granted Congressional charter, which incorporated the National Council of the USO, a separate volunteer arm, into the regular USO organization. Eleven years later the USO was again on the battle scene at the beginning of American involvement in the Persian GULF WAR when it opened two centers in Bahrain and in the United Arab Emirates. During peacetime the USO operates with minimum staff and volunteer help, maintaining approximately two hundred off-post clubs and hospitality centers for servicemen. The organization is financed by direct public contributions raised through United Fund and other campaigns.

— *Martin J. Manning*

■ United States: 1865-1916

Period between the Civil War and American entry in World War I

Following the Civil War the United States experienced rapid social, economic, and political changes that greatly facilitated the growth of propaganda. The number and circulation of NEWSPAPERS grew steadily, and magazines became a major mass medium. An increasingly urbanized society, bound together by improving transportation and communications, presented ready AUDIENCES for a tide of advertising that gradually led to more sophisticated methods for influencing the public. At the same time a variety of social causes sprang up, each with its own message to be spread to these new mass audiences.

The task of reuniting North and South was paramount after the Civil War. The idea of national unity was widely promoted, and Americans were encouraged to give their highest loyalty to their flag and country. Dozens of patriotic organizations were founded, the promotion of patriotism became a part of the public school curriculum, and the American flag was given a central place in the symbolism of national pride and loyalty. Through the efforts of such Southerners as Henry Grady, the Confederacy became the "New South," an integral part of a united America. An "Americanization" movement became the order of the day, and newly arrived immigrants were called upon to transfer their loyalty to their new country. At the turn of the century the SPANISH-AMERICAN WAR was used as an illustration of how North and South had come together against a common foe. In these ways America was given a sense of unity that proved vital to its role as a player on the world scene in the twentieth century.

The populist movement generated considerable propaganda in the 1890's as its adherents sought a stronger voice for the average citizen. Fearful of the growing power of bankers and industrialists, and hard hit by the depression of 1893, workers and farmers formed a receptive audience for the populist message of reform. In 1896 populism was embraced by the DEMOCRATIC PARTY, and the issue of silver versus gold took on a central symbolic importance through the stirring rhetoric of William Jennings BRYAN, whose "Cross of Gold" speech electrified his audience, though it failed to elevate him to the presidency. As populism gave way to progressivism in the early 1900's, further reforms were expedited by the writings of such "muckrakers" as Lincoln Steffens and Ida Tarbell, who used magazines as a vehicle for attacking the nation's social and economic evils. Propaganda demonstrated its own capacity to be used for evil, how-

The emotions unleashed by D. W. Griffith's *The Birth of a Nation* in 1915 revealed the potential power of motion pictures as social propaganda in the United States. (*Museum of Modern Art, Film Stills Archive*)

ever, as illustrated by the way in which D. W. Griffith's epic film *The Birth of a Nation* (1915) was linked by racists to their revival of the KU KLUX KLAN in Georgia.

PROPAGANDA FOR WAR Beginning in 1895, the plight of CUBA captured the American public's attention. The oppression by Spain of its Cuban colony lent itself perfectly to exploitation by the sensational YELLOW JOURNALISM of the American press at the turn of the century, and such newspapers as Joseph Pulitzer's *New York World* and William Randolph HEARST's *New York Journal* were eager to expand their already large circulations by exciting readers with atrocity propaganda about Spanish efforts to suppress the Cuban revolt. Most American newspapers belonged to the Associated Press, which facilitated the reporting of stories about Cuba throughout the United States, but Spanish CENSORSHIP of news from Cuba made it more difficult to tell fact from fiction. By 1898, when the battleship *Maine* exploded while visiting Cuba, American public opinion was ready to give enthusiastic support to a war with Spain, and the resulting Spanish-American War was heralded by the press as a glorious adventure, replete with such heroes as Theodore Roosevelt and Admiral George Dewey.

Moreover, the war gained for the United States its first overseas colonial empire, a result that served the goals of business interests that provided financing and advertising for the leading newspapers of the day.

By the time WORLD WAR I broke out in Europe, the United States was in its heyday of newspaper journalism, with nearly twenty thousand daily and weekly newspapers across the country. Although President Woodrow WILSON steered a neutral course for the country between 1914 and 1917, the American press came to display a distinct pro-British, anti-German bias that was shared by politicians, bankers, industrialists, clergy, and other opinion leaders. Because NEUTRALITY was the nation's official stance, the theme of "preparedness" was adopted as a way of promoting increased defense expenditures and mobilizing a militant citizenry. Led by such prominent Americans as Theodore Roosevelt and his former comrade-in-arms General Leonard Wood, this preparedness movement portrayed the Germans as a threat to world peace. By 1916 the movement had attracted thousands of men and boys to summer camps for voluntary military training. General Wood wrote a book, *Our Military History: Its Facts and Fallacies* (1916), in which he argued that preparing for war meant preserving peace, and that universal military training was necessary if Americans were to be sent into battle with any chance of victory. Motion pictures, America's newest and still fledgling mass medium, also took up the preparedness theme, turning out such productions as *The Battle Cry of Peace* (1916), which showed a Germanic enemy army landing on American shores and waging war without respect for civilian life

(*see* WORLD WAR I). The stories reported by the American press about German atrocities in Europe, and the outrage over the sinking of the oceanliner *Lusitania* in 1915, made the American public all too willing to believe the Germans capable of such cruelties. Beginning with a march in New York City in May, 1916, mass parades were also a tool for spreading the preparedness theme across America. In these ways public opinion was prepared, as it had been in the late 1890's, to embrace a war against a foreign power.

SUGGESTED READINGS:

Curti, Merle. *The Roots of American Loyalty*. New York: Athenum, 1968.

Erikson, Robert S., and Kent L. Tedin. *American Public Opinion: Its Origins, Content, and Impact*. 5th ed. Boston, Mass.: Allyn and Bacon, 1995.

Ross, Stewart Halsey. *Propaganda for War: How the United States Was Conditioned to Fight the Great War of 1914-1918*. Jefferson, N.C.: McFarland, 1996.

Viault, Birdsall S. *American History Since 1865*. New York: McGraw-Hill, 1989.

— *Lawrence W. Haapanen*

■ United States: 1919-1941

Following its involvement in World War I the United States experienced a cultural revolution born of its military victory and subsequent economic prosperity

Like other Western countries during the period following WORLD WAR I, the United States pursued a policy of isolationism in foreign affairs that is typified by its noninvolvement in the LEAGUE OF

NATIONS and nonintervention in the SPANISH CIVIL WAR. Politically, the period was marked by competing conservative, socialist, and communist movements. Government intervention in all areas of American life became especially evident in the 1930's with the NEW DEAL programs of the administration of President Franklin D. ROOSEVELT.

Propaganda representing a variety of viewpoints played an important role in every aspect of American life, and virtually no group, community, or individual escaped its influence. The United States Constitution has generally been interpreted as granting nearly absolute rights of free speech and free association, and the propaganda campaigns of the interwar period ranged from the subtle (ADVERTISING and FILM), to the excessive (marches and demagogic use of the RADIO). It was not until the New Deal Era in the 1930's that American propaganda began taking a much more "official" role in the lives of the American public. Even then, private propaganda campaigns still littered the landscape.

EDUCATION AND RELIGION The most easily recognizable effects of propaganda on average Americans were in the twin pillars of most communities: the schools and the churches. Following World War I, new ways of educating the young began to be explored. "Progressive EDUCATION" emphasizing method over content began to take hold. The curriculum was concerned with four broad areas: health, "fundamental processes," civics and social relations, and recreation. Colleges saw an increase in enrollment and soon found home economics and physical education creeping into the traditional curriculum.

Conservative media and organizations of the period, including the Hearst papers, the Veterans of Foreign Wars, and the Daughters of the American Revolution, pushed to have the schools purged of "Bolsheviks" and return to teaching traditional national values. By the 1930's most colleges were considered by conservatives to be havens of BOLSHEVISM or at least to be decidedly "pink" (left-leaning).

Religion became more militant and overtly political during the interwar period, particularly during the Great Depression. Members of the clergy of nearly all denominations preached socialism in one form or another from the pulpit, a situation which aided communist organizers in their strike efforts, since they found a certain amount of ready support from the workers. Most workers did not support the COMMUNIST PARTY but did support some communistic causes in the light of the support of the churches. These types of propaganda efforts were not organized and reflected more of a gradual attitudinal or educational reorientation. The American ROMAN CATHOLIC CHURCH was more organized in its efforts to continue the isolationist priorities of American politics. The church and its members opposed any involvement in Europe, particularly if it would affect such Catholic countries as Spain or the Vatican.

THE MASS MEDIA With the postwar business boom came a revolution in the use of mass media. Advertising pushed business concerns in all areas, effecting changes in cultural mores and attitudes. Women were encouraged to "reach for a Lucky instead of a sweet" as the tobacco companies entered an entirely new market. Radio was born in the postwar boom and was an immediate success: Sixty million dollars' worth of sets were sold in 1922, the second year of regular broadcasts. By 1925 the figure had reached $430 million; it was $842 million by 1929. Nearly a third of the country listened to the radio every night, forming a captive audience for advertisers of soap, toothpaste, and stocks. The radio was first used in campaigning in 1928 and was later used with great success by President Franklin D. Roosevelt, both in campaigning and in his "fireside chats" during the Great Depression.

Newspapers and magazines in the 1920's reflected the times in their somewhat sensational styles. The tabloid, a format imported from Great Britain, became popular, and even more established papers such as *The New York Times* succumbed to the sensationalizing attitudes. Photography was an important part of this new sensationalism. This shift recognized the need to cater to the growing semi-literate populations of most urban areas. Newsmagazines such as *Time* were aimed at the growing population of college graduates, and literary magazines such as *Smart Set*, edited by social critic H. L. Mencken, introduced American readers to such authors as D. H. Lawrence, James Joyce, and F. Scott Fitzgerald. By the 1930's and the Great Depression, newspapers had begun to fall back to their more conservative roots. Becoming more pro-business and timid in their coverage, American newspapers did little to cover controversial public issues. The interwar period saw a growing sophistication in American films.

As with the rest of the country, the excesses of the 1920's caught up with the film industry. By the 1930's the film business had become more conservative in its outlook. Overt sexuality and violence were rigidly censored by the studios via the Motion Picture Production Code. Most of the content of American films by the middle of the 1930's was fantasy and escapist in orientation. They upheld the status quo instead of criticizing or examining it.

POLITICAL AGITATION All over the world the interwar period was a time of dislocation and revolution. The United States experienced this, albeit in a more muted tone, all throughout the 1920's and 1930's. Left-wing agitators, primarily communists and socialists, organized strikes, wrote pamphlets, and founded magazines. They also used the new media to their advantage. By the 1930's, with the advent of portable equipment, film and photo leagues started in most major cities. These groups produced revolutionary and critical NEWSREELS countering the more conservative films produced by Hollywood. Many of these revolutionary newsreels covered events ignored by the mainstream media.

Right-wing groups developed their own propaganda. The most notable and typical was the demagogic Father Charles E. COUGHLIN, an anti-Semite and later supporter of FASCISM in Italy and Nazi Germany. In the 1930's Father Coughlin was a popular radio broadcaster and organizer who did much to help maintain the United States' commitment to isolationism and used his United Christian Front to propagandize in favor of Italy and Germany.

The government staged its own propaganda campaigns. Some had legitimate purposes, such as election campaigning; others, however, such as New Deal arts organizations, were more partisan and clearly political in nature. Radio, which grew rapidly throughout the 1920's, was regulated in 1927 by the Herbert Hoover administration, which gave the government control of doling out radio frequencies and regulating content. The government also became involved in filmmaking, financing many educational films, usually of low quality. In the 1930's Pare Lorentz made *The Plow That Broke the Plain* and *The River.* The former warned farmers of the dangers of soil erosion, and the latter was a lyrical political tract justifying the creation of the Tennessee Valley Authority (TVA). By the New Deal era, the government was engaged in a much more activist role in the arts and funded several writers and artistic groups and theaters. Many of these groups reflected the Roosevelt administration's left-leaning politics and championed explicitly leftist programs.

SUGGESTED READINGS:

Alexander, William. *Film on the Left: American Documentary Film from 1931 to 1942.* Princeton, N.J.: Princeton University Press, 1981.

Cashman, Sean Dennis. *America in the Twenties and Thirties: The Olympian Age of Franklin Delano Roosevelt.* New York: New York University Press, 1989.

Freidel, Frank. *America in the Twentieth Century.* 3d ed. New York: Alfred A. Knopf, 1970.

Kirkendall, Richard S. *The United States 1929-1945: Years of Crisis and Change.* New York: McGraw-Hill, 1974.

McDonald, Forrest. *The Torch Is Passed: The United States in the Twentieth Century.* Reading, Mass.: Addison-Wesley, 1968.

Parrish, Michael E. *Anxious Decades: America in Prosperity and Depression, 1920-1941.* New York: W. W. Norton, 1992.

— *C. A. Wolski*

■ United States: Since 1945

Period after World War II when the United States became a world power and the leader of the noncommunist world in the Cold War waged against the Soviet bloc

Following the end of WORLD WAR II the U.S. government for the first time in its history began to employ official propaganda in peacetime. Given the recent negative example of Nazi propaganda, the United States took pains to insure that its propaganda would show a respect for the truth and be aimed at foreign rather than domestic audiences. President Harry S Truman gave the State Department responsibility for these propaganda activities, which rapidly expanded as the COLD WAR intensified. With RADIO FREE EUROPE the United States carried an anticommunist message to countries behind the Iron Curtain. VOICE OF AMERICA continued its wartime function of dissemination to the world a favorable picture of American life, politics, and culture. After the explosion of the first Soviet atomic bomb and the outbreak of the Korean War in 1950, Truman set up a psychological strategy board to coordinate the U.S. propaganda activities and portray the Soviet Union as a nation that was prepared to use force to spread communism worldwide. To the extent that this propaganda encouraged Americans to believe in the existence of an international communist conspiracy, it indirectly aided the anticommunist crusade led by Senator Joseph MCCARTHY and fed the nationwide "Red scare" of the early 1950's—in fact, McCarthy even attacked the U.S. propaganda effort as being infiltrated with communists and weak in its opposition to the

Soviet Union, charges that despite their falsehood had demoralizing effects—but it did not prove effective in preventing communism from taking hold in many areas of the world.

THE EISENHOWER YEARS Upon assuming the presidency in 1953 Dwight D. Eisenhower set out to revitalize American propaganda. He abolished the Psychological Strategy Board, put a new Operations Coordinating Board in charge of foreign propaganda activities, and established the UNITED STATES INFORMATION AGENCY (USIA) as the State Department's propaganda arm. A committee chaired by William Jackson advised the Eisenhower administration to soften the strident tone of U.S. propaganda and to have the Voice of America broadcast more "objective, factual news." Eisenhower set the theme himself for this new variety of propaganda in his "Chance for Peace" address in 1953, followed soon afterwards by a speech in support of "Atoms for Peace." The peace theme was pursued by all U.S. propaganda agencies, and achieved a considerable degree of success throughout the 1950's. After 1956, when the Soviet Union violently suppressed the Hungarian revolt (see HUNGARY), U.S. propaganda abandoned the goal of inciting peoples behind the Iron Curtain to rise against their oppressors, and more emphasis was placed on cultural exchanges and programs addressing individuals. The ultimate step in this direction was the visit by the Russian premier Nikita Khrushchev to the United States in 1959, after which a friendly spirit prevailed until the Soviets shot down a U.S. spy plane in 1960 (that was an embarrassment to the U.S. propaganda agencies, which were hard pressed to explain why Soviet airspace had been invaded in violation of international law) and the Paris summit conference collapsed in acrimony.

During the 1950's, while official U.S. propaganda was being aimed abroad, the American public received a steady flow of unofficial propaganda. Such Hollywood films as *My Son John* (1952) and such television programs as *I Led Three Lives* (1953-1956) depicted American communists as traitors to their country, and dozens of films—many made with the cooperation of the PENTAGON—portrayed the U.S. military as the free world's strongest shield against communist aggression (see FILM). Although sometimes viewed as overblown by critics, these productions proved effective in instilling an anticommunist conviction in the American public. In some instances the propaganda campaign for world opinion had an indirect effect on domestic political issues. The propaganda success scored by the Russians in putting *Sputnik* into orbit in 1957 resulted for example in a vigorous U.S. effort to accelerate its space program. The Eisenhower administration also pursued progress on behalf of the CIVIL RIGHTS MOVEMENT with an eye toward the effect such progress would have on world opinion, although the interests of social justice and redress of past injustices were given as the primary grounds.

THE KENNEDY-JOHNSON YEARS John F. Kennedy was elected president in 1960 on his promise to "get the country moving again." His activist approach led him to direct the USIA "to persuade, not inform." To guide the agency firmly in this more persuasive direction, he appointed

Edward R. Murrow as its new director. Like his predecessors, Murrow stressed the importance of truth in America's propaganda activities, but he also orchestrated firm support for Kennedy's foreign policy goals. The agency strenuously criticized the Soviet Union for its support of the Fidel CASTRO regime in CUBA, but tried to put the best possible face on the U.S. backing of the Cuban exiles in the BAY OF PIGS INVASION. Elected, in part, on the strength of the argument that American prestige had slipped in the world under Eisenhower, Kennedy sought to persuade the world that the United States was making progress in the areas of civil rights and space exploration. The USIA portrayed the federal government as doing all it could to promote integration and further civil rights, and the successful missions of the Mercury astronauts were presented as evidence that the United States was leading the Soviet Union in the race to reach the moon first. After the Cuban Missile Crisis in 1962, which nearly precipitated a nuclear war, Kennedy and Khrushchev both sought a relaxation in tensions. One of the tangible results of this was the termination in 1963 of Soviet jamming of Voice of America broadcasts.

Lyndon B. Johnson, who assumed the presidency in 1963 after Kennedy's assassination, found himself facing a less threatening Soviet Union and a more threatening communist insurgency in South Vietnam. As the American military role in the Vietnam War rapidly escalated, so did the level of both foreign and domestic propaganda. For perhaps the first time in American history, a large-scale propaganda campaign supporting the country's war effort was countered by vigorous propaganda from an antiwar campaign. Faced with both official and unofficial propaganda in support of the war, the antiwar activists learned to attract public attention with such methods as AGITPROP and CIVIL DISOBEDIENCE. As the war progressed the mainstream news media began to express more doubts about its ultimate success, especially after the communists' Tet Offensive in 1968. Johnson's decision not to seek another term as president was a tacit admission that he had lost the domestic propaganda battle.

THE NIXON-FORD-CARTER YEARS Elected president in 1968 amid widespread doubts about the wisdom of American involvement in Vietnam, Richard M. NIXON managed to continue the war another five years while actually enhancing his public support. This was accomplished in no small part by his willingness to compete aggressively with the American news media for the public's attention and trust. His administration's efforts to discredit the television networks as news sources and to prevent newspaper publication of the Pentagon Papers were part of Nixon's ongoing campaign to instill public faith in himself and deny it to his critics. His election to a second term in 1972 demonstrated the success of these efforts during his first term, just as his resignation in disgrace in 1974 showed that no amount of propaganda could undo the damage to his reputation that resulted when the media, Congress, and the courts exposed the White House cover-up of the Watergate scandal.

The presidency of Nixon's successor, Gerald Ford, was noteworthy for two failed propaganda efforts. He first failed to convince a majority of Americans that his pardon of Nixon was an appropriate exercise of presidential prerogative. Toward the end of his presidency he likewise failed to persuade the public of the merits of his program to combat inflation, epitomized by the slogan for "whip inflation now" and the "WIN" button that he used as a campaign symbol (*see* WIN CAMPAIGN). These failures led to the election in 1976 of Jimmy Carter, who waged a propaganda war against two adversaries, the Soviet Union and Iran, after the Soviet invasion of Afghanistan and the Iranian seizure of American hostages in 1979. While Carter was successful in painting a more menacing picture of the Soviets, which he underlined with a grain embargo and a boycott of the 1980 Olympic Games in Moscow, no amount of anti-Iranian propaganda could secure the release of the hostages held in Iran.

THE ERA OF PUBLIC DIPLOMACY The inauguration of Ronald REAGAN as president in 1981 launched an era of public diplomacy in which the government placed as much value on communication with individuals as the more traditional diplomacy with other governments. A major five-year-long overhaul of the Voice of America was launched in 1982, as a result of which its worldwide audience doubled by 1987. The USIA was once again made an integral part of the government's foreign policy apparatus; its specific charge was making public opinion more receptive to the placing of intermediate-range nuclear weapons in Western Europe. The Soviets played into the hands of this American propaganda campaign when in 1983 they shot down the Korean Airlines flight 007 and handled the subsequent public relations clumsily. Although the plane had not been identified as a civilian

airliner, the Soviets were made to look like cold-blooded murderers by the carefully orchestrated efforts of the USIA. At the same time, because new American telecommunication technology had made television a worldwide propaganda medium, satellites were able to bring live broadcasts of Reagan's speeches to foreign viewers, an innovation that was beyond the Soviets' ability to match or retard. To counter the Soviet Union's use of disinformation, which went so far as to claim that the ACQUIRED IMMUNODEFICIENCY SYNDROME (AIDS) virus was an American biological weapon, the USIA disseminated a conspiracy theory that the Soviets were behind the attempted assassination of Pope John Paul II in 1981. Possibly the most effective disinformation campaign of the Cold War was the promotion of the Strategic Defense Initiative, also known as "Star Wars," as a perfect defense against Soviet nuclear missiles. By using carefully staged test firings that gave an exaggerated impression of precision and effectiveness, the United States convinced the Soviet Union that only by bankrupting their economy could they compete in a new high-technology arms race.

Communism in the Western hemisphere also regained prominence as a target for American propaganda during this time. RADIO MARTÍ, patterned after Radio Free Europe and directed at Cuba, went on the air in 1985, and a television version followed. Voice of America briefly transmitted to Nicaragua in support of the CIA-backed anti-Sandinista rebels. In the case of Grenada, where a Marxist regime was overthrown by U.S. military intervention in 1983, the USIA made every effort to justify that action by documenting Grenada's drift into the Cuban orbit, and during the civil war in El Salvador in the early 1980's the Reagan administration used the American news media as a vehicle for promoting military aid to that country on the grounds that the rebels were backed by the communists. After the fall of communism in the Soviet Union in the early 1990's, the communist regime in Cuba remained the target of incessant U.S. propaganda.

During George BUSH's presidency the most intense use of propaganda was aimed at Iraq's leader Saddam HUSSEIN, who invaded KUWAIT in 1990. At the same time that official U.S. propaganda demonized Hussein as a brutal dictator and aggressor, the government of Kuwait contracted with an American public relations firm to help sway opinion against Hussein in Congress and in the public at large. Broad public support was won for the GULF WAR, which liberated Kuwait and temporarily humbled but did not topple Hussein. After the end of the Cold War the threat of communism was no longer a dependable propaganda tool for domestic political purposes. The 1992 presidential election that placed Bill Clinton in the White House turned much more on domestic issues than on foreign policy. The increased stridency of partisan political propaganda on taxes, the budget, and a variety of social issues may have been due, at least in part, to the decrease in propaganda directed abroad; enemies now had to be sought at home rather than abroad to sustain the battle for the public's loyalties. In the 1990's, as a result, propaganda was disseminated with new intensity in such areas as the ABORTION DEBATE, the assault on the TOBACCO INDUSTRY, and the immigration controversy (*see* IMMIGRATION CONTROVERSIES).

SUGGESTED READINGS:

Bogart, Leo. *Cool Words, Cold War: A New Look at USIA's Premises for Propaganda.* Rev. ed. Lanham, Md.: American University Press, 1995. Summarizes and puts into context a report originally prepared by the USIA in the early 1950's on propaganda goals and methods.

Carpenter, Ted Galen. *The Captive Press: Foreign Policy Crises and the First Amendment.* Washington, D.C.: Cato Institute, 1995. Describes how the U.S. government has influenced press coverage of foreign policy crises since World War II.

Green, Fitzhugh. *American Propaganda Abroad.* New York: Hippocrene Books, 1988. Provides an insider's view of the work of the USIA.

MacDonald, J. Fred. *Television and the Red Menace: The Video Road to Vietnam.* New York: Praeger, 1985. Describes the role of network television programming in bolstering the American public's anticommunist attitudes during the Cold War.

McGaffin, William, and Erwin Knoll. *Anything But the Truth: The Credibility Gap—How the News Is Managed in Washington.* New York: G. P. Putnam's Sons, 1968. Cites examples, from the U-2 incident to the Gulf of Tonkin incident, of the government's lying to the public and manipulating the press.

Simpson, Christopher. *Science of Coercion: Communication Research and Psychological Warfare, 1945-1960.* New York: Oxford University Press, 1994. Traces the contributions made by social scientists to government-funded research on psychological warfare during the early years of the Cold War.

Snyder, Alvin A. *Warriors of Disinformation: American Propaganda, Soviet Lies, and the Winning of the Cold War, An Insider's Account.* New York: Arcade, 1995. Gives the recollections of an official of USIA on American propaganda during the Reagan presidency.

Sorensen, Thomas C. *The World War: The Story of American Propaganda.* New York: Harper & Row, 1968. Excellent history of American propaganda from the end of World War II to the Vietnam War.

— *Lawrence W. Haapanen*

■ United States Information Agency

U.S. government agency established in 1953 as a propaganda and news service in other countries

The purpose of the United States Information Agency (USIA) is to disseminate the values and policies of the United States to people in other nations and to inform U.S. leaders about foreign public opinion. Activities of the agency include mass communications through media reports and the operation of libraries, cultural exhibits, and exchange programs between the United States and other countries. Known abroad as the United States Information Service (USIS), the organization is involved at different times and places in diplomatic, economic, and other forms of propaganda that serve the objectives of U.S. foreign policy.

AGENCY HISTORY AND STRUCTURE In the years before the creation of the USIA the United States practiced international propaganda through various governmental bodies. Foremost among these as predecessors of the USIA were the COMMITTEE ON PUBLIC INFORMATION (CPI) and the OFFICE OF WAR INFORMATION (OWI).

Congressional passage of the Smith-Mundt Act in 1948 called for a new information service to promote U.S. interests overseas and led to the USIA as an independent and autonomous source of propaganda. The agency is overseen by a director appointed by the president and a staff of foreign-service professionals and media experts involved in the planning of propaganda strategies. Field offices located in more than one hundred countries are responsible for the development and implementation of materials and tactics specific to different parts of the world.

During the COLD WAR years the USIA was particularly active in anticommunism propaganda and with efforts to offset TASS, the Soviet propaganda organization. After the Cold War the agency's emphasis shifted slightly toward information and education functions in the Newly Independent States (NIS) of the former Soviet Union and other parts of the world, but propaganda remained central to its activities.

The USIA works closely with the Department of State in Washington, D.C., with embassy missions abroad, and at times with defense and intelligence arms of the U.S. government. USIA attention and spending are devoted to different parts of the world according to the propaganda and information needs of U.S. foreign policy at any particular time and according to the philosophy and concerns of the administration in power.

In 1978 reorganization resulted in the USIA's taking on additional responsibilities for cultural matters at overseas posts. At that time the agency was renamed the International Communication Agency. In 1982 the agency reverted to its original name, but its duties continued to include cultural work and educational exchange as well as more overt forms of propaganda.

PROGRAMS AND ACTIVITIES Always working toward the objective of communicating American values and supporting U.S. foreign policy, the USIA uses a variety of methods and media. Those that most directly involve the use of propaganda include an extensive program of broadcasting services, an international news-wire service, and publications prepared and produced in the languages of their target audiences. The agency is also involved in arranging lecture tours and producing NEWSREELS, films, and comic books for propaganda purposes. With very few exceptions, propaganda materials prepared for use overseas are not made available for examination or dissemination in the United States.

The most famous USIA broadcast service is probably VOICE OF AMERICA (VOA), the network of radio programs aired in more than thirty different languages around the world via AM, FM, and SHORTWAVE RADIO signals. RADIO MARTÌ and TV Martì are special services within VOA whose broadcasts are targeted exclusively to Cuban audiences. The agency also operates RADIO FREE EUROPE, Radio Free Asia, and RADIO LIBERTY as surrogate broadcasters carrying news and programming in certain countries where they disseminate views purported to represent the opinions of dissidents in those countries.

Worldnet is the name of the satellite television network run by USIA. Like the radio services, Worldnet transmits news and programs with propaganda objectives in different languages around the world. Most of the Worldnet content originates

from USIA studios in Washington, D.C., although some programming is acquired from such outside sources as U.S. commercial and public television networks. Worldnet is also involved with interactive video conferences between journalists and leaders around the world and supplies videotape propaganda materials for use by USIS offices in different countries.

The Bureau of Information within USIA is responsible for the production and distribution of most of the agency's printed propaganda. This includes pamphlets on topics with implications for U.S. government policy, security, and planning interests in other countries, as well as literature, magazines, and books intended to convey a more general pro-American message. A news service called the Wireless File provides continuous updates and releases on government actions and positions for use by foreign media. The agency also attempts to spread propaganda through the international press with its Foreign Press Centers, which serve as host offices to visiting foreign journalists in major U.S. cities. Web sites and Internet pages on various subjects are maintained by the USIA in different countries; they, like USIA propaganda in older media, are not accessible within the United States.

More indirect propaganda tools of the USIA include the Fulbright Program and other academic exchange arrangements; overseas tours by American musicians, performers, and artists; and the sponsorship of speakers, exhibits, and festivals dealing with American culture. In many countries the USIA is involved in the translation of selected American books and in the teaching of English and courses about the United States. Such activities are based at least in part on EDU-CATION AS A PROPAGANDA RATIONALE.

SUGGESTED READINGS:

Bogart, Leo. *Cool Words, Cold War: A New Look at USIA's Premises for Propaganda.* Washington, D.C.: The American University Press, 1995.

Elder, Robert E. *The Information Machine: The United States Information Agency and American Foreign Policy.* Syracuse, N.Y.: Syracuse University Press, 1968.

Hansen, Allen C. *USIA: Public Diplomacy in the Computer Age.* New York: Praeger, 1989.

Rubin, Ronald I. *The Objectives of the U.S. Information Agency.* New York: Praeger, 1966.

— *Kevin L. Keenan*

■ Universum-Film-Aktiengesellschaft

German film propaganda company established in 1917

During WORLD WAR I GERMANY was faced with a crisis of identity. Allied countries, during and immediately after that war, produced a series of effective propaganda films portraying the German nation in a negative light. Germany had largely destroyed or ignored its cinema during the war, but on December 18, 1917, General Erich Ludendorff, commander-in-chief of the German army, merged the remnants of Germany's studios into one national film production center named Universum-Film-Aktiengesellschaft (UFA). Its purpose was as a twofold COUNTERPROPAGANDA weapon: to build German morale at home and to promote German ideals abroad.

By the time the UFA was fully organized, the war was over. The UFA thereupon entered on a period of bold and imaginative activity during the Weimar Republic with the production of films that simultaneously entertained and elevated their audiences. UFA-sponsored films sought to be original and progressive, and they employed innovative lighting, fluid-camera movement, and atmospheric settings. In the process they popularized three distinct film genres: historical spectacle, stylized fantasy/horror tales, and psychological street films. By the mid-1920's Germany rivaled Hollywood as the world's most innovative film market.

The UFA's decline began when in 1927 controlling stock in the company was purchased by Alfred Hugenberg, a conservative newspaper owner and later supporter of Adolf HITLER. Under Joseph GOEBBELS, Hitler's minister of propaganda, the UFA became a compliant propaganda weapon for the National Socialists. Films produced during this time include Leni RIEFENSTAHL's *Triumph of the Will* (1935). The studio ceased to exist with the defeat of the Third Reich. Ironically, Erich Pommer, who had headed the UFA during its glory days in the 1920's but who had been forced to flee to the United States in the 1930's, returned to Germany in 1945 as a U.S. soldier and was responsible for the de-Nazification and restructuring of the shattered German film industry.

— *Terry Theodore*

V

■ Viereck, George Sylvester

December 31, 1884, in Munich, Germany—March 18, 1962, in Holyoke, Massachusetts: German American journalist and apologist for Germany during both world wars

George Sylvester Viereck's family emigrated to the United States in 1897. Viereck graduated in 1906 from the College of the City of New York, then began his lifetime work on newspapers and his overzealous commitment to political journalism and social controversy. During World War I he was employed by the German embassy to organize anti-British and pro-German propaganda and act as an apologist compelled to defend his native land against a hostile and misinformed American press.

Viereck was considered an excellent journalist. The appearance of his editorial in May, 1915, however, warning Americans not to sail on British ships—which appeared shortly before the *Lusitania* was torpedoed by a German submarine—generated not only strong anti-German feelings in the United States but also the incorrect belief that the German embassy had known the ship was to be sunk. During the 1920's Viereck wrote for William Randolph HEARST's press. The 1930's were his "Nazi interlude," when he enthusiastically supported Adolf HITLER, edited a Nazi news magazine, and organized covert propaganda on behalf of Germany National Socialist regime. Viereck was not an anti-Semite, however, and he refused to write anti-Semitic or anti-American propaganda.

In 1943 Viereck was convicted for violation of the Foreign Agents Registration Act and sentenced to prison for one to five years for his activities on behalf of Nazi Germany; he served four years. In his writings—which include several books, including *Confessions of a Barbarian* (1910), *My First Two Thousand Years: The Autobiography of the Wandering Jew* (1928), and *Men into Beasts* (1952)—Viereck emphasized four major propaganda themes: the importance of maintaining U.S. neutrality; the promotion of closer U.S.-German commercial and political ties; the dangers of an entangling alliance with Great Britain; and the exposure of a pro-Allies bias in the American news media.

— *Martin J. Manning*

■ Vietnam War: Communist-bloc propaganda

Philosophical differences between China and the Soviet Union marked the years of the Vietnam War

The Vietnam War occurred during the height of the Sino-Soviet split, at a time when CHINA and the Soviet Union (*see* Russia: 1953-1991) struggled for domination of the communist bloc and leadership of the international communist movement. Both China and the Soviet Union took advantage of the Vietnamese conflict between communist North Vietnam and the Republic of South Vietnam to propagandize against each other and to promote their own national interests. United States propaganda depicted the communist movement as a monolithic force that threatened the free world, but Vietnamese communists found themselves at times in opposition to the policies of both China and the Soviet Union. For example, China's rapprochement with the UNITED STATES in 1972 and the Soviet policy of peaceful coexistence under Premier Nikita Khrushchev were viewed unfavorably in Hanoi. Such policies posed a problem for the communist government of North Vietnam, which needed the support of the two communist giants and did not want to offend either government or be caught in a power struggle between the two. Despite official Chinese and Soviet propaganda that supported the communist struggle in Vietnam, the Vietnamese were extremely wary of China and of the Soviet Union and found the idea that the entire communist world was united behind North Vietnam was much closer to propaganda than to truth.

ANTI-AMERICAN PROPAGANDA Communist nations, however, exploited the Vietnamese conflict to embarrass the West and win favor among Third World countries and nonaligned nations. Communist propaganda portrayed the United States and its multinational corporations as a threat to the integrity and independence of smaller nations. The tone of communist propaganda was anticolonial and anti-imperialist and aimed at the United States, especially after President Lyndon B. Johnson committed U.S. ground troops to Vietnam and escalated the war

in the mid-1960's. The United States was depicted as a capitalist superpower that sought to suppress or undermine revolutionary struggles throughout the world. The United States and its South Vietnamese allies were villains, the North Vietnamese and the communist Viet Cong heroic underdogs. Communist propaganda portrayed the Republic of South Vietnam as a puppet regime of the United States. North Vietnam was portrayed as a brave country that fell victim to American aggression, including the brutal bombing of its cities and countryside. Vietnamese communists were depicted as the true patriots and the liberators of Vietnam. As early as 1959, the Beijing *People's Daily* said the "people of Vietnam would eventually smash the U.S. schemes of aggression."

China and the Soviet Union, true to Marxist ideology, wanted to be perceived as being in the vanguard of the struggle for national liberation and world socialism. In addition to carrying out propaganda campaigns, each country also sent extensive military aid to Vietnam, including technicians and, in the case of China, troops. Although China and the Soviet Union did not always agree with the tactics and policies of the Hanoi regime, both countries realized in the mid-1960's that the Vietnam War had become the focal point in the battle between communism and democracy and that it was incumbent to show support for the Vietnamese. Even so, the Sino-Soviet split came through in propaganda.

The Chinese were more aggressive in their propaganda than the Soviets, who believed, or said they believed, in peaceful coexistence. In opposition to the Chinese and Vietnamese, who had already begun the war against the South, a Soviet article in 1963 pointed out that the peaceful transition to socialism represented a form of revolution and that "opportunists" were wrong to claim that the transition to socialism needed to be achieved by violent methods. Yet, a year later, the Communist Party of the Soviet Union declared its support for the Vietnamese people's struggle "against the U.S. imperialists in South Vietnam." The Soviets condemned American bombing of North Vietnam in 1964, calling them provocations. The more militant Chinese went further; they organized a demonstration against the American embassy in Moscow on March 4, 1965, in which a number of demonstrators were hurt after police and soldiers were called in to disperse the demonstration. The Chinese accused the Soviet government of being more interested in placating the United States than in supporting the Vietnamese.

BEIJING VERSUS MOSCOW As the Sino-Soviet split widened, China and the Soviet Union intensified their propaganda campaigns against each other regarding the Vietnam War. The Chinese declared that the Soviets were collaborating with the United States and undermining the Vietnamese communists. Beijing opposed negotiations to end the war and said that the American bombing halts to promote peace talks were tricks of the Americans in alliance with the Soviets. The Chinese demanded that the Americans withdraw completely from Vietnam before peace talks could be held. Soviet propaganda countered the Chinese charges of betrayal by pointing out that the Soviets were Vietnam's main supplier of sophisticated military equipment and that the Chinese were stealing equipment shipped through China that was intended for Viet-

nam. The Soviets charged that the Chinese campaign aided American imperialism and hurt the war effort, accusations that the Chinese denounced as slander. Both sides accused each other of collusion with the United States.

The Vietnam War served as a propaganda backdrop for the two communist giants to lash out at each other and at the United States when it served their individual interests. North Vietnam as a result struck an independent foreign policy. Beneath the Marxist façade of a unified front against the capitalist class and world imperialism, fissures developed between the communist nation states. Despite the war in Vietnam, China and the Soviet Union both reached an accommodation with the United States.

SUGGESTED READINGS:

Harrison, James P. *The Endless War*. New York: Columbia University Press, 1989.

Karnow, Stanley. *Vietnam: A History*. New York: Viking Press, 1983.

Smyser, W. R. *The Independent Vietnamese: Vietnamese Communism Between Russia and China, 1956-1969*. Athens: Ohio University Center for International Studies, 1980.

— *Jeffrey Brody*

■ Vietnam War: North Vietnamese propaganda

Propaganda was crucial to the political goals of Ho Chi Minh and North Vietnam as early as the 1920's

The vital importance of propaganda as part of the North Vietnamese war effort dates to the early days of the Communist Party in the 1920's, when its leader, Ho

Vietnamese nationalist leader Ho Chi Minh at a reception in France in June, 1946; Ho proclaimed Vietnam's independence ten months earlier, but France did not recognize the nation's independence until years later. (*National Archives*)

CHI MINH, developed a strategy to rid Vietnam of French colonial rule (*see* ANTI-COLONIAL MOVEMENTS). Ho set out to build a national movement that would capture the spirit of Vietnamese patriotism and blend Marxism with the communal aspects of peasant life. He recognized that a communist movement would never predominate in Vietnam without a coherent, ongoing propaganda campaign to discredit not only the French but also noncommunist, anticolonial Vietnamese.

EARLY HISTORY Ho started the Revolutionary Youth League of Vietnam in 1925 to galvanize political support and founded a journal, *Thanh Ninh* (youth), to spread revolutionary thought. Following the example of the Russian Revolution in 1917, the league called for the destruction of French imperialism and the creation of a dictatorship of the proletariat. The writing in the journal, and Ho's call for independence and freedom, helped recruit Vietnamese tired of French rule to the communist cause. As the anticolonial movement grew in the 1940's, the communists organized the Vietnam Liberation Army Propaganda Unit as an integral part of their military campaign. Vo Nguyen Giap, the communist commander in chief, stressed the importance of political indoctrination. Giap called political work—educating soldiers in the philosophy of the Communist Party—the "soul of the army." Like the Russian army, the Vietnamese army used political officers to indoctrinate the troops.

After the French defeat at Dien Bien Phu and the establishment of communist rule in North Vietnam in 1954, Ho capitalized on his success as a propagandist in the emerging war against the newly formed Republic of South Vietnam and its ally, the United States. To Ho, the battle for the South, was a war of liberation that necessitated sacrifice on the part of North Vietnamese. The Communist Party exercised tight control—including censorship of the press—over the dissemination of information and the nature of political discourse in North Vietnam. When North Vietnamese troops conquered South Vietnam in April, 1975, they were surprised by the prosperity of the South and the level of development they saw—the soldiers had been told by the communist leadership that their brethren in the South were starving and on the brink of economic collapse.

THE WAR AGAINST THE SOUTH Communist military tactics against the Republic of South Vietnam emphasized the use of propaganda to foster rebellion and to turn peasants, soldiers, and intellectuals against the Saigon government by appealing to nationalistic and patriotic sentiment. The North Vietnamese used the National Front for the Liberation of South Vietnam (or Viet Cong) to engage in political warfare. Agitation and political warfare teams, trained by North Vietnamese cadres, infiltrated villages controlled by the South Vietnamese government and promised freedom, independence, and land reform. They delivered speeches, distributed hand-

bills, and put up banners and signs in villages denouncing the republic as an illegitimate regime that was the puppet of the United States. Building on their successful resistance to the French, the North Vietnamese communists and their Viet Cong allies stressed that their movement represented the true national aspirations of the Vietnamese people and that the Vietnamese were pawns of the American imperialists. The Viet Cong units also portrayed themselves as commoners willing to make the same sacrifices they asked of the people—unlike government officials and landlords who lived in the cities, the Viet Cong teams resided in rural villages, set up bases in the countryside, and recruited peasant children to join in the war effort. They treated the peasants with respect, but if persuasion failed to win over villagers, the Viet Cong were not above using terrorist tactics such as executing government teachers and those suspected of being disloyal.

The North Vietnamese encouraged Republican soldiers to surrender their arms and join the "people's struggle" for the liberation of their homeland. They repeatedly attacked the legitimacy of the Saigon regime in the South, denouncing it as a brutal, military dictatorship, and persuaded intellectuals that the communists would end foreign domination, establish democracy and realize the Vietnamese dream of independence.

THE WAR AGAINST THE AMERICANS When American troops entered the war, communist propaganda portrayed the United States as the "real enemy of the Vietnamese people" and communist troops as the true patriots. Radio Hanoi's "Voice of Vietnam" broadcast news of American atrocities, such as the My Lai massacre, and depicted American soldiers as blood-thirsty conquerors bent on destroying their land, raping children, and turning women into prostitutes. The Americans were depicted as an occupying power similar to the French colonialists and the Japanese who had controlled Vietnam during World War II.

Hanoi also attempted to win over world opinion by portraying itself as an underdog fighting against American aggression. North Vietnam took advantage of the media, releasing pictures of slain civilians and homes destroyed by American warplanes. They portrayed North Vietnam as a Third World country being unmercifully destroyed by the most technologically advanced country in the world. The North Vietnamese displayed photographs of bomb damage to win sympathy from people and governments in the free world. Their strategy was to undermine international (and American) support for the war by portraying American actions in support of South Vietnam as unjust and immoral.

SUGGESTED READINGS:

Harrison, James P. *The Endless War*. New York: Columbia University Press, 1989

McAlister, John T., Jr., and Paul Mus. *The Vietnamese and Their Revolution*. New York: Harper & Row, 1970.

— *Jeffrey Brody*

■ Vietnam War: South Vietnamese propaganda

The Republic of South Vietnam relied on propaganda to bolster its very existence

The Republic of South Vietnam faced a "credibility gap" from the time the coun-

try was created by the partition of Vietnam in 1954, to the end of the war in 1975. The communist Vietnamese in the North, led by HO CHI MINH, carried the nationalist mantle and claimed to be the true Vietnamese patriots because they had defeated the French during the colonial period and later resisted the Americans who bolstered the Saigon regime in the South.

From the very start of the republic, the South Vietnamese government of Ngo Dinh Diem found itself on the defensive in the battle for public opinion. Diem had to fend off North Vietnamese propaganda attacks that played on the historic animosity of Vietnamese toward foreign domination. A major dilemma that Diem, and the regimes that succeeded him, faced was that the more they depended upon American aid, the more they dug themselves into a hole in terms of the Viet Cong's propaganda campaign. The South claimed that it was fending off aggression from the communist North; the North claimed that it was fighting a war of liberation. The American buildup of a half million troops stationed in and outside cities—fighting all over the countryside—played into communist hands. South Vietnamese leaders had the unenviable task of convincing their people that they were in charge of the war and that the Americans, who were engaged in most of the fighting, were guests. This became exceedingly difficult as Americans took up an even larger part of the fighting.

HEARTS AND MINDS The South Vietnamese government needed to persuade the peasantry, which comprised 80 percent of the nation's population, that it represented the national aspirations of

A photographer's capturing on film of South Vietnamese general Nguyen Ngoc Loan shooting a man he suspected of being a Viet Cong did irreparable damage to American support for the South Vietnamese regime. (*AP/Wide World Photos*)

the Vietnamese. As John T. McAlister, Jr., and Paul Mus note in *The Vietnamese and Their Revolution* (1970), the recurrent pattern of more than two decades of warfare in Vietnam has been the "struggle by pro-Western, urban oriented governments to gain control over the countryside from village-based revolutionaries." To do so, the Republic of South Vietnam waged a campaign against communism that portrayed North Vietnam in COLD WAR terms as an evil client state of the Soviet Union and China. The ideological battle between the Free World and communism mattered little to Vietnamese villagers, however. As American researchers discovered, the tenets of Marxism (such as "from each according to his ability, to each according to his needs") blended better with the communal nature of peasant life than did capitalism, with its absentee landlords and tax collectors representing the Saigon regime. It was only after the North Vietnamese victory in 1975 when the communist state took away private ownership of land and private incentives to produce that the peasantry turned against the communist leadership. During the war, the South Vietnamese government was unable to win the hearts and minds of the rural people. Despite the assistance of American public relations experts and psychological warfare teams, the South Vietnamese government failed to sway public opinion in the countryside.

The South Vietnamese and Americans tried to influence opinion by producing films, television shows, radio broadcasts, newspapers, and pamphlets warning of the dangers of communism and the threat of domination by Moscow and Peking. Propaganda teams, including minstrels, spoke and performed in villages. In 1965, for example, the government dispatched some 7,450 psychological warfare workers to villages in the Mekong Delta, according to a 1967 American University study. The purpose was to offset the Viet Cong, which had its own agitation and propaganda teams.

The South Vietnamese attempted to undermine communist morale by encouraging North Vietnamese and Viet Cong to desert in the Chieu Hoi program, which offered assistance and amnesty to soldiers who fled. South Vietnamese and American pilots dropped leaflets over North Vietnam, urging villagers to rebel against the communists. Commando teams infiltrated the North by land, sea and air, but the South Vietnamese were unsuccessful in fomenting resistance or building a mass movement against the Hanoi regime.

EFFECTS ON THE AMERICAN PRESS Because of the repressive nature of South Vietnamese regimes from Ngo Dinh Diem to Nguyen Van Thieu, and the presence of an American press corps that operated throughout Vietnam without censorship, South Vietnam was fighting a losing battle for American public support.

The South Vietnamese, and the American military, attempted to portray South Vietnam as a free world bastion of democracy defending itself against communist aggression. In the early days of the war, correspondents wrote sympathetic stories, but as South Vietnamese forces suffered defeats on the battlefield and brutally suppressed dissent by Buddhists and students campaigning for democracy, many correspondents eventually turned against the South Vietnamese government and wrote critical accounts of the war that contradicted official pronouncements from Saigon and Washington. Pictures of Buddhists setting themselves on fire and of troops beating students led Americans to question the purpose of the war. Later, television footage of American troops burning South Vietnamese villages and communist troops sweeping into cities during the Tet Offensive of 1968 helped erode American support for the war. Reporting by the American media raised doubts about the official South Vietnamese and American military message that the North Vietnamese were being defeated on the battlefield and that there was "light at the end of the tunnel."

Correspondents scoffed at South Vietnamese government reports that the army of the Republic of South Vietnam (ARVN) was an effective fighting force. While the South Vietnamese attempted to show that their soldiers were as tough as their North Vietnamese counterparts, correspondents quoted American soldiers saying they had more respect for the communist troops than for their South Vietnamese allies.

The South Vietnamese finally fell victim to their own propaganda. They had always maintained that the United States would never desert them and that the Americans would send troops or bomb North Vietnam if Saigon were threatened. As the end drew near, in the final offensive of the war, however, American troops had withdrawn. The Republic of South

Vietnam found itself alone; on April 30, 1975, it surrendered to North Vietnamese troops.

SUGGESTED READINGS:

Area Handbook for South Vietnam. Washington, D.C.: U.S. Government Printing Office, 1967.

Harrison, James P. *The Endless War.* New York: Columbia University Press, 1989.

McAlister, John T., Jr., and Paul Mus. *The Vietnamese and Their Revolution.* New York, Harper & Row, 1970.

— *Jeffrey Brody*

■ Vietnam War: U.S. propaganda

The United States government relied heavily on propaganda to defend its military intervention in Vietnam

In order to justify the sacrifices and expenditures that accompany a nation's decision to go to war, government officials usually resort to the use of various propaganda techniques that stress that the conflict is a "just" war. Through the use of deception and distortion, these efforts utilize favorable ideas, SLOGANS, and doctrines and attack the credibility of the opponent's argument. During the Vietnam War, the United States adopted these tactics to neutralize the support Ho CHI MINH and the Viet Cong received from the American public following the U.S. military guarantee to defend its ally in South Vietnam.

ESTABLISHING LEGITIMACY, 1954-1963 After the French defeat in Vietnam in 1954, the United States undertook the responsibility of establishing an anticommunist government in the South. This task created a burdensome problem for American policymakers. Ho Chi Minh and the Vietminh's victory was directly related to their ability to depict themselves as the dominant nationalist force in Vietnam, and according to the Geneva accords, unified general elections were to be held in 1956. Thus any government that the United States supported in the South not only would be considered illegitimate and in violation of an international agreement but also would inevitably be viewed as a puppet government that had forsaken Vietnamese independence and favored a return to foreign imperialism.

Once the United States installed Ngo Dinh Diem as prime minister of Vietnam, it needed to create the impression that Diem enjoyed widespread support in the South and was not simply a figurehead who adhered to directives issued by the United States. This assignment was turned over to a former advertising executive and a CENTRAL INTELLIGENCE AGENCY official from the U.S. Air Force, Colonel Edward Lansdale, who devised and implemented a psychological warfare program in order to secure a solid bloc of support for Diem. Since more than a million Roman Catholics resided in the North, Lansdale utilized propaganda techniques to convince this group that they could only enjoy religious freedom if they relocated to the South and acknowledged Diem's leadership. Lansdale prompted this exodus by reminding northerners that Diem was also Catholic, and he distributed leaflets stating that "Christ has gone South" and that "the Virgin Mary has departed from the North." He also exacerbated Catholics' fears by stating that the communists would institutionalize atheism. Lansdale's propaganda

Vietnam

CHINA

MYANMAR
(BURMA)

Hanoi ★

LAOS

THAILAND

CAMBODIA

South

China

Sea

A n d a m a n

S e a

Ho Chi Minh City
(Saigon)

Vietnam in Southeast Asia

MALAYSIA

promised refugees land and livestock in return for political support, and he insinuated that the United States would eventually attack the North with nuclear weapons. These techniques convinced approximately a million Catholics to vote with their feet and become loyal Diem supporters in the South.

Psychological warfare continued to play a prominent role in American policy after this exodus. Playing upon the Vietnamese penchant for fortune telling, Lansdale published a book that predicted extreme horrors if the North succeeded in unifying the Vietnamese government under communist leadership. He also purchased space in Saigon's leading newspapers and helped published articles linking communism with antipatriotism. In 1956, along with Diem's brother Ngo Dinh Nhu, he helped establish Diem's claim to legitimacy by manufacturing a fraudulent political victory during South Vietnam's first national elections. Later on, radio transmitters were distributed throughout the countryside as American policymakers attempted to demoralize Ho's cadres in the South by broadcasting erroneous remarks and attributing them to the North. These practices continued throughout the war. In 1962, American officials sponsored an essay contest that awarded monetary prizes to those individuals who could describe the enemy in the most pejorative terms. Matchbook covers were also used to convey pro-government sentiments, and falsified documents were released indicating that a communist victory would result in forced labor, confiscation of property, and economic restrictions. While these endeavors produced limited results, they are a clear indication that the United States attempted to win the hearts and minds of the Vietnamese through the use of psychological warfare and military propaganda.

THE GULF OF TONKIN INCIDENT Before the United States formally committed ground troops in 1965, it supported and directed South Vietnamese commando raids against North Vietnamese coastal targets to gather intelligence and to convince Ho Chi Minh's government that it remained committed to a southern victory. Military advisers regularly participated in these exercises, and American warships steadily patrolled the northern coast off the Gulf of Tonkin.

On August 2, 1964, the American destroyer *Maddox* encountered three small North Vietnamese patrol ships. After these boats reportedly fired a series of torpedoes at the destroyer, the *Maddox* opened fire and chased the patrol back to shore. The aircraft carrier *Ticonderoga* launched a number of jets to pursue the boats, but the battle quickly ended. (There has been considerable debate, and no clear answer, as to whether the patrol boats actually fired on the *Maddox*.) The United States reacted by ordering a second destroyer, the *Turner Joy*, into the Gulf of Tonkin and began initiating additional commando raids against the North's coastal defenses. On August 4, both destroyers reported additional torpedo attacks from the North. As a result, President Lyndon B. Johnson asked Congress to grant him additional power to prosecute the war. The Gulf of Tonkin Resolution passed the House by a vote of 416-0 and the Senate, 88-2, and this act enabled Johnson to strengthen America's military role and to send ground troops to Vietnam.

Former U.S. general William C. Westmoreland at a press conference in January, 1982, refuting charges made a week earlier on *CBS Reports* that he had falsified reports on U.S. casualties during the Vietnam War. (*AP/Wide World Photos*)

The "incident" was essentially an act of American propaganda. During the debate over the resolution, the administration informed Congress that the attacks were un-

provoked, since the destroyers were in international waters. More important, no mention was made of the commando raids. Thus Johnson used deception to convince Congress to intensify the United States' commitment to the war, and after the conflict it was revealed that the second attack never occurred. Throughout the conflict, the American public remained unaware of the administration's efforts to incite hostilities with the North since the official explanation asserted that the United States was following a defensive, rather than an offensive, role in the Gulf.

SELLING THE WAR, 1965-1968 By the beginning of 1965 President Johnson and his advisers agreed that the United States should escalate its bombing missions and accept full responsibility for the prosecution of the war. The administration, however, needed to justify its intervention to the American public and offset some of the dissenting opinions coming from certain leading journalists and university professors.

On February 17, 1965, Johnson and the State Department released a White Paper, *Aggression from the North: The Record of North Viet-Nam's Campaign to Conquer South Viet-Nam,* which outlined its reasons for the additional commitment of air and ground troops for the war. Representative of classic military propaganda, this document was extremely selective and self-serving. It overlooked all the developments in Vietnam prior to 1954. It failed to mention the long-standing history of French and Japanese imperialism in Vietnam. It disregarded Ho Chi Minh's efforts to defeat the Japanese during World War II. This document also ignored the 1954 Geneva accords, which stipulated that national elections were to occur in 1956 to unify the country. Emphasizing the defensive nature of the American mission, this paper indicated that the United States was

simply protecting the democratic aspirations of the South Vietnamese people and that, like the Korean conflict, the war was a result of a Soviet- and Chinese-sponsored invasion to further the spread of international communism. Ho was portrayed as a socialist ideologue who was willing to wage a campaign of terror against the peaceful democratic government in the South. The document contained no material regarding American nation-building efforts or its relationship with Ngo Dinh Diem.

Meanwhile, domestic opposition continuing to grow, prompting President Johnson to answer his critics with his own propaganda campaign, "Target: College Campus," to counterbalance the aggressive and influential activity of the student antiwar movement. This plan called for government officials, members of Congress, and sympathetic college professors to visit campuses and speak on behalf of the administration's war efforts. The president also obtained outside funding for some college students to visit Vietnam in order to work with local youth groups and, it was hoped, to return to the United States and present a more favorable image of American activities on college campuses. Johnson's agenda led to a national conference at Michigan State University on June 1, 1965, with Vice President Hubert Humphrey as one of the featured speakers. Overall, however, such activities failed to erode opposition to the government's was policies.

From 1965 to 1967 the American military consistently stated that the United States was winning the war. Concerned with the emerging strength of the antiwar movement, President Johnson arranged for the commander of U.S. ground troops

■ Vietnam War: History at a Glance

Year	Event
1930	Ho Chi Minh founds the Vietnam Communist Party (VCP).
1945	August: Ho Chi Minh seizes power from the country's colonizing power, France, and proclaims the formation of the Democratic Republic of Vietnam (DRV); an eight-year-long war follows.
1954	July: After the French defeat, the Geneva Accords partition Vietnam into North and South. The VCP take over the North; the U.S. administration of Dwight D. Eisenhower soon begins to support the anticommunist government of Ngo Dinh Diem in the South.
1957	North Vietnam begins guerrilla incursions into South Vietnam.
1959	July 8: The first U.S. military advisers are killed in a Viet Cong raid.
1960	The North Vietnamese National Liberation Front (NFL) is formed.
1961	The United States begins to arm and supply South Vietnamese troops.
1962	President John F. Kennedy sends more military advisers and noncombatant troops to Vietnam.
1963	November 1: South Vietnamese leader Ngo Dinh Diem is killed in a military coup supported by the United States; an extended period of instability follows.
1964	General Nguyen Khanh becomes president of South Vietnam.
	General William C. Westmoreland is placed in command of U.S. troops in South Vietnam.
	August 2-4: North Vietnamese patrol boats attack U.S. destroyers in the Gulf of Tonkin incident.
1965	Military coup puts generals Nguyen Cao Ky and Nguyen Van Thieu in power in South Vietnam.
	March 7-9: First U.S. ground combat troops arrive in Danang
	March 30: The Viet Cong bomb the U.S. embassy in Saigon.
1966	Buddhist protests against the South Vietnamese government are repressed.
	April 12: First bombing raid by B-52s stationed in Guam; U.S. troops number almost 400,000 by the end of the year.
1967	First U.S. mining of North Vietnamese rivers; first B-52s to be stationed in Thailand arrive.
1968	January 30-February 29: Communist Tet offensive, a coordinated, simultaneous attack on many South Vietnamese.
	March 16: My Lai massacre of about 200 Vietnamese villagers by U.S. troops.
	March 31: President Lyndon B. Johnson halts U.S. attacks on North Vietnam north of the 20th parallel.
	May 10: Paris peace talks begin.
	William Westmoreland is replaced by Creighton Abrams as military commander in South Vietnam.
1969	"Vietnamization" of the war begins, with U.S. forces making South Vietnamese forces (ARVN) increasingly responsible for combat.
	February 23-March 29: Spring communist offensive; combated by massive B-52 bombing attacks northwest of Saigon and near Cambodia.
	April: U.S. troop number reaches its highest level, about 543,000.
	May 14: President Richard M. Nixon orders some U.S. troops withdrawn.
	North Vietnamese leader Ho Chi Minh dies in September.
1970	The United States admits that U.S. forces have been involved in combat in Laos; President Nixon announces further troop withdrawals.
	U.S. and ARVN troops invade Cambodia's border region.
1971	Publication of the Pentagon Papers in the United States provides information about the extent of U.S. involvement in the war.

1971 (cont.)	U.S. security adviser Henry A. Kissinger begins secret negotiations with the North Vietnamese.
	By the end of the year U.S. troops in Vietnam number 158,000, and all ground combat has been turned over to the South Vietnamese.
1972	March 30: Communist spring offensive begins.
	May 8: Nixon orders the mining of North Vietnamese harbors.
	October 26: Kissinger announces tentative agreement on peace plan.
	December: Talks are suspended, which leads to resumption of massive U.S. bombing raids.
1973	January 28: Cease-fire goes into effect.
	April 1: Last U.S. troops are withdrawn from Vietnam, leaving only civilian technicians.
1975	January: North Vietnam's final offensive.
	April 29: The last Americans are evacuated.
	April 30: South Vietnam surrenders to North Vietnam.
1976	July: National elections formally unite North and South.

and the person responsible for America's "search-and-destroy" philosophy, General William Westmoreland, to speak before the National Press Club in Washington, D.C., in November of 1967. The general reassured the audience that he was waging a successful war of attrition and that the Viet Cong and the North Vietnamese could no longer sustain high levels of troop involvement. This theory backfired, however, when the Viet Cong staged a dramatic uprising and attack, the Tet offensive of January, 1968. The United States quickly squelched this attack and systematically destroyed a considerable amount of the enemy's intelligence network and guerilla structure, but because of Westmoreland's earlier false optimism, public opinion was negative, the Johnson administration experienced another propaganda nightmare, and the antiwar movement gained additional momentum.

PROPAGANDA FILMS During the Vietnam War, the antiwar and draft resistance movements generated considerable morale problems for the American military (*see* ANTIWAR CAMPAIGNS). In addition, media reports were increasingly highly critical and indicated that the United States was losing the war. To sell the war to reluctant draftees, the Defense Department produced several propaganda films to enhance its reputation and to convince the soldiers that the successful prosecution of the war was within the national interest.

To offset the charge that the United States was pursuing an imperialistic foreign policy in Vietnam, the Defense Department released the film *Why Vietnam?* in 1965. This picture justified American intervention and argued that the war was not an indigenous civil war but part of an international communist conspiracy. It indicated that the National Liberation Front, or Viet Cong, lacked support in the South and depended upon Russian and Chinese sponsorship for its success. The film also contained compassionate images of American soldiers caring for Vietnamese children, and it concluded with a plea for a peaceful settlement from President Johnson. Throughout the film, the United States is portrayed as the defender of freedom and democracy in Vietnam while Ho Chi Minh and the North Vietnamese are compared to Germany's Adolf HITLER and other fascist regimes from WORLD WAR II.

Other films were intended to prepare soldiers for their tour of duty in Vietnam. Highlighting the various social and cultural differences between the two states, these films were an attempt to educate Americans about Vietnamese life. Both *The Unique War* (1966) and *Vietnam Village Reborn* (1967) contain footage of American technical, medical, and educational aid and are filled with Vietnamese statements regarding American kindness. These pictures, moreover, personify the Vietnamese culture as being childlike and lacking in sophistication, thus lending credibility to the paternalistic belief that Vietnam needed American aid for survival and development.

A third type of propaganda film featured American military campaigns and aspired to counteract media reports that implied that the United States was losing the war. *The First Infantry Division in Vietnam: 1965-1970* (1971) spotlighted one of the nation's most famous divisions, the Big Red One. After mentioning that this division had been fighting aggression since the American Revolution, the film focuses upon several encounters that resulted in enormous Viet Cong casualties. It also suggested that American involvement was necessary since the United States was the only superpower who possessed the firepower to thwart international communist expansion. *The Battle of Khe Sanh* (1969) contained similar ideas. The battle was criticized by the news media as being unnecessary, but this film represents the classic story of the American underdog. It shows how six thousand Marines were able to withstand an onslaught from more than twenty thousand North Vietnamese. Commentary by Khe Sanh's commanding officer, Colonel David Lownds, attacked the media and stated that the servicemen found their duty at the base to be personally rewarding and strategically important. But more important, by contrasting this battle with the French defeat at Dien Bien Phu in 1954, this film insinuated that the United States would succeed where the French had failed.

All these films were efforts to paint a more favorable picture of American intervention. They underscored the humanitarian aspects of the war, downplayed Vietnamese hostility toward the United States, and chastised the media for its analysis of the war. All contained numerous examples of the classic propagandistic techniques of deception and distortion.

NORTH VIETNAMESE PROPAGANDA AND THE AMERICAN PUBLIC Ho Chi Minh's government also utilized various propaganda techniques and established informal diplomatic ties with some of the antiwar movement's leadership in order to offset the Johnson Administration's interpretation surrounding the origins of the war. The North viewed their conflict as part of a larger democratic revolutionary crusade inspired by the American war for independence, and they realized that Johnson's White Paper overstated the roles of the Soviet Union, China, and international communism in Vietnam. By inviting antiwar activists to Vietnam and maintaining a permanent relationship with leading antiwar activists, Ho believed that he could convince the American public that the majority of Vietnamese opposed the U.S.-backed government in the South and desired unification with the North.

In July, 1965, a delegation from the Women Strike for Peace traveled to Indonesia and conducted meetings with senior members of the North Vietnamese government and with Viet Cong women. These officials presented a sharp contrast to Johnson's views. They produced evidence outlining American bombing of civilian targets including the complete destruction of schools, churches, and villages. They claimed that superior American firepower did not discriminate between innocent children and Vietnamese cadres, and more important, they refuted Johnson's claims of outside aggression. During Christmas, 1965, antiwar activists Tom Hayden, Staughton Lynd, and Herbert Aptheker journeyed to Hanoi and met northern representatives. After this trip, they published a book, *The Other Side*, which contained numerous reports of carnage and indiscriminate devastation from northern citizens and accused Johnson of thwarting the North's desire for peace. Additional antiwar missions followed, and in 1972, actress Jane FONDA was photographed with a North Vietnamese antiaircraft gun. Whether these propaganda efforts were successful remains debatable. Some historians claim that the antiwar movement's ties with the North actually helped drum up support for the war.

SUGGESTED READINGS:

Anderson, David L. *Trapped by Success: The Eisenhower Administration and Vietnam, 1953-1961.* New York: Columbia University Press, 1991. In addition to its extensive coverage of Eisenhower's policy in Vietnam, this book contains several examples of Edward Lansdale's propaganda activities during the 1950's.

Capps, Walter H. *The Unfinished War: Vietnam and the American Conscience.* Boston: Beacon Press, 1982. This book includes some especially helpful information on the 1965 White Paper and how both the American public and the North Vietnamese reacted to the Johnson administration's military propaganda.

Gibbons, William Conrad. *The U.S. Government and the Vietnam War: Executive and Legislative Roles and Relationships.* Part III: January-July 1965. Princeton, N.J.: Princeton University Press, 1989. This is the third volume in an ongoing series and serves as the official governmental source on the war.

Gitlin, Todd. *The Sixties: Years of Hope, Days of Rage.* New York: Bantam Books, 1987. Although it focuses more upon domestic politics than the Vietnam War, this publication reveals how the North Vietnamese attempted to influence the American antiwar movement through the use of its own propaganda machine.

Greene, Graham. *The Quiet American.* London: Heinemann, 1955. A classic fictionalized account of Lansdale's clandestine activities in South Vietnam during the 1950's.

Rowe, John Carlos, and Rick Berg, eds. *The Vietnam War and American Culture.* New York: Columbia University Press, 1991. An excellent source for articles on American military propaganda and how cultural perceptions have shaped American perceptions of the war.

Tang, Truong Nhu. *A Viet Cong Memoir: An Inside Account of the Vietnam War and Its Aftermath.* New York: Vintage Books, 1985. A helpful source on how the Viet Cong tried to reassure the American public that its victory would not produce a bloodbath in the South.

Young, Marilyn B. *The Vietnam Wars, 1945-1990.* New York: HarperCollins, 1991. One of the best overall accounts of the war, this source contains numerous accounts of American propaganda and psychological warfare.

— *Robert D. Ubriaco, Jr.*

■ Voice of America

U.S. international radio broadcast service formed in 1942

The Voice of America (VOA) is a branch of the United States Information Agency (USIA). In 1996 the VOA broadcast news and information programs around the globe in forty-seven languages on more than two thousand affiliated stations. The VOA, with more than three thousand employees by the mid-1990's, remains one of the largest propaganda organizations operated by the U.S. government.

ORIGINS The Voice of America was formed in response to Nazi propaganda during World War II. Concerned that German RADIO broadcasts were influencing the course of the war, officials in the Franklin D. ROOSEVELT administration urged the president to authorize an American propaganda effort. Roosevelt agreed, and the Office of the Coordinator of Information (COI), modeled after the British Special Operations Executive, was formed in July, 1941. The first COI director, William J. Donovan, and Robert E. Sherwood of the Foreign Information Service initially focused their energies on SHORTWAVE RADIO broadcasts, and the first program was broadcast in German in February, 1942. Programs in English, French, and Italian were quickly added to the broadcast schedule, and within two

months programs were airing twenty-four hours a day. More shortwave stations were acquired and the number of broadcasts increased throughout that year. In June, 1942, bureaucratic reshuffling placed the radio broadcasting operations within the U.S. Information Service, a branch of the OFFICE OF WAR INFORMATION (OWI). The international broadcast service eventually became known as the Voice of America (VOA).

In contrast to the bland reporting style employed by network news reporters, VOA's producer, John Houseman, favored dramatic and vigorous presentations that were intended to bolster the listener's morale. Because the VOA adhered to a policy of accurate reporting, broadcasts during the early years of the war often contained news of Allied losses. To counter the depressing effects of such news, VOA also included programs contrasting democratic values with the evils of fascism. The broadcasts also encouraged resistance in such occupied countries as France. After Houseman's departure in 1943 VOA broadcasts turned to a neutral presentation of news much like that of network broadcasts. New programs targeted at specific audiences such as women or workers were added to the broadcast schedules.

At its height during the war VOA broadcasted 168 hours of daily programming in more than forty languages. At the end of World War II some government officials called for an end to the program. President Harry S Truman abolished the OWI but advocated a continuing, though limited, broadcasting effort to inform the international community about American society and policies. Funding and staff reductions diminished the size and effectiveness of the broadcast service, and the future of the VOA was in jeopardy. With the perception of a new threat to America's security, however, the agency was revitalized in the late 1940's.

THE COLD WAR After World War II Americans had become increasingly anxious about the intentions of their former ally, the Soviet Union. Government officials were concerned that Soviet leader Joseph STALIN planned to dominate Western Europe. Moreover, Soviet news broadcasts to European nations had grown increasingly negative toward the United States. In response VOA aired its first Russian-language program in February, 1947. The following year Stalin ordered the jamming of VOA broadcasts to Eastern Europe. As relations between the two countries worsened, the United States stepped up its radio propaganda efforts, and VOA appropriations increased from $6.9 million in 1946 to $21.7 million in 1953. The United States also created additional broadcast services such as RADIO FREE EUROPE and Radio Free Asia.

The VOA audience included people in nations aligned with the United States, in areas such as Latin America, nations considered neutral in the ideological struggle between communism and democracy, and people in Eastern Europe living under Communist rule. VOA maintained its policy of accurate reporting, but it also engaged in political commentary aimed at the failures of communism. Writers were encouraged to use restraint in their comments but to present a positive and exciting presentation to their listeners. Some American politicians regarded the policy of restraint as misguided and called for a more strident anticommunist format.

However, concern that the international broadcasts might inspire political rebellion that the United States could not support led to a return to moderation in reporting in the mid-1950's. About the same time Congress and President Dwight D. Eisenhower cut the budgets of many government programs, including that of VOA, to cut government spending.

Renewed tensions between the superpowers in the early 1960's led to increased funding for the VOA. The new president, John F. Kennedy, showed a strong interest in international affairs and supported the broadcast service. The new director of the USIA, Edward R. Murrow, regarded objective reporting as a limitation. He believed that VOA should directly influence international attitudes and opinions. However, this period of renewal was short-lived. Kennedy's successor in the White House, Lyndon B. Johnson, had little interest in VOA programs. Moreover, increasing divisiveness in American politics over foreign-policy goals led to reduced congressional funding for VOA programs.

DETÉNTE AND THE REAGAN YEARS The status of the VOA did not improve during the 1970's and the agency's budget, when adjusted for inflation, remained static. Presidents Richard M. NIXON and Jimmy Carter attempted to improve relations with the Soviet Union in a policy known as détente, which caused confusion about the VOA mission. Opponents of the détente policy called for continued criticism of the Soviet Union and its policies. Supporters of the policy wanted the VOA to reduce its coverage of Soviet affairs so as not to endanger relations between the two nations; this position ran counter to the VOA policy of objective reporting. As a result of these conflicts Congress and other observers began to question both the role and importance of the VOA in American foreign policy.

The abandonment of the détente policy and the return to an intense ideological conflict between the United States and the Soviet Union in the 1980's again invigorated the VOA. President Ronald REAGAN, who had a high regard for the power of the media and propaganda, employed the VOA in his foreign policy efforts. The Reagan administration also created a new radio propaganda outlet aimed at Cuba, RADIO MARTÍ. Budget appropriations for the VOA increased, and a $1.6 billion modernization program of the VOA's facilities was undertaken. By 1986 VOA stations were broadcasting 2,353 hours of programming per week, with two hundred hours a week in Russian and other languages spoken in the Soviet Union. A 1987 report concluded that 129 million people around the world listened regularly to VOA broadcasts.

The Soviet Union took the VOA broadcasts seriously. During the détente era the Soviet government had stopped jamming VOA broadcasts, but the practice was resumed during the 1980's. The Soviet Union spent approximately $300 million annually to jam VOA and other foreign broadcasts. In 1987, as another thaw in superpower relations occurred, the U.S.S.R. again stopped jamming the programs.

The history of the Voice of America reveals an ongoing conflict regarding its mission. Recognizing that accurate reporting was essential for gaining the trust of its audience, the VOA committed itself to objective reporting. However, as an agency of the United States government it was also a propaganda instrument for American policies. The clash between objectivity and support for U.S. foreign policy became a particularly serious issue during the détente era, when many VOA reporters believed their agency was censoring stories on aggressive Soviet actions. During eras when the United States was unified in its concern over national security, appropriations for the VOA increased; thus, during World War II, the Korean War, and the crisis years of the early 1960's, the VOA received additional funding and support from the White House and Congress. During eras when national security was not as pressing an issue, or support for foreign policy was not unified, support for the VOA waned; the late 1950's and the decade of the 1970's were periods of limited support for the VOA. Though support for the Voice of America has waxed and waned, it seemed unlikely that in the age of mass communication the United States would abandon its radio broadcast propaganda efforts.

SUGGESTED READINGS:

Alexandre, Laurien. *The Voice of America: From Detente to the Reagan Doctrine.* Norwood, N.J.: Ablex Publishing, 1988.

Alexeyeva, Ludmilla. *U.S. Broadcasting to the Soviet Union.* New York: U.S. Helsinki Watch Committee, 1986.

Hansen, Allen C. *USIA: Public Diplomacy in the Computer Age.* New York: Praeger, 1989.

Shulman, Holly Cowan. *The Voice of America: Propaganda and Democracy, 1941-1945.* Madison: University of Wisconsin Press, 1990.

Tyson, James L. *U.S. International Broadcasting and National Security.* New York: Ramapo Press, 1983.

— *Thomas Clarkin*

W

■ Walesa, Lech

Born September 29, 1943, in Popowo, Poland: Polish labor leader, founder of the Solidarity movement, and statesman

Lech Walesa, an electrician at the Lenin Shipyard in Gdansk, Poland, was an activist in the free trade movement that evolved into the Solidarity movement. Like many Poles, Walesa was a nationalist and ardent Roman Catholic who resented the satellite status of communist Poland. Deteriorating economic conditions in the 1970's and 1980's, coupled with the demoralized Polish Communist Party, led to a widespread and profound lack of confidence in a government that was seen as repressive and corrupt. Political activists were able to mobilize these feelings to create a broad-based political structure, the Solidarity movement, that challenged the legitimacy of the government.

Solidarity was committed to nonviolent struggle as a means of resistance to the weakened TOTALITARIANISM of the Polish regime. Its main goal was to provide a cure for the economic, political, and religious distress of the nation. Its program included demands for civil liberties and rights, the rule of law, and the end of submission and passivity. It promised a kind of social pluralism that would provide the Polish people with the necessary conditions for "physical, mental, and moral development."

The Solidarity movement needed more than political organization to succeed in its vision; it needed to publicize its aims and activities. When Solidarity organizers began to lead a series of paralyzing strikes, the world press took increasing note. The movement's visibility in the world MEDIA, a result of the ease of MASS COMMUNICATIONS, made it difficult for the government to proceed against it physically, nor was it possible to control the dissemination of information about Solidarity-led events. Martial law was imposed in the country and Walesa was arrested, but Solidarity SLOGANS such as "there is no freedom without Solidarity" contributed to the successful mobilization of political unity in Poland and public opinion in the West.

Walesa made good use of the media during the rise of Solidarity. As leader of Solidarity, he debated Prime Minister Mieczslaw Rakowski on Polish television on November 30, 1988, an unprecedented event that was watched by an estimated 78 percent of Polish adults. The media also publicized the support of the Polish pope, John Paul II (Karol Wojtlya), who served as a source of inspiration, unity, and caution during the rise, repression, and rebirth of Solidarity. The pope's intervention in this deeply Catholic country was of inestimable value and contributed to preventing the Soviet Union from taking stronger action against the movement than it did (*see* RUSSIA: 1953-1991).

Central to the success of Solidarity was the personality of Lech Walesa. He was a model example of a charismatic personality and had a natural empathy with ordinary people. Walesa was able to personify resistance; he once declared, "Go down to the shipyards. Talk to any man there. Everyman's story is my story." This rapport was genuine and reciprocal. Moreover, Walesa's humble working-class roots, his religiosity, and his willingness to take personal risks put him in the tradition of the romantic rebel, an appealing type in Polish culture. This image was reinforced by a rough-hewn appearance that many perceived as being typically Polish.

Walesa's skills as labor leader, activist, and statesman are indisputable. His successful leadership of the Solidarity movement was recognized by many international awards, including the Nobel Peace Prize in 1983, and culminated in his being elected president of Poland in 1990.

— *Melvin Kulbicki*

■ Wallace, George

Born August 25, 1919, in Clio, Alabama: Governor of Alabama

George Wallace became active in DEMOCRATIC PARTY politics in the 1940's and 1950's; he served in the state assembly (1947-1953) and as a district court judge (1953-1959). He ran for governor of Alabama in 1962 as a staunch segregationist, vowing to resist the federal government's order to integrate Alabama's schools (*see* CIVIL RIGHTS MOVEMENT).

Wallace came to national attention when he remained true to his campaign promise. In June, 1963, he barred the way of two black students attempting to enter the University of Alabama. Wallace's high-profile confrontation personalized the race issue and made him a populist hero in his own

region. By stepping forward so conspicuously he made himself the symbol of all those forces in the South that were resisting federal authority and promoting what they called states' rights. Many other Southern politicians had done battle with the federal government, but none had so vividly shaped the public mood as the scrappy, charismatic Alabama governor.

Although Wallace was initially viewed as merely one of many Southern segregationists, his appeal began to extend to Northerners who opposed the effects of court-ordered integration in their areas. Wallace's adamant claim that a people had a right to resist government programs and edicts became popular in the North as well.

As a propagandist, Wallace was an excellent entertainer and manipulator. He loved confrontations with long-haired student demonstrators. He enjoyed twitting Northern liberals about their ideas. His down-to-earth style and his use of name-calling and CHARACTER ASSASSINATION (a favorite technique of propagandists) made him a powerful and dangerous speaker who was able to excite strong emotions among both his followers and detractors.

In 1968 Wallace ran for president in a THIRD-PARTY MOVEMENT. Although he had no real chance to win the election, he did well in several Northern democratic primaries. He ran not as a segregationist but as a populist who claimed to be expressing the will of the people against "pointy-headed liberals" and their sympathizers in the media. One of his strongest appeals was for law and order. Because his campaign came during a turbulent decade that saw many mass demonstrations in the streets, those voting for Wallace believed they were supporting a position that would restore civil order to the country.

Wallace campaigned for president again in 1972. By this time, during President Richard NIXON's administration, the term "silent majority" had been coined, and Wallace could capitalize on a strong conviction in the country that he had united the regions in their opposition to unjust federal authority. He drew large crowds who were familiar with his style, and he could dismiss his liberal critics with an epithet.

Wallace's presidential campaign ended when Arthur H. Bremer attempted to assassinate him, leaving him paralyzed below the waist. Wallace continued his political career, but the virulence of his political positions and especially his propagandistic skewing of peoples' emotion gradually ended. Later in life he apologized for his early segregationist positions, but his reputation remains that of a brash politician who tried to foment tensions between the races by appealing to anger and fear.

— *Carl Rollyson*

■ War bonds

Fund-raising device used by national governments in wartime

President Franklin D. ROOSEVELT purchased the first Defense Savings Bond from Secretary of the Treasury Henry Morgenthau, Jr., on April 30, 1941. This led to an appeal to all Americans, both civilian and military, to purchase bonds to help finance the war effort during World War II.

War bonds, as U.S. Treasury bonds came to be known in February, 1942, were sold in different ways. Initially they were sold in denominations of twenty-five, fifty, one hundred, five hundred, and one thousand dollars. They could be bought outright for 75 percent of their face value, or by collecting Savings Stamps until the bond value was attained. In this way everyone, from the wealthy to children and those barely getting along, could save for bonds. War bonds paid 2.9 percent interest and matured in ten years.

The government relied heavily on propaganda to sell the bonds. One of the principal arguments was that everyone in the country had the means to support the war effort. People who were unable to fight could still do their part by buying war bonds to preserve the country's future.

Bond sales were promoted by companies, communities, CHURCHES, and war-finance committees. There were usually speakers and music connected with promotions. Notable persons gave speeches and sang patriotic songs, and even Boy Scouts and Girl Scouts sponsored campaigns to sell bonds.

Organizers of bond rallies periodically broadcast appeals on the radio and in newspapers, playing on the emotions of those listening and appealing to their listeners' feelings of guilt, pity, and sympathy. Advertising campaigns also promoted the sale of war bonds. Patriotic posters depicting battle scenes with patriotic slogans of how the individual could support the war effort appeared everywhere, from billboards, match book covers, and magazine advertisements to the folders that held the savings stamps. Slogans to buy bonds appeared on almost everything that was produced in print. Local film theaters advertised war bond sales with all films that were shown. War bond advertising was a common feature of everyday life during the war.

Howard Chandler Christy's war bonds painting is typical of the mildly provocative "Christy girl" posters he produced during World War I. (*National Archives*)

The sale of war bonds appealed not just to patriotism but also to economic self-interest. Some of the advertising raised the specter of what disasters the future could hold if war bonds were not purchased to support the armed forces. Purchasing war bonds allowed the participants to believe they had joined others in a common effort.

— *Larry N. Sypolt*

■ War casualties

Inaccurate casualty reports can serve as effective propaganda in wartime

The first casualty of war is TRUTH. From time immemorial, imprecise or inaccurate casualty figures have been used as propaganda. The destructiveness of war, coupled with inaccurate records of the numbers of people involved in conflicts, makes it inherently difficult to verify or establish accurate counts of war casualties. Inaccurate or deliberately false STATISTICS can easily serve to minimize losses and exaggerate those of the enemy and thus change the way a conflict is perceived.

Understating combatant casualties hides an enemy's effectiveness both from that enemy and from the troops facing the enemy. Minimizing figures helps to keep up morale among the troops and on the home front, and when used together with CENSORSHIP can cover up mistakes in command or hide deaths that have resulted from "friendly fire." Both sides in the two world wars minimized their casualties to keep the public in ignorance of the true situation and for covert propaganda purposes.

Some propagandists deny war casualties altogether: There are those who reject as propaganda the fact that millions of Jews and others died in Nazi concentration camps (*see* GERMANY: 1918-1933). Belligerents often dismiss the number of noncombatants killed during war, by claiming that the numbers offered by the enemy cannot be either believed or verified. Disagreements over the numbers of people obliterated as a result of the HIROSHIMA AND NAGASAKI BOMBINGS have been used in nuclear weapons debates to create scenario estimates of the number of people who may die in the event of a future nuclear war. Understating or inflating the projected casualties in an imagined nuclear war can serve a partisan advantage.

To establish or increase domestic support for war, governments and other propaganda agitators have chosen falsely to inflate the numbers of their troops killed or to exaggerate the horror of the manner of their deaths by fabricating stories of brutal and barbaric massacres. During the VIETNAM WAR the U.S. Defense Department accused the Viet Cong of atrocities that were meant to increase domestic support for the war; the department was also accused of padding its reports of Vietnamese "body counts" to create a false image of success.

Even when governments, or the military, report combat casualties accurately, they may do so in a manipulative way. They may, for example, issue reports of the numbers killed in irregular installments. The first, partial, casualty number, even when followed by other, more complete, numbers, is sufficient to create a false first impression that remains in the public mind.

The evasive practice of reporting casualties with vague statistical adjectives such as "light" or "moderate" rather than with actual numbers is used to disarm domestic opposition to a conflict. Military language likewise draws on euphemism to camouflage noncombatant causalities. DOUBLE-SPEAK terms such as "collateral damage" and "circular error probability" create confused impressions about a war and leave people puzzled but too uninformed to protest. The "kill ratio" is a method that avoids using accurate percentile numbers in favor of fuzzy proportions.

Manipulating combat losses may support a lost cause, protect a general's reputation for effective command, or glorify a monarch's reign. Some of the casualties depicted in MURAL ART found in the tombs of the pharaohs are revealed by a form of propaganda art that entirely omits the fact of defeats and portrays stalemates as victories.

— A. J. L. Waskey

■ War crimes

Because propaganda often precedes the commission of war crimes, it has been used as part of the proof of intent to commit such crimes

War crimes are defined as crimes against humanity and as violations of international humanitarian law. The modern history of war crimes begins with the Charter of the International Military Tribunal in 1945. The tribunal was formed to try the leaders of Nazi GERMANY for war crimes committed before and during WORLD WAR II. The major Nazi leaders were tried in Nuremberg, Germany, beginning in 1946, in a series of trials known as the Nuremberg Trials. These were followed by trials elsewhere involving other Germans, and

similar trials were conducted against leaders who had determined policy in JAPAN during World War II.

The Charter of the International Military Tribunal defined four acts that are central to war crimes law. Crimes against peace include planning, preparing, initiating, and waging wars of aggression as well as wars that violate treaties and international agreements. War crimes involve violations of the laws and customs of war; such violations include the murder, ill-treatment, or deportation to slave labor of civilians, the murder or ill-treatment of prisoners of war, the killing of hostages, the plunder of public and private property, and the wanton destruction and devastation of cities and towns without military necessity. Crimes against humanity involve the murder, extermination, enslavement, deportation, and other inhumane acts committed against civilians; persecution on political, racial, and religious grounds is also a crime against humanity. Last, a common plan or conspiracy to commit any of the foregoing crimes is itself a criminal act.

War crimes have been further defined by the UNITED NATIONS. A 1948 convention provides for the punishment of genocide. The Geneva Conventions of 1949 provide for the protection of civilians, prisoners of war, and the sick and wounded in time of war. In 1993 and 1994 the United Nations created international tribunals to prosecute persons responsible for violations of international humanitarian law in Rwanda and the former Yugoslavia.

Because propaganda has often been used to set the stage for war crimes, the 1948 convention to punish genocide also makes it illegal to incite anyone to commit genocide. Propaganda figured promi-

Nazi war criminals on trial at Nuremberg after World War II. (*AP/Wide World Photos*)

nently in the proof of war crimes at the Nuremberg Trials. The Indictment of the Military Tribunal listed doctrinal techniques of the common plan and conspiracy to commit war crimes, among them inciting others to join in the conspiracy by disseminating doctrines about the German "master race" and its right to subjugate, dominate, and exterminate other peoples. The tribunal's definition was based on the fact that German propaganda prepared the way for the persecution of entire groups such as the Jews and Slavs and that it paved the way for the Nazis' waging war against peoples they considered not part of the master race.

Similar forms of propaganda emerged during the 1980's and 1990's in the former nations of Yugoslavia, particularly Serbia and Bosnia. In the BOSNIAN CIVIL WAR "ethnic cleansing" was directed against the Bosnian Muslims by their Serb neighbors, which resulted in genocide and the forced relocation of entire populations.

— *David E. Paas*

■ Wells, H. G.

September 21, 1866, in Bromley, England—August 13, 1946, in London, England: British writer and futurologist

Most of the more than 150 books and pamphlets by H. G. Wells are concerned with the possibilities open to humankind to refashion itself and shape its own future by the power of will and imagination. Following in the steps of T. H. Huxley, the eminent Victorian biologist Under whom he studied at the Normal School of Science in London, Wells early in his career as writer and teacher espoused a theory of evolution that set nature against human beings and emphasized the potential of the human mind to conquer nature by initiating and controlling change. Partly as a result of the resounding popular success of his scientific romances *The Time Machine* (1895) and *The War of the Worlds* (1898), Wells came to assume the role of leading prophet to his age. In a long series of prophetic writings, from *Anticipations* (1901) and *A Modern Utopia* (1905) to *The Outline of History* (1920), *The Salvaging of Civilization* (1921), and *The Shape of Things to Come* (1933), he undertook both to warn against the fate in store for humankind should it remain passive before the forces of nature and to map out a plan for political, social, and moral reform based on a scientific model of education that would lead to the greatest possible happiness for humanity as a whole. In the writings of his middle years Wells dramatically argues the need to establish "the World State," a new order in which all frontiers, including such obstacles to an enlightened humanity as nationalism, ignorance, superstition, and subconscious fears, would be overcome. His work as president of the International Association of Poets, Playwrights, Editors, Essayists, and Novelists (PEN) in the 1930's was largely devoted to encouraging its members to create a new vision of the world by spreading the message of the World State as he imagined that state should and might be. All writers, as he urged in his essay "Democracy Under Revision" (1927), should strive not to serve art for art's sake but to produce "creative propaganda" intended to serve humanity's practical needs. Aware though he was of the dangers built into that philosophy of writ-

ing—his novel *The Autocracy of Mr. Parkham* (1930), for example, tells the story of a university don whose dream of "making" rather than documenting history is associated with Benito Mussolini's vision of conquest—Wells insisted that literature should not reflect things as they are or have been but express the most progressive ideas and embody the will of humankind. In his own writings he favored the use of catchwords, SLOGANS, and vivid phrases, techniques he imitated from the practice of newspaper journalists and writers of political speeches. As indicated in his *An Experiment in Autobiography* (1934), Wells preferred to think of himself as a "journalist." In the last years of his life Wells observed that he had overemphasized the potential of the human will and the power of creative propaganda to shape the future. The triumph of nature over human beings prominently figures in his philosophical meditation *The Conquest of Time* (1942), and in *The Mind at the End of Its Tether* (1945) he reckons that the "story" of humankind is "played out," that all possibilities have been exhausted.

— *Camille R. La Bossiere*

■ White propaganda

Open and straightforward propaganda that makes no pretense at being anything but propaganda is called white. Such INFORMATION has a positive function, as in sustaining morale in wartime, improving the health and security of a nation (*see* IMMUNIZATION CAMPAIGNS), or ending the mistreatment of animals (*see* PEOPLE FOR THE ETHICAL TREATMENT OF ANIMALS). It is the opposite of black propaganda, which is aimed at external targets and pretends to be other than what it is. White propaganda includes recruiting posters, health campaigns, materials promoting a cause, and commercial ADVERTISING.

■ Why We Fight

Series of training films produced by the United States Army to prepare American soldiers for battle in World War II

The United States entered WORLD WAR II suddenly, following the Japanese attack on Pearl Harbor in December, 1941. Many Americans were relatively uninformed about the specifics of the conflict, in part because the war was being fought on another continent. This lack of information made it more difficult to motivate soldiers to enlist and to fight.

In 1942 the chief of staff of the U.S. Army, General George C. Marshall, requested the film director Frank CAPRA to develop a series of documentaries to convey six specific messages to recruits: the rightness of the cause; the difficulty of the job; confidence in their comrades and leaders to win the war; confidence in the integrity and fighting ability of the Allies; resentment of enemies; and a belief that military victory would result in a better world.

Capra eventually produced seven films, each approximately fifty minutes long, whose titles indicate his approach to the task: "Prelude to War"; "The Nazis Strike"; "Divide and Conquer"; "The Battle of Britain"; "Battle of Russia"; "Battle of China"; and "War Comes to America." The films provided both long- and short-range analyses of the conflict. Overviews of World

War I, of the rise of National Socialism in Germany, of the growth of fascism in Italy, and of the evolution of imperial rule in Japan provided a context for world affairs, whereas extensive explanations of the philosophies of the Axis and the Allied powers drew a sharp distinction between the two groups. Analysis of recent military and political activity, such as the Polish campaign and the German occupation of Denmark and Norway, showed the power and aggression of the Axis powers.

Capra faced a significant challenge in developing propaganda for people who were being asked to make an enormous sacrifice. He had to demonstrate that the enemy was so powerful and menacing that the forces of good (the Americans and their allies) needed to make every sacrifice to overcome them. At the same time, the director had to show soldiers that the American side had not only the resolve but the ability to win the war. He achieved this delicate balancing act by producing a brilliant amalgamation of images drawn from a variety of sources: official news releases and authoritative speeches from government officials, map montages, and vignettes from the home front and the war zone. Capra included existing footage from NEWSREELS, created new film as needed, and even borrowed from the propaganda films of Axis powers to reinforce the effect of realism. Although the tone of the documentaries could be highly emotional, with spirited background MUSIC and editing to heighten the differences between the two sides, the overall effect was that of a "factual" presentation.

The *Why We Fight* series was a significant propaganda tool in World War II, but it also served as the stimulus material for one of the seminal studies in the history of mass communication research. Researchers who measured the effectiveness of the films found that they were extremely useful in improving the soldiers' factual knowledge about the war but far less useful in altering their attitudes or behavior.

— *Edward J. Lordan*

■ Wilson, Woodrow

December 28, 1856, in Staunton, Virginia—February 3, 1924, in Washington, D.C.: President of the United States (1913-1921)

From his days as a professor of politics at Princeton University until his entry into national affairs in the election of 1912, Wilson studied how a leader might shape public opinion. Throughout his first term as president, Wilson used personal speeches to Congress, press conferences, and speaking tours to get his views across to the American people. He spoke of the need of the president to take "common counsel" with the electorate, and he promised "pitiless publicity" in the conduct of national affairs. While he employed the resources of the Democratic Party in the elections of 1914 and 1916, he did not develop any explicit agencies within the government to convey the administration's positions to its citizens.

Once the U.S. war with Germany began in April of 1917, however, Wilson established the COMMITTEE ON PUBLIC INFORMATION, headed by the former journalist George CREEL. The agency's charge was to guide and shape public attitudes about the war while avoiding direct censorship and interference with the press. The Creel committee focused most of its attention on its domestic audience. It enlisted speakers, especially the "Four-Minute MenFOUR-MINUTE MEN" who gave speeches of that length, provided films and phonograph records, and distributed literature that praised the nations allied with the United States. Creel called it "the world's largest adventure in advertising." It also represented the first official propaganda agency in the nation's history. In important ways, however, the reliance on the CPI undermined Wilson's larger purposes of an expanded American role in world affairs. Since the committee offered a simplified and melodramatic interpretation of the conflict—in which the Germans were unadulterated evil—it became difficult for Wilson to convince Americans of the need for overseas involvement once the war was over.

On the world scene Wilson proved an effective propagandist on his own during WORLD WAR I. His speeches on behalf of "peace without victory" and his Fourteen Points captured the imagination of a world weary of fighting. Once he arrived at the Paris Peace Conference in 1919, however, Wilson seemed to forget most of the lessons of news management he had once known. Reporters received very little news about the workings of the conference, and Wilson kept most of the information to himself. As a result, the impressions in the United States about the resulting Treaty of Versailles and the League of Nations allowed the president's opponents to define the debate. When the Senate seemed likely to block the treaty, Wilson engaged in his last great propaganda campaign with a speaking tour on behalf of the League of Nations. He seemed to be making headway with the public when he collapsed physically.

At the post-World War I peace conference in Paris in 1919, British premier David Lloyd George (left), Italian premier Vittorio Emanuele Orlando, French premier Georges Clemenceau, and U.S. president Woodrow Wilson constituted the "Council of Four." (*Library of Congress*)

Although the treaty failed in the Senate, the force of Wilson's ideas regarding the United States' place in the world remained powerful and attested his skill as a spokesman for his own philosophy. In that sense, Wilson showed himself to be one of the most effective users of propaganda in the modern world.

— *Lewis L. Gould*

■ WIN campaign

President Gerald Ford's "Whip Inflation Now" campaign

The UNITED STATES experienced economic downturns in the 1970's, and economic forecasts and assessments predicted a gloomy future. Industrial production was low and unemployment high, and there was a growing trade deficit. Consumer confidence was said to be the lowest it had been in twenty-eight years. According to a Gallup poll, 51 percent of Americans believed the United States faced a major depression, and 70 percent saw worsening economic times in the near future. Moreover, the gross national product (GNP) declined and inflation accelerated to an adjusted annual rate of 11.5 percent. From the economic morass, inflation was singled out as the main culprit by Congress and the president.

Proposals to fight inflation were submitted by members of the DEMOCRATIC PARTY and REPUBLICAN PARTY. Because Democrats were calling for government controls on wages and prices, President Ford offered an alternative economic plan. Ford's campaign adopted the slogan "Whip Inflation Now," known by the acronym WIN; it was set up to work as a voluntary effort without resorting to governmental intervention.

Overall the Ford agenda was reminiscent of the rhetoric of World Wars I and II. He called for an all-out homefront mobilization, warning in his October 15, 1974, speech on television that "we will not be out of the economic trenches by Christmas." President Ford's administration hoped that their form of economic propaganda would steer public opinion toward a favorable reaction to administration economic policies.

— Daniel L. Mitchell

■ Wodehouse, P. G.

October 15, 1881, in Guildford, England—February 14, 1975, in Southampton, New York: British writer who was accused of collaborating with the enemy in World War II

Probably the most popular writer of humorous fiction in the twentieth century, Pelham Grenville Wodehouse in 1941 became involved in a controversy in which he was widely thought to have willingly served as an agent of Nazi propaganda.

Wodehouse was living in France at the outbreak of WORLD WAR II. After failing to heed warnings of danger, he was trapped there when the German army invaded in May of 1940. Two months later he was placed in internment as an enemy alien and summarily shipped off to a series of makeshift prison camps, arriving at the last of them, a converted insane asylum in southeast GERMANY, in September, 1940. Here he settled down as best he could to write and await his sixtieth birthday, upon which date he was to be automatically released.

In May, 1941, Wodehouse wrote a humorous article on his experiences as a civilian internee and showed it to one of the camp officials, who suggested that he might do a series of RADIO broadcasts to the then-neutral UNITED STATES to let his American readers know how he was faring. Wodehouse replied that there was nothing he would like better. On June 21—four months before turning sixty—he was surprised to find himself released from internment and taken to Berlin, where the idea of radio talks was again suggested. Wodehouse readily agreed and, writing in the same light-hearted vein as his earlier article, prepared and then recorded five talks, the first of which was broadcast via SHORTWAVE radio to America on June 28, 1941.

When it became known in England—which was then under nightly attack by Luftwaffe bombers—that Wodehouse had spoken over radio from Berlin, the reaction was immediate and furious. Although almost no one in GREAT BRITAIN knew anything of the broadcasts' innocuous content, the simple fact of his having made them sufficed to justify accusations of TREASON. Undoubtedly the most damaging attack was that of journalist William Connor, who in a widely heard radio commentary accused Wodehouse of becoming a propagandist for the Nazis in return for his release from internment. Made at a time when the truth was unknown to all but a handful of people, Connor's attack so effectively turned public opinion against Wodehouse that to this day it is widely believed that he had been a willing and knowing collaborator.

At first taken by surprise by the violent reaction to his seemingly harmless broadcasts, Wodehouse soon came to realize that he had committed a grievous error in judgment. Cut off for a year from all news of the progress of the war, he had had no conception of the reaction that an English people enduring nightly air raids and fearing possible invasion would have regarding any semblance of enemy collaboration by a well-known figure. A too-trusting nature and an apparent temperamental disinclination to dwell on life's less pleasant aspects left Wodehouse ill-prepared to deal with the cynical manipulation he met with in Nazi hands.

Wodehouse moved to Paris later in the war and was living there with his wife when the city was liberated by Allied forces in August, 1944. After a lengthy interrogation by Major Edward Cussen of British Military Intelligence, who found him guilty of nothing save extreme foolishness, Wodehouse was released with the advice not to return to England—which in fact he never did. Moving to the United States in April, 1947, Wodehouse continued to write until his death in 1975 at the age of ninety-three. Official British forgiveness had come a few weeks earlier in the form of a knighthood, but Major Cussen's exonerating report was not publicly released until five years later. Wodehouse scholar Richard Usborne has speculated that

Wodehouse may have been making an oblique rueful comment when he had a character in his novel *Joy in the Morning* remark, "You can never trust a writer not to make an ass of himself."

— *Allen Crocker*

■ Woman suffrage movement

International campaigns to gain the vote for women

The goal of the woman suffrage movement was to gain the right of women to vote in political elections. This right included voting in local and state as well as national elections and was often achieved incrementally. The movement was international; however, individuals and organizations in the United States and Great Britain are the best known and were the most influential.

ORIGINS OF THE MOVEMENT An early, possibly the first, appeal for voting rights came from Margaret Brent of the Maryland colony in 1647. Women in New Jersey who met the required property or residence criteria briefly held the right to vote from 1790 to 1807. However, the first significant public action in the United States came in 1848. At the Seneca Falls, New York, Convention, Elizabeth Cady Stanton included in her "Declaration of Sentiments and Resolutions" the controversial resolution calling for the "sacred right to the franchise."

The British movement had its initial voice in Mary Wollstonecraft's *Vindication of the Rights of Woman*, published in 1792. Its second important proponent was Harriet Taylor Mill, wife of John Stuart Mill.

The headquarters of a woman suffrage referendum campaign in Ohio in 1912. (*Library of Congress*)

He submitted an amendment to the Reform Bill of 1866 that would have given English women the vote, but it failed to gain Parliament's support.

Although the movement ebbed and flowed through the nineteenth century, the period between the 1890's and 1920's was the most active period for both the supporters and opponents to the enfranchisement of women. The earliest victory occurred when national voting rights were given to women in New Zealand in 1893. Australia followed in 1902.

The controversy over woman suffrage and its advocacy was based on social and political criteria. The propaganda techniques on both sides of the issue took various approaches, so while the goal of each group was clear, the means for achieving it varied from educational tracts to dramatic public demonstrations. Differing ideological and militant stances were especially apparent within groups working for enfranchisement and found expression in print and speeches—some serious and reasoned, others emotional, others humorous and witty. Public meetings, editorial cartoons, poster art, and both peaceful and aggressive marches and demonstrations were all part of the myriad propaganda techniques employed to bring the issue to the attention of the politicians and the public who would eventually determine the woman suffrage issues.

SUFFRAGE IN THE UNITED STATES The differing ideological approaches of the suffragists in the United States have been summarized by scholars as the "natural right" or justice position and the "expediency" argument. The natural right argument had its roots in the philosophical principle that "all men are created equal" and was extended to women by its advocates because they too were human beings. The expediency rationale recognized the Natural Right or justice position but extended it to include any rationale which would accomplish their goal, the vote for women. Early advocates of woman suffrage espoused the natural right or justice approach and had their chief spokesperson in Elizabeth Cady Stanton and their prime activist in Susan B. Anthony. The expediency advocates were led by Carrie Chapman Catt, who assumed the presidency of the National American Woman Suffrage Association (NAWSA) in 1900. Catt's leadership, the involvement of younger women, and the beginning of the Progressive movement in American politics brought a revitalization and activism to the American movement. The constituency of the suffragist membership broadened to include an appeal to women and men from a wide spectrum of the population. The causes supported moved from the solely political sphere to the arena of social action—for example, the passage of child labor laws.

Activism, with its concomitant publicity and public display and controversy in the press, was accelerated by Alice Paul and the National Woman's Party (NWP). Their goal was specifically political and was concentrated at the national level. Their focus was the DEMOCRATIC PARTY, the 1916 election, and a constitutional amendment providing the right to vote for women. The issue where the two organizations (the NAWSA and the NWP) met in policy and strategy was that of a constitutional amendment giving women the right to vote, which was finally achieved in the United States in 1920.

Opponents of woman suffrage were popularly known as the "antis" (from "antisuffragists"). They too had several strains of emphasis and their own internal differences; however, their argument centered on several basic themes. They began with a basic disapproval of the concept of the right of women to vote and found a voice in churches, the press, and prominent public figures. As the suffragist movement strengthened its organizational base, opponents recognized the need for state groups and finally for the National Association, a women's group opposed to woman suffrage, and its male counterpart, the Man-Suffrage Association. The thrust of the opponents' argument was mainly ideological. Their view can be briefly described in the following way: A woman's proper sphere for exercising her influence on society's morals is home and motherhood; moreover, women do not have the physical capacity to enter or participate fully in the political process. Darwinism became a vehicle for antisuffragist propaganda, as did examples of early women leaders who negatively affected their countries, such as Cleopatra and Marie Antoinette. The antis' publicity vehicle was a journal, *The Woman's Protest*.

SUFFRAGE IN GREAT BRITAIN In Britain the movement for enfranchisement of women involved local organizations and was the subject of parliamentary debate during the last half of the nineteenth century. In 1903 serious organization and militancy began when Emmeline Pankhurst founded the Women's Social and Political Union. British suffragists differed from their American counterparts in their political approach. They chose to act independently of all political parties and opposed the government in power prior to the granting of the vote. In addition to speeches, publications, and rallies, their technique may also be described as "vigorous agitation." This was perhaps most dramatically demonstrated by Emily Wilding Davison, who died as a result of throwing herself in front of the king's horse.

Great Britain too had its "antis" movement. Its leader was Mrs. Humphrey Ward, who was influential in founding the Woman's National Anti-Suffrage League in 1908. Its publicity vehicle was *The Anti-Suffrage Review*. By 1911 it had merged with the Men's League and became the National League for Opposing Woman's Suffrage. British opposition differed from that in the United States in two ways: The women members were largely upper class, and the leadership against suffrage came mainly from prominent and influential men.

World War I was an important milestone for the British suffragist movement. The suffragists focused their energies in support of the war effort and were therefore sympathetically received by the populace. In 1918 the vote was granted to women age thirty or over, and by 1928 the age limit was changed to twenty-one or over.

SUGGESTED READINGS:

Camhi, Jane Jerome. *Women Against Women: American Anti-Suffragism, 1880-1920*. Brooklyn, N.Y.: Carlson, 1994. Comprehensive discussion of the anti-suffragist theories and tactics, including a chapter on the well-known writer Ida Tarbell.

Harrison, Brian. *Separate Spheres: The Opposition to Women's Suffrage in Britain*. New York: Holmes & Meier, 1978. Contains examples of propaganda, humorous and serious, used by suffragists and antis.

Kraditor, Aileen S. *The Ideas of the Woman Suffrage Movement, 1890-1920*. New York: Columbia University Press, 1965. Comprehensive coverage, including historical background, the arguments and ideologies of the pro- and anti-suffrage leaders, and constituencies to which they both appealed.

Rover, Constance. *Women's Suffrage and Party Politics in Britain, 1866-1914*. London: Routledge & Kegan Paul, 1967. This thorough study of the suffrage movement in Britain covers the arguments and tactics of the constitutional societies and the militants, and those of the anti-suffragists.

Tickner, Lisa. *The Spectacle of Women: Imagery of the Suffrage Campaign, 1907-1914*. Chicago: University of Chicago Press, 1988. Provides extensive examples of cartoon art, banners, photographs, and posters showing the wide spectrum of propaganda employed in England.

Wheeler, Marjorie Spruill, ed. *One Woman, One Vote*. Troutdale, Ore.: New Sage Press, 1995. Nineteen articles covering important topics on the woman suffrage movement in the United States. This volume is the companion text to the "One Woman, One Vote" production in the Public Broadcasting Service's *American Experience* series.

— *Ann Thompson*

■ Works Progress Administration

Federal Depression-era program created in 1935

The Works Progress Administration (WPA) was a NEW DEAL program created during the administration of Franklin D. ROOSEVELT in response to the economic crisis of the Great Depression. Headed by Harry Hopkins, the WPA provided jobs to nearly three million unemployed Americans until it ceased operations in 1943. While some WPA assignments involved construction or building restoration, agency officials also created several innovative cultural programs. Because critics charged that WPA jobs were of no real value, Hopkins and his staff employed propaganda techniques to improve the agency's image.

PUBLICITY EFFORTS Propaganda efforts of the WPA had two goals: to secure popular support for its programs and to counter charges that it was a make-work agency that wasted or stole public funds. Under Hopkins's capable leadership, the WPA ran an effective publicity program that used a variety of communications methods. As one of the largest New Deal agencies, the WPA had an accordingly large publicity division, which in 1937 had forty employees. Publicity was divided into two departments: press and information. Employees responded to public telephone calls and letters for information and developed programs using publications, posters, exhibits, and films to disseminate information about specific projects. The agency also possessed a news ticker in order to keep abreast of any press reports, positive or negative, regarding the WPA. Each state had a publicity agent, who re-

ceived assistance from one of the six regional publicity officials. The extensive publicity department did not escape public scrutiny. Referring to the agency's publicity efforts in 1937, one congressman accused the WPA of issuing propaganda.

Agency publications included *Our Job with WPA*, a pamphlet distributed to agency workers, and the *Digest*, which collected and organized press reports of WPA activities for use by agency officials. The WPA also used motion pictures to promote its projects. Harry Hopkins wanted to use the agency's Motion Picture Record Division to produce newsreels depicting agency successes. When this proved impossible, he turned to a private filmmaking company, which received a contract in 1936 to produce and nationally distribute thirty newsreels about agency programs. This venture received considerable criticism from members of the motion picture industry, many of whom were uncomfortable with the use of private companies to produce newsreels that were obviously propaganda. Because of the controversy, Hopkins did not repeat the experiment. The WPA produced its own short films, including titles such as "Work Pays America" and "We Work Again," and encouraged film theater owners to show them to the public.

Perhaps the most effective publicity tool was the various projects that the WPA organized. The Federal Theatre Project presented plays, puppet shows, and other performances, often to audiences which had never attended the theater. The project also produced the "Living Newspapers," which dramatized contemporary events and often portrayed the Roosevelt administration in a positive light. By the end of 1936 an estimated sixteen million

Americans had attended a project performance, and by 1939, the year the program ended, some thirty million Americans had attended an event. The Federal Art Project allowed artists to decorate public buildings with murals and teach art and crafts classes to the general public. Music performances across the country drew millions of listeners, and radio broadcasts attracted millions more. Finally, the Federal Writers' Project published hundreds of books, including ethnic studies and city and state travel guides which were popular with the general public. Though these innovative programs drew the wrath of critics who saw no reason for the government to sponsor such activities, the cultural programs appealed to many Americans, placed the agency in a positive light, and increased public support for both the WPA and the New Deal.

In addition to the cultural programs, WPA projects of a more practical nature served to broaden agency support. In 1936 the WPA responded to disastrous floods that inundated parts of the Northeast. Approximately fifty thousand WPA workers battled rising waters, assisted the homeless, and cleaned and repairs towns devastated by the floodwaters. Agency cameramen recorded the WPA relief efforts, and press releases touted the efforts of the workers.

DEFENDING THE WPA The WPA became one of the best-known of the New Deal programs, so it received criticism from opponents of Roosevelt's policies. Attacks increased as the 1936 presidential election neared; Republicans hoped that discrediting the WPA would cost Roosevelt votes. Despite projects such as the flood relief operations, critics charged that WPA workers received paychecks for leaning on shovels instead of engaging in productive activity. They also claimed that agency officials were corrupt, giving work to their friends and pocketing money. Given the size of the agency and its numerous projects, examples of waste or fraud were not difficult to find. In addition, Harry Hopkins had become a public figure, and his prominence made him a target for the critics. Like President Roosevelt, Hopkins projected a dynamic image that some Americans enjoyed and others detested. His opponents charged that Hopkins was using the WPA to build a political machine.

Recognizing the need to maintain a positive public image, WPA officials responded with a press campaign to prove that many popular stories about WPA mismanagement were incorrect. Hopkins defended this practice in Congress, arguing that people in a democracy had the right to accurate information. He also made radio addresses and speeches refuting his critics, often accusing them of partisan interests.

SUGGESTED READINGS:

Adams, Henry H. *Harry Hopkins*. New York: G. P. Putnam's Sons, 1977.

Leuchtenburg, William E. *Franklin D. Roosevelt and the New Deal*. New York: Harper & Row, 1963.

McCamy, James L. *Government Publicity: Its Practice in Federal Administration*. Chicago: University of Chicago Press, 1939.

McJimsey, George. *Harry Hopkins: Ally of the Poor and Defender of Democracy*. Cambridge, Mass.: Harvard University Press, 1987.

Steele, Richard W. *Propaganda in an Open Society: The Roosevelt Administration and the Media, 1933-1941*. Westport, Conn.: Greenwood Press, 1985.

— *Thomas Clarkin*

■ World War I

1914-1918: International conflict in which the United States, Great Britain, France, and their allies defeated Germany, Austria-Hungary, and the Ottoman Empire

The systematic use of propaganda as a modern weapon of war began with World War I. The war began with the assassination of the Archduke Franz Ferdinand, heir to the throne of the Austro-Hungarian Empire, by a Serbian nationalist on June 28, 1914. The Austrians made several demands on Serbia and issued an ultimatum. When Serbia did not reply satisfactorily by July 28, Austria-Hungary declared war. GERMANY entered the war in support of its ally, Austria-Hungary. RUSSIA entered to support Serbia, and FRANCE and GREAT BRITAIN entered to support Russia and oppose Germany. By early August of 1914 all of Europe was at war.

PROPAGANDA IN EUROPE From the beginning, all the warring nations organized campaigns to win the support of their own people for the war effort. In Germany a group of staff officers at the High Command was assigned to generate propaganda on the home front. They began by issuing completely fictitious news bulletins about the French, British, and Russians sabotaging German water supplies and invading Belgium. They managed to convince most German citizens that the German armies were acting in self-defense.

The British enlisted the support of their citizens by issuing stories of German atrocities in Belgium. Many stories included such horrors as the rape and mutilation of children. Most of these stories were later proved to be exaggerations, if not complete inventions, but they served their purpose. As the war went on, propaganda techniques became more sophisticated and a wide variety of media were used. Carefully edited personal accounts of battle found their way into the popular press. The reports of war correspondents were also censored to present an optimistic picture of the progress of the war. Cartoons and drawings published in magazines and NEWSPAPERS often portrayed enemy atrocities.

In the days before mass media like RADIO and TELEVISION, POSTER ART was considered one of the most effective ways to get a message across to a large number of people. All the warring nations produced many posters for recruiting purposes. Some became very well known, as thousands of copies were produced and distributed.

Photographs were used extensively during World War I (*see* PHOTOGRAPHY AND PHOTOJOURNALISM). The invention of small, lightweight cameras and color film made photography a valuable tool of World War I propagandists. Photographs were censored by all the warring nations, and most nations had war photographers who were assigned to produce officially approved photos. Scenes of immaculate trenches and neat, smiling soldiers were often posed by the photographers. Public demand for pictures was high, and there was often a short supply, so newspapers and magazines used many photos of dubious authenticity. Many photographs were falsely captioned, and a few were complete fakes. Films, too, were used by all the warring parties. Official filmmakers carefully cut in scenes shot in training or staged after battles to make sure that the public saw only positive images.

PROPAGANDA IN THE UNITED STATES
Both German and British propagandists flooded the United States, which was at first officially neutral in the conflict, with art and literature designed to enlist support for one side or the other. The Germans targeted recent German immigrants to the United States and Irish Americans who might be hostile to the British. The British appealed to the traditional cultural ties between the United States and Great Britain. British propaganda, which usually portrayed the Germans as vicious monsters, played an important part in drawing the United States into the conflict in 1917.

The United States entered World War I as a result of unrestricted submarine warfare by the Germans in the north Atlantic. War was declared after several U.S. ships were sunk in the early spring of 1917. President Woodrow WILSON created the COMMITTEE ON PUBLIC INFORMATION by executive order one week after Congress declared war. It was headed by George CREEL, and its purpose was to mobilize American public opinion in favor of the war. The committee instituted voluntary press censorship, produced films, hired speakers, commissioned posters, and bought newspaper ads. It was extremely successful in its efforts, both at home and in Europe. Leaflets were dropped from airplanes and even shot from guns to get the American message to the German people.

Posters were an important feature of the American propaganda campaign. More than nine million posters were printed in 1918 alone (*see* POSTER ART). The artist Charles Dana Gibson coordinated a volunteer effort called the Division of Pictorial Publicity, which met weekly in New York City and in a year and a half produced almost fifteen hundred designs for posters, postcards, buttons, and banners. Most of the posters were upbeat and patriotic, but some portrayed the Germans as brutal monsters. Their intent was both to enlist support for the war effort and to stir up negative feelings against the enemy. Probably the most famous wartime poster was American painter James Montgomery Flagg's "I Want You" (1917), which shows "UNCLE SAM" pointing a finger directly at the viewer. This poster was used in both world wars and eventually more than four million copies were distributed.

The Committee on Public Information also hired seventy-five thousand "FOUR-MINUTE MEN," whose job was to give talks at public gatherings to sell WAR BONDS and recruit soldiers. Their speeches and poems stirred up patriotic fervor with accusations of murder and treachery by the Germans and the invocation of the blessing of God on the American war effort.

These activities were undertaken by all parties in the name of winning the war. In Germany propaganda efforts began to fail only near the end of the war, when food was scarce and defeat became inevitable. Only then did a majority of Germans turn against the war. In the United States the efforts were enormously successful, and the American public overwhelmingly supported the war throughout U.S. involvement. Most British and American citizens were willing to relinquish a measure of freedom to assure allied victory in the war, and most were willing to accept the assertion of British author and the propagandist Hillaire Belloc that "[i]t is sometimes necessary to lie damnably in the interests of the nation."

SUGGESTED READINGS:

Asprey, Robert B. *The German High Command at War: Hindenburg and Ludendorff Conduct World War I.* New York: William Morrow, 1991.

Gilbert, Martin. *The First World War: A Complete History.* New York: Henry Holt, 1994.

Haythornthwaite, Philip J. *The World War One Source Book.* London: Arms and Armour, 1992.

— *Deborah D. Wallin*

■ World War I: British propaganda

Great Britain developed an effective propaganda organization in the course of the war

GREAT BRITAIN entered World War I with little preparation to wage an effective propaganda war. Nevertheless, by 1918 Britain's propaganda organization was widely recognized as the world's finest. Over the four years of the war British propaganda efforts contributed significantly to the final victory of the Allies over the Central Powers. British propaganda targeted four chief constituencies: domestic public opinion (designed to attract recruits into the army and bolster civilian support for the war), Britain's wartime allies, neutral opinion (especially in the UNITED STATES; *see* NEUTRAL COUNTRIES DURING WAR), and the morale of the enemy.

ORGANIZATION During the first two years of World War I British propaganda efforts were marked by a number of competing and overlapping agencies that included the War Propaganda Bureau (known as Wellington House), the News Department, operating out of the Foreign Office, and the Neutral Press Committee at the Home Office. Other propaganda offices worked out of the War Office, in particular the military intelligence division called MI7, and the Admiralty. By 1917 Prime Minister David Lloyd George ordered the creation of a Department of Information to concentrate propaganda efforts. Finally, in March of 1918 British propaganda operations were centralized in the MINISTRY OF INFORMATION, headed by the Canadian newspaper magnate Max Aitken (Lord Beaverbrook). The Enemy Propaganda Department, known as Crewe House, came into being under the British newspaper editor and proprietor Lord NORTHCLIFFE. Yet even with these administrative changes, responsibility for various aspects of the propaganda war remained split. Crewe House handled propaganda directed at enemy countries, while the National War Aims Committee (NWAC) oversaw domestic propaganda. Wellington House had responsibility for all other operations.

CONDUCT From the beginning of World War I Great Britain instituted measures designed to mobilize public opinion and to repudiate German propaganda. CENSORSHIP was imposed on the press. Measures were taken to reassure allies of Britain's contribution and commitment to the war. British propaganda stressed the heroism of the British soldiers, contrasted with those who decided to remain safely at home, and the barbarism of the Germans. The earliest propaganda campaign in the war operated by the Parliamentary Recruiting Committee (PRC) sought to raise volunteers for the British army. Leaflets, mass rallies, and posters (*see* POSTER

ART) were used to encourage enlistment. Military bands and speakers toured the country to rally support for the war.

Along the western front a battle of leaflets developed (a practice introduced by the Germans). In October, 1914, the British Army distributed propaganda leaflets along sections of the western front. Wellington House employed noted writers, among them G. K. Chesterton and Sir Arthur Conan Doyle, to write pamphlets with titles such as *To Arms* (1914) and *Letters to an Old Garibaldian* (1914). Under the auspices of the War Office, MI7 distributed millions of leaflets and single-sheet newspapers over enemy lines by airplane, balloon, and combat patrols. German soldiers were forbidden to have enemy propaganda material in their possession. British propaganda aimed at weakening the morale of the German combat soldiers by trying to convince them that their chances of victory were slight. The kaiser was a popular target for British propaganda. More than eight million leaflets were distributed, chiefly by balloon, during the final three months of the war.

Films played a significant role in the propaganda war (*see* FILM: WORLD WAR I). Mobile cinema vans employed by the PRC toured Britain, showing patriotic films such as *Our Navy* and *With the Royal Flying Corps in France. Britain Prepared* (1915) and *Battle of the Somme* (1916) proved effective propaganda films for domestic and overseas use. Wellington House also distributed postcards, cigarette cards, and photographs. Posters served as a highly effective medium as well with millions printed and displayed. A cadre of artists made contributions through their war paintings and exhibits.

The United States was the focus of the most important propaganda campaign in a neutral country. From the start of World War I American opinion divided along three lines: pro-German, pro-Allied, and proneutrality. Hampered by the severing of overseas cable lines by the British, German propaganda in the United States was inept and clumsy. Common ties of language and culture gave a great advantage to the British in the conduct of the American propaganda war. German actions also provided a ready-made supply of material for British propagandists. The sinking of the *Lusitania* in 1915 and the disclosure of the Zimmermann telegram of 1917 played into British hands. British propaganda portrayed the Germans as brutal barbarians and as aggressors lusting for world conquest. Germany's resort to unconditional submarine warfare reinforced these negative images. After the entry of the United States into the war in 1917, the British Bureau of Information, later renamed the British Pictorial Service, opened in New York; it made wide use of film.

ATROCITIES ATROCITY PROPAGANDA played a significant role in the propaganda war. The invasion of Belgium at the beginning of the war placed Germany on the moral low ground from the outset; Germany's violation of international law and treaty obligations outraged world opinion. Stories of German atrocities in Belgium surfaced after the invasion: civilians shot or deported to Germany as forced labor; the looting and destruction of innocent villages; the raping of women and young girls, the bayoneting of babies, and torture. Although many of these stories were fabricated or exaggerated, Germany's disregard of international law and the brutal treatment of Belgian civilians provided ample fodder for propaganda.

Germany's October, 1915, execution of Edith Cavell for assisting Allied soldiers in Belgium was afterward used as a powerful propaganda weapon against the Central Powers—particularly because Cavell had also nursed German soldiers. (AP/Wide World Photos)

A number of atrocities were central to the propaganda war. The execution of British nurse Edith Cavell by a German firing squad for giving aid to Allied soldiers trying to elude capture shocked world opinion. Germany's destruction of the medieval town of Louvain, with its great churches and libraries, was used to furnish further evidence of German barbarity. On May 7, 1915, the sinking of the British passenger liner *Lusitania* by a German submarine with the loss of 1,198 lives, 128 of them American, outraged American opinion. The Germans defended the sinking by claiming that the ship was carrying munitions (which in fact it was). Subsequently, when the Germans unwisely commissioned a

medal to commemorate the sinking, British propagandists produced and distributed a replica of the medal to fuel anti-German sentiment. These events, coupled with the resumption of German unconditional submarine warfare and the Zimmermann telegram, all played a part in the eventual American entry into the war. By late in the war, stories appeared in the British Press reporting the operation of "corpse factories" behind the German lines utilizing bodies in the production of glycerine. The Ministry of Information did little to block or discourage these fabricated stories. Following the war, disillusionment set in among the British public. Portions of the wartime propaganda campaign were exposed as either false or exaggerated. This situation contributed later to the widespread disbelief of stories about atrocities against Jews in Nazi Germany and later reports of the death camps.

PROPAGANDA IN ENEMY COUNTRIES   British propaganda became increasingly offensive in nature as the tide of the war began to turn in favor of the Allies. Propaganda from Crewe House helped foment the already great internal tensions among the various nationalities of the Austro-Hungarian Empire. With the failure of Germany's 1918 spring offensive (designed to win the war before the Americans arrived in large numbers), British propaganda concentrated its attention on the battle-weary German soldiers. The Allies often captured German soldiers with British propaganda material in their pockets.

British propaganda contributed to the mobilization and maintenance of public support for the war effort. It was a significant factor in the entry of the United States into the war, and in the last months of the war sophisticated British propaganda probably did help accelerate the collapse of Germany. Ultimately, however, although propaganda played an important role in the war, it was not a war-winning weapon. The British propaganda organization was quickly dismantled following the war. Not until the threat of Adolf Hitler's Germany emerged in the 1930's did Britain begin once again to prepare for a major propaganda war.

SUGGESTED READINGS:

Bourne, J. M. *Britain and the Great War, 1914-1918.* London: Edward Arnold, 1989.

Roetter, Charles. *Psychological Techniques in the World War.* New York: Stein & Day, 1974.

Sanders, M. L. "Wellington House and British Propaganda During the First World War." *Historical Journal* 18 (1975).

Sanders, M. L., and Philip M. Taylor. *British Propaganda During the First World War.* London: Macmillan, 1982.

Taylor, Philip. "The Foreign Office and British Propaganda During the First World War." *Historical Journal* 23 (1980).

Wilson, Trevor. "Lord Bryce's Investigation into Alleged German Atrocities in Belgium, 1914-1915." *Journal of Contemporary History* 14 (1979).

————. *The Myriad Face of War: Britain and the Great War, 1914-1918.* Cambridge, England: Polity Press, 1986.

— *Van Michael Leslie*

■ World War I: Central Powers propaganda

The propaganda disseminated by Germany, Austria-Hungary, Bulgaria, and the Ottoman Empire was predominantly defensive

The Central Powers of World War I—Germany, Austria-Hungary, Bulgaria, and the Ottoman Empire—waged largely defensive propaganda campaigns as they responded to charges of atrocities. Since film remained a fledgling medium and radio had not yet been invented, printed material such as books, pamphlets, newspaper articles, and posters dominated these efforts.

In May of 1915 the British government published the Bryce Report (nicknamed the "blue book" for the color of its cover), which purported to document the Turkish massacres of Armenians (*see* ARMENIAN GENOCIDE). Though made to look like the product of disinterested academic research, the document often relied upon dubious sources. In response the Central Powers began to compile and publish their own annual atrocity reports. The German "white books" were culled from diplomatic and army dispatches, often as shocking as they were unsubstantiated. The allegations ranged from British use of "dum-dum" bullets to French and Belgian civilians gouging out the eyes of wounded German soldiers. As the war progressed, the white books paid special attention to the treatment of German prisoners of war in French and Russian camps. The French were accused of plundering and murdering German prisoners; one report even claimed that a French Turk had traveled the country displaying the decapitated head of a German prisoner. Though many of the accusations were based upon sworn testimony of imprisoned German officers, they often constituted little more than "hearsay" evidence. Following suit, Austria-Hungary created its "red book." The initial edition of 1915 detailed Serb emasculations and mutilations of prisoners of war and in one instance even accused them of roasting a pro-Austrian civilian alive. The red book of the following year charged the Montenegrins with cutting off the noses and ears of Austrian wounded and the Italians with committing mass rapes in the "liberated" town of Friuli.

Although Germany and Austria-Hungary dominated the Central Powers' international propaganda effort, Bulgaria waged a smaller, and perhaps ultimately more successful, propaganda campaign that succeeded in dissuading the United States from declaring war on the small Balkan nation. The Bulgarians directed their propaganda efforts through a pair of American missionaries visiting their country: the two returned home and convinced key members of the U.S. Congress and State Department that the Bulgarian people were overwhelmingly pro-American, had no interest in Germany's imperial ambitions, and simply wanted to regain territories lost in the Balkan Wars. The Bulgarians subsequently established a propaganda bureau in Washington to combat anti-Bulgarian materials disseminated the Serbian and Greek legations.

In contrast, the propaganda efforts of the Ottoman Turks were more successful with the domestic than the international audience. Perhaps the boldest move by the Ottoman sultan was to reinvent his flagging Turkish Empire as a pan-Muslim state: On November 15, 1914, he declared a *jihad*, or holy war, against the Balkan "infidels" to whom the empire had ceded territory only the year before. During this same period the Turks waged a fairly successful propaganda campaign to encourage mass emigration of Muslims from cession areas in the Balkans such as Montenegro. However, the sultan showed the hollowness of his pan-Muslim ideal when he used the banner of religious orthodoxy brutally to put down insurrections by rebellious Muslim populations within his empire. Less than a month after the sultan had declared his *jihad*, a pan-Arabic movement (*see* PAN-ARABISM) centered in Mecca had declared its own holy war against him. If Turkish propaganda had little appeal in the Muslim world, it had even less among the Allied nations, which were horrified by reports of the collective deportation and massacres of Armenians in 1915. The Allies did not accept Turkish propaganda that sought to justify its genocidal measures on the basis of Armenian atrocities—for example, the reported burning to death of all five hundred members of a Muslim village in the province of Van. The atrocity stories disseminated by the Turkish news agency seldom saw print in European newspapers beyond Germany; a bias against Islam no doubt contributed to Europeans' willingness to believe the worst of the Turks while ignoring unsettling reports about the Christian Armenians.

THE PAMPHLET WAR German propaganda centered on the writing and speechmaking activities known as *Publizistik*, or "pamphleteering." These efforts were directed at both domestic and international audiences. At home, pamphleteers stirred up anti-Russian feeling by portraying the czar's regime as ignorant and barbaric; one pamphlet reported that Russian soldiers had shot Red Cross workers after mistaking their white hats for those of enemy officers. However, most pamphlet activities were directed abroad to encourage pro-German sympathies and pacifist movements in neutral countries such as the United States (which did not enter the war until April, 1917). To undermine American support for the Allied cause, the German Propaganda Ministry reprinted as pamphlets Pro-German newspaper articles written by prominent German American academics and boasting titles such as *Germany's Just Cause* and *Current Misconceptions About the War*. The ministry relied upon American "front" organizations to distribute the pamphlets to target groups of legislators, clergyman, and financiers (*Thou Shalt Not Kill* was directed at clergyman, *The Imperial Russian Finances* at Wall Street). Reasoning that propaganda would be more effective if paid for by the consumer, the Propaganda Ministry often insisted that its pamphlets be sold through legitimate news companies and independent bookstores. A number turned out to be inadvertant best-sellers; one of these was *The War Plotters of Wall Street*, which revealed the close relationship between American bankers and Allied war loans.

In addition to pamphlets, German propagandists coordinated the publication of pro-German books by legitimate American publishers. Perhaps the greatest propaganda coup in this vein was Macmillan's publication of Hugo von Mach's pro-German review of the atrocity reports of all the belligerent nations. To counteract the "Hun" image, the Propaganda Ministry promoted the accomplishments of German *Kultur* by subsidizing projects such as the American publication of *German Classics*, a twenty-volume work edited and translated by the Harvard professor Kuno Francke.

PEACE PROPAGANDA Central Powers propagandists became provocateurs when they tried to rouse PACIFIST MOVEMENTS within American labor unions. German propagandists created a front organization named Labor's National Peace Council, consisting primarily of pro-German workers. In 1915 the council passed a resolution recommending that President Woodrow WILSON prohibit the sale and shipment of munitions to all belligerent nations. In April, 1916, the council flooded the U.S. Congress with telegrams advocating the nation's continued neutrality; the German Propaganda Ministry underwrote the cost of sending an estimated five million telegrams.

Germany's allies also contributed to these subversive campaigns. Prior to the United States' entrance into the war, the Austro-Hungarian ambassador orchestrated attempted to foment strikes among pacifists working in American munitions plants; when his plans were discovered by U.S. authorities he was recalled to his homeland. Austro-Hungarian propagandists even financed a film scenario that dramatized Hungarian immigrants in the United States making the shells that would kill their relatives on the European battlefront.

PROPAGANDA BLUNDERS Germany suffered a major propaganda defeat in the United States after sinking the *Lusitania*, a British cruise liner carrying American passengers, on May 7, 1915. Swayed by Allied propaganda, the American public did not accept the German contention that the ship was carrying a military cargo—despite considerable evidence to that effect. An even greater blow to Germany came with the publication of the Zimmermann note (or telegram) in early 1917. This diplomatic message, which proposed an alliance between Germany and Mexico against the United States, brought an end to German sympathies even among the most ardently pro-German Americans. These catastrophes were merely the climax of a series of mistakes and miscalculations made by the German Propaganda Ministry. For example, earlier in the war Germany had missed an opportunity to score an international propaganda victory against the British naval blockade: Fearful of admitting any domestic vulnerability, the Propaganda Ministry had undermined a "milk-for-German-babies" campaign begun in the then neutral United States. Similarly, the German obsession with secrecy prevented the Propaganda Ministry from purchasing the *New York Evening Post* and other major American newspapers; instead, it quietly sponsored small pro-German and pro-Irish papers whose cumulative propaganda effect was negligible.

ANTICOLONIAL AND RACIST PROPAGANDA
Perhaps the Central Powers' most effective propaganda targeted the Allies' history of colonial hegemony. When Great Britain accused the Germans of wartime atrocities, the Germans countered with pamphlets on British atrocities during the SOUTH AFRICAN WAR, in which more than twenty thousand Boer women and children had died; one pamphlet featured a cover illustration showing Boers hanging lifeless on a camp's electrified barbed wire. Moreover, although the Germans did little to aid Ireland's abortive Easter Uprising in 1916, their Propaganda Ministry did capitalize on the execution of Roger Casement and other Irish revolutionaries, primarily in the hopes of stirring up anti-British feeling among Irish Americans during a presidential election year.

Racism played a major part in the Central Powers' propaganda. For example, the Austro-Hungarians defended their attack on the Serbs by condemning them as a race of regicides. It was the Germans, however, who most consistently resorted to racial themes. The Propaganda Ministry made much of the "black peril"—the French and British use of colonial troops in combat positions, the American use of African Americans, and so on. The Germans reported as fact rumors that the Ghurkas and Sikhs fighting for the British used poisoned knives and occasionally slipped across no-man's land to slit the throats of the enemy in order to drink their blood. Such racist propaganda allowed Germany to cast itself in the hardly credible role of protector of Western civilization. Indeed, the Germans argued that the use of "inferior races" on the battlefield constituted a form of genocide as primitive, undrilled colonials were used as cannon fodder. However, such propaganda eventually boomeranged on the Germans when the valor and discipline of black and colonial regiments in the Allied armies became widely publicized. Late in the war, for example, African American units such as the U.S. Army's 92nd Regiment and 167th Artillery Brigade won special commendation from General Pershing for their frontline activities.

SUGGESTED READINGS:

Ferro, Marc. *The Great War, 1914-1918.* London: Routledge & Kegan Paul, 1977.

Mackenzie, A. J. *Propaganda Boom.* London: John Gifford Limited, 1938.

Petkov, Petko. *The United States and Bulgaria in World War.* New York: Columbia University Press, 1991.

Ponsonby, Arthur. *Falsehood in War-Time.* New York: E. P. Dutton, 1929.

Read, James Morgan. *Atrocity Propaganda: 1914-1919.* New Haven, Conn.: Yale University Press, 1941.

Viereck, George Sylvester. *Spreading Germs of Hate.* New York: Horace Liveright, 1930.

— *Luke A. Powers*

■ World War I: French propaganda

France had little propagandistic organization in place before war broke out

French civilian and military authorities began World War I with little thought of propaganda. By war's end, however, FRANCE had built a vast network of organized persuasion and control, influencing later propaganda techniques in authoritarian regimes such as Bolshevik RUSSIA and National Socialist GERMANY.

In August, 1914, Germany invaded neutral Belgium to attack France, the speed and aggression of the campaign designed to knock out the French as quickly as possible. A French call to the "sacred union" galvanized the country against a nearly successful German drive to Paris. From the beginning, CENSORSHIP of the press was part of the union, but only after offensives and counteroffensives led to a bloody stalemate on the western front did French leaders begin to see a need to preserve morale. Suddenly it was realized that the war was going to last longer than the expected few weeks.

THE SERVICE D'INFORMATION The first small steps toward organized propaganda came not from civilian leaders but from the military. By the end of October, 1914, the French high command saw that the silence of military commanders was harming home front morale and, just as bad, was tarnishing France's reputation in neutral countries. In response the war ministry set up the *Service d'information* under the mobilized journalist and politician André Tardieu. Its mission was to prepare morale-boosting stories from the front and distribute them to the press. (At this time JOURNALISTS themselves were still banned from reporting at the front.) Tardieu established a system of officer-correspondents to submit stories, similar in concept to the "country correspondents" of small American weeklies. Throughout 1915 a flurry of published human-interest stories in French newspapers describing "life at the front" showed the initial success of this informal soldier/writer system. Stories emphasized cheerful troops happy to do their duty despite sometimes muddy trenches and uncomfortable beds. The horrific truth of trench warfare was not part of these reports, leaving civilians mostly unaware of the real experiences of loved ones at the front.

Unfortunately for the service, these correspondents, being combatants themselves, did not file stories during battles, when the press most needed information. On February 21, 1916, Germans attacked French fortifications at Verdun. The service initially produced little information on this battle so symbolically critical to French morale, and military authorities became alarmed by what they considered to be morale-damaging rumors circulating around the home front. A hastily assembled small corps of soldiers who could also write were dispatched to the battlefield, charged not with fighting but with writing. For several months the only news from Verdun came from these soldiers, who wrote captivating and spirited articles showing the heroism and gritty resistance of French troops. Verdun legends created by these early propagandists endure today.

The role of the army's *Service d'information* was reduced at the end of 1916, and by 1917 civilian journalists were finally allowed controlled access to the French front. In addition the service established a second division, the *Bureau d'information militaire.* That office took on new services for the press, including preparation of photographs, films, briefings for journalists, radio transmissions, daily communiqués, and an army-published newspaper, *Bulletin des armées.* The French high command, initially so skeptical of any kind of publicity, had clearly seen how useful carefully controlled information could be to civilian morale as the war dragged into a fourth year.

PROPAGANDA HEADQUARTERS OPENS Civilian leaders in France, too, were beginning to see the benefits of propaganda. At the beginning of 1916, the government announced the opening of a new bureau to help journalists cover the war, the *Maison de la presse.* Housed in an exclusive, six-story Paris townhouse formerly occupied by the United States embassy, the *Maison* became a clearinghouse for a huge network of worldwide French propaganda. The center, under the direction of French politician Philippe Berthelot, was separated into four offices: diplomatic department, military department, department of translation and analysis of the foreign press, and propaganda department. The propaganda department was again divided into three sections: allied countries, neutral countries, and general ideas. The agency was staffed by diplomats, journalists, university professors, and disabled war veter-

ans. It was particularly concerned with persuading neutral countries, notably the United States, to join the allied side (*see* NEUTRAL COUNTRIES DURING WAR). Staff worked closely with British propagandists to promulgate the stories of German atrocities (*see* ATROCITY PROPAGANDA) so effective in turning many Americans against Germany. After the war, journalists discovered that many of the atrocity stories were false.

The *Maison* was operated by the foreign ministry. The country's censorship bureau, controlling literally every word printed in France, was still under the war ministry, although journalists who approached that bureau directly were usually referred to the *Maison*. Censors, too, had clearly seen the value of their work to a propaganda mission by the end of 1917. A report from the office late that year noted that if journalists were provided with more material from the censorship office, "little by little they would fall into the habit of waiting for us to give them the most interesting information, and in this way they would naturally become agents for our propaganda."

After the United States entered the war on the side of the Allies in April, 1917, American military and government leaders consulted with the *Maison* for tips on how to handle the press. Nearly three years of experience had brought France from silence to science, applying modern technology and knowledge to public persuasion. In fact, the system served the government so well that French authorities were slow to abandon it after the war ended, not eliminating the last censorship control until nearly a year after armistice. In establishing its sweeping propaganda organization France showed how wartime propaganda could play a central role in victory. It treated public communication as an industry like any other to be mobilized and controlled for national defense. Subsequent totalitarian governments clearly took lessons from the propaganda successes of France and GREAT BRITAIN, proving to the world the power of modern, scientific propaganda to move masses.

SUGGESTED READINGS:

Collins, Ross F. "The Development of Censorship in World War I France." *Journalism Monographs* 131 (February, 1992).

Knightley, Phillip. *The First Casualty*. London: Pan Books, 1975.

Lasswell, Harold D. *Propaganda Technique in World War I*. 1927. Reprint. Cambridge, Mass.: MIT Press, 1971.

— *Ross F. Collins*

■ World War I: U.S. propaganda

After first remaining neutral, the United States entered World War I in 1917

The United States embarked upon a three-fold program to mobilize civilian support for the war, create a moral fighting spirit in the military, and divide and demoralize the enemy war effort.

When war broke out in Europe in 1914, the United States remained neutral. The president, Woodrow WILSON, urged the nation not to become attached to either side because there was no essential difference in either side's war aims. Wilson was reelected in 1916 on the platform "He kept us out of war."

The American population contained large minorities of Germans, Austrians, Poles, and Russians whose loyalties were thought to be in question. In addition pacifism was a significant strain in the American political scene in 1917 (*see* PACIFIST MOVEMENTS). In short, American PUBLIC OPINION was divided along several lines concerning American entry into World War I, and when Wilson and Congress finally declared war against Germany, general American support for the war was not assured.

THE HOME FRONT In order to unify American opinion in favor of war—to turn the United States from an antimilitaristic nation into a fully organized warmaking society—President Wilson created the COMMITTEE ON PUBLIC INFORMATION (CPI) on April 1, 1917. To head the committee he appointed George CREEL, a writer and editor with experience as a crusading progressive newspaper journalist. Creel, like most progressives, believed that mass education was the method by which the social order could be improved. The CPI, led by Creel, would embark on a program designed to educate the American people about the war so that they would voluntarily join into a unity of opinion supporting the war.

One of the primary functions of the CPI was to advertise the reasons for American participation in the war. Virtually all American NEWSPAPERS voluntarily ran articles proclaiming America's fight as a "war to end all wars." Other CPI-sponsored articles engaged in in-depth descriptions of the war as a battle between the forces of light and darkness, good and evil, DEMOCRACY and tyranny. That job was made infinitely simpler when the autocratic czar of Russia was overthrown and Russia was taken out of the French and English alliance.

Another function was to unify American opinion against the enemy in general, and the Germans in particular. Cartoons developed by the CPI and published in nationwide newspaper chains depicted the German Kaiser as somewhat less than human. Kaiser Wilhelm was often drawn with slightly slanted eyes, slumped shoulders, and an evil grin. Often he had his long fingers around the throat of a woman entitled "Liberty" or of a baby entitled "Humanity" or "Democracy."

The motion picture was a new technology, and the CPI used it in its attempt to unify American opinion against the Germans. In one classic film short produced by the CPI, an actor dressed as the German kaiser attempted to abduct an actress made up as the Statue of Liberty. Although it was not specifically stated, the lecherous grin on the kaiser and the nervous way in which he rubbed his hands together suggested that he was about to force himself upon the statue. The image of the rapists of Liberty was precisely the one the CPI wanted Americans to believe of Germans.

On May 10, 1917, the American government began to publish the *Official Bulletin* in order better to control the dissemination of information concerning the war. The headlines and articles in that publication were usually positive and upbeat in order to maintain a high level of morale in the general public. American defeats in battle or large-scale German advances were minimized, glossed over, or ignored. Also, the *Official Bulletin* tended to emphasize the moral components of the causes of the war. The German enemy's blame for the war was stressed, whereas the British and French allies' contribution to the causes of the war were minimized.

In an age before radio and television, the CPI developed an ingenious method to spread information to the American public. The FOUR-MINUTE MEN were a group of about seventy-five thousand individuals scattered throughout the United States who gave preapproved speeches about a wide variety of war issues. From conservation of scarce resources to the importance of security issues, the Four-Minute Men were amazingly successful in helping achieve a unity of opinion about war issues throughout America.

THE MILITARY World War I necessitated the building of the largest military establishment up to that time in American history. Men and women from the civilian sector found themselves in the military and were subjected to typical military indoctrination. These new members of the Army and Navy were expected to fight, and quite possibly to die, in an unknown land. For that reason, the American government decided it was necessary to educate the new military on the reasons behind the war.

The Four-Minute Men had a military unit comprised of officers who spoke to the soldiers, formally and informally, about the causes of the war. Again, the moral implications of German aggression were stressed, while the contributing factors of English and French imperialism were minimized. As in the civilian sector, the themes of a "war to end war" and to "make the world safe for democracy" emerged as the primary reasons to fight the war. The CPI was actively engaged in the indoctrination of the American military. To this end the *Army Bulletin* was published. With titles such as "Why We Are Fighting" and "Back of the Trenches,"

W. A. Rogers' caricature of Kaiser Wilhelm wiping his bloody hands on the American flag typifies anti-German propaganda of World War I. (*Library of Congress*)

articles in the *Army Bulletin* reinforced the moralistic reasons for the war. These articles typically stressed the evil nature of the German mind. German atrocities were publicized; English and French "mistakes" were minimized.

The government found it simpler to achieve a unity of opinion about the war within the ranks of the military than in the civilian population at large. The military traditionally offers an enclosed environment of uniform activities, uniform clothing and uniform thinking where the dissemination of propaganda becomes almost natural. If soldiers are going to die in battle, the more readily they accept moralistic reasons for that death, the easier it becomes to gloss over the more tawdry nationalistic and economic reasons.

Governments generally depict their wartime enemies as somewhat less than human. Characterizing the Germans as "Huns," "rats," or "spiders" made it easier for American soldiers to kill them in battle. Propaganda was the tool with which the American government persuaded Christian young Americans to annihilate Christian young Germans.

THE ENEMY CAMP By the time of American entry into the war, the European belligerents had been fighting for almost three years. The war had degenerated into a deadlock, with both sides digging deeper and deeper into their resources. One of those resources was the use of propaganda in attempts to demoralize and divide the enemy coalition, and the United States was quick to take up that weapon.

For the front-line propaganda effort, the American Military Intelligence Branch was formed. One of the ideas developed was the delivery of pamphlets emphasizing American moral war aims to the enemy soldiers at the front. The messages again listed the reasons America fought, stressing the themes of democracy, freedom, and moral political activities. These messages were delivered via trench mortar, balloon, rocket, and airplane.

Other pamphlets delivered to the German soldiers attempted to exploit their poor material conditions in 1917-1918. Lists of equipment carried by the typical American soldier were sent in order to create dissent in German ranks. Mess menus were sent in order to exploit the hunger within the German ranks in an attempt to increase resentment and create an attitude of defeatism. Tactical and strategic maps were delivered to the German soldiers, some truthful, some exaggerated, in order to convince German combat soldiers that they were in an untenable military situation.

The German High Command displayed a high degree of respect for the effectiveness of trench propaganda, as evidenced by the enactment of an automatic death sentence for any German soldier caught reading American propaganda leaflets. That forced the Americans to redesign the propaganda they sent, making the pamphlets smaller and easier to hide and pass among German troops. Simpler messages were devised, with shorter messages in larger type, so that less time would be spent reading them, limiting the German soldiers' exposure to danger.

The CPI was able to affect enemy morale on the enemy home front by publishing moralistic war aims in the newspapers of European neutral countries. German newspapers were quick to pick up news releases through neutral capitals. Even though the German newspapers were subject to strict censorship, the CPI was able to inject rumors of war aims and generous surrender terms into the enemy populations.

Although France, England, and the United States were allies, and the war effort was a joint enterprise, the Allied propaganda effort was anything but unified. Officially organized as "Allied Propaganda," French and English attempts to treat Americans in a junior capacity resulted in the reality of an almost unilateral propaganda campaign on the part of the United States.

SUGGESTED READINGS:

Brown, James A. Campbell. *Techniques of Persuasion, from Propaganda to Brainwashing.* Baltimore: Penguin Books, 1963.

Kennedy, David M. *Over Here: The First World War and American Society.* New York: Oxford University Press, 1980.

Mock, James R. and Cedric Larson. *Words That Won the War.* New York: Russell & Russell, 1939.

Sorensen, Thomas C. *The World War: The Story of American Propaganda.* New York: Harper & Row, 1968.

Wiegand, Wayne A. *An Active Instrument for Propaganda: The American Public Library During World War I.* New York: Greenwood Press, 1989.

— *Tim Palmer*

■ World War II

1939-1945: World-wide conflict in which the United States, Great Britain, the Soviet Union, and their allies defeated Germany, Italy, and Japan

Propaganda was more important during World War II than during any previous wars for several reasons. RADIO and films (*see* FILM: WORLD WAR II) had reached new heights of influence, and the world was increasingly separating into one mass democracies and mass dictatorships; under either system millions of people had to be led, cajoled, and manipulated to achieve desired national ends. Moreover, unlike WORLD WAR I, this war was a conflict of clashing ideologies, those of DEMOCRACY, FASCISM, and communism, and in each system all forms of propaganda were highly valued. Finally, the old forms of propaganda, specifically NEWSPAPERS, magazines, LITERATURE, and POSTER ART, were more influential than ever before because European literacy had expanded dramatically in the course of the century.

ALLIED PROPAGANDA The Allied powers described themselves as the victims of aggression who were righteously seeking revenge for dastardly attacks, democratic societies protecting their way of life from states aiming to extinguish freedom and impose slavery. These countries held out a vision of greater freedom and greater prosperity for their populations after victory. The best example of Anglo-American propaganda was the proclamation of the Atlantic Charter's four freedoms: freedom of speech, freedom of worship, freedom from fear, and freedom from want.

U.S. propaganda stressed how people from many different nationalities cooperated in the country, and it emphasized that the fruits of liberty were readily apparent in the tremendous output of American business and industry. If Europeans could learn the lessons of American experience, Europe too would be able to enjoy freedom and prosperity after the war.

GERMANY'S WAR PRODUCTION DRIVE IS DIFFERENT

Despite the deadly seriousness of the issues it raised, American wartime propaganda was not above the use of humor. (*Robert McClenaghan*)

British propaganda had its own points of emphasis, stressing how Great Britain had stood alone against tyranny and how the country had stemmed the tide of Axis victory in the Battle of Britain and in North Africa before the U.S. entry into the war. Great Britain proclaimed itself,

with its centuries of experience dealing with Europe, to be more qualified than the United States to lead a democratic Europe after the war.

AXIS PROPAGANDA There were two distinct thrusts, one for home consumption and one for overseas distribution, in the propaganda employed by the Axis powers. Propaganda was extremely important to mobilize the masses to support dictatorships such as Adolf HITLER's National Socialist regime, which relied on a brilliant specialist in propaganda, Joseph GOEBBELS. Fascism is an extreme form of aggressive nationalism under dictatorial leadership, and fascist rule included the proclamation that government was capable of ending corruption, bringing order out of chaos, imposing justice, and bringing cooperation to all sectors of the economy. National destiny also required that the superior race assert itself over inferior races and purge the intermingled international power of the Jews and of the BOLSHEVIKS, as the communists were usually called. War, often a necessary means to this end, allowed the race to reveal some of its most noble virtues: bravery, endurance, and determination. A special twist of Italian Fascist Party propaganda was the recollection of the glory of the ancient Roman Empire and the need for the Italian people to reassert themselves over some of Rome's old territory.

Axis propaganda beamed overseas changed its emphasis once Germany invaded the Soviet Union in June, 1941. Before that, Axis propaganda expounded that Europe was being liberated from corruption and stagnation. Once the Soviet Union was attacked, the war was depicted in Axis propaganda as a crusade of European civilization against the barbarism of international BOLSHEVISM. Men from all over occupied Europe were urged to join on the Axis side.

Soviet wartime propaganda was completely mobilized and controlled by the Communist Party (*see* RUSSIA: 1855-1918). Before the German invasion the propaganda had been mostly anti-Polish and anti-British. After June, 1941, the keynote was uncompromising vengeance against those who had unleashed the unprovoked attack. Unlike the Axis and Allied powers, the Soviets dwelt upon the suffering of their people. They also stressed the heroism of the "little man," the unity of various Soviet nationalities, and historical examples of thwarted invasions, such as Napoleon's campaign of 1812.

Japanese propaganda justified both it's attack on Allied possessions and the expansion of the Japanese empire across Asia. Japan's enemies were described as imperial powers determined to keep Asians in colonial subjection. These imperial powers had sought to encircle Japan and to deny its access to resources so as to limit Japanese power and influence in Asia. Japan also emphasized that it had liberated millions of Asians and brought them into a new order called the Greater East Asia Co-Prosperity Sphere. Japan professed to be saving Asians from Western exploitation and decadence and, in the case of China, preventing both a communist takeover as well as exploitation by selfish warlords.

All belligerent nations during World War II used propaganda to maximize their victories and minimize their defeats. Lost battles and the prospect of defeat were usually denied. As defeat began to loom for the Axis powers, their enemies were depicted as vicious fiends to stimulate the armies to renewed efforts.

SUGGESTED READINGS:

Cole, Robert. *Propaganda in Twentieth Century War and Politics: An Annotated Bibliography.* Lanham, Md.: Scarecrow Press, 1996.

Herzstein, Robert Edwin. *The War That Hitler Won: The Most Infamous Propaganda Campaign in History.* New York: G. P. Putnam's Sons, 1978.

Short, K. R. M., ed. *Film and Radio Propaganda in World War II.* Knoxville: The University of Tennessee Press, 1983.

— *Henry Weisser*

■ World War II: British propaganda

After Germany invaded Poland in September, 1939, Great Britain realized the need for preparing for war and establishing a propaganda policy

The outbreak of the second European war in 1939 placed GREAT BRITAIN before a new responsibility for foreign and domestic persuasion that necessitated the marshalling of public consent for war aims at home and the management of neutral powers (*see* NEUTRAL COUNTRIES DURING WAR) and allies in Europe. To facilitate this, the Foreign Publicity Directorate was formed on September 4, 1939, under the control of the domestic MINISTRY OF INFORMATION (MOI), to make British war aims acceptable abroad. The Ministry of Information, for its part, was responsible for directing public thinking into channels that would make the war acceptable.

The German invasion and conquest of Poland in September, 1939, caught Great

Britain off guard, but the lull allowed the British to establish a rudimentary propaganda machine.

Opinion in Whitehall was divided. Propaganda was not seen as a substitute for a rational foreign policy regarding Europe, but a powerful and vocal opposition emerged to counter the rationalists. Under the guidance of Sir Robert Vansittart, chief diplomatic advisor, and Sir Stephen Talents, public relations controller at the BRITISH BROADCASTING CORPORATION (BBC) and principal MOI planner, the need for an active role in anti-Axis persuasion was eventually accepted as a compromising necessity.

FOREIGN PUBLICITY DIRECTORATE The formation of the Foreign Publicity Directorate (FPD), under the leadership of Sir Ronald Charles, had the dual role of producing anti-German propaganda and at the same time strengthening the resolve of Britain's European allies. The agency also attempted to make sure that the neutral powers remained neutral and did not stray into the Axis camp. Great Britain sought to secure its own continuance as a dominant force during and after the war by suggesting that the British held the paramount moral and political vision that would prevail, defeat Nazi Germany militarily, and secure eventual peace in Europe.

The FPD supervised area specialists who were responsible for regional planning and policy formation, and it also established press attachés at overseas missions. With the help of the Foreign Office, the BBC, and various intelligence organizations, the FPD produced a steady stream of propaganda overseas. However, after the German invasion of Denmark, Norway, France, Belgium, and Holland. In April, 1940, British military forces were withdrawn in 1941.

By December, 1941, Great Britain essentially stood alone in Europe, as most of its allies had been overrun by Germany. The fact that the neutral countries in Europe were now restricted to Sweden, Switzerland, SPAIN, and PORTUGAL was particularly trying for the FPD, especially since these countries were afraid of a German invasion themselves and imposed stringent CENSORSHIP on British propaganda to avoid incurring Nazi retaliation. While some, like Spain, were openly hostile to Britain, the remaining neutral nations vacillated wildly in their belief in British leadership.

To push the British line harder, Prime Minister Winston CHURCHILL reorganized the propaganda machine by appointing Brenden Bracken as the new minister of information in July, 1941. Bracken, a journalist and a politician, was clearly suited for his new role, and he set about clarifying and rationalizing propaganda policy and tailoring aims to specific markets.

The entrance of the Soviet Union and the United States into the war on the British side affected propaganda aims. With the influx of American resources into the beleaguered British camp, the FPD made clear to the neutral nations that Britain was invincible despite earlier military setbacks. The FPD suggested that the crushing defeats suffered by Germany at the hands of the Red Army indicated that the National Socialists were a dwindling force.

By 1942 it was clear that the Allies would eventually win the war, and Great Britain began to focus on propaganda with which to win the European peace. Fearful of American and Russian dominance in European affairs, Britain presented itself as the only real representative of strictly European interests and thus a bulwark of freedom against fascist aggression. These propaganda aims were continued after 1945 through attempts to build cooperation with newly liberated local governments. After it became clear that both the United States and the Soviet Union were pursuing their own propaganda campaigns in Europe, Britain had to recognize its dwindling influence over the emerging postwar Europe.

DOMESTIC PROPAGANDA On the domestic front propaganda was directed by the Ministry of Information, which sought to secure civilian morale and, perhaps more important, produce a willingness in the British public to contribute to the war effort. In the same way that foreign propaganda had to appeal without implicit threat, so domestic propaganda had to navigate difficult questions of social and political import. Hampered by the class-bound politics of the propagandists themselves, the construction of a united front had to appeal beyond traditional political conservatism and take into consideration emerging socialist voices in the British political establishment.

Whereas the slow start to the war had provided time for the emergence of the FPD, the conditions on the home front were a different matter. With the collapse of Poland after a month of fighting, the British public were expectant, yet confused. After Britain's declaration of war, it seemed at first that there would be no war and that there was no tangible enemy. However, by May, 1940, World War II had become a reality. When the invasion and defeat of France, as well as the collapse of the British military initiative, was followed by hysterical fears of invasion by German forces, the MOI began a propaganda campaign to maintain order and instill faith in the national leadership. The British retreat at Dunkirk promoted a defensive civilian posture, both against the German threat and against fears of internal sabotage. The inclusion of working-class voices in propaganda messages, posters, and cartoons, was a response to fears that many in the British middle class were considering collaborating with the Nazis.

The MOI also tried to arouse direct hatred for the Germans with an "anger campaign" in 1940. With the cooperation of twenty to thirty influential journalists, the agency attempted to craft feature stories that would explore the German psychology and deflate Adolf HITLER's seeming omniscience and military invincibility. These stories were essentially tailored to the class prejudices of the reader, and implied the material and social losses inflicted by a German occupation.

The anger campaign showed only mixed results, and general hatred of the Germans was aroused more by the air-attacks on British cities after September, 1941. While the Blitz strengthened British resolve, it also produced class antagonism, especially when it became apparent that the wealthy could avoid potential target cities by fleeing to the countryside. In response, the MOI appealed to reasonableness and community spirit, even when this was far from the truth. As an ironic aside to this, the MOI avoided propagandizing Nazi treatment of the Jews, because of growing incidents of anti-Semitism amongst the British urban population over issues of wealth abuse, favoritism, and avoiding food rationing. While the ugliness of the British reaction to air raids was played down, the Germans were condemned as terrorists, and the raids themselves were hailed as promoting the indomitable British spirit.

At the same time MOI propaganda

made erroneous appeals to a sense of fair play and historical tradition that assiduously avoided all mention of political relations in Britain at the time. By 1942 it was clear that the Allies would win the war, yet the propaganda avoided meaningful discussion of the postwar world. While there were claims that the British public would be rewarded for their efforts in a grinding, protracted war, discussion of reconstruction aims was limited. Similarly, Britain's alliance with the Soviet Union avoided all mention of the international nature of the communist movement, and instead hailed their example in nationalist terms for fear of legitimating an alternative form of political identity.

While British propaganda was successful in a limited fashion, the combination of German military threat and successful Red Army resistance played a more significant role in propaganda reception. At home the turmoil of postwar politics and rejection of the status quo indicated that domestic propaganda had outlived its usefulness by 1945.

SUGGESTED READINGS:

Addison, Paul. *The Road to 1945*. London: Lawrence and Wishart, 1975.

Cole, Robert. *Britain and the War of Words in Neutral Europe, 1939-1945: The Art of the Possible*. New York: St. Martin's Press, 1990.

————. *Propaganda in Twentieth Century War and Politics: An Annotated Bibliography*. Lanham, Md.: Scarecrow Press, 1996.

Cruikshank, Charles. *The Fourth Arm: Psychological Warfare, 1938-1945*. Oxford: Oxford University Press, 1981.

McLaine, Ian. *Ministry of Morale: Home Front Morale and the Ministry of Information in World War II*. London: Allen & Unwin, 1979.

— *Paul Hansom*

■ World War II: French propaganda

French wartime propaganda was produced by the pre-armistice government, the Vichy regime, the Free French, the political parties, and other groups

During World War II the range of messages and styles of propaganda reflected the ideological and political divisions of the French people. Until the humiliating defeat in June, 1940, most factions supported the goal of defending the country against Germany. After General Henri Pétain signed an armistice on June 22, German troops occupied the northern and western parts of France, while Pétain's government, located in the spa town of Vichy, ruled over the "free zone" in the southeast. General Charles de GAULLE repudiated the armistice and fled to London to establish a government in exile, which was called Free France. France's large Communist Party reluctantly supported Germany until the Soviet Union was invaded in 1941; thereafter the party's propaganda activities supported the Free France movement.

UNTIL JUNE 22, 1940 During the interwar period the liberal laws of FRANCE's Third Republic allowed for the expression of almost all points of view in newspapers, magazines, and films, with only mild controls over radio broadcasts. The government conducted few propaganda activities, other than explaining and defending official policy. The Ministry of Foreign Affairs organized a bureau to promote French culture, but it avoided political propaganda. When faced with the threat of a major war, however, Prime Minister Edouard Daladier on July 29, 1939, created the General

LES MENTEURS DE BERLIN

Captioned "The Liars of Berlin," this French wartime cartoon is an example of antipropaganda propaganda. (*Library of Congress*)

Commission of Information, which was given authority to regulate national broadcasting and to organize a campaign of mass propaganda. The writer Jean Giraudoux was appointed director of the commission.

With the outbreak of the war the French government instituted a broad policy of CENSORSHIP over the mass media. The parliament made it illegal to distribute communist and fascist publications, as well as any expressing criticism of official policy. Giraudoux's commission also banned about sixty films that advocated PACIFISM, and it provided licenses as well as some financial support for about thirty-five patriotic films, most of which were never completed. In addition the commission launched a monthly magazine that summarized NEWSREELS shown in the cinemas. Despite such efforts, historians generally agree that the commission did not have enough time to organize effective MASS COMMUNICATIONS.

THE OCCUPIED ZONE The German Military Command enforced strict rules of CENSORSHIP, threatening torture, imprisonment, and even death for anyone caught with materials hostile to the German cause. At the same time, applying Joseph GOEBBELS' techniques, the command's large propaganda section maintained its own staff of journalists, disseminating newspapers, magazines, books, and posters and sponsoring profascist films, rallies, and expositions. Although most French people remained anti-German and anti-Nazi, many were predisposed to believe propaganda about Bolshevik and Jewish threats. Until early 1943, moreover, most were persuaded that German dominance over the new Europe was inevitable.

Many citizens in Paris and elsewhere were willing to collaborate actively with the German occupation. The prominent journalist Philippe Henriot had an extraordinary effect on the audiences of Radio Paris. George Suarez, the editor of the Paris daily *Aujourd'hui,* denounced multiparty democracy and warned about the dangers of communist aggression. Several right-wing and Fascist parties enthusiastically advocated French integration into the National Socialists' new order. Jacques Doriot, a superb orator who headed the French Popular Party, was especially effective before the large audiences that flocked to his Parisian rallies. Other talented communicators of fascist-like doctrines included Marcel Déat, Pierre Drieu la Rochelle, and Robert Brasillach.

THE UNOCCUPIED ZONE The Vichy government, led by Henri Pétain and Pierre Laval, was able to exercise considerable freedom of action, at least until German intervention late in 1942. Rather than being committed fascists, leaders in the southern zone generally agreed to collaborate with Nazi Germany because they believed it was necessary for the survival of France. Pétain, a military hero of World War I, was tremendously popular with the public, and Vichy propaganda tended to emphasize his personal appeal. Patriotic posters with the general's image were ubiquitously displayed. Elementary-school teachers were required to assign their students to write letters and poems to Pétain, who was then shown receiving them in emotional ceremonies.

The Vichy government tried to convince citizens that it was conducting a "national revolution" based on the slogan "Work, Family, Fatherland," and it denounced Soviet, British, and American war aims. The government pursued a policy of sending dissidents to prison, and its

Ministry of Information and Propaganda maintained rigid controls over the press, radio, and cinema. During the Vichy period private groups produced about two hundred feature films and four hundred news documentaries, most upholding the official values. To support its anti-Jewish legislation, the regime encouraged the showing of anti-Semitic films and expositions. In late 1943 it increased its propaganda budget and put Philippe Henriot in charge of the ministry. The underground resistance, recognizing Henriot's great skill in using the media, assassinated him in the summer of 1944.

FREE FRANCE General De Gaulle was a strong believer in the power of mass propaganda. He and his chief radio spokesman, Maurice Schumann, knew how to use radio effectively from London to proclaim that the flame of French resistance would not be extinguished. Free French programs, titled "Honor and Fatherland," were always introduced by the national anthem and other patriotic SYMBOLS. Many people in the occupied zone were willing to risk the threat of arrest to listen to these broadcasts. In addition to radio broadcasts, de Gaulle's London-based organization coordinated the propaganda activities of many resistance movements throughout France. Clandestine newspapers such as *Combat* and *Libération* provided information from an anti-German, anti-Vichy point of view, and their availability sent a clear message of the French determination for national independence.

SUGGESTED READINGS:

Dank, Milton. *The French Against the French: Collaboration and Resistance*. New York: J. B. Lippincott, 1974.

Paxton, Robert. *Vichy France: Old Guard and New Order, 1940-1944*. New York: Knopf, 1972.

Pryce-Jones, David. *Paris in the Third Reich: A History of the German Occupation, 1940-1944*. New York: Holt, Rinehart, and Winston, 1981.

Short, Kenneth, ed. *Film and Radio Propaganda in World War II*. Knoxville: University of Tennesee Press, 1983.

Strebel, Elizabeth. "French Cinema, 1940-1944, and Its Socio-Psychological Significance." *Historical Journal of Film, Radio, and Television* 1 (1981): 33-47.

— *Thomas T. Lewis*

■ World War II: German propaganda

Nazi Germany had a tightly controlled propaganda organization during the war

Wartime propaganda in the Third Reich during World War II (*see* GERMANY: 1933-1945) was a state-sponsored effort that aimed to exploit diplomatic, military, cultural, and political aspects of life in what Adolf HITLER termed the "Thousand-Year Reich." In 1925, in his blueprint for world conquest titled *Mein Kampf* (my struggle), Hitler wrote that one of the chief aims of propaganda was "to disintegrate the present state of affairs and to infiltrate it with new doctrine."

ORGANIZATION AND AIMS The Nationalsozialistische Deutsche Arbeiter Partei (NSDAP), or National Socialist German Workers' Party (also known as Nazi Party), the propaganda apparatus was directed by Joseph GOEBBELS who was appointed by Hitler to the title of Minister of Public Enlightenment and Propaganda on March 13, 1933. The actual ministry of the same name came into being in Berlin on June 30,

After Germany's occupation of France in June, 1940, Adolf Hitler (center)—who had once aspired to be an architect—had himself and his architect, Albert Speer (left), filmed in front of Paris' Eiffel Tower—a powerful symbol of France. (*National Archives*)

1933. Goebbels' entire propaganda empire operated on the simple principle that people could be made to believe anything if, in Goebbels' words, "you tell it to [them] in the proper way." It was the minister's uncanny effectiveness in the propagandizing of the Nazi cause "in the proper way" that absorbed his entire career.

When the National Socialists came to power in 1933 they immediately set about the task of organizing state and local mind control on an unprecedented scale. In the Third Reich state-sponsored propaganda flowed from three agencies: the Reich Ministry of People's Enlightenment and Propaganda; the Central Propaganda Office of the Nazi Party; and the Reich Chamber of Culture. Of these three the Ministry of People's Enlightenment and Propaganda was the epicenter of German propaganda throughout World War II.

By 1938 the ministry consisted of five departments: administration; propaganda; broadcasting (radio); press; and theater and adult education. By 1942 these original five had been expanded to a total of fourteen, but it was the propaganda department that developed and oversaw the distribution by press, radio, leaflet, word of mouth, and other means of the virulent Nazi racial and anti-Semitic propaganda. This propaganda prepared the mind-set for the "final solution to the Jewish question," a Nazi code phrase for the implementation of plans for the extermination of the European Jews.

The government ordered huge numbers of radio sets—called *Volksempfänger,* or people's receivers—to be made available to the public for about seventy-six Reichmarks, or approximately thirty dollars in American currency. These radios were inexpensive enough to allow millions of ordinary Germans to buy them and tune in to political, cultural, and military broadcasts in aid of the Nazi cause. Compared to other nations at the time, Nazi Germany had the highest number of household radio ownership of any country in the world. In order to reach even further into all aspects of German life, the

Nazi Party also employed local political leaders called *Gauleiter* (the term comes from the German word *Gau,* or province) to insure that NSDAP propaganda was reaching its intended audience. There were thirty-six *Gauleiter* in the original Reich before the war, but by the end of World War II the Nazis had placed *Gauleiter* in all conquered territories. They oversaw the so-called *Ortsgruppenleiter,* local Nazi Party organizers and group leaders; the lowest propaganda official was the *Blockwart* or block warden. The *Blockwart* was assigned a specific geographical territory to supervise. No police state can exist if it does not proclaim certain values and norms of correct and incorrect behavior. The Nazi propaganda effort was so organized that all individual ideas and thoughts were subordinated to those of the state under the führer, or leader. An espoused principle of "national freedom"—from the Jews, from the Communists, from the decadent democratic ideology of the West, and from "racial mongrelization"—propelled German propaganda efforts in the war years.

PROPAGANDA IN A TWO-FRONT WAR
When World War II commenced with the German invasion of Poland in the early morning hours of September 1, 1939, Nazi propaganda was directed at the Eastern European nations that Germany coveted for its expanded *Lebensraum,* or living space (Soviet Russia was excepted because of the Non-Aggression Pact signed between Hitler and Joseph STALIN in August, 1939). One of the main early techniques of German propaganda used in aid of military conquests was to allege dark and sinister plots being concocted by Germany's adversaries in both Poland

and the West. German military intervention was often excused or explained with
the pretense that Germany had to take
preemptive action to protect the Reich.
The occupation of neutral Belgium and
Holland, for example, was justified on the
premise that these two small nations were
not, in fact, neutral but controlled by the
governments of France and Great Britain.
In a dramatic effort to prove its point the
Reich Ministry of Propaganda quoted a
report by a German war correspondent
that a German officer had "discovered"
32,000 German maps of the Third Reich
in Holland; the Germans deduced that an
invasion of the fatherland was imminent.

On May 10, 1940, Germany invaded the
Netherlands and Belgium, and with that
the war in the West began. Nazi propaganda efforts attempted to neutralize
world opinion for this invasion because,
in Germany's view, Belgium and Holland
had violated their officially neutral stance.
With the invasion of France shortly after
the Belgium-Holland incursion, German
propaganda revived anti-French clichés,
especially accusing France of "race-mixing"
with inferior racial stock from French colonial Africa. In Belgium, the Netherlands,
and France the Germans unleashed the
same new military tactic that had been so
successful in Poland: Blitzkrieg, or light-
ning warfare. Although the French had
the largest and one of the best-equipped
armies in Europe, German military organization and tactics quickly seized the initiative and France fell to the German onslaught on June 24, 1940. The swift victories
abolished the long-held notion in the interwar years of German military inferiority,
and the Reich Ministry for Propaganda
made the most of the startling military
collapse of the French.

The British were next to bear the brunt
of both military action and propaganda
assaults. The *Luftwaffe*, or air force, subjected Great Britain to a relentless across-
channel air assault during the fall of 1940;
they were eventually repelled by the Royal
Air Force (RAF). By late fall, 1940, however, the German battle against Great
Britain had been lost, largely because of
the false conviction of supremacy engen-
dered by German propaganda. The early
victories in Poland had blinded German
propagandists to believe in the invincibility of the *Luftwaffe* pilots and their aircraft, and Goebbels' ministry had seriously underestimated the effectiveness of
the RAF's Spitfire and Hurricane fighter
squadrons as well as the British early-
warning radar system. The night-bombing
of British cities between October, 1940,
and May, 1941, called the blitz, was largely
ineffective in breaking the English will to
fight, and German propaganda steadily
shifted its focus away from an English invasion scenario when the German Balkan
campaign got under way in April, 1941.

Between June 22, 1941, the invasion of
the Soviet Union, and January 31, 1943,
the German Sixth Army's defeat at Stalingrad, Nazi propaganda against the Russians reached new heights of intensity.
Like the Blitzkrieg victories in Poland and
the West, the initial German military superiority over the Soviets provided the
Reich's propaganda machinery material
with which to extol the superiority of Germany and to marginalize the military
prowess of the decadent Slavs. Hitler was
convinced that Germany only had to "kick
the door in" to Russia, whereupon the nation would crumble from within. The Red
Army and Air Force proved otherwise.
From the German defeat at Stalingrad

during the brutal winter of 1942-1943 until the fall of Berlin into Russian hands on May 4, 1945, German propaganda continued the big lie (*see* BIG-LIE TECHNIQUE) that the Russians would be halted on the banks of the Oder River.

Nazi Germany unconditionally surrendered to the Allies in a schoolhouse in Rheims, France, at 2:41A.M. on the morning of May 7, 1945. The war in Europe was over, and the Third Reich and its totalitarian propaganda paraphernalia vanished into history five years, eight months, and seven days after the invasion of Poland in 1939.

SUGGESTED READINGS:

Boelcke, Willi A. *The Secret Conferences of Dr. Goebbels: The Nazi Propaganda War, 1939-1943.* New York: E. P. Dutton, 1970.

Bramsted, Ernest K. *Goebbels and National Socialist Propaganda, 1925-1945.* East Lansing: Michigan State University Press, 1965.

Goodspeed, D. J. *The German Wars, 1914-1945.* New York: Bonanza Books, 1985.

Shirer, William L. *The Rise and Fall of the Third Reich: A History of Nazi Germany.* New York: Simon & Schuster, 1960.

Toland, John. *Adolph Hitler: A Bibliography.* New York: Anchor Books-Doubleday, 1976.

— *John C. Watkins, Jr.*

■ World War II: Italian propaganda

Italian wartime propaganda reflected the ideals of the Fascist state

Benito Mussolini allied Italy with Nazi Germany with the Rome-Berlin Axis in 1936 and the Pact of Steel in May, 1939, and in June, 1940, he intervened in World War II on the side of Germany. As WORLD WAR II proceeded, Benito MUSSOLINI's fierce determination to be seen as the sole military as well as the political leader of ITALY—il Duce—and as a genius without compare, led to one military disaster after another. As a result of appointing weak-willed subordinates his cabinet rarely challenged him.

Wartime Italian propaganda was therefore principally pivoted around Mussolini's status, and this propaganda's weakness derived precisely from the gulf that opened up between his bombastic assertions of Italian military prowess and the grim reality of repeated defeat. When Mussolini was arrested by order of the king, Vittorio Emmanuele III, in July, 1943, there was practically no response, even from Fascists; most of the people had already become utterly skeptical of his pronouncements. The puppet republic of Salò set up by Mussolini's Nazi rescuers in September, 1943, until his capture in April, 1945, did nothing to restore his credibility.

MUSSOLINI'S MILITARY ACTIONS The first sign of war was Mussolini's decision in 1940, motivated by his passion to have a military victory to compete with Hitler's, to invade and colonize Greece. This attempt was preceded by propaganda urging Italians to see Greeks as racially inferior Balkans and as incapable of withstanding superior Italian force; at the same time Mussolini wildly overexaggerated the numbers of troops and weapons at his disposal. His naval and air chiefs feebly tried to dissuade him from the adventure, but his army chief of staff learned of the invasion from radio news. The Greeks drove the Italian forces back into Albania in a week, and for the next

Italian ambassador Dino Alfieri with German propaganda minister Joseph Goebbels in Berlin in May, 1939—four months before Germany invaded Poland to start World War II. (*AP/Wide World Photos*)

three months the Italian troops fought a purely defensive battle.

Mussolini himself eventually went to Albania in 1941 for three weeks to direct the war there. When the Greeks did not budge, he was compelled to return. His military bulletins claimed, however, that the Greek army had virtually been annihi-lated, and he himself announced that he had been commanding "the greatest and most bloody battle in modern history." To those who knew the truth, he claimed he had gone simply to reconnoitre the situation and to reward the troops—troops who at other times he claimed were being defeated because of their racially suspect stock, since many came from southern Italy and some auxiliary units were Albanian. Mussolini seemed to have little notion that over time his contradictory definitions would undermine his leadership.

When Germany intervened and overwhelmed the Greek army one month later, Mussolini claimed that the Greeks had already been in full flight. This, too, contributed to the credibility gap. Mussolini's habit of speaking of war as a "sublime holocaust," in which the mettle and superiority of a people were forged, stood out clearly as the monstrous fantasy it was. In the same month Allied troops captured Ethiopia and Italy's other East African colonies with hardly a struggle. What Mussolini had described as "the pearl of the Fascist regime" was now lost.

At later stages in the war Mussolini several times instructed one of his generals to retreat from a given location, only to announce in public that the position had been lost through the incompetence, cowardice, and treachery of the general in question. He used this ploy to protect the MYTH of his own leadership.

During the fascist era it was required that the people listen to Mussolini's war bulletins while standing up. His speeches were read on ceremonial occasions as though religious utterances—sometimes as much as one million copies were printed of a single speech—and his writings were translated into thirty or more languages, including a ten-volume Japanese edition.

Yet in January, 1943, the Italian army was expelled from Libya by Allied forces, and by February, 1943, some army units were without boots. The weaponry available had shrunk to a minimal level to resist the invasion that had begun in Sicily

in July of that year. The British, previously characterized as a weak and timid force terrified of an Italian invasion, were now labeled barbaric monsters who would destroy all Italians if they took control of the country.

CINEMA AND PROPAGANDA As a result of Mussolini's obsession with personally controlling all details and the impossibility that he actually do so, it was often possible to subvert his policies in various ways. One of the realms in which this was increasingly evident during the war was cinema. During the 1930's, at the time of the invasion of ETHIOPIA, procolonial epics and other highly ideological films had been produced. Mussolini established the huge Cinecittà studios in Rome in 1938 to expand propagandistic cinema production. Yet as the war dragged on films came to be made that, while not overtly attacking fascist propaganda or tenets, nevertheless often sidelined them. The emphasis, increasingly, was on survival strategies, on sexual and class conflicts, and on questions of interpersonal violence. Even in films with clichéd happy endings, the overall content was often far from schematic.

Indeed, the roots of postwar Italian cinema, especially the so-called neorealist style that sought to reflect the everyday lives of ordinary people, and also so-called *film noir*, with its emphasis on the disturbing and harsh aspects of social life, are to be found in this period. Italian cinema moved further and further from its assigned role to echo the real direction of Italian life and culture.

SUGGESTED READINGS:

DiScala, Spencer M. *Italy: From Revolution to Republic.* Boulder Colo.: Westview Press, 1995.

Landy, Marcia. *Fascism in Film: The Italian Commercial Cinema, 1931-1943.* Princeton N.J.: Princeton University Press, 1986.

Smith, Denis Mack. *Mussolini.* New York: Vintage Books, 1983.

— *John D. H. Downing*

■ World War II: Japanese propaganda

The Japanese government referred to its official wartime propaganda efforts as "thought war"

In 1933 Japan withdrew from the LEAGUE OF NATIONS over the Manchurian crisis; the following year it abrogated its commitments under the Washington Naval Treaty, and in 1936 it signed the Anti-Comintern Pact with Germany (*see* GERMANY:1933-1945), which was followed in 1940 by the Tripartite Pact with Italy (*see* ITALY: 1922-1945) and Germany (*see* JAPAN: 1912-1945). With that Japan became one of the Axis powers. Following the fall of France (*see* FRANCE:1871-1940), Japan invaded French Indochina in 1940, occupying Saigon on July 27, 1941. In retaliation the United States restricted its trade with Japan, as did Great Britain and the Netherlands, imposing embargoes on the export of oil to Japan. The United States made Japanese withdrawal from China and Indochina a condition for any agreement with Japan.

General Hideki Tojo, a former chief of staff in Manchuria, became the Japanese prime minister on October 17, 1941. Nicknamed the "Razor," he was instrumental in preparing for the attack on Pearl Harbor on December 7, 1941, which brought the United States into World War II as a combatant power. A series of swift Japanese victories in Southeast Asia followed with the taking of Hong Kong on Christmas Day, 1941, and, shortly after, the PHILIPPINES. The following year Japanese forces also captured Singapore, Malaya, Burma, and the Dutch East Indies, INDONESIA.

The battle for the command of the Pacific depended on naval air power, and at the start the odds favored the Japanese. However, the United States secured naval victories in the Pacific Ocean over Japan in the Battles of the Coral Sea (off New Guinea in May, 1942) and Midway Island (in June, 1942), which halted Japan's military successes. A further naval defeat for Japan occurred in the Solomon Islands in August, 1942. In November, 1942, the United States and Japan fought a bitter naval war at Guadalcanal in the Solomons, where Japan, despite heavy losses, continued its determined resistance until February, 1943. In May, Japanese troops engaged in suicidal attacks against victorious American forces in the Aleutian Islands. The United States gained ground gradually in the Marshall Islands in February, 1944; the Marianas in June; and in Guam and New Guinea in July. That same year a Japanese invasion of India resulted in a resounding defeat at the hands of Indian and British forces. On July 18, 1944, Prime Minister Tojo resigned, and Japan withdrew from Burma soon after. On October 20, 1944, General Douglas MacArthur attacked the Philippines, following a Japanese naval defeat at Leyte Gulf (this three-day clash became famous for the suicide missions of Japanese kamikaze pilots who crashed their planes into American warships), and Manila fell to the Allies on March 3, 1945. By December, 1944, United States forces attacked the island of Iwo Jima, which they invaded on February 19 and had captured by March, 1945. Meanwhile British and Indian forces took Burma on March 19, 1945, and on April 1, 1945, the United States invaded Japan at Okinawa, conquering the island by June 22. The tenacious Japanese resistance resulted in the loss of more than one hundred thousand Japanese and seven thousand Americans.

Japan continued to resist peace and rejected the Potsdam Declaration of July 26, 1945, which directed unconditional surrender. On August 6, 1945, the United States dropped the atomic bomb on Hiroshima and followed this with a second bomb on Nagasaki on August 9 (*see* Hiroshima and Nagasaki bombings). One day before the Nagasaki bombing, the Soviet Union declared war on Japan. In an unprecedented radio broadcast to his subjects, Emperor Hirohito proclaimed the surrender of Japan on August 15, 1945, and the Japanese government surrendered officially on September 2, 1945.

JAPANESE PROPAGANDA According to Harold D. Lasswell in his *Propaganda Technique in the World War* (1972), "modern war must be fought on three fronts: the military front, the economic front, and the propaganda front. The economic blockade strangles, the propaganda confuses, and the armed force delivers the coup de grace." The Japanese government, which rarely used the word propaganda, referred to this aspect as "thought war."

Japanese propaganda during World War II was intended to influence its own populace to provide unquestioning support for the war effort. This was achieved by exaggerating the Japanese victories and minimizing their defeats. Japanese naval losses in the Pacific were not reported accurately inside Japan, and a campaign of deliberate misinformation kept the news of American victories from the Japanese people. The emperor's nationwide radio announcement on August 15, 1945, of Japan's surrender to Allied powers therefore came as a shock to most Japanese.

Within their conquered territories in China and Southeast Asia, the Japanese occupation forces also sought to isolate the public from the truth about the progress of the war. Instead they focused on the benefits of the Greater East Asia Co-Prosperity Sphere—a scheme to oust colonial rule from Asia, substitute Japanese hegemony in the region, and provide a source for cheap raw materials and markets for Japan. Loyalty to the emperor-God was the fundamental basis of all Japanese propaganda, and it sought to inspire Japanese troops, including the kamikaze pilots engaged in suicidal bombing missions, with the belief that they were dying for their ruler.

Propaganda was in the hands of various governmental departments, and although there was a general air of confusion and a multiplicity of sources, the message was similar. Whether the propaganda emanated from the Ministry for Greater East Asiatic Affairs or from the Information Bureau or the Army Press Section, the information presented the Japanese as beleaguered, peace-loving people fighting a just war against colonial powers and their American allies. In the occupied territories the Japanese imposed severe censorship, including raids on homes to ensure that no foreign news was being disseminated.

Emperor Hirohito inspecting damage done to Tokyo by U.S. bombing raids toward the end of the war. Pictures such as this were seen by few Japanese until after the war. (*AP/Wide World Photos*)

Every available technological and communication means was used by Japan, including RADIO, the press (*see* JOURNALISM), LITERATURE, telephones, cables, and FILM (NEWSREELS and motion pictures) to convince the Japanese people of the government's propaganda aims, to demoralize Allied troops, and to control the inhabitants of the conquered territories.

The historian Leo Margolin has stated that "[t]he Japanese used propaganda as a double-barrelled weapon," and he suggests that Japan wanted to convince its people about the benefits of its imperial ventures and, prior to 1941, to ensure that the United States remained neutral while Japan conquered most of Asia. Hence the propaganda emphasized the Japanese dedication to peace and to the end of colonial oppression in Asia (*see* AN-

TICOLONIAL MOVEMENTS). Because the Japanese people were legally banned from owning SHORTWAVE RADIO sets after 1933, they had little access to foreign news broadcasts. A similar policy was followed in the conquered territories during the war.

Following its attack on Pearl Harbor, Japan concentrated its propaganda on efforts to demoralize U.S. forces through its radio broadcasts. The best-known of these broadcasters was the notorious Tokyo Rose (*see* TOKYO ROSE AND AXIS SALLY) on N.H.K. (the Japanese broadcasting corporation), who played American music for foreign troops and appealed to the loneliness and homesickness of American soldiers. Japan also attempted to alienate Australians from their American allies through radio propaganda.

The United States retaliated with radio broadcasts from Hawaii to Japan and Southeast Asia with the Allied version of the progress of the war. As Japanese defeats in the Pacific arena continued, Americans resorted to leaflet propaganda against Japan. The German general Erich Ludendorff, who was prominent in WORLD WAR I, once wrote that "[t]here are times and situations when one ton of propaganda leaflets—skillfully prepared and properly placed—can do more damage than one hundred tons of high explosive."

Japanese propaganda was all-encompassing and presented a totally false picture of the progress of World War II; it minimized defeats, misinformed the Japanese about casualties, and failed to warn the people about the real possibility of eventual surrender until the emperor made the announcement in August, 1945. The Japanese fought the propaganda war as ferociously as they fought the military war. With consummate skill they wove a web of misinformation to their own people and DISINFORMATION to the outside world. Ultimately their thought war was not able to conceal the grim reality of military defeats, foreign invasion, and enormous battlefield casualties. It has been suggested that the propaganda war had the ultimate effect of turning the Japanese public away from war and in favor of world peace.

SUGGESTED READINGS:

Daniels, Gordon. "Japanese Domestic Radio and Cinema Propaganda, 1937-1945: An Overview." In *Film and Radio Propaganda in World War II*, edited by K. R. M. Short. Knoxville: University of Tennessee Press, 1983.

Grant, Neil. *Illustrated History of Twentieth Century Conflict*. London: Hamlyn, 1992.

Nornes, Abe Mark, and Fukushima Yukio, eds. *The Japan/American Film Wars: World War II Propaganda and Its Cultural Contexts*. Langhorne, Pa.: Harwood Academic Publishers, 1994.

Taylor, Philip M. *Munitions of the Mind: War Propaganda from the Ancient World to the Nuclear Age*. Wellingborough, England: P. Stephens, 1990.

— *Ranee Panjabi*

■ World War II: Neutral nations

The participants in the war engaged in energetic propaganda efforts to recruit neutral nations or at the very least persuade them to stay neutral

The belligerent powers of World War II carried out vigorous propaganda campaigns in Sweden, PORTUGAL, SPAIN, and Switzerland. The two chief antagonists in this propaganda war were Germany (*see* GERMANY: 1933-1945 and WORLD WAR II: GERMAN PROPAGANDA) and Great Britain (*see* WORLD WAR II: BRITISH PROPAGANDA) although the United States made a major propaganda effort after entering the war as an ally of the British in December of 1941 (*see* WORLD WAR II: U.S. PROPAGANDA). The three powers used different propaganda approaches to gain influence in the neutral nations. Germany typically made brazen claims for the invincibility of its war machine and the inevitability of the expansion of the Third Reich. The British used more subtle approaches that focused on respect for the national traditions of the neutral nations and their historic ties to Great Britain. The United States used methods that fell somewhere between German bombast and British subtly, often relying on Hollywood films (*see* FILM: WORLD WAR II) to influence the public in neutral nations.

The neutral governments usually did not mount extensive propaganda campaigns themselves but instead used various forms of CENSORSHIP to protect their NEUTRALITY by limiting the flow of external communications.

German propaganda had considerable potential in Sweden, where the public distrusted Russia and generally approved of Germany's invasion of that communist nation. Aware of the Swedish point of view, British propagandists followed a carefully designed pattern that expressed respect for the Swedish nation and encouraged Swedish neutrality. London effectively contrasted Germany's strident, warmongering pronouncements with Great Britain's long-standing economic and cultural ties to Sweden. In 1943 Great Britain and the United States scored significant propaganda triumphs in the Swedish public's responses to news articles and motion pictures, notably Hollywood's *The Moon Is Down* (involving Norway's antifascist underground movement). The Swedish government tilted its policies and public statements toward the Allies during the last two years of the war as Germany's defeat became more likely.

PORTUGAL AND SPAIN The strategically located Iberian peninsula was dominated by two fascist governments—the regimes of Antonio Salazar in Lisbon and Francisco FRANCO in Madrid—but the peoples of these two nations were inclined to support the British. This tension between governments and general populace, in addition to the peninsula's vital location made these two nations into propaganda battlegrounds. German propaganda seemed to thrive in Portugal during the 1939-1941 period of Blitzkrieg successes. The British were concerned about Salazar, whose main role in the propaganda struggle was the selective enforcement of censorship laws, often against messages from London. The Germans, however, were unable to compete with popular British films, London's appeals to traditional Christian values, and the historic ties between the two nations. Nazi propagandists resorted to the tactic of demonizing their opponent while lauding the military might of the German divisions, an approach that converted few Portuguese and apparently alienated many. After German defeats in North Africa and Russia in 1942-1943 the British gained the upper hand in most Portuguese media with the tacit approval of Lisbon.

Franco's regime had received crucial military aid from Germany and Italy during the SPANISH CIVIL WAR. British and U.S. observers feared that Franco would make an alliance with the fascist powers. The German defeat of France in June, 1940, stimulated a wave of pronouncements from the Falange Party that created the impression that Spain was turning away from neutrality toward the Axis powers. British propaganda efforts in print and film met formidable barriers in Spanish censorship, and the anticommunist Franco was emboldened by early German victories in the Soviet Union. Anti-British demonstrations in front of the British embassy in Madrid in the summer of 1941 was probably the low point for London's diplomatic propaganda campaign in Spain. The British ambassador Sir Samuel Hoare protested Spanish censorship of information from British sources but chose not to engage in full-blown condemnations of fascism for fear of pushing Franco further in the direction of the Axis. In 1942 and 1943 U.S. ambassador Carlton J. H. Hayes initiated a carefully pointed campaign to reinforce Spanish neutrality that stressed the differences between the extremists in the Falange and the Spanish citizenry. Hayes was concerned about Spanish influence in the Western Hemisphere—especially in Argentina where a pro-Axis military government held power. Hayes encountered problems, however, when criticisms of fascism drew complaints from the Franco regime. Only in the last months of the war, with Germany's collapse imminent, did British and U.S. propagandists operate without serious Spanish government interference.

SWITZERLAND Located in the Alps between Germany and Italy, Switzerland posed special problems for British propaganda. London's agents had difficulty in transporting film and printed matter into this mountainous nation, whereas German-language feature films and newsreels enjoyed large audiences. In spite of the Nazis' obvious advantages in capturing the attention of the German-speaking portion of Switzerland's population, British propaganda specialists reported that Berlin's appeals had little lasting impact on the independent-minded Swiss. The British did not gain many propaganda victories, but they were content to accept the steadfastness of Swiss neutrality as a positive sign for the Allied cause. In the last two years of the war German propaganda lost much of its appeal when German forces met defeat on the battlefield.

Propaganda did not convert the neutral nations to either the Axis or the Allied camps, but it did reinforce existing preferences for the democratic civility of Great Britain and the United States over the militaristic hyperbole of Nazi Germany. The most protracted struggle was in Spain, where the British and the United States overcame the barriers laid down by the profascist Falange and the vacillating Franco government to strengthen that nation's neutralist tendencies. Given Spain's strategic location and the recent triumph of fascism there, this hard-won propaganda advantage was no small triumph.

SUGGESTED READINGS:

Balfour, Michael. *Propaganda in War, 1939-1945: Organizations, Politics, and Publics in Britain and Germany*. London: Routledge & Kegan Paul, 1979.

Cole, Robert. *Britain and the War of Words in Neutral Europe, 1939-1945*. New York: St. Martin's Press, 1990.

Hayes, Carlton J. H. *Wartime Mission in Spain, 1942-1945*. New York: Macmillan, 1945.

Herzstein, Robert Edwin. *The War That Hitler Won: The Most Infamous Propaganda Campaign in History*. New York: G. P. Putnam's, 1978.

— *John A. Britton*

■ World War II: Soviet propaganda

The Soviet Union's propaganda messages changed as the country's diplomatic ties shifted

Anglo-French appeasement of Nazi Germany (*see* GERMANY: 1933-1945), coupled with continued isolationism by the United States (*see* UNITED STATES: 1919-1941), caused the Soviet Union (*see* RUSSIA: 1918-1953) to abandon its policy of

ЮНОШИ и ДЕВУШКИ,
ЗАЩИЩАЙТЕ СВОБОДУ, РОДИНУ и
ЧЕСТЬ, ЗАВОЕВАННЫЕ ВАШИМИ ОТЦАМИ
1917

Soviet wartime poster appealing to young men and women to "defend the freedom, the nation, and the honor fought for by your fathers." (*Library of Congress*)

collective security and sign, on August 23, 1939, a Non-Aggression Pact with Germany. At that point Soviet propaganda ceased urging an antifascist coalition of all democracy-loving nations and instead hailed the pact as a peace move designed to prevent international conflagration. Nine days later Germany attacked Poland, causing the outbreak of World War II.

ONSET OF WAR With the outbreak of war the COMINTERN replaced its slogans urging popular front and collective security, which had served for the preceding five years, and made posters (*see* POSTER ART) denouncing "the new imperialist war." At the same time Joseph STALIN used the opportunity provided by the Non-Aggression Pact to recover those

parts of the former czarist empire that had been lost in the Bolshevik Revolution: East Poland, the Baltic states, and Finland. Soviet aggression was rationalized as national security, and Poland was dismissed as "the monster child of the Treaty of Versailles."

During the period of the Non-Aggression Pact, the Soviet Union made few favorable statements about the Nazi regime, and there were no organized rallies in support of the pact or cultural exchanges with Adolf HITLER's Germany. Instead, in a rather defensive posturing, Soviet propaganda touted the Red Army as the finest in the world and proclaimed that Russian industry was capable of high output. Warnings to Stalinist Russia during the late spring, 1941, about an impending and monumental German attack were denounced as absurd rumors spread by anti-Soviet interests. Blinded by his own propaganda, Stalin did not act immediately even when Germany invaded on June 22, 1941. Initial reports from the front were met with inaction and disbelief.

A *Pravda* editorial on June 23 announced a "fatherland war" to be launched by the people of the Soviet Union against the Nazi invader. The term "fatherland war" became firmly planted, as did the emphasis on traditional Russian nationalism, which replaced themes related to building a communist utopia. Ten days after the invasion Stalin in a radio address called for a patriotic war of liberation against the fascist enslaver. He ordered a scorched-earth policy and the formation of partisan bands in occupied territories. Allusions were made to past Russian greatness, including the victory over Napoleon in 1812, the historic greatness of czarist generals such as Prince Suvorov and Prince Kutuzov, and the victory seven centuries earlier of Alexander Nevsky. *Pravda* and *Red Star* (the military newspaper) were used to fan the flames of hatred, preaching "no mercy to the German invaders! Death to the German invaders!" Patriotic poems were published, along with news highlights about the bravery of individual soldiers and units, as a substitute for actual news about what was happening on the individual battlefronts.

Faced with a struggle for its very existence, the full propaganda potential of Soviet Russia was unleashed as a weapon of war. Radio Moscow and Leningrad used news reporting to increase public confidence in ultimate victory. There were readings of letters from the front, letters from partisans, inspirational poems, patriotic LITERATURE, nationalistic songs, and innumerable speeches by Stalin, who emerged as the omniscient engineer of the ultimate victory; soon the slogan "For our Country and Stalin" was in general use (*see* SLOGANS). Artists were instructed to use their creativity to portray Germans in posters as demonic and sadistic criminals, as well as predatory animals and spiders. Atrocities were highlighted and righteous revenge underscored. Songwriters drew on nationalistic feelings by using traditional Russian folk melodies, to which they set new words that depicted defence of motherland, hometown, and heroism in battle. "Sacred War, a patriotic hymn urging Russians to rise up against the invaders dark hoard, became the semiofficial national anthem during the course of the war. Classical composers created magnificent new works among them Dmitri Shostakovich's Seventh Symphony, called the *Leningrad* Symphony, and Sergei Prokoviev's *War and Peace* (*see* MUSIC).

Playwrights (*see* THEATER AND DRAMA) devoted their talents to historical dramas to inspire national pride, the most famous being Konstantin Simonov's *The Russian People* and *Wait for Me* (1942). In stressing the love of Russia and hatred of Germany, Ilya Ehrenberg, author of the popular poem "Kill Him," proved to be Russia's most powerful wartime writer.

FILM PROPAGANDA Particularly effective for propaganda was Russian FILM; filmmakers produced more than seventy films and documentaries during the war, and NEWSREELS such as *Defeat of the Russian Armies near Moscow* and *A Day of the War, June 1942* produced pride in the Soviet military. Feature-length films dealt with themes such as the courage of Soviet partisans, as in *The Rainbow*, and of female heroes, as in *She Defends the Motherland* and *Zoia*. In the last-named the heroine is hanged by Nazis but dies smiling in a superimposed closeup as Soviet tanks and fighter planes move westward to victory.

By 1943 themes related to communism had all but disappeared from Soviet propaganda. Dressed in a marshal's uniform, Stalin sought to embody traditional Russian nationalism. In September 1943 the Russian Orthodox church was rehabilitated and the Patriarchate reestablished. In return Patriarch Sergei proclaimed Stalin "the divinely anointed." Medals, orders, and even military academies were named after heroes from the czarist past. The "Communist Internationale" was no longer the Soviet national anthem, and the Comintern was dissolved to allay lingering Allied fears. Communists throughout Europe were ordered to cooperate with all antifascist elements in popular front resistance movements. Winston CHURCHILL and Franklin D. ROOSE-

VELT were often complimented as being part of the united front for freedom against slavery; similarly, in the United States Stalin became "Uncle Joe."

Following the invasion of Normandy, however, after the victory at Stalingrad, Stalin began to fear contact with the armies of his allies. Articles began to appear in *Pravda* and *Red Star* warning Russians about the false glitter of bourgeois culture. At the end of the war Stalin informed a party meeting that "the war on fascism ends, the war on capitalism begins." Soon the United States had replaced Nazi Germany as the embodiment of imperialist aggression, and the Soviet propaganda machine once again shifted gears.

SUGGESTED READINGS:

Nation, R. Craig. *Black Earth, Red Star: A History of Soviet Security Policy, 1917-1991.* Ithaca, N.Y.: Cornell University Press, 1992.

Raack, R. C. *Stalin's Drive to the West, 1938-1945.* Stanford, Calif.: Stanford University Press, 1995.

Stites, Richard, ed. *Culture and Entertainment in Wartime Russia.* Bloomington: University of Indiana Press, 1995.

Werth, Alexander. *Russia at War, 1941-1945.* New York: E. P. Dutton, 1964.

— *Irwin Halfond*

■ World War II: U.S. propaganda

American wartime propaganda covered topics ranging from many aspects of daily life to carefully structured governmental policy

U.S. propaganda strategies and tactics during World War II reflected many characteristics of overall American society.

Propaganda efforts, which were largely a merger of capitalist and democratic ideals and practices, tended to be extensive, complex, and diverse. Propaganda efforts were frequently a combination of private initiative and public policy. The needs of government, business, and the public were often simultaneously addressed.

Unlike the persuasive efforts of those in totalitarian societies such as Nazi Germany, Japan, and the Soviet Union, U.S. propagandists rarely spoke with a single voice. Instead, their propaganda stressed American economic productivity, power, and commitment to the war effort, as well as focusing on the somewhat nebulous American "way of life" through countless vignettes of everyday activities such as baseball and gardening. Optimism was frequently combined with hard truth, such as reporting threatened labor strikes or racial disturbances as examples of the democratic process in action. Government agencies, the military, businesses, and civilian organizations were involved in propaganda campaigns during the war.

GOVERNMENT PROPAGANDA SOURCES Two federal agencies were most responsible for U.S. propaganda efforts—the Office of Censorship (OC) and the OFFICE OF WAR INFORMATION (OWI). The OC, established in December, 1941, was directed by Byron Price, a former executive news editor of the Associated Press. The office, staffed by more than fourteen thousand people, monitored all communications between the United States and other countries, and it monitored domestic information originating from military installations or businesses with military contracts. The organization's censorship of most domestic communication, including mass media, relied on voluntary compliance. In January, 1942, the OC issued the *Code of Wartime Practices for the American Press*, which detailed what constituted improper reporting of military activities; a similar code was presented to RADIO stations. Throughout the war nearly all American news operations closely followed the codes.

The Office of War Information (OWI), formed in June, 1942, to coordinate war-related information, superseded several government agencies such as the Office of Facts and Figures. Elmer DAVIS, a network radio commentator and former *New York Times* staff member, directed the organization. Divided into domestic and overseas branches, the OWI provided news about war policies and activities, and it also developed propaganda campaigns to bolster the war effort. By May, 1945, the agency employed 9,600 people worldwide.

The OWI news bureau offered to the nation's media a steady diet of news stories, weekly digests, features, cartoons, and photographs. The OWI also coordinated promotional campaigns. Print journalists, columnists, advertisers, cartoonists, broadcasters, and film personnel were regularly given background information concerning government objectives. The OWI sent monthly guides to media and advertising personnel suggesting themes and topics that promoted the war effort. In addition, the organization produced its own films, such as *Get a War Job*, and reviewed and helped distribute Hollywood war films to domestic and overseas audiences (*see* FILM: 1939-1945). By the war's end much of the OWI budget was devoted to its SHORTWAVE RADIO broadcasts overseas, known as the VOICE OF AMERICA.

MILITARY PROPAGANDA SOURCES Propaganda from the branches of the U.S. military took two forms: the production of words, photographs, and films; and the withholding of communication. The production of messages had several purposes, depending on the audience. Some stories, photographs, and films by military personnel were released to the American public, usually to bolster morale; the best example of this is Frank CAPRA's *Why We Fight* series. Other communications targeted overseas audiences, particularly those in Axis-held territory. Here military personnel often worked with the OWI and its Voice of America radio broadcasts, as well as with intelligence agencies such as the Psychological Warfare Service (PFS) and the Office of Strategic Services (OSS), which after the war evolved into the CENTRAL INTELLIGENCE AGENCY (CIA). The OSS and PFS produced materials such as radio programming and leaflets meant to affect the morale of enemy troops.

However, most military communication was produced for the American troops. Almost every major military unit had its own publication, and some publications, such as *Stars and Stripes* and *Yank*, developed circulations in the millions. The Army, Army Air Corps, Navy, and Marine Corps also had their own film and photographic units, which by war's end had produced millions of feet of film footage, much of which was meant to help train soldiers. The Army Signal Corps' Pictorial Service produced more than 2,500 training films during the war, among them *Trench Foot* and *Conservation of Clothing and Equipment*. Film units also produced many morale-building films for soldiers, such as *Know Your Ally Britain*,

Caricatures of the leaders of the Axis powers typically depicted them as objects of ridicule. (*National Archives*)

produced early in the war, and *Two Down and One to Go*, produced after the fall of Italy and Germany in order to prepare troops for an invasion of Japan. Feature-length documentary films— such as *Memphis Belle*, a film about a bomber crew's experiences in the skies of Europe—were shown to military units and the general public.

Much of this military material, particularly photographs and film footage, never reached the American public. Although the War and Navy Departments were required to consult with the OWI about withholding specific information from the public, the services could override OWI recommendations and often did. The OWI often wanted material—especially photographs and film footage depicting the horrors of war— that the military refused to release. Images of dead American soldiers in grotesque positions were censored, as were those showing details of wounds. Likewise pictures indicating that American soldiers treated enemy dead with contempt, such as one showing a dead German soldier whose body was embellished with American playing cards, were withheld.

Early in the war America's various media usually followed the War Department's lead and practiced self-censorship. Starting in 1943, however, images of American dead began to appear, as when *Life* magazine published photographs of dead American troops on a New Guinea beach. Such images did not come close to fully revealing the horrors of war, however.

CIVILIAN PROPAGANDA SOURCES Civilian propaganda often originated with directives from government or military organizations such as the OWI. Print, radio, and film media not only voluntarily censored their stories, images, and programs, they actively promoted the war effort in a variety of ways. The War Advertising Council, formed in late 1941 by advertisers, agencies, and media, worked closely with the OWI and other government agencies such as the Treasury Department. The council organized many campaigns to promote the war effort. Selling war bonds, boosting military recruitment, increasing the number of women and minority workers in factories, and persuading citizens to ration and grow their own "victory gardens" were some of the goals of the War Advertising Council. Although the government paid for recruitment advertising, all other campaigns were paid for by business and media donations.

Radio, NEWSREELS, magazines, and NEWSPAPERS also promoted the war effort in news and feature and entertainment stories. Producers, commentators, editors, writers, and columnists often produced materials under OWI guidelines. For example, starting in December 1942, mass media began promoting the recruitment of women into war-industry jobs (*see* ROSIE THE RIVETER). This promotional effort originated with recommendations from the OWI, the federal War Manpower Commission, and the War Department. The campaigns used advertising such as posters (*see* POSTER ART), billboards, and magazine advertisements, but they also used magazine feature stories, newspaper articles, short films, and radio programs, both fictional and nonfictional. Campaigns promoting war-bond sales used similar tactics (*see* WAR BONDS).

The federal government and Hollywood developed a close but wary relationship during the war years. The motion picture industry, distrustful of government because of an ongoing antitrust case against film companies, nevertheless organized the War Activities Committee in 1941. Through the committee the film industry worked with the War Department and OWI in producing hundreds of feature-length motion pictures that in some way promoted the war effort. By war's end the OWI had reviewed 1,652 Hollywood film scripts. During the war the committee also distributed 43,000 prints of Hollywood films free of charge to American troops.

Hollywood cooperated closely with the military in the production of many war films from 1941 through 1945. Film companies had to work with the military in order to use military facilities, equipment, and film footage in their own war productions. As a result throughout the war nearly all Hollywood motion pictures presented a positive view of the American war effort. In such films as *Thirty Seconds over Tokyo*, *Guadalcanal Diary*, and *The Fighting Seabees*, class and racial differences in society evaporated; Allied bombing rarely killed civilians except for war workers; military units were close-knit teams; the Japanese were racially inferior; the Nazis were simply evil; and the American "way of life" was the most virtuous in the world.

SUGGESTED READINGS:

Doherty, Thomas. *Projections of War: Hollywood, American Culture, and World War II*. New York: Columbia University Press, 1993.

O'Brien, Kenneth, and Lynn Parsons, eds. *The Home-Front War: World War II and American Society*. Westport, Conn.: Greenwood Press, 1995.

Roeder, George. *The Censored War: American Visual Experience During World War II*. New Haven, Conn.: Yale University Press, 1993.

Rupp, Leila. *Mobilizing Women for War: German and American Propaganda, 1939-1945*. Princeton, N.J.: Princeton University Press, 1978.

Soley, Lawrence. *Radio Warfare: OSS and CIA Subversive Propaganda*. New York: Praeger, 1989.

Winkler, Allan. *The Politics of Propaganda: The Office of War Information, 1942-1945*. New Haven, Conn.: Yale University Press, 1978.

— *Charles Lewis*

X

■ Xenophobia

The term literally means the fear or hatred of strangers and foreigners. It may be inspired by misunderstanding or racial prejudice, and it is made to order for PROPAGANDISTS who draw upon paranoia, fear, LABELING, or jingoistic language in their campaigns (*see* PARANOIA PROPAGANDA, FEAR CAMPAIGNS, and JINGOISM). Xenophobia is a regular feature of political, social, and war propaganda. Two examples are KU KLUX KLAN propaganda that portrays Jews and Catholics as representing foreign conspiracies against American values, and African Americans as not actually being Americans; and Nazi propaganda that encouraged Germans to be antiforeigner, especially after the outbreak of WORLD WAR II.

Y

■ Yellow journalism

Traditionally understood to mean news reporting that attracts and influences readers through cheap sensationalism and unscrupulous methods, this kind of journalism is not concerned with accuracy or honesty. Historically associated with the late nineteenth century press magnates Joseph Pulitzer and William Randolph HEARST, yellow journalism more recently has come to be associated with the tabloid press and such "investigative" television programs as *Inside Edition* and *Current Affair*. That such programs attract large audiences and that the tabloid press sells to a wide readership suggests a general public that is less than critical in its consideration of journalism that purports to be telling the "TRUTH." Yellow journalism need not be propaganda, but it often draws upon similar techniques, among them LABELING, CONSPIRACY THEORY, and DISTORTION.

■ Yom Kippur War

1973: Israeli war against Egypt and Syria

The fourth Arab-Israeli war, also known as the October War, the War of Ramadan, and the Yom Kippur War, began on Saturday, October 6, 1973. SYRIA and EGYPT coordinated assaults along two fronts, the Golan Heights and the Sinai Peninsula.

THE CAUSES OF THE WAR AND WORLD REACTION In 1971 and 1972 Anwar al SADAT secretly began making plans for war. Seven months after the war's end Sadat, speaking before an audience at the University of Alexandria, declared: "I knew I had to fight when I took office." He began by purging the Soviets from Egypt for "freedom of maneuver," as he explained, and he made renewed alliances with such Arab neighbors as Jordan, LIBYA, Syria, and SAUDI ARABIA, attempting to cajole Syria's President Assad and Jordan's King Hussein into agreeing to wage war against ISRAEL.

One of Sadat's objectives was to gain control of the wealth provided by the tolls of the Suez Canal. A second objective was to recapture Israeli-occupied areas of Syria, Jordan, and Egypt. Ostensibly, however, the main reason for war was the restoration of the rights of Palestinian Arabs.

At a Cairo summit, which Sadat called to unite Syria, Jordan, and Egypt into a military alliance, Hussein appealed for resolution through diplomacy. After the adjournment of the summit, as a result of Sadat's effective use of propaganda, with which he veiled his real objectives, Hussein persuaded himself that Egypt and Syria were in agreement with him.

In a sense the war was a proxy between the two great superpowers, the UNITED STATES and the Soviet Union, in which Israel and Egypt served as quasi-client states (*see* COLD WAR). Although Sadat was an avowed socialist, his stance toward the Soviet Union was ambivalent. After expelling the Soviets from Egypt he tried to minimize the damage to the diplomatic relations; he wanted no interference from the Soviets, but he also wanted to secure the supply of Soviet arms. The Soviet Union advised nonmilitary action to resolve the Mideast conflict. Israel had the moral support of the United States, but the secretary of state, Henry Kissinger, was afraid to give military support for fear of an armed conflict with the Soviet Union.

Despite being alert to belligerent action on the part of any of its Arab neighbors, Israel was under the mistaken belief that such action would only be spurred by a Palestinian uprising. On June 12, 1971, Sadat and Assad agreed on joint military action. The Egyptian and Syrian military leaders rejected the idea of a Blitzkrieg assault and instead opted for a war of attrition, called by Egypt's General Ahmed Ismail in the periodical *Al Ahram* a "meat-grinder" war.

On the holiest day of the Jewish liturgical calendar, Yom Kippur, the Day of Atonement, a day of fasting and repentance, Egypt and Syria coordinated a surprise attack on Israel. Egypt attacked the Israeli-held Sinai Peninsula, opening the campaign with an assault across the Suez Canal, and Syria attacked the Golan Heights. While the UNITED NATIONS attempted to pass resolutions calling for a cease-fire, the United States hesitated over whether to provide Israel with military supplies. The Soviet Union, by contrast, was quick to assist the Arabs with a massive airlift. News of the Soviet airlift galvanized American support for Israel, even though the United States had to consider its growing dependency upon Arab oil.

When Israel, having suffered heavy losses, contemplated using its nuclear capabilities against its Arab antagonists, the United States and the Soviet Union stepped up their efforts for a cease-fire. Both the superpowers feared being pulled deeper into the conflict. Hesitant to use nuclear force, Golda Meir spoke on television to express her willingness to talk about a cease-fire with the Arabs, though she felt threatened by Assad's words that spoke of liberating the whole land. If by whole land he meant all of Palestine, then the Israelis would be willing to use ultimate force to maintain their existence as a nation-state. Speaking to the Knesset, Israel's parliament, Meir claimed that the Arabs meant to retake all of Israel, and she also rebuked the Soviets for their assistance to the Arabs. Assad explained on television that the war's objective was to restore confidence and dignity to Arabs. At first the Egyptian offensive was successful, but it was quickly repulsed by the Israeli military under the leadership of Ariel Sharon. Through efforts by the UNITED NATIONS, the United States, and the Soviet Union, Israel and the Arab nations agreed to a cease-fire.

THE ARAB OIL WEAPON Even though the Arabs were defeated militarily, they were successful economically. The great oil embargo of 1973 was a weapon of enormous impact. It could very well be said that the oil embargo was a continuation of the 1973 war. The United States, Europe, and Japan were hurt by the embargo.

In fact, the Arab nations, through the ORGANIZATION OF PETROLEUM EXPORTING COUNTRIES (OPEC) planned to use oil as a weapon and, by means of cutting supply and increasing prices, to arrive at a resolution of the Palestinian problem. About 90 percent of the world's oil supplies were owned and controlled by OPEC. The United States was particularly vulnerable because of its dependency upon foreign oil producers. The United States claimed only 6 percent of the world's population but consumed 30 percent of the world's oil. Moreover, between 1969 and 1972 U.S. oil imports increased by 83 percent. Libya's Muammar al-Qaddafi spurred Arab nations to cut off oil supply. Saudi Arabia's King Faisal threatened in a television broadcast that the U.S. support of ZIONISM would lead him to cut off the oil supply. OPEC promised to restore oil supply when the rights of the Palestinians were restored.

One result of the Arab-Israeli War of 1973 was the unification of the Arab nations—an objective that not even Gamal Abdel NASSER had been able to achieve. To prevent a similar war in the future, it appeared that Israel must accept the existence of a Palestinian state, and Arab nations must accept the existence of a Jewish state in Palestine.

SUGGESTED READINGS:

Choueiri, Youssef. *Islamic Fundamentalism*. Boston: Twayne, 1990.

Lippman, Thomas. *Understanding Islam: An Introduction to the Moslem World*. Rev. ed. New York: New American Library, 1990.

The Yom Kippur War. New York: Doubleday, 1974.

— *Michael R. Candelaria*

■ Youth movements

Propaganda has played an important role in mass youth movements around the world, in both democratic and authoritarian societies

Organized by a central authority and often used to propagate specific ideological values, youth movements are aimed at young people ranging in age anywhere from six to their late twenties. Youth organizations in democratic societies generally reflect the dominant societal values and rely upon voluntary membership. In contrast, mass youth organizations in authoritarian societies reflect the values of the ruling party and depend to a greater or lesser extent on coercive measures to increase their membership.

PURPOSE AND CHARACTERISTICS Mass youth organizations in democratic societies are often organized around a core of civic virtues, secular values, or religious belief systems. The purpose of these organizations is to instill in their members the appropriate ideals and attitudes so as to transmit respective values or belief systems from one generation to the next. Through thus appropriating young people's leisure time, the proponents of one belief system can prevent young people's being exposed to other belief systems. Although there is usually no formal tie in democratic societies between youth organizations and the state, conservative governments generally favor and support their work as long as it propagates the appropriate values or civic virtues and thus contributes to the stability of the government.

Youth organizations in totalitarian societies are generally characterized by a pronounced militaristic and ideological flavor. Governments are involved, either directly or through the ruling party, in the organization and management of youth organizations; membership is often not voluntary, and governments use a variety of coercive measures to gain and to keep new members. Mass youth organiza-

Members of the Yugoslav Youth Labor Brigade marching with farm tools and a portrait of Marshall Tito. (*National Archives*)

tions in authoritarian societies generally claim a monopoly on all organized youth activities and serve as the training ground for future party members and for military and political leaders. Their purpose is to ensure the strengthening of the ideological foundation of the regime and the perpetuation of a party's teachings from generation to generation. Members are controlled and manipulated by a system of rewards, such as preferential treatment in admission to training or educational programs. Other characteristics of mass youth organizations in totalitarian societies include rituals of loyalty and the awarding of honors and military-style decorations to selected members. In some instances members of mass youth organizations are entrusted with specific tasks in the community, including police and surveillance tasks.

SCOUTING MOVEMENTS The most prominent mass youth movement in democratic societies is the scouting movement. About four million Boy Scouts and nearly one and a half million adult leaders are active in scouting in the United States alone. In more than one hundred countries worldwide more than ten million scouts and their leaders participate in a variety of scouting activities.

The Boy Scout movement was founded in 1907 by Robert BADEN-POWELL, a British army officer. The Boy Scout movement in the United States, which offers programs for boys from age eight through high-school age was established in 1910. The movement emphasizes duty to God and country, character development, physical and mental fitness, and good citizenship—qualities that are addressed in "The Scout Oath" and the "Scout Law." Boy Scots of America, since 1977 referred to as Scouting/USA, features an organizational structure that allows boys to meet a series of qualifying proficiency tests and to earn awards and merit badges with which they can advance to the highest rank, that of Eagle Scout. Throughout the process Scouts are involved in many activities that stress self-sufficiency, citizenship, personal honor, and leadership.

Girl Scouts of the USA, earlier known as Girl Guides, were organized in 1912 and today represent the largest voluntary organization for girls in the world. The program offers a variety of programs for girls from the ages of six to seventeen, and it stresses service to country, God, and humankind, which is expressed in the "Girl Scout Promise" and the "Girl Scout Law." Particular emphasis is placed on such areas as self awareness, awareness of various cultures, the arts and technology, and career awareness and exploration.

SOCIALIST YOUTH MOVEMENTS The most important mass youth movement in socialist countries, and in many respects the prototype of socialist youth movements around the world was the Komsomol, or All-Union Leninist Communist Youth.

Founded in 1918, the Komsomol became the principal organ for the spread of communist teaching and for the mobilization, indoctrination, and control of Soviet youth. As such the Komsomol became the primary training ground for politically reliable members of the Communist Party and virtually all important institutions of the nation. Following the Russian Revolution, during which its members were active as saboteurs and shock troops, the Komsomol played a major role in the campaign to collectivize agriculture and to assist in the drive to industrialize the nation. In addition, Komsomol members were involved in social and cultural activities and assisted the Communist Party in various tasks. During World War II the Komsomol again took up military and political duties, but it returned to civilian tasks after the war, when its members participated in massive construction tasks and agricultural projects. With the collapse of communism in the Soviet Union, the Komsomol voted in 1991 to dissolve.

Among the imitators of the Komsomol in other socialist nations was the Freie Deutsche Jugend (FDJ), or Free German Youth, established in the German Democratic Republic in 1946. The FDJ and its associated organizations, like the Young Pioneers, soon achieved a monopoly on all youth organizations in the country. Although the purpose of the FDJ was to see to it that all members mastered the teachings of Marxism-Leninism, the FDJ also declared that this did not require its members to be atheists. Like the Komsomol in the Soviet Union, the FDJ prepared young people for membership in the Socialist Unity Party (SED) and assisted in carrying out the policies of the SED whenever appropriate.

FASCIST YOUTH MOVEMENTS The earliest fascist youth movement of any consequence emerged in Italy. Under the guidance of the Fascist Party two major organizations emerged: the Gioventú universitaria fascista (GUF), which was specifically designed for university students and the less elitist and more broadly based Gioventú italiana del littorio (GIL). The emphasis in these organizations was primarily on glorifying war and imperialism and on instilling in its members the kinds of soldierly virtues reflected in the fascist motto "Believe, Obey, Fight." Although these organizations also appealed to girls, the ideal fascist woman was apolitical and expected to devote herself to more traditional tasks.

Like Italian FASCISM, German National Socialism also placed great importance on the indoctrination of youth. The principal organization and, after several years the only organization, for youth was the Hitler Jugend (HJ), or Hitler Youth, designed for boys aged fourteen through eighteen, and its counterpart for girls, Bund deutscher Mädchen (BDM), or League of German Maidens. Beginning in 1931 two organizations were added to accommodate boys and girls in the age group ten to fourteen. As of December, 1936, membership in these organizations was compulsory.

The purpose of the HJ and the BDM was to integrate German youth into the structure of the National Socialist state and to provide a training ground for the future leaders of the National Socialist Party and the state. Members of the Hitler Youth, in particular, were seen as soldiers of the National Socialist ideology. Their function was to guarantee the future of the Third Reich.

The indoctrination of German youth was achieved through a variety of programs that emphasized collective activities, including sports, hiking, and ideological instruction. The emphasis was on comradeship, racial awareness, and service to the *Volk*. With the outbreak of World War II the character of the HJ began to change as greater emphasis was placed on paramilitary instruction. The growing influence of the Schutzstaffel (SS) eventually led to the creation of the 12th SS Panzer division "Hitler Youth," which saw action in Normandy. The division was made up of about 10,000 boys, many of whom were not yet seventeen.

SUGGESTED READINGS:

Egorov, Vladimir. *Seventy Years of the Soviet Komsomol.* Moscow: Novosti Press Agency Publishing House, 1988. Provides a brief look at the Russian Communist youth organization.

Kasza, Gregory J. *The Conscription Society: Administered Mass Organizations.* New Haven, Conn.: Yale University Press, 1995. Analyzes the structures and functions of mass organizations in Japan, Germany, Italy, and the U.S.S.R.

Koch, H. W. *Hitler Youth: The Duped Generation.* New York: Ballantine Books, 1972. Survey of the history, training, and function of the Hitler Youth by a former member.

Rempel, Gerhard. *Hitler's Children: The Hitler Youth and the SS.* Chapel Hill: University of North Carolina Press, 1989. Explores the institutional and social processes through which the SS manipulated the Hitler Youth.

Soto, Carolyn. *The Boy Scouts.* New York: Exeter Books, 1987.

_____. *The Girl Scouts.* New York: Exeter Books, 1987. Basic overview of scouting in the United States, Canada, and the United Kingdom. Extensive pictorial coverage.

Tannenbaum, Edward R. *The Fascist Experience: Italian Society and Culture, 1922-1945.* New York: Basic Books, 1972. Contains a useful and readable summary of the Fascist socialization of Italian youth.

— *Helmut J. Schmeller*

■ Yugoslavia

Southeast European nation that in 1991 split into the separate nations of Croatia, Slovenia, Yugoslavia (Serbia and Montenegro), Macedonia, and Bosnia-Herzegovina

From its founding in 1918 to its collapse in 1991, Yugoslavia was the focus of propaganda campaigns. Although heir to a glorious history, the modern state (called Yugoslavia from 1929) began as the Kingdom of Serbs, Croats, and Slovenes in 1919, after the end of World War I.

In the century before WORLD WAR I the area was subject to occupying powers (Austria-Hungary and the Ottoman Empire) and native liberation movements. The Serbs, wishing to become free of Ottoman domination, directed their propaganda efforts to their coreligionist Russians, hoping to involve Russia in a war of liberation against the Turks. The Croats, though loyal to the Habsburg monarchy, suffered discrimination from both Austrians and Hungarians. Hostile relations between Austria-Hungary and Serbia developed after 1908, when Austria annexed

■ Yugoslavia: History at a Glance

Year	Event
1914	World War I is precipitated by the assassination in Sarajevo of Francis Ferdinand, Archduke of Austria. The assassin is a Serbian nationalist; although Serbia is independent at the time, other regions of what would become Yugoslavia are part of the Austro-Hungarian Empire.
1918	The Kingdom of the Serbs, Croats, and Slovenes is created in a region long divided by various political powers and ethnic nationalities.
1929	The country is renamed Yugoslavia by its king, Alexander. Croatian and Macedonian nationalists urge autonomy for their regions.
1931	A constitution is adopted.
1934	King Alexander is assassinated.
1941	Yugoslavia is invaded by Germany. Resistance fighters include Josip Broz Tito, a communist.
1945	Tito, with the support of the U.S.S.R., wins factional disputes among the resistance leaders and becomes the leader of Yugoslavia after the Germans are ousted.
1948	Tito breaks some ties with Moscow, instituting his own communist foreign and domestic policy.
1980	Tito dies after bringing a period of stability to the region. A system is initiated by which the presidency rotates among ethnic groups.
1991	Croats and Slovenians vote for independence. Civil war among ethnic groups begins.
1992	The Yugoslav federation dissolves; Yugoslavia formally ceases to exist. The nations of Slovenia and Croatia are created.
1992	The United Nations intervenes to halt Serbian forces invading Bosnia-Hercegovina.
1993	Civil war continues as three principal groups—the Serbs, the Croats, and the Muslims—fight for territory.
1994	United States forces enter into the Bosnian conflict, bombing Serbian positions.

Bosnia, an area occupied by Moslems, Serbs, and Croats. The assassination in 1914 of the Austrian archduke, Franz Ferdinand, by a Bosnian Serb triggered World War I.

The interwar years witnessed strife between the Serbs and Croats. In 1934 Alexander Karageorgevic, the king of Yugoslavia, was assassinated by a Croat Ustasha (an extreme nationalist organization) agent. Terrorist activities relating to Macedonia and various political parties were frequent.

The 1930's brought the rise of National Socialism in Germany, fascism in Italy, and communism in Yugoslavia. During World War II, when the Yugoslavian monarchy made a pact with Adolf HITLER's Nazi government, the Yugoslavs refused to accept it. Hitler retaliated by bombing Belgrade in April, 1941. He also set up the puppet state of Croatia under the leadership of Ustasha terrorists. Thus began a civil war that engulfed Yugoslavia until after the end of the war.

World War II opened the way to the dictatorship of Josip Broz TITO, a COMINTERN agent for the Soviet Union and a military leader of great ability. Tito's partisans, by an effective propaganda campaign directed against the Serbian Chetniks and their commander Draza Mihailovic, as well as their own military success against both Chetniks and Germans, convinced the Allies that they should be given military aid.

Following the war, with Tito installed as leader of the country, Yugoslavia pursued its own path to communism. Tito managed, through skillful use of the media in Yugoslavia, and his own public-relations efforts, to break away from the Soviet bloc, set up loan and trade agreements with the West, and liquidate his own internal political enemies. He convinced noncommunist countries that his initiatives, including worker self-management, promotion of the tourist trade, and strategic alliances with other nonaligned powers, benefited world peace. Yugoslavia was also the first Soviet-bloc country to abandon SOCIALIST REALISM as an artistic creed.

Tito's death in 1980 and the lack of a strong leader caused Yugoslavia to drift into economic and social chaos, culminating in the country's dissolution. Slobodan Milosevic and Franjo Tudjman, who became the leaders of the Serbs and Croats, respectively, pursued a significantly more aggressive policy of DISINFORMATION and control of the media than had Tito.

— *Gloria Fulton*

Z

■ Zilliacus, Konni

September 13, 1894, in Kobe, Japan—July 6, 1967, in London, England: British Peace advocate and member of Parliament

Konni Zilliacus was one of the most important and influential propagandists for the LEAGUE OF NATIONS in the 1920's and 1930's and, later, as a British Labour Party Member of Parliament from 1945 to 1949 and from 1955 to 1967. He was an indefatigable advocate for peaceful coexistence with the Soviet Union and for nuclear disarmament. Zilliacus was the son of the daring Finnish Nationalist revolutionary propagandist Konni Zilliacus, Sr., who, in the name of Finnish independence, had published underground newspapers, smuggled literature, and run guns to the Bolsheviks. Zilliacus learned well his father's craft and internalized his father's sense of mission and devotion to a cause.

During World War I his cause became the League of Nations. Zilliacus, like his mentor Sir Norman ANGELL, a leading propagandist for the UNION OF DEMOCRATIC CONTROL in 1915, was a Radical-Liberal rationalist who believed that peo-

ple supported war out of ignorance and because of government distortion or suppression of important foreign policy information. As a democratic internationalist, Zilliacus made it his mission to end secret diplomacy. While in Siberia in 1919, as an unwilling participant in the British war against bolshevism, Zilliacus, as cipher officer, discovered secret information concerning Great Britain's military plans for a major offensive only days after Winston CHURCHILL had told Parliament that the country would not carry out offensive action but was only seeking withdrawal. Incensed, Zilliacus risked court-martial by sending copies of military orders and other classified material to Leonard Woolf and Josiah Wedgwood, to be used in the press and in Parliament to block Churchill's intervention.

In 1920, after returning to Britain, Zilliacus joined the League of Nations. When it became evident to him that the League's two most powerful members, Great Britain and France, sought to ignore the Covenant, Zilliacus decided to break League rules and began a propaganda campaign. From 1922 until 1938, writing under a number of pseudonyms—including "Roth Williams" and "Vigilantes"—Zilliacus wrote hundreds of letters to newspaper editors, scores of articles, and seven books in support of greater powers for the League, including *The League of Nations Today* (1923) and *Inquest on Peace* (1935). He was such a prolific propagandist that the historian A. J. P. Taylor has commented: "It is a safe rule which I present to future researchers that anyone writing in the nineteen-thirties under a name other than his own was Konni Zilliacus." Zilliacus was a highly skilled propagandist; while writing under one pseudonym he often quoted himself writing under a different pseudonym, thus attempting to create the impression that his views were widely shared.

By the 1930's Zilliacus had concluded that world history after 1917—including the League's failure to halt aggression and Western democracies' diplomatic policy of appeasement—was a function of capitalist hostility toward, and fear of, the Soviet Union and social revolution. Capitalism, he argued, was structurally violent and incapable of maintaining world peace, which he had come to define as social justice. As did many in 1930's, Zilliacus viewed the Soviet Union as peace-seeking, and he therefore sought to align the League and the British Labour Party's foreign policy more closely with Soviet policies.

In 1945 Zilliacus was elected to Parliament, and by 1946 he had become the Labour government's most vocal foreign policy critic. He waged an unrelenting propaganda campaign against his own government's emerging pro-American COLD WAR policy. Writing in journals ranging from the British communist *Labour Monthly* to the American liberal *New Republic*, Zilliacus pushed for peaceful coexistence with communism and a sharing of nuclear secrets with the UNITED NATIONS. In 1948 he traveled to the United States for a speaking tour to support Henry Wallace's anti-Cold War Progressive Party presidential bid. By 1949 his activities had so angered British and American officials—the FEDERAL BUREAU OF INVESTIGATION (FBI) kept him under surveillance throughout his 1948 tour—that the Labour Party expelled him for holding communist sympathies in their own MCCARTHY-like witch hunt. At the same

time, ironically, Zilliacus was targeted as an enemy of the Soviet Union for siding with Josip Broz TITO in YUGOSLAVIA's break with the Soviet bloc, and he was once nearly assassinated in France. In the early 1950's, as a result of his efforts to create a noncommunist social democratic Left, Zilliacus was labeled by the Soviet Union as the chief Western-capitalist-Titoist conspirator in the infamous Slansky show trials in Czechoslovakia. By the mid-1950's both the Labour Party and the Soviet Union had "rehabilitated" him, and in 1955 Zilliacus was returned to Parliament. From 1955 until his death in 1967 he continued to lobby and write articles and books in which he hoped to convince Western politicians and public opinion of the dangers in Cold War diplomacy and a nuclear arms race.

— *Ken Millen-Penn*

■ Zionism

Modern movement to return the world's Jews to their ancestral homeland in the Middle East

The term "Zionism" is derived from the word "ZION," the biblical reference to Jerusalem and a modern-day synonym for the state of Israel and its Jewish citizenry. The term was coined by Nathan Birnbaum in the late 1800's to refer to the ideology and subsequent activism that proclaimed the unity of Jewish people everywhere and preached participation in what was deemed a continuum evolving from biblical times and culminating in the creation of a Jewish sovereign state.

HISTORY Theodore Herzl (1860-1904), a Jewish journalist covering the trail of Captain Alfred Dreyfus for a Viennese newspaper (*see* FRANCE: 1871-1940 and TREASON), was impressed with the blatant anti-Semitism the Dreyfus affair uncovered even in such a modern society as France. Herzl wrote a pamphlet entitled *The Jewish State* in 1896 in which he stated that the sole antidote to Jewish persecution was Jewish self-sufficiency in the guise of national sovereignty for the Jews. Herzl wrote

> No human being is wealthy or powerful enough to transplant a people from one place of residence to another. Only an idea can achieve that. The State idea surely has that power. The Jews have dreamed this princely dream throughout the long night of their history.

To this end Theodore Herzl founded modern political Zionism. Herzl was instrumental in advancing the concept that anti-Semitism was a political problem and could only be addressed through political solutions. He convened approximately two hundred of his followers in Basel, Switzerland, in August, 1897, to form a political convention to address this problem—the World Zionist Organization.

Herzl's initial plan called for the establishment of a Jewish national homeland in either Argentina or Palestine. Traditionalists among his followers voiced strident objections to the suggestion that Argentina could provide an adequate national base. Citing biblical, historical, and religious ties to Palestine, the group was adamant in its insistence that Palestine was the political tool which could both motivate Jews worldwide and provide the historical nexus to make a compelling

geopolitical argument in the international arena. The First Zionist Congress concluded with the issuance of the Basel Program, which resolved that a Jewish sovereign state would be established in Palestine, "secured by public law."

THE RHETORIC AND OPPONENTS OF ZIONISM The philosophy of Zionism is so prevalent among Jews today that most assume that its basic historical appeal was universal among Jews. This was not the case. The Basel Program was vehemently denied and castigated on pulpits throughout the world. The concept of Judaism as a nationalistic movement rather than a purely moral and ethical spiritual movement was anathema to many Jewish leaders. In fact, nationalistic fervor was seen as diametrically opposed to the Messianic ideal espoused by religious leaders. Literature was disseminated throughout Europe and the Americas disavowing nationalistic zealots and calling upon Jews to proclaim allegiance to the state of their citizenship and denying any nationalistic ties to Jews outside the boundaries of their home state. Such views were espoused by various scholars of the time, including Ludwig Geiger in his "Die Stimme der Wahrheit" (1905), Lucien Wolf, Laurie Magnus, and Claude Montefiore.

Anti-Zionist propaganda was further disseminated by major educational groups such as the Kultusgemeinden, which controlled Jewish education in Germany, and the Alliance Israelite Universalle in France, the Anglo-Jewish Association in England, and the Reform Movement's Central Conference of American Rabbis.

During his tenure, Herzl founded a variety of organizations under the umbrella of the Zionist organization to raise money and acquire land for the furtherance of a Jewish national homeland in Palestine. Much like a modern-day Moses, Herzl did not live to see the fruition of his dream. Nevertheless, the many ideals raised and promoted by the Zionist movement may be traced to his conceptions. Zionism promoted concepts of pride and unity among Jews as Jews and directly resulted in efforts to promote Jewish cultural identity and Jewish self-defense organizations. External factors, primarily the discriminatory and persecutory actions taken against Jews in nations all over the world, gave impetus to this newly raised Jewish consciousness. Not only did anti-Semitism promote Jewish identity among Jews, but it also motivated Christian Zionists, who recognized an essential element of Herzl's call for a Jewish state—that the dehumanization of any people dehumanizes humankind.

MODERN ZIONISM   Modern-day Zionism evolved for the particular purpose of creating a national homeland for the Jews in Palestine. It provided a counterpoint to the Nazi atrocities and provided a salve for the international conscience when those atrocities came to light. The state of Israel was created in 1948, and Zionism subsequently played a role in the evolution of the state. Zionism served as a rallying cry for Jews worldwide to assist the fledgling state in meeting the various threats to its existence imposed by a hostile environment.

Zionism was denounced as racist ideology by a UNITED NATIONS resolution, later repealed. It is viewed even by many Israelis as obsolete, detrimental, and at worst, a barrier to normalization of relationships between Israel and its Arab neighbors. At best, some argue, it is inaccurate, as it is based on the concept of world Jewry constituting a distinct nation. Zionists counter that Zionism, as an ideology for a social order based on biblical text and evolved as a social ideology aspiring to the highest ideals of democracy, has continuing validity. Israeli prime minister Benjamin Netanyahu, has argued that contemporary anti-Zionistic sentiment is equivalent to Nazi rhetoric.

SUGGESTED READINGS:

Edelheit, Abraham J. *The Yishuv in the Shadow of the Holocaust: Zionist Politics and Rescue Aliya, 1933-1939*. Boulder, Colo.: Westview Press, 1996.

Klieman, Aaron S., ed. *Zionism as an Issue in Interwar Politics*. New York: Garland, 1990.

Neusner, Jacob. *Who, Where, and What Is "Israel"?: Zionist Perspectives on Israeli and American Judaism*. Lanham, Md.: University Press of America, 1989.

Shimoni, Gideon. *The Zioist Ideology*. Hanover: University Press of New England, Brandeis University Press, 1995.

Shindler, Colin. *Israel, Likud, and the Zionist Dream: Power, Politics, and Ideology from Begin to Netanyahu*. New York: Tauris, 1995.

— *Murray Henner*

■ Filmography

This selective listing of films with propaganda themes is arranged chronologically within the subject headings listed below. In instances in which films are known to have been released under more than one title, the alternative titles are given in parentheses.

— *Betty Richardson*

Alcohol, Drugs, and Addiction

1894: *Chinese Opium Den* may be first film (a Kinetoscope loop) to document the (then legal) drug trade.

1908: *Father and Drunkard*, among the earliest of many films to show the dangers of alcohol, dramatizes the transformation of a decent man into a gambler.

1912: D. W. Griffith's *For His Son* is among earliest films to show dangers of narcotics. *The Opium Smugglers* shows the opium smuggling business, which began after opium importing became illegal in 1909.

1914: *The Cocaine Traffic* (Lubin, *The Drug Terror*) and *The Drug Traffic* depict the dangers of drugs and ways of circumventing new drug laws. Lois Weber directed *John Barleycorn*, an antialcohol film based on Jack London's autobiographical novel.

1915: *The Secret Sin* stars Blanche Sweet as twins, one a morphine addict. *Prohibition* (Photo Drama for Prohibition Film Corporation), an antialcohol film, was made by James Halleck Reid, father of the film star and narcotics victim Wallace Reid.

1923: *Human Wreckage*, an antidrug message picture, was sponsored by Dorothy Davenport, widow of the Hollywood star Wallace Reid, after Reid's death from drug addiction.

1928: *The Pace That Kills*, part melodrama, part documentary, shows the actual preparation and peddling of drugs.

1938: *Reefer Madness* dramatizes the evils of marijuana.

1945: Actor Ray Milland won an Academy Award for his realistic portrayal of an otherwise decent and sensible man consumed by alcoholism in *The Lost Weekend*.

1949: *Wild Weed* (Kroger Babb, *Devil's Weed*, *She Should'a Said No!*), was made to exploit the arrest of the film star Robert Mitchum for marijuana use; led to the overturning of Pennsylvania's forty-six-year-old censorship law when the film was banned there.

Disease and Medicine

1904: *The Inner Struggle* is set in a leper colony; even there human emotions survive.

1913: *The Price of Human Lives* dramatizes the deception of public by those selling false cures for tuberculosis.

1911: *The Awakening of John Bond*, a collaboration between the Edison Company and the U.S. government, shows the dangers of contracting tuberculosis in overcrowded slums and the need for uncontaminated milk. *The Sins of the Fathers*, borrowed from Henrik Ibsen's play *Ghosts*, deals with the destructiveness of venereal disease.

1915: U.S. version of *Damaged Goods*, the much censored play (*Les Avariés*) about venereal disease by Eugène Brieux, which shows the destruction of a respectable family by syphilis; British version appeared in 1919.

1916: First World War I antivenereal disease campaign film *Fit to Fight* (*Fit to Win*), distributed by the U.S. Public Health Service.

1917: Joseph Best's *Whatsoever a Man Soweth* graphically documents the physical effects of venereal disease.

1919: Warner Brothers' *Open Your Eyes* shows the effects of venereal disease on a middle-class family. Edward H. Griffith's *End of the Road*, based on a report by Katherine Bement Davis, a New York commissioner of corrections, is directed primarily at women and shows women infected with venereal disease.

1934: *Tomorrow's Children* deals with involuntary sterilization laws passed in U.S. states between 1907 and 1937 and their effects, drawing an analogy between practices toward "inferior races" in Nazi Germany and those in the United States.

1938: *The Birth of a Baby*, documenting pregnancy from the first awareness of pregnancy to birth, was compiled by American Committee for Maternal Welfare and backed by major medical organizations, including the U.S. Public Health Service, American Medical Association, and American Association of Obstetricians and Gynecologists.

1941: The German *Ich klage an* (I accuse) treats the question of euthanasia from the Nazi point of view, justifying state control of decisions over fitness to live.

1946: John Huston's *Let There Be Light*, documentary commissioned by the U.S. War Department (which later suppressed it), dramatizes the treatment of shell-shocked war veterans.

1948: Olivia de Havilland stars in *The Snake Pit*, the first Hollywood film to treat seriously the plight of patients in public mental institutions; the film is based on Mary Jane Ward's account of her own eight-and-a-half-month experience.

1967: *Titicut Follies* documents the treatment of the insane in a Massachusetts hospital.

1975: Director Milos Forman's adaptation of Ken Kesey's novel *One Flew over the Cuckoo's Nest* won all the major Academy Awards for its year and raised public consciousness of abuses of the mentally ill in institutions.

1989: German filmmaker Rosa von Praunheim's *Ein Virus kennt keine Moral* (a virus has no morals) satirizes reactions to acquired immunodeficiency syndrome (AIDS), including that of the gay community.

1990: *Longtime Companion*, directed by Norman Rene, dramatizes the devastation of AIDS in a homosexual community, combining a fictional story with informational material.

1992: Director Jonathan Demme's *Philadelphia* portrays a homosexual attorney who is fired when his firm learns that he has AIDS.

Environmentalism and Urban Planning

1936: Pare Lorentz's *The Plow That Broke the Plains*, produced under the U.S. Government Resettlement Administration, documents the land mismanagement that led to the Dust Bowl, the resulting poverty, and the subsequent federal land management efforts.

1937: *The River*, produced by Pare Lorentz for the Farm Security Administration, documents land mismanagement along the Mississippi River and its tributaries, the resultant erosion and floods and their effects, and the Tennessee Valley Authority reclamation effort; the film contains footage of the disastrous 1937 flood.

1939: Willard Van Dyck and Ralph Steiner's *The City*, a documentary concerning urban planning, was prepared for showing at the New York World's Fair of 1939.

1979: Seen by many as a somber warning of the potential dangers of nuclear power plants, *The China Syndrome* is a story about a power company's cover-up of a serious operational flaw. The film's release around the time of a nuclear accident at Three Mile Island in Pennsylvania added strength to its message.

1983: Based loosely on a true story, *Silkwood* is about a nuclear processing plant worker who dies in a mysterious accident before she is scheduled to tell a newspaper reporter about a safety problem in the plant.

Homosexuality

1961: When Lillian Hellman's play *The Children's Hour* was filmed as *These Three* in 1936, the lesbian theme was unacceptable to censors; the theme was reintroduced in the 1961 remake.

1970: *The Boys in the Band*, based on a stage play by Matt Crowley who produced the film version, introduced a compassionate treatment of homosexuality to screen comedy.

1989: Black British filmmaker Isaac Julien's *Looking for Langston*, a study of the African American poet Langston Hughes, was a part-documentary study of racial and sexual consciousness.

Political Ideologies

1916: *The Cossack Whip* presents a favorable view of the Russian Revolution revolutionary forces against the backdrop of czarist Russia.

1917: *The Fall of the Romanoffs* portrays the fall of czarist Russia; the central characters are Rasputin, adviser to the czar, and Iliodor, his opponent, who portrays himself. Documentary footage of the February, 1917, revolution in Petrograd became *The Great Days of the Russian Revolution from February 28 to March 4, 1917*; footage compiled for an American audience opened in New York as *Russia to the Front.*

1919: *Bolshevism on Trial*, based on *Comrades*, a novel by Thomas Dixon (on whose *The Clansman* the film *The Birth of a Nation* was based), satirizes the novelist Upton Sinclair's socialist experiment in California. *Burning Question*, among the first films produced for nonprofit viewing in Roman Catholic church parish halls, attacks foreign-born agitators, associating them with socialism, bolshevism, and anarchism.

1920: Basil Thomson, director of the British Secret Service Special Branch, helped produce *Land of Mystery*, a drama made in Lithuania, to counteract Russian Bolshevik propaganda. George Barr Baker, a publicist for Herbert Hoover's American Relief Administration, worked on and funded *Starvation*, a documentary designed to show that communism is not the solution to world hunger.

1921: The Russian immigrant and Goldwyn studio employee Herman Axelbank assisted Friends of Soviet Russia to produce *Russia Through the Shadows* for Soviet famine relief.

1923: Hall Caine's 1900 novel *The Eternal City* describes a state created on Christian Socialist principles; Samuel Goldwyn, filming the novel in Rome, was forced by Benito Mussolini to change the novel to a celebration of Fascist power.

1925: Sergei Eisenstein's *Bronenosets Potemkin* (*The Battleship Potemkin*), based on the attempted 1905 revolution in Odessa, Russia, was made to celebrate the twentieth anniversary of that event.

1928: Herman Axelbank's *Tsar to Lenin* (released in 1937), made with the assistance of Max Eastman, traces the Russian Revolution and includes footage of the revolutionary leader Leon Trotsky.

1930: *L'Age d'Or* (France; the golden age), filmed by the artist Salvador Dali and the surrealist Luis Buñuel, attacks bourgeois culture, the Roman Catholic church, and fascism.

1932: Luis Buñuel's *Las Hurdes* (Spain; *Terre sans pain*, or land without bread; released 1937) describes the sufferings and ignorance of rural Spain under totalitarian government.

1932: Director Fritz Lang's *Das Testament des Dr. Mabuse* (Germany; the last will of Dr. Mabuse) equates insane and criminal behavior with Nazism. William Randolph Hearst's *Gabriel over the White House* urged the need for dictatorial authority in the United States.

1934: *Hitler's Reign of Terror* (*The Reign of Nazi Terror*) documents Cornelius Vanderbilt's visit to Germany and Austria and was first film to show, through newsclips and dramatization, what was happening under Adolf Hitler's regime.

1935: Leni Riefenstahl's *Triumpf des Willen* (Germany; *Triumph of the Will*) shows the September, 1934, Nazi rally at Nuremberg.

1937: *Lenin in October*, made by Mikhail Romm at Joseph STALIN's request, celebrates the twentieth anniversary of the Russian Revolution, portraying Stalin as the rightful heir of the revolutionary leader V. I. Lenin. *The Spanish Earth*, with narration written and spoken by the novelist Ernest Hemingway and music by Virgil Thomson and Marc Blitzstein, shows the attempts of villagers to survive the devastation of the Spanish civil war.

1938-1939: The two-part *A Great Citizen* (U.S.S.R.), made by Friedrich Ermler, focuses on internal enemies of communism as propaganda to pave the way for the murder of Joseph Stalin's enemies. *Professor Mamlock* (U.S.S.R.) dramatizes both Nazi anti-Semitism and the struggles of those, especially communists, opposed to Nazism. Leni Riefenstahl's *Olympische Spiele* (Germany; *Olympiad, Olympia*), film of the 1936 Berlin Olympic Games, links ideals of the event with those of Adolf Hitler's Third Reich.

1939: *Confessions of a Nazi Spy*, directed by Anatole Litvak and starring Edward G. Robinson, was the first major Hollywood film to document the threat posed by Adolf Hitler. *The 400 Million*, with narration by Frederic March, attempted to introduce Western audiences to the 1937 war between China and Japan and to publicize the role of Chinese communists in fighting Japanese.

1940: In *The Great Dictator*, Charlie Chaplin plays a Jewish barber and his look-alike, Adenoid Hynkel (the "Furor"), dictator of Tomania, in a satiric treatment of Adolf Hitler's political policies and anti-Semitism; a parody of *Triumph of the Will.*

1943: *Mission to Moscow*, made at the request of President Franklin D. Roosevelt to educate the public about Russia, then a war ally, features Walter Huston as Joseph E. Davies, U.S. ambassador to Russia from 1936 to 1941, contrasting brutality of life under Adolf Hitler with life in Russia and showing Russian women at work at a time when U.S. women were urged to work outside of the home. RKO's *Hitler's Children* shows forced child-breeding and sterilization and indoctrination of young people under Hitler. *Watch on the Rhine* (Warner Brothers), based on Lillian Hellman's play, warns of American complacency that allowed European and American Nazism to develop.

1944: Released as World War II ended, *Wilson*, a biography of the U.S. president Woodrow Wilson, who urged the need for a League of Nations after World War I; the film was attacked by conservative forces as propaganda for President Franklin D. Roosevelt's election to a fourth term and was banned in all U.S. troop camps until Congress amended the Soldier's Voting Act, which had been used to prohibit any showing.

1951: Warner Brothers' anticommunistic *I Was a Communist for the F.B.I.* dramatizes the exploits of an actual undercover agent.

1954: George Orwell's *Animal Farm*, anticommunist satiric treatment of barnyard animals who overturn their authoritarian farmer only to find their revolution ending in fascism again, was produced as an animated feature-length cartoon.

1964: Emile de Antonio's *Point of Order* is a compilation film that reduces thirty-six days of testimony to a one-hundred- minute film, documenting the fall of the virulent anticommunist Joseph McCarthy at televised hearings aimed at accusing the U.S. Army of harboring subversives.

1965: *The East Is Red* is a filmed Maoist

stage musical with a cast of three thousand, in which Mao Zedong was celebrated as the savior of the Chinese people, contrasting the misery of the Chinese poor under capitalism with a finale in which jubilant audience members join actors in celebrating Mao.

1966: Director Melville Shavelson's *Cast a Giant Shadow* covers the months before the Israeli war of independence and focuses on the need to build a strong military force.

1968: Octavio Getino and Fernando Solanes's three-part *La Hora de los Hornos* (Argentina, *The Hour of the Furnaces*), advocates revolution, as in Cuba, as a response to neocolonial exploitation.

1975: *Chronique Des Années De Braises* (Algiers, *Chronicle of the Burning Years, Chronicle of the Years of the Brazier, Chronicle of the Years of Embers*) depicts Algerian history between 1939 and 1954 and the rebellion against French colonialism.

1976: Andrzej Wajda's *Czlowiek z marmurur* (Poland, *Man of Marble*) attacks power, especially communist power.

1984: One of the most blatantly propagandist films of the Cold War era, *Red Dawn* follows the exploits of a band of teenage American guerrilla fighters who resist a Soviet-Cuban occupation of the United States.

1985: Claude Lanzmann's *Shoah*, an almost ten-hour study of Nazi extermination camps in Poland, presents recollections of the Holocaust by Nazi extermination camp survivors, witnesses, and German officials.

1993: *Schindler's List* is an adaptation of an award-winning novel about a German industrialist using slave labor from concentration camps who found, in the process, that he had a conscience. The film's critical and commercial success made it one of the most influential films ever made about the Holocaust. German filmmaker Ray Müller wrote and directed *The Wonderful, Horrible Life of Leni Riefenstahl* (*Die Macht der Bilder*), which documents the career of the woman who made *Triumph of the Will*. Using extracts from Riefenstahl's films and an extended interview with her, the film raises the question of what crime, if any, she was guilty of committing.

1994: *Strictly Propaganda* is a compilation by the German director Wolfgang Kissel of educational film produced by the communist East German government during the four decades prior to its collapse in 1989.

Labor, Management, and Working Conditions

1904: *The Coal Heavers* (American Mutoscope and Biograph) was based on the Colorado miners' strike of 1903-1904 that led to the formation of the Industrial Workers of the World led by Bill Haywood.

1908: D. W. Griffith's *The Song of the Shirt* shows the struggle of the poor to survive; the film features Florence Lawrence, the earliest identified U.S. film star, as an orphaned seamstress forced to support an ill sister.

1911: The American Federation of Labor produced *A Martyr to His Cause* to defend John J. and James B. McNamara, labor leaders charged with dynamiting the *Los Angeles Times* building in 1910.

1912: *Children Who Labour*, starring Viola Dana, makes a case for legislation to limit factory work for children. In collaboration with the National Association of Manufacturers, Edison produced *The Crime of Carelessness*, urging workers to take responsibility for their own factory safety, probably as a reaction to the 1911 Triangle Shirtwaist Factory fire in which approximately 150 workers lost their lives. The antilabor *The Agitator*, with its portrayal of a labor leader as a drunken outside agitator, brought protests from the American Federation of Labor.

1913: *The Cry of the Children*, taken from

1908 book by the reformer Mrs. John Van Voorst, portrays poverty conditions that force families to put their children to work. Attorney Clarence Darrow played himself in *From Dawn to Dusk*, an account of the McNamara dynamiting and trial sympathetic to labor. *An American in the Making* was produced under the direction of United States Steel Company for the U.S. Bureau of Mines; a safety film, it told an immigrant success story set in the safety of American industry.

1914: *The Strike at Coaldale*, dramatizing a railroad strike, was banned in Pennsylvania and Ohio as too prolabor. *The Jungle*, based on Upton Sinclair's indictment of conditions in the meat-packing industry, shows the effect of those conditions on workers and poisoned the public. *The Locked Door*, a drama produced in cooperation with the New York fire and police departments, uses the Triangle Shirtwaist Factory fire to point to the need for safe working conditions.

1915: *The Blood of the Children*, written by Bess Meredyth, portrays child labor in cotton factories where lint was a health hazard.

1916: *The Blacklist*, written by William deMille and Marion Fairfax and starring Blanche Sweet, dramatizes a system whereby mining companies exchange information about employees suspected of union activities; it was based on the 1914 Ludlow Massacre of more than forty people during a strike at Colorado Fuel and Iron Company.

1920: *The Woman God Sent*, written by the reformer Sophie Irene Loeb, deals with efforts to outlaw child factory labor.

1921: *The New Discipline* was the first release of the Federation Film Corporation of Seattle, an organization of trade unionists and political radicals; the film shows the successful takeover of a mill by workers.

1925: *Labor's Reward* supported the American Federation of Labor recruiting campaign.

1926: Strikers produced *The Passaic Textile Strike* using profits to support the strike. *Metropolis* (Germany), made by Fritz Lang and Thea von Harbou, offers an antiutopian vision of a futuristic city providing great luxury for a population sustained by a race of underground slaves, and the final breakdown between labor and management.

1928: King Vidor's *The Crowd* shows the alienation and isolation of a young couple trapped in the anonymity of the urban world.

1940: Willard Van Dyke's *Valley Town* documents the hardships of workers made obsolete by changing technology.

1976: *Manthan* (India; *The Churning*), filmed by Shyam Benegal, was produced by 500,000 Gujarat farmers, each of whom invested two rupees; film shows how a farm cooperative allows farmers to oppose avaricious landlords.

1979: Sally Field's strong portrayal of a courageous union organizer made *Norma Rae* a triumph of both labor and feminist values.

1989: Michael Moore's *Roger & Me* documents the effects of the automobile factory closings in Flint, Michigan.

Marriage and Family

1918: Echoing President Theodore Roosevelt's opposition to divorce, William Fox's *Blindness of Divorce* aroused public opinion to oppose divorce.

1928: *Companionate Marriage*, starring Betty Bronson, is a study of a couple who contract a marriage with an understanding that it may be terminated; Judge Ben Lindsey, whose controversial theory of companionate marriage allowed for divorce by mutual consent, makes a brief appearance in the film.

1979: The stark title of *Kramer vs. Kramer* conveys some of the feeling of writer-director Robert Benton's film about a child-custody battle.

Politics and Corruption

1915: In director Lois Weber's *The Hypocrites*, politicians are paid off by gangsters, police, saloonkeepers, madams, and drug dealers. Impeached New York Governor William Sulzer stars in *The Governor's Boss* (*The Governor's Decision*) which ends not, as in reality, with impeachment, but with the defeat of Sulzer's Tammany Hall enemies and the restoration of justice to New York.

1939: James Stewart plays a political innocent appointed to the U.S. Senate who uncovers high-level political corruption in Frank Capra's *Mr. Smith Goes to Washington*. Some U.S. politicians feared that releasing the film in Europe would damage U.S. prestige, but because the film allows democratic values to triumph, the film actually raised American prestige abroad.

1962: One of the most controversial American films of its time, *The Manchurian Candidate* is a taut thriller about an American soldier who returns from the Korean War as a hero, when in fact he had been captured by the communists and brain-washed to serve their needs as an assassin.

1976: *All the President's Men*, directed by Alan J. Pakula, was a widely seen adaptation of Carl Bernstein and Bob Woodward's account of the journalistic exposé of the Watergate scandal that helped bring down Richard M. Nixon's presidency.

Poverty, Hardship, and Crime

1902: *The Girl Who Went Astray* shows the life of a prostitute controlled by a pimp. *A Legal Holdup* attacks police abuse.

1904: In *Decoyed* young girls are warned about agents of the so-called white slave (involuntary prostitution) traffic.

1905: Director Edwin S. Porter's *Kleptomaniac* dramatizes the different legal treatment of rich and poor.

1909: D. W. Griffith's *A Corner in Wheat*, taken from the 1904 Channing Pollock novel *The Pit*, dramatizes how speculation in grain raised prices and increased poverty and hunger.

1910: *The Ex-convict*, filmed by Edwin S. Porter, shows the rejection of a released prisoner by his community and his difficulty in avoiding a return to crime. D. W. Griffith's *The Usurer* (Biograph) contrasts the extravagant life of money lenders with the lives of the poor from whom they reap profits. *Emigranten* and *Amuletten* (Sweden) portray poverty and crime in America, an attempt to discourage emigration from Sweden.

1911: *Life at Hull House* shows the assistance the Chicago settlement house brought to its neighboring slum population.

1912: Made by Thanhouser Films and the New York Association for Improving the Condition of the Poor, *The Other Half Lives* dramatizes slum conditions originally publicized by the reformer Jacob Riis in *How the Other Half Lives* (1890). Essanay's *The Virtue of Rags* shows the awakening social conscience of a slum landlord. *For the Commonwealth* dramatizes the effect of convict labor in lowering wages among the urban poor. *Land Beyond the Sunset*, a collaboration with the Children's Fresh Air Fund, shows the fund-sponsored visits to the country designed to save slum children from tuberculosis. Edison and Russell Sage Foundation produced *The Usurer's Grip*, which attacks the exploitation of the poor by moneylenders.

1913: *Children of the Tenements*, based on a 1904 book by Jacob Riis, reports on the lives of slum children. *Traffic in Souls*, falsely claimed to dramatize a report by John D. Rockefeller, Jr., about New York vice and the white slave traffic. *Inside the White Slave Traffic* was endorsed by law enforcement officers, U.S. justices, and such feminist leaders as Charlotte Perkins Gilman and Carrie Chapman Catt; produced by the Social Research Film Corporation, it includes documentary footage of prostitutes. *Saved by the Juvenile Court (Fighting Crime)* dramatizes Judge Ben Lindsey's attempt to form a separate juvenile system for young criminal offenders; Lindsey appears in the film. *The Wages of Sin*, based on a story by F. E. Farnsworth, attacks gambling. *The Fight for Right*, written by the reformist James Oppenheim, shows how a factory is forced to shut down because of competition by convict labor.

1914: Judge Willis Brown, the founder of boys' communities for reformation in Michigan and Indiana, directed *A Boy and the Law*, which dramatizes his efforts. *The Silent Plea for a Widowed Mother's Allowance*, made in cooperation with the East Side Protective Association, argues for assistance programs to permit widowed mothers to remain at home with their children. A policewoman and a chief of police appear in *Dregs of the City*, which shows the attempt to close a red-light district of Chicago, an attempt that ended in a battle between two groups of police.

1915: Cecil B. DeMille's *Kindling* (Paramount) protests against the exploitation of children.

1916: *Public Opinion* condemns the U.S. press's tendency to prejudice the public against criminal defendants before trials begin. Lois Weber's *The People v. John Doe (God's Law)*, protests against capital punishment. Edward Sloman directed the socialist drama *Dust*, which portrays the poor both as dust beneath their employers' feet and as dying of factory dust.

1917: *The Public Be Damned* and *The Food Gamblers* protested against the manipulation of food prices after the United States entered World War I, blaming the manipulations for increased retail prices that brought the poor close to starvation.

1919: Thomas Mott Osborne of the New York State Prison Reform Commission collaborated with Edward MacManus to produce *The Gray Brother*, which contrasts traditional penal management with the results of Mutual Welfare League procedures advocated by Osborne.

1925: *Capital Punishment*, starring Clara Bow and Margaret Livingston, argues against capital punishment by showing the ease with which an innocent man can be convicted.

1926: *The Red Kimono* was made by Mrs. Wallace Reid, the second of her crusading "Sins of the World" series; written by the future director Dorothy Arzner and directed by Walter Lang, the film depicts New Orleans' Storyville, the red light district that was shut down in 1917.

1929: Piel Jutzi's *Mutter Krausens Fahrt ins Glück* (Germany; Mother Krausen's journey) shows the bleak lives of poor people contending with unemployment, housing shortages, and indifferent authorities; hope is offered through film shots of marching young workers.

1932: Paul Muni stars in Mervyn Leroy's *I Am a Fugitive from a Chain Gang*, based on the experiences of a fugitive who, in articles and a book, dealt with the intolerable conditions he had experienced when convicted of theft; the film condemns prison conditions and legal injustice.

1934: King Vidor's *Our Daily Bread* dramatizes a group of itinerant, unemployed people who succeed, despite opposition, in establishing a collective farm.

1940: *Power and the Land*, produced by Pare Lorentz for the U.S. Film Service, shows the hardship of farm life, the need for electrification, and the transformations electrification provided. Although director John Ford's adaptation of John Steinbeck's novel *The Grapes of Wrath* was based on a toned-down screenplay by Nunnally Johnson, it was nevertheless a powerful indictment of the problems faced by "Okies" whose farms were ruined by the Dust Bowl conditions of the Great Depression. Adolf Hitler is reported to have regarded the film as an accurate depiction of American conditions generally.

1952: Giuseppe De Santis' *Roma Ore 11* (*Rome, 11 O'Clock*) dramatizes an actual disaster that shows the neediness among working classes; two hundred girls apply for a single job, and the staircase on which they are standing collapses.

1978: The Turkish film *Enemy* dramatizes the lives of the dispossessed underclass.

Race and Religion

1903: Edwin S. Porter filmed Harriet Beecher Stowe's anti-slavery novel *Uncle Tom's Cabin*.

1908: *The Hebrew Fugitive* was the first U.S. film to depict Russian pogroms, government-sanctioned massacres of Jews.

1910: Edwin S. Porter's *Russia, Land of Oppression* portrays a Cossack raid on a Jewish community at Passover.

1913: William F. ("Buffalo Bill") Cody filmed a reconstructed version of the Battle of Wounded Knee from a point of view sympathetic to Native Americans; the film was made in cooperation with the U.S. government but withheld from general release by the government. Prejudice against Native Americans is addressed in Sidney Goldin's *The Friendless Indian*. *How the Jews Care for Their Poor* was a drama showing the work of Jewish philanthropic societies.

1914: *A Passover Miracle*, made in cooperation with the Bureau of the Jewish Community of New York, realistically shows Jewish religious rituals in a film released to coincide with the Passover holidays and designed to counter religious and racial stereotyping. *The Birth of a Nation*, based on Thomas Dixon's *The Clansman*, blames the Civil War and its aftermath on African Americans and corrupt politicians.

1915: Among several early attempts to film Native American customs with sympathy and respect is Rodman Wanamaker's thirteen-reel *History of the American Indian*, made in cooperation with tribal officials of the Crow Reservation near Sheridan, Wyoming; reconstructed battle scenes were scrutinized for accuracy by the tribal officials.

1916: William Randolph Hearst's racist serial *Patria*, the first feature film to be advertised in a monthly magazine, presents Mexicans and Japanese as U.S. enemies; it starred famed dancer Irene Castle, but brought protests from the Japanese and Mexican governments.

1919: D. W. Griffith's *Broken Blossoms*, based on a story from Thomas Burke's *Limehouse Nights* and starring Lillian Gish, shows the contrast between sympathetic and compassionate Chinese and brutal English; Griffith was countering "Yellow Peril" films featuring sinister Asian villains.

1920: Oscar Micheaux's *Within Our Gates* (*La Negra*) illustrates lynching in America.

1922: Lon Chaney portrays a Chinese victim of racial prejudice in *Shadows*, which exposes small-town hypocrisy. *Hungry Hearts* is based on autobiographical short stories by Anzia Yezierska, who told of Jewish refugees and their struggles in New York.

1928: *The Scar of Shame* documents the African American middle class.

1929: *Disraeli*, one of the first of a series of feature films attacking anti-Semitism, records the life of the British prime minister Benjamin Disraeli (played by George Arliss) and his contributions to British history.

1937: Warner Brothers' *The Life of Émile Zola* focuses on the novelist's defense of Alfred Dreyfus, the French military officer convicted of espionage because of anti-Semitism.

1940: *Jud Süss*, part of an official German anti-Semitic media campaign launched in 1939 with the comedy *Robert und Bertram*, was followed by *The Eternal Jew* (*Der ewige Jude*), which blames Jews for depravity, disease, and the threat of war; a specially edited and adapted French version opened in Paris on July 6, 1942, ten days before the mass roundup of Jews began there.

1944: *The Negro Soldier*, produced by Frank Capra's War Department film unit, undertook to explain the role of African Americans in a segregated army being sent to fight a war against Nazi racial inequity.

1947: *Crossfire*, directed by Edward Dmytryk, studies anti-Semitism. Darryl Zanuck's *Gentlemen's Agreement*, based on the novel by Laura Z. Hobson, depicts a gentile newspaperman who poses as a Jew and for the first time realizes the extent of racial and religious prejudice in the United States.

1949: *Pinky*, directed by Elia Kazan, the story of an African American who attempts to pass for white, explores various African American strategies for coping with racism.

1959: *The Diary of Anne Frank*, based on the diary kept by a young Jewish girl shortly before she was arrested and killed by the Nazis (and on the stage play by Frances Goodrich and Albert Hackett), was the first U.S. feature film fully to treat the persecution of the Jews under Hitler.

1961: Stanley Kramer's *Judgment at Nuremberg* questions how fascism gained public allegiance, whether a person can be excused on the grounds of having merely followed orders, and how crimes against humanity should be punished; the film, which focuses on four Germans who represent the ninety-nine actually tried at Nuremburg, contains documentary footage.

1965: Documentary filmmakers Michael Roemer and Robert Young made their first feature film, *Nothing But a Man*, to show the problems of an African American family deprived of dignity and civil rights in a Southern town.

1968: *Koshikei* (Japan; death by hanging), produced by Nagisa Oshima, attacks racism in Japan.

1971: Melvin Van Peebles' *Sweet Sweetback's Bad Asssss Song* was a milestone in the cinematic expression of African American anger.

1992: Leading African American filmmaker Spike Lee's *Malcolm X* (with Denzel Washington in the title role) is a powerful treatment of the black nationalist's life, taken principally from Malcolm X's own autobiography.

War

1898: Filmed immediately after the outbreak of the Spanish-American War to generate support for the newspaper-supported invasion of Cuba, John Stuart Blackton's *Tearing down the Spanish Flag* may be the world's earliest propaganda film.

1915: John Stuart Blackton's anti-German *Battle Cry of Peace* (*An American's Home*), strongly supported by Theodore Roosevelt, shows a German invasion of New York and the city's destruction.

1916: *The Battle of the Somme*, made on the western front in 1916 by the war correspondents J. B. McDowell and G. Malins, gave as true a picture of World War I battle conditions as censorship allowed; the film was intended to encourage home-front efforts. *Germany on the Firing Line*, presenting the war from the German point of view, was widely shown in the United States.

1917: The producer Robert Goldstein was convicted under the 1917 Espionage Act for showing his opposition to U.S. entry into World War I by portraying British troops during the American Revolution as the equivalent of German troops in World War I in his Revolutionary War drama *The Spirit of '76*. D. W. Griffith's *Hearts of the World* (in part filmed under British government sponsorship) showed civilians, including the star Lillian Gish, being mistreated under German occupation; the film boosted military recruitment in the United States. First film to be produced by British government money was *Life of Nelson*, which urged British suffering in World War I to reflect on the courage of the famous admiral of Napoleonic conflicts. In *To Hell with the Kaiser*, written by June Mathis, Satan encourages the German kaiser Wilhelm II to use poison gas and bomb Red Cross hospitals.

1919: The pacifist *J'accuse* (France) was filmed on World War I battlefields; Abel Gance used troops returned from the front to portray the dead rising from their graves to protest the horrors. The film was remade in 1937 to protest the threat of World War II.

1920: *On the Red Front*, a two-reel propaganda film made by Lev Kuleshov under the direction of V. I. Lenin, portrays everyday lives of men fighting for revolution.

1925: King Vidor's *The Big Parade*, a top box-office hit of the silent film era, is an anti-war drama showing three recruits who enlist because of social pressure and gradually realize the horrors of war.

1928: Sybil Thorndike starred in *Dawn* (England), an anti-German film about the nurse Edith Cavell who was shot by Germans as a spy in World War I.

1930: Lewis Milestone's *All Quiet on the Western Front*, which shows the folly of war from the perspective of German soldiers, presented so unglamorized a picture of war that Nazi riots prevented the film's showing in Germany.

1933: Reacting to the rise of fascism in Europe, the Marx Brothers' *Duck Soup* shows Groucho as the dictator of Fredonia, leading his country into a ridiculous war.

1937: Herbert Kline's *Heart of Spain*, made for the American-Canadian relief commission, shows the plight of bombed Spain.

1938: Sergei Eisenstein's *Alexandr Nevskii* (U.S.S.R.; *Alexander Nevsky*) depicts the thirteenth century victory of Russians over German invaders to boost Russian resistance to Nazi Germany.

1940: *London Can Take It*, made by Humphrey Jennings and Harry Watt, focuses on Londoners' reactions to the German Blitz; it was one of the first documentaries to be produced by the Crown Film Unit of the British Ministry of Information. *Feuertaufe* (Germany; *Baptism of Fire*) is a documentary of combat, showing Allied forces as the aggressors.

1942: The U.S. War Department's series of *Why We Fight* documentaries include *Prelude to War, The Nazis Strike, Divide and Conquer, The Battle of Britain, The Battle of Russia*, and *The Battle of China*; Hollywood filmmakers in charge of the project included Frank Capra and Anatole Litvak. *In Which We Serve* documents the lives of officers and crew of the HMS *Torrin* in a celebration of British values and of the British navy's courage; written by Noel Coward, it was directed by Coward and David Lean. The Oscar-winning Soviet documentary *Razgrom nemetzkikh voisk pod Moskvoi* (defeat of the German armies near Moscow) shows the Soviet defense of Moscow in 1941.

1943: In *Der Fuehrer's Face* Donald Duck, living in a Nazi-occupied country, faces Nazi might in a film commissioned by the U.S. Treasury Department to show the importance of paying taxes. Humphrey Jennings' *Fires Were Started* uses actual footage to show the work of fire brigade personnel in defending London against German incendiary bombs.

1944: In Alfred Hitchcock's *Lifeboat*, based on a John Steinbeck story, survivors of various races and classes find themselves succumbing to totalitarian leadership as they attempt to survive after their ship has been torpedoed.

1947: Charlie Chaplin's *Monsieur Verdoux* turns the story of a wife killer into an antiwar statement.

1961: Adapted from a television play, *Judgment at Nuremburg* is a dramatization of the post–World War II trials of Nazi war criminals.

1962: *PT 109*, made during John F. Kennedy's presidency, dramatizes Kennedy's wartime heroism and ability as leader. *Mourir à Madrid* (to die in Madrid) combines documentary and newsreel footage from six countries and contemporary footage to reexamine the Spanish civil war.

1964: *Dr. Strangelove: Or, How I Learned to Stop Worrying and Love the Bomb*, written by Stanley Kubrick, Terry Southern, and Peter George, and directed by Kubrick, shows how technology and bungling bureaucrats could produce world destruction.

1965: British documentary filmmaker Peter Watkins' *The War Game*, which warns of the inadequacies of civil defense in case of nuclear disaster, was banned from BBC broadcast until 1985. *Why Vietnam?*, produced by the U.S. Department of Defense, justifies the Vietnamese military buildup to service personnel; includes speeches by President Lyndon B. Johnson and Secretary of State Dean Rusk. *Morir en España* offers a defense of the Spanish dictator Francisco Franco.

1967: *Loin de Vietnam* (far from Vietnam) compiles reflections on the Vietnam War by nine directors, including Jean-Luc Godard, Alain Resnais, Agnès Varda, and Jacques Demy.

1968: John Wayne starred in, produced, and codirected *The Green Berets*, in which he justified the Vietnam War and celebrated the bravery of Special Forces there.

1969: *Oh! What a Lovely War*, Richard Attenborough's adaptation of Joan Littlewood's play, placing it in the context of the Vietnam War, contrasts the horrors of World War I with the popular-culture platitudes that encourage men to enlist. Emile de Antonio's *In the Year of the Pig* (*Vietnam in the Year of the Pig*), an attack on American involvement in Vietnam, incorporates unusual historical film footage.

1975: The Vietnam War is documented in *Introduction to the Enemy*, directed by Haskell Wexler, Tom Hayden, and Jane Fonda.

1978: *Coming Home* was one of the first major feature films to deal with the special problems that veterans of the Vietnam War faced on their return to the United States. The same year also saw director Michael Cimino's *The Deer Hunter*, about the impact of service in the war on the lives of three young men from a small Pennsylvania town.

1979: Director Francis Ford Coppola's *Apocalypse Now* adapts the theme of Joseph Conrad's novella *Heart of Darkness* (1902) to the Vietnam War to create a chilling indictment of the amorality of U.S. involvement in the war.

1983: This year saw two films about the aftermath of nuclear attacks on the United States. *Testament* focused on the impact of a blast on a small California town. *The Day After* was one of the most widely viewed television films in history.

1986: Writer-director Oliver Stone's first film about the Vietnam War, *Platoon*, depicts the brutal realities of the war for infantrymen.

1989: *Born on the Fourth of July*, director Oliver Stone's second film about the Vietnam war, is based on a true story of a veteran disabled in combat who joins the antiwar movement.

1993: Oliver Stone's third exploration of the Vietnam War, *Heaven and Earth*, tells the story of a Vietnamese girl who grows up amid the horrors of the war and then adjusts to settling in America.

Women's Issues

1912: *Votes for Women*, made in cooperation with the National American Women Suffrage Association, directed by Hal Reid, includes appearances by Jane Addams of Hull House and other feminist leaders, as well as footage of the 1912 New York suffrage parade; it contrasts the high-principled leaders of the suffrage movement with corrupt mainstream politicians.

1913: *The Fight for Right*, written by the reformer James Oppenheim, shows how the woman's reform movement was able to change the prison system; the film was endorsed by the National Committee on Prison Labor and popularized idea of prison reform. The feminist leaders Emmeline Pankhurst and Harriet Stanton Blatch appear in *Eighty Million Women Want*—written by B. P. Schulberg, which shows a suffragist who rescues her attorney sweetheart from political corruption. *Die Suffragette* (Germany; *The Militant Suffragette*), starring Asta Nielsen, portrays the violence of the British suffrage movement.

1914: *Your Girl and Mine*, backed by Ruth Hanna McCormick, president of the National American Woman Suffrage Association, shows the inequality of the law as it can affect even the most respectable and wealthiest of women. To prove that policewomen serve important functions, policewoman Alice Stebbins Wells was hired for the lead in *The Policewoman*. Laura Oakley, police chief of Universal City, stars in the comedy *When the Girls Joined the Force*, which shows women cleaning up a graft-ridden police department.

1916: Director Lois Weber dramatizes abortion and birth control issues in *Where Are My Children? The Woman in Politics* features a woman health inspector who overturns a city's corrupt political machine.

1917: Margaret Sanger acted in and cowrote *Birth Control* (*The New World*), a study of her campaign to make birth control information available. Director Lois Weber based *The Hand That Rocks the Cradle* on Sanger's campaign and imprisonment.

1923: *Married Love* (England; *Maisie's Marriage*) was produced as a vehicle for Dr. Marie Stopes, who advocated birth control and sex education.

1927: *The Women's Bureau* shows the activities of the U.S. Department of Labor Women's Bureau, formed in 1920.

1931: Marie Dressler stars in *Politics* as a servant who rises to political power, defeating a corrupt mayor with the support of society women.

1940: Pare Lorentz's *The Fight for Life* dramatizes a physician's realization of the need for prenatal care, sterile conditions for delivery, and sanitation, all made virtually impossible by the squalor and poverty of the slums.

1946: Kenji Mizoguchi's *Josei no Shori* (Japan; *Women's Victory*), shows women overcoming difficulties in pursuing legal careers.

1947: Two Japanese films, *Joyu Sumako no Koi* (*The Loves of Actress Sumako*) and *Joyu* (*The Actress*) pay tribute to the actress Sumako Matsui, who had taken up the cause of women's rights by appearing in Henrik Ibsen's dramas.

1950: Director Ida Lupino's *Outrage* was the first U.S. film under production code to treat rape realistically.

1957: *Nara Livet* (Sweden; *So Close to Life, Brink of Life*) depicts three women in a maternity ward; directed by Ingmar Bergman, it deals with questions of miscarriage, abortion, and the desire for children.

1986: *Rosa Luxemburg* (West Germany) retells the life of the Polish-born German Jewish revolutionary from a feminist perspective.

■ Bibliography

Abrams, Mark. "Opinion Polls and Party Propaganda." *Public Opinion Quarterly* 28 (1964): 13-19.

Abrams, Ray H. *Preachers Present Arms: The Role of the American Churches and Clergy in World Wars I and II, with Some Observations on the War in Vietnam.* Scottdale, Pa.: Herald Press, 1969.

Adam, Peter. *Art of the Third Reich.* New York: Harry N. Abrams, 1992.

Adler, Leo K., and Thomas G. Paterson. "Red Fascism: The Merger of Nazi Germany and Soviet Russia in the American Image of Totalitarianism, 1930's-1960's." *American Historical Review* 75 (April, 1970): 1046-1064.

Akzin, Benjamin. *Propaganda by Diplomats.* Washington, D.C.: Digest Press, 1936.

Albert, Ernst. "The Press in Nazi Germany." *Contemporary Review* 154 (November, 1938): 693-699.

Aldgate, Anthony, and Jeffrey Richards. *Britain Can Take It: The British Cinema in the Second World War.* Oxford, England: Basil Blackwell, 1986.

Alexandre, Laurien. *The Voice of America: From Detente to the Reagan Doctrine.* Norwood, N.J.: Ablex, 1988.

Allen, George V. "Are the Soviets Winning the Propaganda War?" *Annals of the American Academy of Political and Social Science* 336 (July, 1961): 1-11.

Allport, Floyd H. "Toward a Science of Public Opinion." *Public Opinion Quarterly* 1 (January, 1937): 7-23.

Allport, Gordon W. *ABCs of Scapegoating.* New York: Anti-Defamation League of B'nai B'rith, 1966.

Allport, Gordon W., and Leo Postman. *The Psychology of Rumor.* New York: Henry Holt, 1947.

Altheide, David L. *Creating Reality: How TV News Distorts Events.* Beverly Hills, Calif.: Sage Publications, 1976.

————. *Media Power.* Beverly Hills, Calif.: Sage Publications, 1985.

Altheide, David L., and John M. Johnson. *Bureaucratic Propaganda.* Boston: Allyn & Bacon, 1980.

Annis, Albert D., and Norman C. Meier. "The Induction of Opinion Through Suggestion by Means of 'Planted Content.'" *Journal of Social Psychology* 5 (February, 1934): 65-81.

The Art and Science of Psychological Operations: Case Studies of Military Application. 2 vols. Washington, D.C.: American Institute for Research, 1976.

Asher, R., and S. S. Sargent. "Shifts in Attitudes Caused by Cartoon Caricatures." *Journal of General Psychology* 24 (1941): 451-455.

Atkin, Charles K., et al. "Quality Versus Quantity in Televised Political Ads." *Public Opinion Quarterly* 37 (Summer, 1973): 209-224.

August, Thomas G. *The Selling of the Empire: British and French Imperialist Propaganda, 1890-1940.* Westport, Conn.: Greenwood Press, 1985.

Bagdikian, Benjamin H. "Congress and the Media: Partners in Propaganda." *Columbia Journalism Review* 12 (January/February, 1974): 3-10.

Bagley, William C. "The Army Tests and the Pro-Nordic Propaganda." *Educational Review* 67 (April, 1924): 179-187.

Baird, Jay W. *The Mythical World of Nazi War Propaganda, 1939-1945.* Minneapolis: University of Minnesota Press, 1974.

Baker, M. Joyce. *Images of Women in Film: The War Years, 1941-1945.* Ann Arbor, Mich.: UMI Research Press, 1980.

Balfour, Michael. *Propaganda in War, 1939-1945: Organizations, Policies, and Publics in Britain and Germany.* London: Routledge & Kegan Paul, 1979.

Barkhausen, Hans. *Filmpropaganda für Deutschland im Ersten und Zweiten Weltkrieg.* Hildesheim, Germany: Olms Presse, 1982.

Barnicoat, John. *A Concise History of Posters.* New York: Oxford University Press, 1972.

Barnouw, Erik. *The Golden Web: A History of Broadcasting in the United States.* Vol. 2, *1933-1953.* New York. Oxford University Press, 1968.

_____. *The Image Makers: A History of Broadcasting in the United States.* Vol. 3, *From 1953.* New York: Oxford University Press, 1970.

Barsamian, David, ed. *Stenographers to Power: Media and Propaganda.* Monroe, Maine: Common Courage Press, 1992.

Beeley, Sir Harold. "The Changing Role of British International Propaganda." *Annals of the American Academy of Political and Social Science* 398 (November, 1971): 124-129.

Bell, P. M. H. *John Bull and the Bear: British Public Opinion, Foreign Policy and the Soviet Union, 1941-1945.* London: Edward Arnold, 1990.

Bem, Daryl J. *Beliefs, Attitudes, and Human Affairs.* Monterey, Calif: Brooks/Cole, 1970.

Benn, David Wedgewood. "Soviet Propaganda: The Theory and the Practice." *World Today* 41 (April, 1985): 112-115.

Berchtold, William E. "The World Propaganda War." *North American Review* 138 (November, 1934): 421-430.

Berelson, Bernard, and S. de Grazia. "Detecting Collaboration in Propaganda." *Public Opinion Quarterly* 11, no. 2 (1947): 244-253.

Berelson, Bernard, and Morris Janowitz, eds. *Reader in Public Opinion and Communication.* New York: Free Press, 1966.

Berezin, Mabel. "The Organization of Political Ideology: Culture, State, and Theater in Fascist Italy." *American Sociological Review* 56 (October, 1991): 639-651.

Bernays, Edward L. "Molding Public Opinion." *Annals of the American Academy of Political and Social Science* 179 (1935): 82-87.

_____. *Propaganda.* New York: Horace Liveright, 1928.

_____. *Public Relations.* Norman: University of Oklahoma Press, 1952.

Best, James J. *Public Opinion: Micro and Macro.* Homewood, Ill.: Dorsey Press, 1973.

Bettinghaus, Irwin P. *Persuasive Communications.* New York: Holt, Rinehart and Winston, 1968.

Beyle, Herman C. "Determining the Effect of Propaganda Campaigns." *Annals of the American Academy of Political and Social Science* 179 (1935): 106-113.

Bishop, Robert L., and LaMar S. Mackay. "Mysterious Silence, Lyrical Scream: Government Information in World War II." *Journalism Monographs* 19 (May, 1971): 1-39.

Bittman, Ladislav. *The KGB and Soviet Disinformation: An Insider's View.* Washington, D.C.: Pergamon-Brassey's, 1985.

_____, ed. *The New Image-Makers: Soviet Propaganda and Disinformation Today.* Washington, D.C.: Pergamon-Brassey's, 1988.

Black, John B. *Organizing the Propaganda Instrument: The British Experience.* The Hague: Martinus Nijhoff, 1975.

Blakey, George T. *Historians on the Home Front: American Propagandists for the Great War.* Lexington: University Press of Kentucky, 1970.

Boelcke, Willi A., ed. *The Secret Conferences of Dr. Goebbels: The Nazi Propaganda War, 1939-1943.* Translated by Ewald Osers. New York: E. P. Dutton, 1970.

Bogart, Leo. *Premises for Propaganda: The United States Information Agency's Operating Assumptions in the Cold War.* New York: Free Press, 1976.

Boyd, Douglas A. "Broadcasting Between the Two Germanies." *Journalism Quarterly* 60 (Summer, 1983): 232-239.

Braestrup, Peter. *Big Story: How the American Press and Television Reported and Interpreted the Crisis of Tet, 1968, in Vietnam and Washington.* Boulder, Colo.: Westview Press, 1977.

Bramstead, Ernest K. *Goebbels and National Socialist Propaganda.* East Lansing: Michigan State University Press, 1965.

Briggs, Asa. *The History of Broadcasting in the United Kingdom*. Vol. 3 in *The War of Words*. London: Oxford University Press, 1970.

Brown, J. A. C. *Techniques of Persuasion: From Propaganda to Brainwashing*. Baltimore: Pelican Books, 1963.

Browne, Donald R. *International Radio Broadcasting: The Limits of the Limitless Medium*. New York: Praeger, 1982.

Brownstein, Ronald. *The Power and the Glitter: The Hollywood-Washington Connection*. New York: Pantheon Books, 1990.

Bruntz, George H. *Allied Propaganda and the Collapse of the German Empire in 1918*. Stanford, Calif.: Stanford University Press, 1938.

Buitenhuis, Peter. *The Great War of Words: British, American, and Canadian Propaganda and Fiction, 1914-1933*. Vancouver: University of British Columbia Press, 1987.

Burden, Hamilton T. *The Nuremberg Party Rallies: 1923-1939*. New York: Frederick A. Praeger, 1967.

Burns, Tom. *The BBC: Public Institution and Private World*. London: Macmillan, 1977.

Buzzi, Giancarlo. *Advertising: Its Cultural and Political Effects*. Translated by B. David Garmize. Minneapolis: University of Minnesota Press, 1967.

Bytwerk, Randall L. *Julius Streicher: The Man Who Persuaded a Nation to Hate Jews*. New York: Stein & Day, 1983.

Calder, Robert Lorin. *W. Somerset Maugham and the Quest for Freedom*. London: Heinemann, 1972.

Callcott, W. R. "The Last War Aim: British Opinion and the Decision for Czechoslovak Independence, 1914-1919." *Historical Journal* 27, no. 4 (1984): 979-989.

Campbell, Craig W. *Reel America and World War I: A Comprehensive Filmography and History of Motion Pictures in the United States, 1914-1920*. Jefferson, N.C.: McFarland, 1985.

Campbell, Donald T. "Stereotypes and the Perception of Group Difference." *American Psychologist* 22 (October, 1967): 817-829.

Cantril, Hadley, ed. *Public Opinion, 1935-1946*. Princeton, N.J.: Princeton University Press, 1951.

_____. *Soviet Leaders and Mastery over Man*. New Brunswick, N.J.: Rutgers University Press, 1960.

Cantril, Hadley, and Gordon W. Allport. *The Psychology of Radio*. New York: Harper & Row, 1935.

Carr, E. H. *Propaganda in International Politics*. Oxford, England: Clarendon Press, 1939.

Carsten, F. L. *War Against War: British and German Radical Movements in the First World War*. Berkeley: University of California Press, 1982.

Casey, Ralph D. "The National Publicity Bureau and British Party Propaganda." *Public Opinion Quarterly* 3 (October, 1939): 623-634.

_____. "Party Campaign Propaganda." *Annals of the American Academy of Political and Social Science* 179 (1935): 96-105.

Castle, Eugene W. *Billions, Blunders and Baloney: The Fantastic Story of How Uncle Sam Is Squandering Your Money Overseas*. New York: Devin-Adair, 1955.

Cater, Douglass, and Richard Adler, eds. *Television as a Social Force: New Approaches to TV Criticism*. New York: Praeger, 1975.

Catlin, George. "Propaganda and the Cold War." *Yale Review* 43 (September, 1953): 103-116.

_____. "The Role of Propaganda in a Democracy." *Annals of the American Academy of Political and Social Science* 179 (1935): 219-226.

Chaffee, Steven H., and Michael J. Petrick. *Using the Mass Media: Communication Problems in American Society*. New York: McGraw-Hill, 1975.

Chaiken, Shelly, and Charles Stangor. "Attitudes and Attitude Change." *Annual Review of Psychology* 38 (1987): 575-630.

Chakotin, Serge. *The Rape of the Masses: The Psychology of Totalitarian Political Propaganda*. New York: Alliance Book Corporation, 1940.

Chandler, Robert W. *Public Opinion: Changing Attitudes on Contemporary Political and Social Issues.* New York: R. R. Bowker, 1972.

_____. *War of Ideas: The U.S. Propaganda Campaign in Vietnam.* Boulder, Colo.: Westview Press, 1981.

Chappell, Matthew N., and C. E. Hooper. *Radio Audience Measurement.* New York: Stephen Daye, 1944.

Chase, Stuart. *The Tyranny of Words.* New York: Harcourt Brace, 1938.

Chenault, Libby. *Battlelines: World War I Posters from the Bowman Gray Collection.* Chapel Hill: University of North Carolina Press, 1988.

Cherry, Colin. *World Communication: Threat or Promise? A Socio-technical Approach.* Chichester, England: John Wiley & Sons, 1978.

Chester, Edward W. *Radio, Television, and American Politics.* New York: Sheed & Ward, 1969.

Child, Irvin L., and Leonard W. Doob. "Factors Determining National Stereotypes." *Journal of Social Psychology* 17 (1943): 203-219.

Childs, Harwood Lawrence. *An Introduction to Public Opinion.* New York: John Wiley & Sons, 1940.

_____. *Public Opinion: Nature, Formation, and Role.* Princeton, N.J.: D. Van Nostrand, 1965.

_____, ed. *Public Opinion Quarterly* 7 (Spring, 1943). The entire issue is devoted to the "Office of War Information."

_____, ed. *Propaganda and Dictatorship: A Collection of Papers.* Princeton, N.J.: Princeton University Press, 1936.

Childs, Harwood Lawrence, and John B. Whitton, eds. *Propaganda by Short Wave.* Princeton, N.J.: Princeton University Press, 1942.

Chomsky, Noam. *Towards a New Cold War: Essays on the Current Crisis and How We Got There.* New York: Pantheon Books, 1982.

Choukas, Michael. *Propaganda Comes of Age.* Washington, D.C.: Public Affairs Press, 1965.

Christensen, Terry. *Reel Politics: American Political Movies from "Birth of a Nation" to "Platoon."* London: Basil Blackwell, 1987.

Clark, David C. "Radio in Presidential Campaigns: The Early Years (1924-1932)." *Journal of Broadcasting* 6 (Summer, 1962): 229-238.

Clarke, Peter, and Eric Fredin. "Newspapers, Television, and Political Reasoning." *Public Opinion Quarterly* 42 (1978): 143-160.

Clarke, Peter B. *West Africans at War: 1914-1918; 1939-1945: Colonial Propaganda and Its Cultural Aftermath.* London: Ethnographica, 1986.

Clews, John C. *Communist Propaganda Techniques.* New York: Praeger, 1964.

Cockett, Richard. *Twilight of Truth: Chamberlain, Appeasement, and the Manipulation of the Press.* New York: St. Martin's Press, 1989.

Coers, Donald V. *John Steinbeck as Propagandist: "The Moon Is Down" Goes to War.* Tuscaloosa: University of Alabama Press, 1991.

Coggeshall, Reginald. "Diplomatic Implications in International News." *Journalism Quarterly* 11 (June, 1934): 141-159.

Cohen, Arthur R. *Attitude Change and Social Influence.* New York: Basic Books, 1964.

Cohen, Stanley, and Jock Young, eds. *The Manufacture of News: A Reader.* Beverly Hills, Calif.: Sage Publications, 1973.

Colby, Benjamin. *'Twas a Famous Victory: Deception and Propaganda in the War with Germany.* New York: Arlington House Publishers, 1974.

Cole, J. A. *Lord Haw-Haw—and William Joyce.* London: Faber & Faber, 1964.

Cole, Robert. *Britain and the War of Words in Neutral Europe, 1939-1945: The Art of the Possible.* London: Macmillan, 1990.

_____. " 'Good Relations': Irish Neutrality and the Propaganda of John Betjeman, 1941-1943." *Éire-Ireland* 33 (Winter, 1996): 33-46.

_____. *Propaganda in Twentieth Century War and Politics: An Annotated Bibliography.* Lanham, Md.: Scarecrow Press, 1996.

Cole, Taylor. "The Italian Ministry of Popular Culture." *Public Opinion Quarterly* 2 (July, 1938): 425-434.

Collins, Ross F. "The Development of Censorship in World War I France." *Journalism Monographs* 131 (February, 1992): 1-25

Combs, James E., and Dan Nimmo. *The New Propaganda: The Dictatorship of Palaver in Contemporary Politics.* White Plains, N.Y.: Longman, 1993.

Combs, James E., and Sara T. Combs. *Film Propaganda and American Politics: An Analysis and Filmography.* New York: Garland Publishing, 1994.

Constantine, Stephen. *Buy and Build: The Advertising Posters of the Empire Marketing Board.* London: Her Majesty's Stationery Office, 1986.

Converse, Philip E. "The Nature of Belief Systems in Mass Publics." In *Ideology and Discontent,* edited by David E. Apter. New York: Free Press, 1964.

Conway, Flo, and Jim Siegelman. *Holy Terror: The Fundamentalist War on America's Freedoms in Religion, Politics, and Our Private Lives.* Garden City, N.Y.: Doubleday, 1982.

Cook, Sir Edward. *The Press in War-Time: With Some Account of the Official Press Bureau.* London: Macmillan, 1920.

Cook, Fred J. "Radio Right: Hate Clubs of the Air." *Nation* 198 (May 25, 1964): 523-527.

Corcoran, Paul E. *Political Language and Rhetoric.* Austin: University of Texas Press, 1979.

Cornebise, Alfred E. "The Refinement of Allied Propaganda: The Case of *Nachrichtendienst.*" *German Studies Review* 2 (February, 1979): 30-48.

_____. *War as Advertised: The Four Minute Men and America's Crusade, 1917-1918.* Philadelphia, Pa.: American Philosophical Society, 1984.

Cornick, Martyn. "The BBC and the Propaganda War Against Occupied France: The Work of Émile Delavaney and the European Intelligence Department." *French History* 8, no. 3 (1994): 316-354.

Costello, David R. "*Searchlight Books* and the Quest for a 'People's War,' 1941-1942." *Journal of Contemporary History* 24 (April, 1989): 257-276.

Coultass, Clive. *Images for Battle: British Film and the Second World War, 1939-1945.* Newark, N.J.: University of Delaware Press, 1989.

Crawford, Anthony R., ed. *Posters of World War I and World War II in the George C. Marshall Research Foundation.* Charlottesville: University Press of Virginia, 1979.

Creel, George. *How We Advertised America: The First Telling of the Amazing Story of the Committee on Public Information That Carried the Gospel of Americanism to Every Corner of the Globe.* New York: Harper and Brothers, 1920.

Cremieux-Brilhac, Jean-Louis, ed. *Les Voix de la liberté: Ici Londres, 1940-1944.* Paris: La Documentation Français, 1975.

Crew, T. *Health Propaganda (Ways and Means).* Leicester, England: Leicestershire Health Insurance Committee, 1935.

Crofts, William. *Coercion or Persuasion? Propaganda in Britain After 1945.* London: Routledge, 1989.

Crozier, Emmet. *American Reporters on the Western Front, 1914-1918.* New York: Oxford University Press, 1959.

Cruickshank, Charles. *The Fourth Arm: Psychological Warfare, 1938-1945.* Oxford, England: Oxford University Press, 1981.

Culbert, David, ed. *Film and Propaganda in America: A Documentary History.* 4 vols. New York: Greenwood Press, 1990.

_____. "*Reds*: Propaganda, Docudrama, and Hollywood." *Labor History* 24 (Winter, 1983): 125-130.

Cull, Nicholas John. *Selling War: The British Propaganda Campaign Against American "Neutrality" in World War II.* New York: Oxford University Press, 1995.

Curran, James, Michael Gurevitch, and Janet Woollacott, eds. *Mass Communication and Society.* Beverly Hills, Calif.: Sage Publications, 1979.

Curran, James, Anthony Smith, and Pauline Wingate, eds. *Impacts and Influences: Essays on Media Power in the Twentieth Century.* London: Methuen, 1987.

Curtis, Liz. *Ireland: The Propaganda War. The British Media and the "Battle for Hearts and Minds."* London: Pluto Press, 1984.

Dahlin, Ebba. *French and German Public Opinion on Declared War Aims, 1914-1918.* Reprint. New York: AMS Press, 1971.

Dallek, Robert. *Ronald Reagan: The Politics of Symbolism.* Cambridge, Mass.: Harvard University Press, 1984.

Daugherty, William E., and Morris Janowitz, eds. *A Psychological Warfare Casebook.* Baltimore: The Johns Hopkins University Press, 1958.

Davison, W. Phillips. "The Public Opinion Process." *Public Opinion Quarterly* 22 (1958): 91-106.

_____. "Some Trends in International Propaganda." *Annals of the American Academy of Political and Social Science* 398 (November, 1971): 1-13.

Davitz, Joel R., ed. *The Communication of Emotional Meaning.* New York: McGraw-Hill, 1964.

Deacon, Richard. *The Truth Twisters.* London: MacDonald, 1986.

DeFleur, Melvin L., and Sandra J. Ball-Rokeach. "The Effects of Mass Communication." In *Theories of Mass Communications.* 5th ed. New York: Longmans, 1989.

Delmer, Sefton. *Black Boomerang.* New York: Viking Press, 1962.

Demm, Eberhard. "Propaganda and Caricature in the First World War." *Journal of Contemporary History* 28 (January, 1993): 163-192.

Dennis, Everette E., George Gerbner, and Yassen N. Zassoursky, eds. *Beyond the Cold War: Soviet and American Media Images.* Newbury Park, Calif.: Sage Publications, 1991.

DeNoon, Christopher. *Posters of the WPA.* Los Angeles: Wheatley Press, 1987.

The Deportation of Women and Girls from Lille. Translation. New York: George H. Doran, 1917.

Deutschmann, Linda. *Triumph of the Will: The Image of the Third Reich.* Wakefield, N.H.: Longwood Academic, 1991.

Diamond, Edwin, and Stephan Bates. *The Spot: The Rise of Political Advertising on Television.* Cambridge, Mass.: MIT Press, 1992.

Dickinson, Margaret, and Sarah Street. *Cinema and State: The Film Industry and Government, 1927-1984.* London: BFI Publishing, 1985.

Dobyns, Fletcher. *The Amazing Story of Repeal: An Exposé of the Power of Propaganda.* Chicago: Willett, Clark, 1940.

Doherty, Martin. "Black Propaganda by Radio: The German Concordia Broadcasts to Britain, 1940-1941." *Historical Journal of Film, Radio, and Television* 14, no. 2 (1994): 167-197.

Doob, Leonard W. "Propaganda." *International Encyclopedia of Communications.* Vol. 3. Oxford, England: Oxford University Press, 1989.

_____. *Propaganda: Its Psychology and Technique.* New York: Henry Holt, 1935.

_____. *Public Opinion and Propaganda.* 2d ed. Hamden, Conn.: Archon Books, 1966.

Douglas, Roy. *The World War, 1939-1945: The Cartoonists' Vision.* London: Routledge, 1990.

Dovifat, Emil, ed. *Handbuch der Publizistik.* 3 vols. Berlin: Walter de Gruyter, 1968.

Ducat, Stephen. *Taken in: American Gullibility and the Reagan Mythos.* Tacoma, Wash.: Life Sciences Press, 1988.

Dunham, Donald. *Kremlin Target: U.S.A. Conquest by Propaganda.* New York: Ives Washburn, 1961.

Duus, Masayo. *Tokyo Rose: Orphan of the Pacific.* Translated by Peter Duus. Tokyo: Kodansha International, 1979.

Dyer, Murray. *The Weapon on the Wall: Rethinking Psychological Warfare.* Baltimore: The Johns Hopkins University Press, 1959.

Dyer, Sherman H. *Radio in Wartime.* New York: Greenberg, 1942.

Eberle, Matthias. "George Grosz, the Irate Dandy: Art as a Weapon in the Class Struggle." In *World War I and the Weimar Artists.* New Haven, Conn.: Yale University Press, 1985.

Ebermayer, Erich, and Hans-Otto Meissner. Translated by Louis Hagen. *Evil Genius: The Story of Joseph Goebbels.* London: Allan Wingate, 1953.

Ebon, Martin. *The Soviet Propaganda Machine.* New York: McGraw-Hill, 1987.

Edwards, John Carver. *Berlin Calling: American Broadcasters in Service to the Third Reich.* New York: Praeger, 1991.

Ekstein, Modris. *The Limits of Reason: The German Democratic Press and the Collapse of Weimar Democracy.* London: Oxford University Press, 1975.

Ellul, Jacques. *Histoire de la propagande.* Paris: Presses Universitaires de France, 1967.

_____. "Propagande et personnalization du pouvoir." In *La Personnalization du pouvoir,* edited by Léo Hamon and Albert Mabileau. Paris: Presses Universitaires de France, 1964.

Emery, Walter B. *National and International Systems of Broadcasting: Their History, Operation, and Control.* East Lansing: Michigan State University Press, 1969.

Evans, F. Bowen, ed. *Worldwide Communist Propaganda Activities.* New York: Macmillan, 1955.

Evans, Gary. *John Grierson and the National Film Board: The Politics of Wartime Propaganda.* Toronto: University of Toronto Press, 1984.

Fairbanks, Arthur. *Economics or Propaganda?* Dún Laoghaire, Ireland: Boole Press, 1987.

Farago, Ladislas, ed. *German Psychological Warfare: Survey and Bibliography.* New York: Committee for National Morale, 1941.

Farrell, John C., and Asa P. Smith, eds. *Image and Reality in World Politics.* New York: Columbia University Press, 1967.

Ferguson, John. *The Arts in Britain in World War I.* London: Stainer and Bell, 1980.

Festinger, Leonard, and Nathan Maccoby. "On Resistance to Persuasive Communications." *Journal of Abnormal and Social Psychology* 68 (1964): 359-366.

Fielding, Raymond. *The American Newsreel, 1911-1967.* Norman: University of Oklahoma Press, 1972.

_____. *The March of Time, 1935-1951.* New York: Oxford University Press, 1978.

Flavell, M. Kay. "Kitsch and Propaganda: The Blending of Myth and History in Hedwig Courths-Mahler's *Lissa geht ins Glück* (1936)." *German Studies Review* 8 (February, 1985): 65-87.

Ford, Guy Stanton. "The Committee on Public Information." *Historical Outlook* 11 (March, 1920): 97-100.

Ford, Nick Aaron, ed. *Language in Uniform: A Reader on Propaganda.* New York: Odyssey Press, 1967.

Foulkes, A. P. *Literature and Propaganda.* London: Methuen, 1983.

Fraser, Lindley. *Germany Between Two Wars: A Study of Propaganda and Guilt.* London: Oxford University Press, 1945.

_____. *Propaganda.* London: Oxford University Press, 1957.

Frederick, Howard H. *Cuban-American Radio Wars: Ideology in International Telecommunications.* Norwood, N.J.: Ablex, 1986.

Freedman, Jonathan L., and D. O. Sears. "Warning, Distraction, and Resistance to Influence." *Journal of Personality and Social Psychology* 1 (1965): 262-266.

Freeman, Ellis. *Conquering the Man in the Street: A Psychological Analysis of Propaganda in War, Fascism, and Politics.* New York: Vanguard Press, 1940.

Freeman, Judith. "The Publicity of the Empire Marketing Board, 1926-1933." *Journal of Advertising History* 1 (1977): 12-14.

Friedl, Bettina, ed. *On to Victory: Propaganda Plays of the Woman Suffrage Movement.* Boston: Northeastern University Press, 1987.

Friedrich, Carl J. *The Pathology of Politics, Violence, Betrayal, Corruption, Secrecy, and Propaganda.* New York: Harper & Row, 1972.

————. "Propaganda and Education." *The Atlantic* 159 (June, 1937): 693-701.

Friedson, Eliot. "Communications Research and the Concept of the Mass." *American Sociological Review* 18 (June, 1953): 313-317.

Fulbright, Senator J. W. *The Pentagon Propaganda Machine.* New York: Liveright, 1970.

Furhammar, Leif, and Folke Isaksson. *Politics and Film.* Translated by Kersti French. New York: Praeger, 1971.

Fyfe, Hamilton. *Sixty Years of Fleet Street.* London: W. H. Allen, 1949.

Gadberry, Glen W., ed. *Theatre in the Third Reich: Essays on Theatre in Nazi Germany.* Westport, Conn.: Greenwood Press, 1995.

Gallo, Max. "1925-1945: Propaganda and Ideology." In *The Poster in History*, translated by Alfred and Bruni Mayor. Secaucus, N.J.: Wellfleet Press, 1989.

————. "1950-1970: Words and Images." In *The Poster in History*, translated by Alfred and Bruni Mayor. Secaucus, N.J.: Wellfleet Press, 1989.

Garber, William. "Propaganda Analysis: To What Ends?" *American Journal of Sociology* 48 (1942-1943): 240-245.

Garnett, Maxwell. "Propaganda." *Contemporary Review* 147 (May, 1935): 574-582.

Geldern, James von. *Bolshevik Festivals, 1917-1920.* Berkeley: University of California Press, 1993.

George, Alexander L. *Propaganda Analysis: A Study of Inferences Made from Nazi Propaganda in World War II.* White Plains, N.Y.: Row, Peterson, 1959.

George, John. *Nazis, Communists, Klansmen, and Others on the Fringe: Political Extremism in America.* Buffalo, N.Y.: Prometheus Books, 1992.

Gervereau, Laurent. *La Propagande par l'affiche.* Paris: Éditions Syros-Alternatives, 1991.

Gilmour, T. L. "The Government and Propaganda." *The Nineteenth Century* 85 (January, 1919): 148-158.

Ginsberg, Benjamin. *The Captive Public: How Mass Opinion Promotes State Power.* New York: Basic Books, 1986.

Goldie, Grace Wyndham. *Facing the Nation: Television and Politics, 1936-1976.* London: Bodley Head, 1977.

Goodfriend, Arthur. "The Dilemma of Cultural Propaganda: 'Let It Be'." *Annals of the American Academy of Political and Social Science* 398 (November, 1971): 104.

Goodrum, Charles, and Helen Dalrymple. *Advertising in America: The First Two Hundred Years.* New York: Harry N. Abrams, 1990.

Gordon, George N., and Irving A. Falk. *The War of Ideas: America's International Identity Crisis.* New York: Hastings House, 1973.

Gordon, George N., Irving A. Falk, and William Hodapp. *The Idea Invaders.* New York: Hastings House, 1963.

Gordon, Joseph S., ed. *Psychological Operations: The Soviet Challenge.* Boulder, Colo.: Westview Press, 1988.

Gordon, Robbie. *We Interrupt This Program . . . : A Citizen's Guide to Using the Media for Social Change.* Amherst: University of Massachusetts Press, 1978.

Graber, Doris A. *Mass Media and American Politics.* Washington, D.C.: Congressional Quarterly Press, 1993.

Graham, Cooper C. *Leni Riefenstahl and Olympia.* Metuchen, N.J.: Scarecrow Press, 1986.

Grahame, Jeanne. "The Four-Minute Men: Volunteers for Propaganda." *Southern Speech Journal* 32, no. 1 (1966): 49-57.

Grandin, Thomas. *The Political Use of the Radio.* 1939. New York: Arno Press and *The New York Times*, 1971.

Grant, Mariel. *Propaganda and the Role of the State in Inter-War Britain.* Oxford, England: Clarendon Press, 1994.

Graves, W. Brooke, ed. *Readings in Public Opinion: Its Formation and Control.* New York: D. Appleton, 1928.

Green, Fitzhugh. *American Propaganda Abroad.* New York: Hippocrene Books, 1988.

Greenwald, Anthony G., Timothy C. Brock, and Thomas M. Ostrom, eds. *Psychological Foundations of Attitudes.* New York: Academic Press, 1968.

Gregory, G. H. *Posters of World War II.* New York: Gramercy Books, 1993.

Grierson, John. "Propaganda: A Problem for Educational Theory and for Cinema." *Sight and Sound* 2 (1933): 119-121.

Gross, John, ed. *The Age of Kipling.* New York: Simon & Schuster, 1972.

Grothe, Peter. *To Win the Minds of Men: The Story of the Communist Propaganda War in East Germany.* Palo Alto, Calif.: Pacific Books, 1958.

Gruening, Ernest. *The Public Pays: A Study of Power Propaganda.* New York: Vanguard Press, 1931.

Gustainis, J. Justin. *American Rhetoric and the Vietnam War.* Westport, Conn.: Praeger, 1993.

Hachey, Thomas E. "British War Propaganda and American Catholics in 1918." *Catholic Historical Review* 61 (1975): 48-66.

Hale, Oron James. *Publicity and Diplomacy: With Special Reference to England and Germany, 1890-1914.* Gloucester, Mass.: Peter Smith, 1964.

Hall, Alex. "The War of Words: Anti-Socialist Offensives and Counterpropaganda in Wilhelmine Germany, 1890-1914." *Journal of Contemporary History* 11 (July 1976): 11-42.

Hallin, Daniel C. *The "Uncensored War": The Media and Vietnam.* New York: Oxford University Press, 1986.

Halloran, J. D. *The Effects of Mass Communication with Special Reference to Television.* Leicester, England: Leicester University Press, 1965.

Hamlin, Charles Hunter. *Educators Present Arms.* 1939. New York: Garland, 1973.

———. *Propaganda and Myth in Time of War: The War Myth in United States History.* 1927. New York: Garland, 1973.

Hanak, Harry. *Great Britain and Austria-Hungary During the First World War: A Study in the Formation of Public Opinion.* London: Oxford University Press, 1962.

Hansen, Allen C. *USIA: Public Diplomacy in the Computer Age.* New York: Praeger, 1989.

Hanson, Elisha. "Official Propaganda Under the New Deal." *Annals of the American Academy of Political and Social Science* 179 (May, 1935): 176-186.

Hapgood, Norman. "Atrocities." *Harper's Weekly* (July 10, 1915): 28-30.

Harding, T. Swann. "Genesis of one 'Government Propaganda Mill.'" *Public Opinion Quarterly* 11 (1947-1948): 227-235.

Hardy, Alexander G. *Hitler's Secret Weapon: The "Managed" Press and Propaganda Machine of Nazi Germany.* New York: Vantage Press, 1967.

Hargrave, John. *Words Win Wars: Propaganda, the Mightiest Weapon of All.* London: Wells Gardner, Darton, 1940.

Harrisson, Tom. "What Is Public Opinion?" *Public Opinion Quarterly* 11 (1940): 368-383.

Hartsough, Denise. "Soviet Film Distribution and Exhibition in Germany, 1921-1933." *Historical Journal of Film, Radio, and Television* 5, no. 2 (1985): 131-148.

Haste, Cate. *Keep the Home Fires Burning: Propaganda in the First World War.* London: Allen Lane, 1977.

Havighurst, Clark C., ed. *International Control of Propaganda.* Dobbs Ferry, N.Y.: Oceana, 1967.

Hawthorne, Jeremy, ed. *Propaganda, Persuasion, and Polemic.* London: Edward Arnold, 1987.

Hayakawa, S. I. *Language in Thought and Action.* 4th ed. New York: Harcourt Brace Jovanovich, 1978.

Henderson, Edgar H. "Towards a Definition of Propaganda." *The Journal of Social Psychology* 18 (1943): 71-87.

Hennessy, Bernard C. *Public Opinion.* Belmont, Calif.: Wadsworth, 1965.

Herman, Edward S. *Beyond Hypocrisy: Decoding the News in an Age of Propaganda.* Boston: South End Press, 1992.

_____. *The Real Terror Network: Terrorism in Fact and Propaganda.* Boston: South End Press, 1982.

Herz, Martin F. "Some Psychological Lessons from Leaflet Propaganda in World War II." *Public Opinion Quarterly* 13, no. 3 (1949): 471-486.

Hiebert, Ray Eldon. "Public Relations as a Weapon of Modern Warfare." *Public Relations Review* 17 (Summer, 1991): 107-16.

_____. "Public Relations, Propaganda, and War: A Book Review and Essay on the Literature." *Public Relations Review* 19 (Fall, 1993): 293-302.

Higham, Charles Frederick. *Looking Forward: Mass Education Through Publicity.* New York: Alfred A. Knopf, 1920.

Hiley, Nicholas. "Sir Hedley Le Bas and the Origins of Domestic Propaganda in Britain, 1914-1917." *Journal of Advertising History* 10, no. 2 (1987): 30-46.

Himelstein, Morgan Y. *Drama Was a Weapon: The Left-Wing Theatre in New York, 1929-1941.* New Brunswick, N.J.: Rutgers University Press, 1963.

Hobson, J. A. *The Psychology of Jingoism.* London: Grant Richards, 1901.

Hogan, J. Michael. "The Rhetoric of Historiography: New Left Revisionism in the Vietnam Era." In *Argument and Social Practice: Proceedings of the Fourth SCA/AFA Conference on Argumentation,* edited by J. Robert Cox, Malcolm O. Sillars, and Gregg B. Walker. Annandale, Va.: Speech Communication Association, 1985.

Hollander, Gayle Durham. *Soviet Political Indoctrination: Developments in Mass Media and Propaganda Since Stalin.* New York: Praeger, 1972.

Hollins, T. J. "The Conservative Party and Film Propaganda Between the Wars." *English Historical Review* 96 (April, 1981): 359-369.

Holt, Robert T., and Robert W. van de Velde. *Strategic Psychological Operations and American Foreign Policy.* Chicago: University of Chicago Press, 1960.

Honey, Maureen. *Creating Rosie the Riveter: Class, Gender, and Propaganda During World War II.* Amherst: University of Massachusetts Press, 1984.

Hopkin, Deian. "Domestic Censorship in the First World War." *Journal of Contemporary History* 5 (1970): 151-169.

Horak, Jan-Christopher. "Zionist Film Propaganda in Nazi Germany." *Historical Journal of Film, Radio, and Television* 4, no. 1 (1984): 49-58.

Houn, Franklyn W. *To Change a Nation: Propaganda and Indoctrination in Communist China.* New York: Free Press of Glencoe, 1959.

Hovland, Carl I., Arthur A. Lumsdaine, and Fred D. Sheffield. *Experiments on Mass Communications.* Vol. 3 in *Studies in Social Psychology in World War II.* Princeton, N.J.: Princeton University Press, 1949.

Howitt, Dennis. *Mass Media and Social Problems.* Oxford, England: Pergamon Press, 1982.

Hummel, William, and Keith Huntress. *The Analysis of Propaganda.* New York: Dryden Press, 1949.

Huxley, Aldous. "Notes on Propaganda." *Harper's Magazine* 174 (December, 1936): 32-41.

Hyman, Herbert H. "Problems in the Collection of Opinion Research Data." *American Journal of Sociology* 55, no. 4 (1950): 362-370.

Hyman, Herbert H., and Paul B. Sheatsley. "Some Reasons Why Information Campaigns Fail." *Public Opinion Quarterly* 11 (Spring, 1947): 412-423.

Inkeles, Alex. *Public Opinion in Soviet Russia: A Study in Mass Persuasion.* Cambridge, Mass.: Harvard University Press, 1950.

_____. "The Soviet Attack on the Voice of America." *American Slavic and East European Review* 12 (October, 1953): 319-342.

Institute for Propaganda Analysis. *The Fine Art of Propaganda: A Study of Father Coughlin's Speeches.* New York: Harcourt Brace, 1939.

Irion, Frederick C. *Public Opinion and Propaganda.* New York: Thomas Y. Crowell, 1950.

Irwin, Will. *Propaganda and the News: Or, What Makes You Think So?* New York: Whittlesey House, 1936.

Isenberg, Michael T. "The Mirror of Democracy: Reflections of the War Films of World War I, 1917-1919." *Journal of Popular Culture* 9 (Spring, 1976): 878-885.

———. *War on Film: The American Cinema and World War I, 1914-1941.* London: Associated University Presses, 1981.

———. "World War I Film Comedies and American Society: The Concern with Authoritarianism." *Film and History* 5 (September, 1975): 7-15, 21.

Jacobson, David J. *The Affairs of Dame Rumor.* New York: Rinehart, 1948.

Jahoda, Marie, and Eunice Cooper. "The Evasion of Propaganda: How Prejudiced People Respond to Anti-Prejudice Propaganda." *Journal of Psychology* 23 (1947): 15-25.

Janowitz, Morris. "Mass Persuasion and International Relations." *Public Opinion Quarterly* 25 (Winter, 1961): 560-570.

———. "The Technique of Propaganda for Reaction: Gerald L. K. Smith's Radio Speeches." *Public Opinion Quarterly* 8 (Spring, 1944): 84-93.

Jarvie, I. C. "Fanning the Flames: Anti-American Reaction to *Operation Burma* (1945)." *Historical Journal of Film, Radio, and Television* 1, no. 2 (1981): 117-137.

Johnson, Abby Arthur, and Ronald Maberry Johnson. *Propaganda and Aesthetics: The Literary Politics of Afro-American Magazines in the Twentieth Century.* Amherst: University of Massachusetts Press, 1979.

Johnson, Niel M. *George Sylvester Viereck: German-American Propagandist.* Urbana: University of Illinois Press, 1972.

Johnston, Winifred. *Memo on the Movies: War Propaganda, 1914-1939.* Norman, Okla.: Cooperative Books, 1939.

Jones, Barbara, and Bill Howell. "Propaganda and Morale." In *Popular Arts of the First World War.* New York: McGraw-Hill, 1972.

Jowett, Garth S. "Propaganda and Communication: The Re-emergence of a Research Tradition." *Journal of Communication* 37 (Winter, 1987): 97-114.

Jowett, Garth S., and James M. Linton. *Movies as Mass Communications.* 2d ed. Newbury Park, Calif.: Sage, 1989.

Joyce, Walter. *The Propaganda Gap.* New York: Harper & Row, 1963.

Judd, Denis. *Posters of World War II.* New York: St. Martin's Press, 1973.

Juergens, George. *News from the White House: The Presidential-Press Relationship in the Progressive Era.* Chicago: University of Chicago Press, 1981.

Kamins, Bernard Francis. *Basic Propaganda.* Los Angeles: Houlgate House, 1951.

Kapferer, J. N. "A Mass Poisoning Rumor in Europe." *Public Opinion Quarterly* 53 (Winter, 1989): 467-481.

Kaplan, Frank L. "The Communist International's Press Control from Moscow." *Journalism Quarterly* 48 (Summer, 1971): 315-325.

Karlins, Marvin, and Herbert I. Abelson. *Persuasion: How Opinions and Attitudes Are Changed.* New York: Springer, 1970.

Katz, Daniel, et al., eds. *Public Opinion and Propaganda: A Book of Readings.* New York: Dryden Press, 1954.

Kecskemeti, Paul. "The Soviet Approach to International Political Communication." *Public Opinion Quarterly* 20 (Spring, 1956): 299-308.

Kenez, Peter. *The Birth of the Propaganda State: Soviet Methods of Mass Mobilization, 1917-1929.* Cambridge, England: Cambridge University Press, 1985.

Kershaw, Ian. *The "Hitler Myth": Image and Reality in the Third Reich.* Oxford, England: Clarendon Press, 1987.

————. "Ideology, Propaganda, and the Rise of the Nazi Party." In *The Nazi Machtergreifung,* edited by Peter D. Stachura. London: George Allen & Unwin, 1983.

Kingston, Paul J. *Anti-Semitism in France During the 1930s: Organizations, Personalities, and Propaganda.* Hull, England: University of Hull Press, 1983.

Kirwin, Gerald. "Allied Bombing and Nazi Domestic Propaganda." *European History Quarterly* 15 (July, 1985): 341-362.

Knightly, Phillip. *The First Casualty, from the Crimea to Vietnam: The War Correspondent as Hero, Propagandist, and Myth Maker.* New York: Harcourt Brace Jovanovich, 1975.

Knowles, Dorothy. *The Censor, the Drama, and the Film, 1900-1934.* London: George Allen & Unwin, 1934.

Knudson, Jerry W. "The Ultimate Weapon: Propaganda and the Spanish Civil War." *Journalism History* 15 (Winter, 1988): 102-111.

Koppes, Clayton R., and Gregory D. Black. *Hollywood Goes to War: How Politics, Profits, and Propaganda Shaped World War II Movies.* New York: Free Press, 1987.

————. "What to Show the World: The Office of War Information and Hollywood, 1942-1945." *Journal of American History* 64 (June, 1977): 87-105.

Kracauer, Siegfried. *From Caligari to Hitler: A Psychological History of the German Film.* 1947. Reprint. Princeton, N.J.: Princeton University Press, 1974.

Kraus, Sidney, and Richard M. Perloff, eds. *Mass Media and Political Thought.* Beverly Hills, Calif.: Sage Publications, 1985.

Kriesberg, Martin. "Cross-Pressures and Attitudes: A Study of the Influence of Conflicting Propaganda on Opinion Regarding American-Soviet Relations." *Public Opinion Quarterly* 13 (Spring, 1949): 5-16.

Kris, Ernst, and Hans Speier, eds. *German Radio Propaganda: Report on Home Broadcasts During the War.* New York: Oxford University Press, 1944.

Kruglak, Theodore E. *The Two Faces of TASS.* Minneapolis: University of Minnesota Press, 1962.

Lacey, Kate. "From *Plauderei* to Propaganda: On Women's Radio in Germany, 1924-1935." *Media, Culture, and Society* 16 (1994): 589-607.

Lahav, Pnina, and Sue Curry Jansen. "Censorship." *International Encyclopedia of Communications.* Vol. 1. Oxford, England: Oxford University Press, 1989.

Lambert, Richard S. *Propaganda.* London: Thomas Nelson and Sons, 1938.

Landau, Captain Henry. *The Enemy Within: The Inside Story of German Sabotage in America.* New York: G. P. Putnam's Sons, 1937.

Landy, Marcia. *Fascism in Film: The Italian Commercial Cinema, 1931-1943.* Princeton, N.J.: Princeton University Press, 1986.

Lane, Robert E. *Political Ideology: Why the American Common Man Believes What He Does.* New York: Free Press of Glencoe, 1962.

Lang, Gladys Engel, and Kurt Lang. *The Battle for Public Opinion: The President, the Press, and the Polls During Watergate.* New York: Columbia University Press, 1983.

Larson, Cedric, and James R. Mock. "The Lost Files of the Creel Committee of 1917-19." *Public Opinion Quarterly* 3 (1939): 5-29.

Lasswell, Harold D. "The Impact of Public Opinion Research on Our Society." *Public Opinion Quarterly* 21 (1957): 33-38.

————. "The Persons: Subject and Object of Propaganda." *Annals of the American Academy of Political and Social Science* 179 (1935): 187-193.

————. "Propaganda." In *Encyclopedia of the Social Sciences.* Vol. 12. New York: Macmillan, 1934.

————. *Propaganda and Dictatorship.* Princeton, N.J.: Princeton University Press, 1936.

_____. *Propaganda Technique in the World War*. New York: Garland, 1972. Reissue of earlier publication.

_____. "The Theory of Political Propaganda." *American Political Science Review* 21 (August, 1927): 627-631.

Lasswell, Harold D., and Dorothy Blumenstock. *World Revolutionary Propaganda: A Chicago Study*. New York: Alfred A. Knopf, 1939.

Laurence, John C. *Race, Propaganda, and South Africa*. London: Victor Gollancz, 1979.

Lavine, Harold. *Fifth Column in America*. New York: Doubleday, Doran, 1940.

Lavine, Harold, and James Wechsler. *War Propaganda and the United States*. New York: Garland Publishing, 1972.

Lawrence, Raymond D. "Haldeman-Julius Has Made Propaganda Profitable." *Public Opinion Quarterly* 3 (January, 1939): 79-91.

Leab, Janiel J. "How Red Was My Valley: Hollywood, the Cold War Film, and *I Married a Communist*." *Journal of Contemporary History* 19 (January, 1984): 59-88.

Lee, Alfred McClung. *How to Understand Propaganda*. New York: Holt Rinehart, 1952.

Lee, Ivy L. *Publicity: Some of the Things It Is and Is Not*. New York: Industries Publishing, 1925.

Leeper, R. A. "British Culture Abroad." *Contemporary Review* 148 (August, 1935): 201-207.

Leighton, Marian Kirsch. *Soviet Propaganda as a Foreign Policy Tool*. New York: Freedom House, 1991.

Leff, Leonard J., and Jerold Simmons. "*Wilson*: Hollywood Propaganda for World Peace." *Historical Journal of Film, Radio, and Television* 3, no. 1 (1983): 3-18.

LeMahieu, D. L. *A Culture for Democracy: Mass Communication and the Cultivated Mind in Britain Between the Wars*. Oxford, England: Clarendon Press, 1988.

Lemert, James B. *Does Mass Communication Change Public Opinion After All? A New Approach to Effects Analysis*. Chicago: Nelson-Hall, 1981.

Lendvai, Paul. *The Bureaucracy of Truth: How Communist Governments Manage the News*. London: Burnett Books, 1981.

Lenin, N. (Vladimir Ilich). *Agitation und Propaganda*. Vienna: Verlag für Literatur und Politik, 1929.

Lerner, Daniel. "Is International Persuasion Sociologically Feasible?" *Annals of the American Academy of Political and Social Science* 398 (1971): 44-49.

Lichtenberg, Bernard. "Business Backs New York World Fair to Meet the New Deal Propaganda." *Public Opinion Quarterly* 2 (April, 1938): 314-320.

Liebovich, Louis. *The Press and the Origins of the Cold War, 1944-1947*. New York: Praeger, 1988.

Lilly, Carol S. "Problems of Persuasion: Communist Agitation and Propaganda in Post-War Yugoslavia." *Slavic Review* 53 (Summer, 1994): 395-413.

Lindzey, Gardner, and Elliot Aronson, eds. *Handbook of Social Psychology*. 2 vols. New York: Random House, 1985.

Lipsky, Abram. *Man the Puppet: The Art of Controlling Minds*. New York: Frank-Maurice, 1925.

Lodeesen, Jon. "Radio Liberty (Munich): Foundations for a History." *Historical Journal of Film, Radio, and Television* 6, no. 2 (1986): 197-210.

Low, David. *A Cartoon History of Our Times*. New York: Simonn & Schuster, 1939.

Lowell, Abbott Lawrence. *Public Opinion in War and Peace*. Cambridge, Mass.: Harvard University Press, 1923.

Lowry, Montecue J. *Glasnost: Deception, Desperation, Dialectics*. New York: Peter Lang, 1991.

Lumley, Frederick E. *The Propaganda Menace*. New York: Century, 1933.

Lutz, Ralph Haswell. "Studies of World War Propaganda, 1914-1933." *Journal of Modern History* 5 (1933): 496-516.

Lyons, Timothy J. "Hollywood and World War I, 1914-1918." *Journal of Popular Film* 1 (Winter, 1972): 15-30.

MacArthur, John R. *Second Front: Censorship and Propaganda in the Gulf War.* New York: Hill & Wang, 1992.

MacCann, Richard Dyer. *The People's Films: A Political History of U.S. Government Motion Pictures.* New York: Hastings House, 1973.

McCombs, Maxwell E. "Mass Communication in Political Campaigns: Information, Gratification, and Persuasion." In *Current Perspectives in Mass Communications Research*, edited by F. Gerald Kline and Phillip J. Tichenor. Beverly Hills, Calif.: Sage Publications, 1972.

McCombs, Maxwell E., and Donald L. Shaw. "The Agenda-Setting Function of Mass Media." *Public Opinion Quarterly* 36 (Summer, 1972): 176-187.

McCrosky, James C. "A Summary of Experimental Research on the Effects of Evidence in Persuasive Communication." *Quarterly Journal of Speech* 55 (April, 1969): 169-176.

MacDonald, Callum A. "Radio Bari: Italian Wireless Propaganda in the Middle East and British Countermeasures, 1934-1938." *Middle Eastern Studies* 13 (1977): 195-207.

MacDonald, J. Fred. "The Cold War as Entertainment in Fifties Television." *Journal of Popular Film and Television* 7, no. 1 (1978): 3-31.

McDowall, Duncan, ed. *Advocacy Advertising: Propaganda or Democratic Right?* Ottawa: The Conference Board of Canada, 1982.

McEwen, John M. "The National Press During the First World War: Ownership and Circulation." *Journal of Contemporary History* 17 (July 1982): 459-486.

MacKenzie, A. J. *Propaganda Boom.* London: John Gifford, 1938.

MacKenzie, John M., ed. *Imperialism and Popular Culture.* Manchester, England: Manchester University Press, 1986.

_____. *Propaganda and Empire: The Manipulation of British Public Opinion, 1880-1960.* Manchester, England: Manchester University Press, 1984.

McLaine, Ian. *Ministry of Morale: Home Front Morale and the Ministry of Information in World War II.* London: George Allen & Unwin, 1979.

McLaughlan, Andrew Cunningham. "Historians and the War." *The Dial* 62 (May 17, 1917): 427-428.

MacLean, Eleanor. *Between the Lines: How to Detect Bias and Propaganda in the News and Everyday Life.* Montreal: Black Rose Books, 1981.

Mancini, Elain. *Struggles of the Italian Film Industry During Fascism, 1930-1935.* Ann Arbor, Mich.: UMI Research Press, 1985.

Mansell, Gerard. *Let Truth Be Told: 50 Years of BBC External Broadcasting.* London: Weidenfeld & Nicolson, 1982.

Marchand, Roland. *Advertising the American Dream: Making Way for Modernity, 1920-1940.* Berkeley: University of California Press, 1985.

Marett, Sir Robert. *Through the Back Door: An Inside View of Britain's Overseas Information Services.* Oxford, England: Pergamon Press, 1968.

Markham, James W. *Voices of the Red Giants: Communications in Russia and China.* Ames: Iowa State University Press, 1967.

Marks, Melvin R., and Wilson L. Taylor. "A Methodological Study of the Effects of Propaganda." *Journal of Social Psychology* 65 (April, 1965): 269-277.

Marquis, Alice Goldfarb. "Words as Weapons: Propaganda in Britain and Germany During the First World War." *Journal of Contemporary History* 13 (July, 1978): 467-498.

Marrin, Albert. *The Last Crusade: The Church of England in the First World War.* Durham, N.C.: Duke University Press, 1974.

Martin, Kingsley. "Public Opinion: Censorship During the Crisis." *Political Quarterly* 10 (1939): 128-134.

Martin, L. John. "Effectiveness of International Propaganda." *Annals of the American Academy of Political and Social Science* 398 (1971): 61-70.

_____. *International Propaganda: Its Legal and Diplomatic Control.* Minneapolis: University of Minnesota Press, 1958.

Marx, Fritz Morstein. "Propaganda and Dictatorship." *Annals of the American Academy of Political and Social Science* 179 (May, 1935): 211-226.

Meo, L. D. *Japan's Radio War on Australia, 1941-1945.* Melbourne: Melbourne University Press, 1968.

Merton, Robert K. *Mass Persuasion: The Social Psychology of a War Bond Drive.* Westport, Conn.: Greenwood Press, 1946.

Messenger, Gary S. *British Propaganda and the State in the First World War.* Manchester, England: Manchester University Press, 1992.

Metzl, Irvine. "The Poster Goes to War." In *The Poster: Its History and Its Art.* New York: Watson-Guptill, 1963.

Meyer, Michael. "The Nazi Musicologist as Myth Maker in the Third Reich." *Journal of Contemporary History* 10 (October, 1975): 649-665.

Michie, Allan A. *Voices Through the Iron Curtain: The Radio Free Europe Story.* New York: Dodd, Mead, 1963.

Milenkovitch, Michael M. *The View from Red Square: A Critique of Cartoons from Pravda and Izvestia, 1947-1964.* New York: Hobbs, Dorman, 1966.

Millard, Oscar E. *Uncensored: The True Story of the Clandestine Newspaper "La Libre Belgique" Published in Brussels During the German Occupation.* London: Robert Hale, 1937.

Mock, James Robert. *Censorship 1917.* 1941. Reprint. New York: Da Capo Press, 1971.

Mock, James Robert, and Cedric Larson. *Words That Won the War: The Story of the Committee on Public Information, 1917-1919.* Princeton, N.J.: Princeton University Press, 1939.

Molotch, Harvey, and Marilyn Lester. "News as Purposive Behavior: On the Strategic Use of Routine Events, Accidents, and Scandals." *American Sociological Review* 39 (February, 1974): 101-112.

Montague, Ivor. *The Political Censorship of Films.* London: Victor Gollancz, 1929.

Morris, A. J. A. *The Scaremongers: The Advocacy of War and Rearmament, 1896-1914.* London: Routledge & Kegan Paul, 1984.

Moss, Armand. *Disinformation, Misinformation, and the "Conspiracy" to Kill JFK Exposed.* Hamden, Conn.: Archon Books, 1987.

Mould, David H. *American Newsfilm, 1914-1919: The Underexposed War.* New York: Garland, 1983.

Nagorski, Zygmunt, Jr. "Soviet International Propaganda: Its Role, Effectiveness, and Future." *Annals of the American Academy of Political and Social Science* 398 (1971): 130-139.

Nelson, Joyce. "*Mr. Smith Goes to Washington*: Capra, Populism, and Comic-Strip Art." *Journal of Popular Film* 3 (Summer, 1974): 245-254.

Nelson, Richard Alan. *A Chronology and Glossary of Propaganda in the United States.* Greenwood Press, 1996.

Nicholson, Ivor. "An Aspect of British Official Wartime Propaganda." *Cornhill Magazine* 70 (1931): 593-606.

Nielsen, Keith. "Joy Rides?: British Intelligence and Propaganda in Russia, 1914-1917." *Historical Journal* 24, no. 4 (1981): 885-906.

Nieuwenhof, Frans. "Japanese Film Propaganda in World War II: Indonesia and Australia." *Historical Journal of Film, Radio, and Television* 4, no. 2 (1984): 161-177.

Noble, George Bernard. *Policies and Opinions at Paris, 1919: Wilsonian Diplomacy, the Versailles Peace, and French Public Opinion.* New York: Macmillan, 1935.

Noelle-Neumann, Elisabeth. *The Spiral of Silence: Public Opinion—Our Social Skin.* Chicago: University of Chicago Press, 1984.

Odegard, Peter H. *Pressure Politics: The Story of the Anti-Saloon League.* New York: Columbia University Press, 1928.

_____. "Social Dynamics and Public Opinion." *Public Opinion Quarterly* 3, no. 2 (1939): 239-250.

Ogle, Marbury Bladen, Jr. *Public Opinion and Political Dynamics.* Boston: Houghton Mifflin, 1950.

O'Higgens, Paul. *Censorship in Britain.* London: Nelson, 1972.

Orwant, Jack E. "Effects of Derogatory Attacks in Soviet Arms Control Propaganda." *Journalism Quarterly* 49 (Spring, 1972): 107-115.

Osterhouse, R. A., and T. C. Brock. "Distraction Increases Yielding to Propaganda by Inhibiting Counterarguing." *Journal of Personality and Social Psychology* 15 (1970): 344-358.

O'Sullivan, Carol. *Television: Identifying Propaganda Techniques.* San Diego: Greenhaven Press, 1990.

Page, Caroline. *U.S. Official Propaganda During the Vietnam War, 1965-1973: The Limits of Persuasion.* Madison, N.J.: Fairleigh Dickinson University Press, 1994.

Parry, Robert. *Fooling America: How Washington Insiders Twist the Truth and Manufacture the Conventional Wisdom.* New York: William Morrow, 1992.

Parry-Giles, Shawn J. "Propaganda, Effect, and the Cold War: Gauging the Status of America's 'War of Words.'" *Political Communication* 11 (April-June, 1994): 203-213.

Perris, Arnold. *Music as Propaganda: Art to Persuade, Art to Control.* Westport, Conn.: Greenwood Press, 1985.

Peterson, H. C. *Propaganda for War: The Campaign Against American Neutrality, 1914-1917.* Norman: University of Oklahoma Press, 1939.

Peterson, H. C., and Gilbert C. Fite. *Opponents of War, 1917-1918.* Madison: University of Wisconsin Press, 1957.

Petty, Richard E., Gary L. Wells, and Timothy C. Brock. "Distraction Can Enhance or Reduce Yielding to Propaganda: Thought Disruption Versus Effort Justification." *Journal of Personality and Social Psychology* 34 (1976): 874-884.

Phelan, John, ed. *Communications Control: Readings in the Motives and Structure of Censorship.* New York: Sheed & Ward, 1969.

Pielke, Robert G. *You Say You Want a Revolution: Rock Music in American Culture.* Chicago: Nelson-Hall, 1986.

Pirsein, Robert William. *The Voice of America: A History of the International Broadcasting Activities of the United States Government, 1940-1962.* New York: Arno Press, 1979.

Pohle, Heinz. *Der Rundfunk als Instrument der Politik: Zur Geschichte des deutschen Rundfunks von 1923/38.* Hamburg: Hans Bredow Institut, 1955.

Ponsonby, Sir Arthur. *Falsehood in War-Time: Containing an Assortment of Lies Circulated Throughout the Nations During the Great War.* London: George Allen & Unwin, 1928.

Pool, Ithiel de Sola, et al., eds. *Handbook of Communication.* Chicago: Rand McNally, 1973.

Potter, Pitman B. "League Publicity: Cause or Effect of League Failures?" *Public Opinion Quarterly* 2 (July, 1938): 399-412.

Pratkanis, Anthony R., and Elliot Aronson. *Age of Propaganda: Everyday Use and Abuse of Propaganda.* Newark, N.J.: W. H. Freeman, 1992.

Price, Vincent. "Social Identification and Public Opinion: Effects of Communicating Group Conflict." *Public Opinion Quarterly* 53 (Summer, 1989): 197-224.

Pronay, Nicholas. "British Newsreels in the 1930's: Their Policies and Impact." *History* 57 (February, 1972): 63-72.

Pronay, Nicholas, and D. W. Spring, eds. *Propaganda, Politics, and Film.* London: Macmillan, 1982.

Pronay, Nicholas, and Jeremy Croft. "British Film Censorship and Propaganda Policy During the Second World War." In *British Cinema History,* edited by James Curran, and Vincent Porter. Totowa, N.J.: Barnes & Noble Books, 1983.

Pronay, Nicholas, and Philip M. Taylor. "'An Improper Use of Broadcasting . . .': The British Government and Clandestine Radio Propaganda Operations Against Germany During the Munich Crisis and After." *Journal of Contemporary History* 19 (July, 1984): 357-384.

Qualter, Terence H. *Opinion Control in the Democracies.* New York: St. Martin's Press, 1985.

Raack, R. C. "Nazi Film Propaganda and the Horrors of War." *Historical Journal of Film, Radio, and Television* 6, no. 2 (1986): 189-195.

Rappaport, Armin. *The British Press and Wilsonian Neutrality.* Stanford, Calif.: Stanford University Press, 1951.

Rawls, Walton. *Wake Up, America! World War I and the American Poster.* New York: Abbeville Press, 1988.

Read, James Morgan. *Atrocity Propaganda, 1914-1919.* New Haven, Conn.: Yale University Press, 1941.

Reader, W. J. *"At Duty's Call": A Study in Obsolete Patriotism.* Manchester, England: Manchester University Press, 1988.

Reardon, Kathleen Kelley. *Persuasion: Theory and Context.* Beverly Hills, Calif.: Sage Publications, 1981.

Reeves, Nicholas. *Official British Film Propaganda During the First World War.* London: Croom Helm, 1986.

Reid, Franklyn. *The British Press and Germany, 1936-1939.* Oxford, England: Clarendon Press, 1971.

Remington, Thomas. "The Mass Media and Public Communications in the USSR." *Journal of Politics* 43 (August, 1981): 803-817.

Renov, Michael. *Hollywood's Wartime Women: Representation and Ideology.* Ann Arbor, Mich.: UMI Research Press, 1988.

Renshaw, Patrick. "The IWW and the Red Scare of 1917-1924." *Journal of Contemporary History* 3, (October, 1968): 63-72.

Rentschler, Eric. "Ministry of Illusion: German Film, 1933-1945." *Film Comment* 30 (November/December, 1994): 34-42.

Reuth, Ralf Georg. *Goebbels.* Translated by Krishna Winston. New York: Harcourt Brace, 1993.

Reynolds, Mary T. "The General Staff as a Propaganda Agency, 1908-1914." *Public Opinion Quarterly* 3 (July, 1939): 391-408.

Rhodes, Anthony. *Propaganda, the Art of Persuasion: World War II.* London: Angus and Robertson, 1976.

Rice, Arnold. *The Ku Klux Klan in American Politics.* Washington, D.C.: Public Affairs Press, 1962.

Richards, Jeffrey. "The British Board of Film Censors and Content Control in the 1930s: Images of Britain." *Historical Journal of Film, Radio, and Television* 1, no. 2 (1981): 95-116.

Rickards, Maurice. *Posters of Protest and Revolution.* New York: Walker, 1970.

Riegel, O. W. *Mobilizing for Chaos: The Story of the New Propaganda.* New Haven, Conn.: Yale University Press, 1934.

———. "Press, Radio, and the Spanish Civil War." *Public Opinion Quarterly* 1 (January, 1937): 131-136.

———. "Propaganda and the Press." *Annals of the American Academy of Political and Social Science* 179 (1935): 201-210.

Riley, John R., and Leonard S. Cottrell, Jr. "Research for Psychological Warfare." *Public Opinion Quarterly* 21 (1957): 33-38.

Riley, Norman. *999 and All That.* London: Victor Gollancz, 1940.

Robertson, James C. *The British Board of Film Censors: Film Censorship in Britain, 1896-1950.* London: Croom Helm, 1985.

———. "British Film Censorship Goes to War." *Historical Journal of Film, Radio, and Television* 2, no. 1 (1982): 49-64.

Robinson, Michael J., and Andrew Kohut. "Believability and the Press." *Public Opinion Quarterly* 52 (Summer, 1988): 174-188.

Roeder, George H., Jr. *The Censored War: American Visual Experience During World War II.* New Haven, Conn.: Yale University Press, 1993.

Roetter, Charles. *The Art of Psychological Warfare, 1914-1945.* New York: Stein & Day, 1974.

Rogerson, Sidney. *Propaganda in the Next War.* London: Geoffrey Bles, 1938.

Rokeach, Milton. "Attitudes: Nature." *International Encyclopedia of the Social Sciences.* Vol. 1. New York: Macmillan, 1968.

————. "The Nature and Meaning of Dogmatism." *Psychological Review* 61, no. 3 (1954): 194-204.

Rosenberg, William G. *Bolshevik Visions: First Phase of the Cultural Revolution in Soviet Russia.* Ann Arbor, Mich.: Ardis, 1984.

Rosnow, Ralph L., and Edward J. Robinson, eds. *Experiments in Persuasion.* New York: Academic Press, 1967.

Rotha, Paul. *Documentary Diary: An Informal History of the British Documentary Film, 1928-1939.* New York: Hill & Wang, 1973.

Roxburgh, Angus. *Pravda: Inside the Soviet News Machine.* New York: George Braziller, 1987.

Rubin, Bernard. "International Film and Television Propaganda: Campaigns of Assistance." *Annals of the American Academy of Political and Social Science* 398 (November, 1971): 81-92.

Rudnitsky, Konstantin. *Russian and Soviet Theatre, 1905-1932.* Translated by Roxane Permar. New York: Harry N. Abrams, 1988.

Rupp, Leila J. *Mobilizing Women for War: German and American Propaganda, 1939-1945.* Princeton, N.J.: Princeton University Press, 1978.

Saerchinger, César. "Radio as a Political Weapon." *Foreign Affairs* 16 (January, 1938): 244-259.

Sanders, M. L. "Wellington House and British Propaganda During the First World War." *Historical Journal* 18, no. 1 (1975): 119-146.

Sanders, Michael, and Philip M. Taylor. *British Propaganda During the First World War, 1914-1918.* London: Macmillan, 1982.

Sargant, William. *Battle for the Mind: A Physiology of Conversion and Brain-Washing.* London: Pan Books, 1957.

Sayegh, Fayez A. *Zionist Propaganda in the United States: An Analysis.* Pleasantville, N.Y.: Fayez A. Sayegh Foundation, 1983.

Schiller, Herbert I., et al. *The Ideology of International Communications.* New York: Institute for Media Analysis, 1992.

Schnitzer, Luda, Jean Schnitzer, and Marcel Martin, eds. *Cinema in Revolution: The Heroic Era of the Soviet Film.* London: Secker & Warburg, 1973.

Schramm, Wilber, and Donald F. Roberts, eds. *The Process and Effects of Mass Communications.* Rev. ed. Urbana: University of Illinois Press, 1971.

Seldes, George. *You Can't Print That! The Truth Behind the News, 1918-1928.* Garden City, N.Y.: Garden City Publishing Company, 1929.

Selwyn, Francis. *Hitler's Englishman: The Crime of Lord Haw-Haw.* London: Routlege & Kegan Paul, 1987.

Shindler, Colin. *Hollywood Goes to War: Films and American Society, 1939-1952.* London: Routledge & Kegan Paul, 1979.

Short, K. R. M, ed. *Film and Radio Propaganda in World War II.* London: Croom Helm, 1983.

————. "Hewing Straight to the Line: Editorial Control in American News Broadcasting, 1941-1942." *Historical Journal of Film, Radio, and Television* 1, no. 2 (1981): 167-176.

————, ed. *Western Broadcasting over the Iron Curtain.* London: Croom Helm, 1986.

Short, K. R. M., and Richard Taylor. "Soviet Cinema and the International Menace, 1928-1939." *Historical Journal of Film, Radio, and Television* 6, no. 2 (1986): 131-159.

Shover, Michele J. "Roles and Images of Women in World War I Propaganda." *Politics and Society* 5 (1975): 469-486.

Shulman, Holly Cowan. *The Voice of America: Propaganda and Democracy, 1941-1945.* Madison: University of Wisconsin Press, 1990.

Shultz, Richard H., and Roy Godson. *Dezinformatsia: Active Measures in Soviet Strategy.* Washington, D.C.: Pergamon-Brassey's, 1984.

Silverman, Joan L. "*The Birth of a Nation*: Prohibition Propaganda." *Southern Quarterly* 19, nos. 3/4 (Spring/Summer, 1981): 23-30.

Simcovitch, Maxim. "The Impact of Griffith's *Birth of a Nation* on the Modern Ku Klux Klan." *Journal of Popular Film* 1 (Winter, 1972): 45-54.

Singerman, Robert. *Anti-Semitic Propaganda: An Annotated Bibliography and Research Guide.* New York: Garland Publishing, 1982.

Skinner, James M. "Cliché and Convention in Hollywood's Cold War Anti-Communist Films." *North Dakota Quarterly* 46 (Summer, 1978): 35-40.

Smith, Bruce Lannes. "Propaganda." In *International Encyclopedia of the Social Sciences.* Vol. 1. New York: Macmillan, 1968.

_____. "Propaganda Analysis and the Science of Democracy." *Public Opinion Quarterly* 5, no. 2 (1941): 250-259.

Smith, Bruce Lannes, and Chitra M. Smith. *International Communication and Political Opinion: A Guide to the Literature.* Westport, Conn.: Greenwood Press, 1956.

Smith, Bruce Lannes, Harold D. Lasswell, and Ralph D. Casey, eds. *Propaganda, Communications, and Public Opinion: A Comprehensive Reference Guide.* Princeton, N.J.: Princeton University Press, 1946.

Smith, M. Brewster. "Attitudes: Change." In *International Encyclopedia of the Social Sciences.* Vol. 1. New York: Macmillan, 1968.

Smith, Ted J., III, ed. *Propaganda: A Pluralistic Perspective.* New York: Praeger, 1989.

Smith, Woodruff. "The Colonial Novel as Political Propaganda: Hans Grimm's *Volk ohne Raum.*" *German Studies Review* 6 (May, 1983): 215-235.

Soley, Lawrence C. *Radio Warfare: OSS and CIA Subversive Propaganda.* New York: Praeger, 1989.

Sorensen, Thomas C. *The Word War: The Story of American Propaganda.* New York: Harper & Row, 1968.

Sorrels, Charles A. *Soviet Propaganda Campaign Against NATO.* Washington, D.C.: United States Arms Control and Disarmament Agency, 1983.

Southworth, Herbert Rutledge. *Guernica! Guernica! A Study of Journalism, Diplomacy, Propaganda, and History.* Berkeley: University of California Press, 1977.

Sparks, Kenneth R. "Selling Uncle Sam in the Seventies." *Annals of the American Academy of Political and Social Science* 398 (November, 1971): 113-123.

Spitzer, H. M. "Presenting America in American Propaganda." *Public Opinion Quarterly* 11 (1947-1948): 213-221.

Sproule, J. Michael. "Progressive Propaganda Critics and the Magic Bullet Myth." *Critical Studies in Mass Communication* 6 (September, 1989): 225-246.

_____. "Propaganda Studies in American Social Sciences: The Rise and Fall of the Critical Paradigm." *Quarterly Journal of Speech* 73 (February, 1987): 60-78.

Squires, James Duane. *British Propaganda at Home and in the United States from 1914 to 1917.* Cambridge, Mass.: Harvard University Press, 1935.

Stanley, Peter. *What Did You Do in the War Daddy? A Visual History of Propaganda Posters.* Melbourne, Australia: Oxford University Press, 1983.

Stead, Peter. "Hollywood's Message for the World: The British Response in the Nineteen Thirties." *Historical Journal of Film, Radio, and Television* 1, no. 1 (1981): 19-32.

Steele, Richard W. "Preparing the Public for War: Efforts to Establish a National Propaganda Agency, 1940-1941." *American Historical Review* 75 (October, 1970): 1640-1653.

_____. *Propaganda in an Open Society: The Roosevelt Administration and the Media, 1933-1941*. Westport, Conn.: Greenwood Press, 1985.

Stenton, Michael. "British Propaganda and Raison d'Etat 1935-1940." *European Studies Review* 10 (1980): 47-74.

Stevens, John D. "Press and Community Toleration: Wisconsin in World War I." *Journalism Quarterly* 46 (Summer, 1969): 255-259.

Stone, Vernon A. "Individual Differences and Inoculation Against Persuasion." *Journalism Quarterly* 46 (Summer, 1969): 267-273.

Storey, Graham. *Reuters' Century*. London: Max Parrish, 1951.

Strebel, Elizabeth Grottle. "French Cinema, 1940-1944, and Its Socio-Psychological Significance: A Preliminary Probe." *Historical Journal of Film, Radio, and Television* 1, no. 1 (1981): 33-45.

Street, C. J. C. "Propaganda Behind the Lines," *Cornhill Magazine* 48 (1919): 490-495.

Stuart, Sir Campbell. *Secrets of Crewe House: The Story of a Famous Campaign*. London: Hodder & Stoughton, 1920.

Suleiman, Susan Rubin. *Authoritarian Fictions: The Ideological Novel as a Literary Genre*. New York: Columbia University Press, 1983.

Swann, Paul. *The British Documentary Film Movement, 1926-1946*. Cambridge, England: Cambridge University Press, 1989.

Swanson, G. E. "Agitation Through the Press: A Study of the Personalities of Publicists." *Public Opinion Quarterly* 20, no. 2 (1956): 441-456.

Swartz, Marvin. *The Union of Democratic Control in British Politics During the First World War*. Oxford, England: Clarendon Press, 1971.

Tanaka, Yasumasa. "Psychological Factors in International Persuasion." *Annals of the American Academy of Political and Social Science* 398 (1971): 50-60.

Tavin, Eli, and Yonah Alexander. *Psychological Warfare and Propaganda: Irgun Documentation*. Wilmington, Del.: Scholarly Resources, 1982.

Taylor, Edmond. *The Strategy of Terror: Europe's Inner Front*. Boston: Houghton Mifflin, 1940.

Taylor, Philip M., ed. *Britain and the Cinema in the Second World War*. New York: St. Martin's Press, 1988.

_____. "The Foreign Office and British Propaganda During the First World War." *Historical Journal* 23, no. 4 (1980): 875-898.

_____. "If War Should Come: Preparing the Fifth Arm for Total War, 1935-1939." *Journal of Contemporary History* 16 (1981): 27-51.

_____. "Power, Propaganda, and Public Opinion: The British Information Services and the Cold War, 1945-1957." In *Power In Europe?* Vol.2 in *Great Britain, France, Germany and Italy and the Origins of the EEC, 1952-1957*, edited by Ennio Di Nolfo. New York: Walter de Gruyter, 1992.

_____. *The Projection of Britain: British Overseas Publicity and Propaganda, 1919-1939*. Cambridge, England: Cambridge University Press, 1981.

_____. "Techniques of Persuasion: Basic Ground Rules of British Propaganda During the Second World War." *Historical Journal of Film, Radio, and Television* 1, no. 1 (1981): 57-65.

_____. *War and the Media: Propaganda and Persuasion in the Gulf War*. Manchester, England: Manchester University Press, 1992.

Taylor, Richard. "Boris Shumyatsky and the Soviet Cinema in the 1930s: Ideology as Mass Entertainment." *Historical Journal of Film, Radio, and Television* 6, no. 1 (1986): 43-64.

_____. *Film Propaganda: Soviet Russia and Nazi Germany*. London: Croom Helm, 1979.

_____. "A Medium for the Masses: Agitation in the Soviet Civil War." *Soviet Studies* 22 (April, 1971): 562-574.

_____. *The Politics of the Soviet Cinema, 1917-1929*. Cambridge, England: Cambridge University Press, 1979.

_____. "Soviet Cinema: The Path to Stalin." *History Today* 40 (July, 1990): 43-48.

Taylor, Richard, and Nigel Young, eds. *Campaigns for Peace: British Peace Movements in the*

Twentieth Century. Manchester, England: Manchester University Press, 1987.

Thompson, Wayne N., ed. *The Process of Persuasion: Principles and Readings*. New York: Harper & Row, 1975.

Thomson, George P. *Blue Pencil Admiral*. London: Sampson Low, Marston, 1947.

Thornton, Sinclair. "The Nazi Party Rally at Nuremberg." *Public Opinion Quarterly* 2 (October, 1938): 570-583.

Thorpe, Frances, and Nicholas Pronay, eds. *British Official Films in the Second World War: A Descriptive Catalogue*. Oxford, England: Clio Press, 1980.

Thum, Gladys, and Marcella Thum. *The Persuaders: Propaganda in War and Peace*. New York: Athenaeum, 1972.

Turner, Ralph H. "The Public Perception of Protest." *American Sociological Review* 34 (December, 1969): 815-831.

United States Committee on Public Information. *The Creel Report: Complete Report of the Chairman of the Committee on Public Information, 1917, 1918, 1919*. 1920. New York: Da Capo Press, 1972.

Ursprung, Tobias. "The Use and Effect of Political Propaganda in Democracies." *Public Choice* 78 (March 4, 1994): 259-282.

Vaughn, Stephen. *Holding Fast the Line: Democracy, Nationalism, and the Committee on Public Information*. Chapel Hill: University of North Carolina Press, 1980.

Viereck, George Sylvester [George F. Lorners, pseud.]. *Spreading Germs of Hate*. New York: Horace Liveright, 1930.

Waddington, Geoffrey. "Fifth Arm or Fifth Column? Nazi Propaganda Activities in Britain." *Historical Journal of Film, Radio, and Television* 6, no. 1 (1986): 93-99.

Wagnleitner, Reinhold. *Coca-Colonization and the Cold War: The Cultural Mission of the United States in Austria After the Second World War*. Translated by Diana M. Wolf. Chapel Hill: University of North Carolina Press, 1994.

Waley, Daniel. *British Public Opinion and the Abyssinian War, 1935-6193*. London: Maurice Temple Smith, 1975.

Walker, Graham. "The Irish Dr. Goebbels: Frank Gallagher and Irish Republic Propaganda." *Journal of Contemporary History* 27 (January, 1992): 149-165.

Wallace, Stuart. *War and the Image of Germany: British Academics, 1914-1918*. Edinburgh: John Donald, 1988.

Walster, Elaine, and Leon Festinger. "The Effectiveness of 'Overheard' Persuasive Communications." *Journal of Abnormal and Social Psychology* 65, no. 6 (1962): 395-402.

Ward, Larry Wayne. *The Motion Picture Goes to War: The U.S. Government Film Effort During World War I*. Ann Arbor, Mich.: UMI Research Press, 1985.

Warner, Arthur H. "'Sainte-Anastasie': The Censorship in France." *The Outlook* (June 13, 1917): 258-262.

Warren, Allen. "Sir Robert Baden-Powell, the Scout Movement, and Citizen Training in Great Britain, 1900-1920." *English Historical Review* 101 (April, 1986): 376-398.

Wasburn, Philo C. *Broadcasting Propaganda: International Radio Broadcasting and the Construction of Political Reality*. New York: Praeger, 1992.

Weiss, Janet A., and Mary Tschirhart. "Public Information Campaigns as Policy Instruments." *Journal of Policy Analysis and Management* 13 (Winter, 1994): 82-119.

Welch, David. "A Medium for the Masses: UFA and Imperial German Film Propaganda During the First World War." *Historical Journal of Film, Radio, and Television* 6, no. 1 (1986): 85-91.

―――. *Propaganda and the German Cinema, 1933-1945*. Oxford, England: Clarendon Press, 1983.

Wettig, Gerhard. *Broadcasting and Détente: Eastern Policies and Their Implications for East-West Relations*. London: C. Hurst, 1977.

White, Ralph K. "Hitler, Roosevelt, and the Nature of War Propaganda." *Journal of Ab-*

normal and Social Psychology 44 (April, 1949): 157-174.

_____. "The New Resistance to International Propaganda." *Public Opinion Quarterly* 16 (Spring, 1952): 539-551.

_____. "Propaganda: Morally Questionable and Morally Unquestionable Techniques." *Annals of the American Academy of Political and Social Science* 398 (1971): 26-35.

Whitton, John Boardman. "Hostile International Propaganda and International Law." *Annals of the American Academy of Political and Social Science* 398 (November, 1971): 14-35.

_____, ed. *Propaganda and the Cold War.* Washington, D.C.: Public Affairs Press, 1963.

Wildy, Tom. "From the MOI to the COI—Publicity and Propaganda in Britain, 1945-1951: The National Health and Insurance Campaigns of 1948." *Historical Journal of Film, Radio, and Television* 6, no. 1 (1986): 3-17.

Willcox, Temple. "Projection or Publicity? Rival Concepts in the Pre-War Planning of the British Ministry of Information." *Journal of Contemporary History* 18 (January, 1983): 97-116.

Willey, Malcolm M. "Communication Agencies and the Volume of Propaganda." *Annals of the American Academy of Political and Social Science* 179 (1935): 194-200.

Williams, John. *The Other Battleground—The Home Fronts: Britain, France, and Germany, 1914-1918.* Chicago: Henry Regnery, 1972.

Wilson, Charles H. "Hitler, Goebbels, and the Ministry of Propaganda." *Political Quarterly* 10, no. 3 (1938): 83-99.

Wilson, H. H. "Techniques of Pressure: Anti-Nationalization Propaganda in Britain." *Public Opinion Quarterly* 15 (Summer, 1951): 225-242.

Wilson, Trevor. "Lord Bryce's Investigation into Alleged German Atrocities in Belgium, 1914-1915." *Journal of Contemporary History* 14 (July, 1979): 369-383.

Winkler, Allan M. *The Politics of Propaganda: The Office of War Information, 1942-1945.* New Haven, Conn.: Yale University Press, 1978.

Wooddy, Carroll H. "Education and Propaganda." *Annals of the American Academy of Political and Social Science* 179 (1935): 227-239.

Wright, D. G. "The Great War, Government Propaganda, and English 'Men of Letters' 1914-1916." *Literature and History* 7 (1978): 70-100.

Yass, Marion. *This Is Your War: Home Front Propaganda in the Second World War.* London: Her Majesty's Stationery Office, 1983.

Young, John Wesley. *Totalitarian Language: Orwell's Newspeak and Its Nazi and Communist Antecedents.* Charlottesville: University Press of Virginia, 1991.

Young, Kimball, and Raymond D. Lawrence. *Bibliography on Censorship and Propaganda.* Eugene: University of Oregon Press, 1928.

Young, Robert G. " 'Not This Way Please!' Regulating the Press in Nazi Germany." *Journalism Quarterly* 64 (Winter, 1987): 787-792.

Youngblood, Denise J. *Soviet Cinema in the Silent Era, 1918-1935.* Austin: University of Texas Press, 1991.

Younger, Kenneth. "Public Opinion and British Foreign Policy." *International Affairs* 40 (January, 1964): 22-35.

Yu, Frederick T. C. *Mass Persuasion in Communist China.* New York: Frederick A. Praeger, 1964.

Zajonc, Robert B. "Attitudinal Effects of Mere Exposure." *Journal of Personality and Social Psychology Monograph Supplement* 9 (June, 1968): 1-27.

Zeman, Z. A. B. *Nazi Propaganda.* London: Oxford University Press, 1964.

THE ENCYCLOPEDIA OF
PROPAGANDA

Categorized List of Entries

Artistic and Literary Issues
Anthems
Architecture and monuments
Art
Caricature
Documentary Film Movement
Film: Vietnam War
Film: World War I
Film: World War II
Film and politics
Film and social change
Graffiti
Literature
Mural art
Music
Postage stamp art
Poster art
Socialist Realism
Theater and drama

Books, Films, Songs, and Works of Art
Art of War, The
Battleship Potemkin, The
Birth of a Nation, The
Communist Manifesto, The
Grapes of Wrath, The
Green Berets, The
Horst Wessel song
I Led Three Lives
I Was a Communist for the FBI
Lies of Our Times
Mein Kampf
Prince, The
Protocols of the Elders of Zion, The
Psychology of Radio, The
Public Opinion Quarterly
Reefer Madness
Republic
Stars and Stripes
Triumph of the Will
Uncle Tom's Cabin
Why We Fight

Business and Economic Issues
Advertising
Economic propaganda
Gambling
Labor movements
Nuclear power production
Organization of Petroleum Exporting
    Countries
Public utility propaganda

Education and Language Issues
Antipropaganda training
Basic English movement
Civic education
Education as a propaganda rationale
Education as a propaganda tool
Education as an antipropaganda tool
Esperanto
Language policies
Propaganda to promote education

General Concepts and Issues
Activation
Agitprop
Antiwar campaigns
Assessment
Astrology
Asymmetrical definition
Atrocity propaganda
Audiences
Bias
Big-lie technique
Black propaganda
Brainwashing
Censorship
Character assassination
Charismatic leadership
Chauvinism
Civil disobedience
Confederate flag
Confusion
Conspiracy theory
Conversion

Government Bodies and Agencies

INDEX

A page number or range in **boldface** type indicates a full article devoted to that topic.